Talking About Structural
Inequalities in Everyday Life
New Politics of Race in Groups,
Organizations, and Social Systems

Talking About Structural Inequalities in Everyday Life
New Politics of Race in Groups, Organizations, and Social Systems

Edited by

Ellen L. Short
Leo Wilton

INFORMATION AGE PUBLISHING, INC.
Charlotte, NC • www.infoagepub.com

Library of Congress Cataloging-in-Publication Data

The CIP data for this book can be found on the Library of Congress website (loc.gov).

Paperback: 978-1-68123-384-0
Hardcover: 978-1-68123-385-7
eBook: 978-1-68123-386-4

CONTENTS

PART I

STRUCTURAL INEQUALITIES FOR INDIVIDUALS OF COLOR AND MENTAL HEALTH

PART II

STRUCTURAL INEQUALITIES AND INSTITUTIONS

PART III

ORGANIZATIONAL AND GROUP DYNAMICS AND STRUCTURAL INEQUALITIES

ENDORSEMENTS

Talking About Structural Inequalities in Everyday Life: New Politics of Race in Groups, Organizations, and Social Systems is a must have resource for scholars and students of race! The editors have done a masterful job of putting together a collection that not only synthesizes the expansive literature on race, racism, and racial microaggressions, but the work also includes innovative interpretations that advance the field of study. The book is well organized and provides compelling discussions of multiple intersecting identities (race, class, gender, sexual identity, and nationality) and the complex ways in which structural inequalities frame people of colors' lived experiences. The inclusion of concrete strategies and interventions to undermine and disrupt structural inequalities is an important addition to underscore hope for transformation.

Helen A. Neville, Ph.D.
Chair, Counseling Psychology Program
Professor, Educational Psychology and African American Studies

Never have I been as intrigued by the chapter titles and contents of a multicultural book as I have with "Talking About Structural Inequalities in Everyday Life." There are many books on the market that deal with race and cultural issues in society— most of these are reviews of general issues in the multicultural field. Now, finally, this masterfully edited volume by Drs. Ellen Short and Leo Wilton delves deep into the underbelly of racial structures in society to locate the root of racial inequality—ingrained systemic injustice. The editors have recruited an interdisciplinary group of the field's most cutting edge and courageous scholars who unpack the systemic nature of racism, sexism, and homophobia, and lay bare the societal practices that promote the continued oppression of large segments of our population. With structural inequality deconstructed, the book shows the way to a more equitable and just society.

This volume includes 16 concise and well-written chapters organized along three major sections that address structural inequalities as manifested at the individual, institutional, and group levels. Among the timely and pressing topics covered are the diversity within racial/ethnic groups, violence in the lives of African American women and ways of coping with trauma, media representation of Black/African descent women, race, and the prison industrial complex, microaggressions faced by various communities of color, and violence and resiliency in transgender women of color. The book also tackles with precision the thorny issues of inequality in how we conceptualize and measure "intelligence" in racial groups as well as educational disparities in Asian American populations. While reviewing critical areas of cultural study and deconstructing inequality in its many forms, the book also provides pragmatic solutions and hope for the future through the presentation of case studies and model programs directed at dismantling inequality and building resilience. Examples here include the "Project SisterCricle Intervention" for Black/African and Latina adolescent girls, and programmatic initiatives to improve college graduation rates in Black men.

Before we can be effective as clinicians, teachers, administrators, and policy leaders in an increasingly multicultural society mantled on a history of oppression, we must first understand the deep structures that maintain and promote inequality, examine our own roles in the systems in which we live and work, and be moved to action to challenge inequality in its many forms. Drs. Short and Wilton, with their eclectic author team of researchers, clinicians, and activists, have provided us a roadmap to work toward greater equality and justice in society. The ramifications of such an effort for all of society's mental and physical health is profound.

Joseph G. Ponterotto, Ph.D.
Professor and Coordinator, Mental Health Counseling Program
Fordham University, New York, USA
Co-Editor of the *Handbook of Multicultural Counseling* (Sage) and
the *Handbook of Multicultural Assessment* (Wiley)

FOREWORD

I was honored when Dr. Ellen Short and Dr. Leo Wilton invited me to write the Foreword for their edited book *Talking About Structural Inequalities in Everyday Life: New Politics of Race in Groups, Organizations, and Social Systems*. During the course of my life, I have come to believe that most experiences and opportunities are timely and happen for a reason. Therefore, it was rather fortuitous that I had a recent encounter, which underscores the importance and necessity of this book. I participated in a symposium at Brown University and sponsored by the Center for the Study of Race and Ethnicity in America. The title of the symposium was *Young, Gifted, and @ Risk: Symposium on High-Achieving Students of Color and Mental Health*. The symposium was inspired by the suicide of a gifted African American man who was a graduate of Brown. The purpose of the symposium was to provide various expert perspectives on the challenges facing high-achieving students of color during college and emerging adulthood. During the course of the symposium, several references were made to structural racism and its impact on high-achieving students of color. A war metaphor was also used to characterize the ongoing assault on high-achieving students of color. One individual, an accomplished research scientist, approached me afterwards to discuss something that was bothering her. She was disturbed by the war metaphor, and she had no idea what structural racism was. Having adopted a Black girl, she confessed to having no knowledge or understanding of structural racism, and asked me to ex-

Talking About Structural Inequalities in Everyday Life: New Politics of Race in Groups, Organizations, and Social Systems, pages xi–xiii.

plain it to her. She described herself as a White liberal woman; however, she was particularly concerned that using a war metaphor and emphasizing structural racism to characterize the experiences of high-achieving students of color would only serve to promote a victim mentality among these students. She indicated that she did not want to socialize her daughter this way. By this time another African American panelist had eased into the conversation, and her expression conveyed a look of incredulousness (which was confirmed in a later dinner conversation).

Few concepts are more threatening to our democracy that the notion of structural inequalities. In a society where meritocracy and rugged individualism are considered to be core American values, it is deeply disturbing and unsettling to many White Americans that there could be the existence of systemic, structural inequalities that disadvantage certain groups of people. Race is the social construct that serves as the source of much of the structural inequalities in this country. The intersection of race with other social identities such as ethnicity, gender, and sexual identity further compounds the harmful impact of structural inequalities.

The editors have done an outstanding job of conceptualizing the broad impact of structural inequalities at the individual, institutional, and organizational/group levels. The chapters cover a range of populations, including Black/Africana women, Black men, Black gay South African men, Latino/a Americans, Caribbean Americans, Asian Americans and Pacific Islanders, transgender women of color, and Dalits. The chapters also address a range of topics such as racial microaggressions, coping with traumatic life events, educational disparities, the assessment of intelligence, and the prison industrial complex.

A notable feature of the book is its focus on women of color. Six of the sixteen chapters focus on women of color. With all the attention given to males of color as evidenced by President Obama's Brother's Keeper initiative and recent events of police shooting unarmed Black men, the plight of women of color is often ignored. I believe the focus on women of color illustrates that the impact of structural inequalities is particularly harmful when there is an intersection of race, gender, and sexual identity.

Each chapter tells a compelling story. I am particularly drawn to Ch. 13 on *Racial Inequalities and the Assessment of Intelligence*. There is perhaps no better example of the impact of structural inequalities on racial and ethnic minorities than the assessment of intelligence and its role in the inequitable distribution of opportunities and resources, and the permanent consignment of lower status. In many special education programs, Black and Latino/a students make up twice their percentage of the student population, while White students in gifted education often make up more than twice their percentage of the student population. The casual observer may conclude that it is just an unfortunate fact that Black and Latino/a students are simply more likely to have special education needs. However, it is the overreliance of intelligence tests and the failure to understand the role of culture and bias in diagnosis that contributes to the disproportionate placement of racial and ethnic minorities in special education.

I commend Dr. Short and Dr. Wilton for recognizing the need for this book and having the vision to bring together this impressive group of authors. This book will be useful for researchers, clinicians, prevention experts, and policy makers. I highly recommend it for any individual who wants to eradicate structural inequalities and advocate for social justice.

Kevin Cokley, Ph.D.
Director
The Institute for Urban Policy Research & Analysis [IUPRA]
The University of Texas at Austin
Professor of Counseling Psychology and African and African Diaspora Studies
Editor-in-Chief, *Journal of Black Psychology*

PREFACE

As the editors for *Talking About Structural Inequalities in Everyday Life: New Politics of Race in Groups, Organizations, and Social Systems,* we have endeavored to create a book that will provide our readers with critical attention to contemporary, innovative, and cutting-edge issues in group, organizational, and social systems that address the complexities of racialized structural inequalities in everyday life. We also endeavored to create an edited book that has a more comprehensive focus on systemic, societal, and organizational dynamics in multi-faceted contexts that will advance a variety of interdisciplinary fields including human development, psychology, counseling, social work, education, multiculturalism/cultural studies, and organizational consultation. Although we envisioned the target audience for this scholarly book to primarily be researchers, prevention experts, clinicians, and policy makers, it is our hope that our book will be widely read by anyone who is interested in systemic inequalities.

As scholars, researchers, and practitioners, we pose some questions that form the basis of several of the chapters throughout the book: "What's happening now?" "What structural inequalities exist in these domains?" How have communities challenged and moved beyond these imposed structural boundaries? These questions provide the foundation for the book's focus, which incorporate interdisciplinary and intersectional approaches. In our work with groups, organizations and systems, we have found that although much of the literature is important and intriguing, it does not cover a wide enough spectrum regarding the salience of systemic functioning based on socio-cultural contexts in the United States and internationally. We have also found that maintaining a systemic lens across disciplinary boundaries can be very challenging. We believe that our book will provide a focus that will help the reader more fully understand and appreciate systemic perspectives as they are applied in the aforementioned contexts.

Talking About Structural Inequalities in Everyday Life: New Politics of Race in Groups, Organizations, and Social Systems has an impressive roster of talented authors who have written chapters focusing on contemporary issues related to social justice in counseling and psychology. Each chapter authored addresses core areas related to the current state of knowledge in a variety of disciplines.

There are three sections of the book; each section contains chapters whose contents have been conceptualized and written by the authors in ways that will capture the interest and attention of the reader and enlighten them. Part I addresses structural inequalities for individuals of color in mental health and includes chapters focusing on Caribbean Americans and stressors of the immigration and acculturation processes, a meta-ethnographic study on the coping strategies employed by Africana women in response to trauma, a chapter that explores systemic and workplace microaggressions and provides recommendations for best practices for institutions and organizations, and several other chapters devoted to the complexities of structural inequalities in racialized and gendered contexts. Part II of the book explores structural inequalities and institutions and includes chapters examining educational disparities in Asian American and Pacific Islander communities, racialized perspectives on the Prison Industrial Complex, the efficacy of programmatic initiatives on improving graduation rates among Black male college students, racial inequalities and the assessment of intelligence, as well as chapters focusing on structural violence, agency, and resiliency in Black transgender women's communities, and race, sexuality, AIDS and activism in Black same-gender practicing men's communities in post-apartheid South Africa. Part III offers perspectives on organizational and group dynamics as they relate to structural inequalities and includes chapters focusing on social constructions about race and racialized spaces in systems, systemic implications of Black women giving voice publicly regarding experiences of gender-based violence and ethnoviolence, and a group-relations-focused exploration of caste among the Dalit of India.

Finally, *Talking About Structural Inequalities in Everyday Life: New Politics of Race in Groups, Organizations, and Social Systems* (or, TASIIEL, which is the acronym we began using during our work on the book), was truly a labor of love for us; it encompasses an almost two decades long professional and personal relationship that we have with each other, as peers, colleagues, and friends as well as our ongoing commitment to exploring, identifying and naming racialized structural inequalities in everyday life.

Ellen L. Short, Ph.D.
Long Island University, Brooklyn Campus
Brooklyn, New York
January, 2016

Leo Wilton, Ph.D.
State University of New York at Binghamton
Binghamton, New York
January, 2016

PART I

STRUCTURAL INEQUALITIES FOR INDIVIDUALS OF
COLOR AND MENTAL HEALTH

CHAPTER 1

BETWEEN RAGE AND
A HARD PLACE

A Cautionary Tale of Colin Ferguson, Racial
Politics, and Caribbean American Mental Health

Schekeva P. Hall

On December 7th 1993, Colin Ferguson, a 35-year-old Jamaican immigrant, shot
and killed six passengers aboard a Hicksville-bound Long Island Railroad train
and injured nineteen others (McQuiston, 1995). Attempts to explore the reason
for the shooting revealed Ferguson's deep-seated psychological issues. Yet, this
reflected a major historical mass murder trial in the United States (US) with an
overt and provocative racial context. It was fueled by the defendant's perceived
(Oh, Yang, Anglin, & DeVylder, 2014; Soto, Dawson-Andoh, & BeLue, 2011)
and likely experienced (Chae, Lincoln, & Jackson, 2011; Grier & Cobbs, 1968;
hooks, 1996) racial injustice. US-citizens and immigrants alike, including Ferguson, had to consider the position that race and power occupy in the US. They had
to consider how persistently experiencing, witnessing and/or perceiving US racial
discrimination could make a person angry and that this response was a justifiable
response to racism (hooks, 1996).

*Talking About Structural Inequalities in Everyday Life: New Politics of Race in Groups,
Organizations, and Social Systems,* pages 3–23.
Copyright © 2016 by Information Age Publishing
3

As attorneys, psychologists, and the public scrambled to explore reasons for Ferguson's actions, his defense team, Kunslter and Kuby, attempted to use *Black rage* as a proxy for an insanity plea, noting: "We didn't claim Colin Ferguson was sane but, the form the insanity took was what we deemed to be *Black rage"* (Kuby, 2012). Taking a contextual approach grounded in the past, the defense team highlighted Ferguson's experience with US-racism as an immigrant and his adjustment to it, linking it to *Black rage*. Kuby (2012) contended:

> For the first time he began to encounter systematic institutionalized racism in the United States. Didn't encounter it in Jamaica. Had grown up thinking that he was no different than anybody else and soon got to the United States and, and learned differently.

The term *Black rage* was intended to describe feelings felt by Blacks based on their continuous encounters with systematic racism (Grier & Cobbs, 1968). Nonetheless, lawyers Kunslter and Kuby conflated this term with insanity, compromising the term and subsequent understanding of it by the masses. Thus, *Black rage* became synonymous with pathology. Grier and Cobbs (1968), the original authors of the term *Black rage*, cautioned against pathologizing it, noting the importance of looking at the context with which Blacks become enraged. hooks (1996) adds, "That [Black] rage is not pathological. It is an appropriate response to injustice. However, if not processed constructively, it can lead to pathological behavior— but so can any rage, irrespective of the cause that serves as the catalyst" (p. 26).

Historically, Blacks in the US have learned to *play it cool* (Boyd-Franklin, 2003; Sue & Sue, 2012) as a means of survival in an obstinate racist culture with a history of slavery, segregation, lynching, and other forms of racialized violence. This process of *playing it cool* often involves choosing to conceal feelings of anger and rage due to racism or their anger in general. Unfortunately, as long as Black peoples' anger remains unacceptable to Whites, Blacks *play it cool* to avoid being misunderstood and exploited (Sue & Sue, 2012). Those who do become overwhelmed and "lose their cool" after experiencing negative racial experiences may be more likely to be given a mental health diagnosis, such as paranoia or anger control issues (Newhill, 1990). Grier and Cobbs (1968) understood this reality and noted the challenge with experiencing cultural paranoia,

> For a black man survival in America depends in large measure on the development of a 'healthy' cultural paranoia. He must maintain a high degree of suspicion toward the motives of every white man and at the same time never allow this suspicion to impair his grasp of reality. It is a demanding requirement and not everyone can manage it with grace. (Grier & Cobbs, 1968, p. 161)

Ferguson's case demonstrates that the cultural reference and context of both actor and the audience need to be a part of any case exploration in the courtroom, or for that matter in therapy. In fact, scholars indicate that cultural context affects health outcomes including diagnosis (Williams, Lavizzo-Mourey, & Warren, 2004). For instance, Viruell-Fuentes, Miranda, and Abdulrahim (2012) argue that the multiple dimensions of inequality within a given culture can affect health outcomes of individuals. Structural racism found within US culture can affect access to health care, health education, etc., which may directly or indirectly affect health. Moreover, an environment where there are incessant day-to-day experiences of racism or discrimination produces disease (Link & Phelan, 1995).

Ferguson's case is not a classic straightforward case of psychosis and it does not fit any clear psychiatric diagnosis on the basis of rage alone. Nonetheless, it remains clear that there was notable dissension within Ferguson, and there was a need for psychological intervention well before he reached the point of entering the penal system and making national headlines.

As the details of the case emerged, the nation learned that Ferguson had been overtly grappling with US racial politics since his transition to the US, which represents a common theme for many Black immigrants migrating to the US (Vickerman, 2001; Waters, 1999). As a result, Black immigrants can be misdiagnosed with psychotic disorders and/or institutionalized shortly after their transition to a Westernized country (Harrison, Holton, Nielson, & Boot, 1988; Selten, Slaets, & Khan, 1997; Sharpley, Hutchinson, McKenzie, & Murray, 2001).

Scholars contend that this is likely a result of these individuals' immigration and post-immigration experiences (Hutchinson & Haasen, 2004), which most likely can include disorder-engendering racial discrimination (Chae et al., 2011; Oh et al., 2014) among other stressors. This consistent theme also found with other Immigrants of Color (Grant et al., 2004) overall suggest that nativity and the immigrant experience as an Immigrants of Color are associated with "psychiatric morbidity" (Williams et al., 2007). Closer examination of this phenomenon can reveal the psychiatric morbidity common for many US immigrants can be a result of psychological injury (Carter, 2007) from a racist culture and not an innate inability to for immigrants to properly adapt. Carter (2007) notes psychological injury is a better way to account for the interaction between a racist culture and minority bystanders who become ill because it correctly assigns the role of the US in creating psychological unrest. Thus, a realistic appraisal of the dynamic should include the role cultural racism plays in immigrants' adjustment to an inherently oppressive system (Newhill, 1990).

While this case is more than 20 years old, the issues highlighted are not. Given decades of countless accounts of overt institutionalized racism and the recent national cases of Trayvon Martin, Michael Brown, Marissa Alexander, and Eric Garner, we are likely to not only experience racial unrest in the nation but, also, we may begin to see more and more clinical cases where the primary focus for Blacks in the US may be traumatic stress (Franklin-Jackson & Carter, 2007) or psychological injury (Carter, 2007) due to racism. Both of these factors have provided alternate viable cultural explanations for mental health issues among Blacks necessary for culturally competent practice. These and additional undocumented cases between Blacks and racist US institutions have brought about a very public resurgence of rage for many socialized in the US. Blacks migrating to the US may need to make sense of this racialized violence, particularly within a context where they potentially may be a target of individual, institutional and/or cultural racism. Some may choose to cope with racism in ways consistent to how their US peers do (e.g., play it cool, activism, etc.) or not (e.g., ignore, minimize its effects). However, it is likely that coping will not initially include the provision of traditional mental health services. Persons of Color have historically found other means of coping, which can include seeking spiritual guidance within their communities or ignoring or minimizing the effects of stressors (Sutherland, Moodley, & Chevannes, 2014). The historical distrust for Westernized health practices generally also comes into play for many racial minorities, immigrants or US-born citizens. This is especially the case for mental health counseling as there is a long-standing stigma associated with this for Caribbean Americans. As such, Ferguson's provocative case also highlights concerns with the underutilization of mental health resources among Caribbean Americans. It is a cautionary tale of the importance of understanding and exploring racial/cultural dynamics that occur with Caribbean Americans both inside and out of the therapeutic relationship.

The remainder of this chapter is divided into two sections. Part I addresses some relevant dimensions of the cultural history of Blacks of Caribbean ancestry. It includes comparisons between Caribbean and US racial socialization systems and emerging racial identity development. Part II addresses how to engage Caribbean Americans in the US mental health systems. Using Ferguson as an example, it addresses the pertinent issues for this marginalized Black immigrant group. Mental health clinicians can consider these issues in development of culturally inclusive working conceptualizations and practice. The chapter will use Caribbean Americans to denote Black Caribbean Americans from the Anglophone Caribbean.

PART I—THE CONTEXT

When exploring the context for Caribbean Americans like Colin Ferguson, it is imperative to have comprehensive contextualized understandings of the variegated experiences of immigrants. As such, it is important to understand their reasons for migration, and what ideologies immigrants bring with them on their journey.

Coming to the US: Understanding the History and Culture of Emigration

> Young, articulate, ambitious, he [Ferguson] moved to the United States and aspired to the American Dream: college, marriage, jobs with a future. (McFadden, 1993, p. 3)

Immigrants from the African Diaspora coming into the United States steadily increased since the post–1965 wave of immigration with no signs of abating (Thomas, 2012). In fact, the US Black population has grown one-fifth in recent years due to immigration alone (Kent, 2007). This is largely due to significant increases in the Black-Caribbean immigrant population and their US-born children who identify with their parents' birth country (Logan & Deane, 2003). Yet, it is Black immigrants from the Anglophone Caribbean that comprise the majority of US Black Caribbean immigrants (Thomas, 2012), resulting in over one million Black US residents of Caribbean ancestry in 2009 (Thomas, 2012).

Unique independent island histories and diverse racial compositions of some Caribbean countries (e.g., percentage of South Asians in Trinidad and Tobago vs. Jamaica) may affect immigrants' multiracial views. Even so, general inferences can be made relevant to Black West Indian immigrants' acculturation experiences in the US. These include reasons for travel, expectations for and reactions to US culture and racial climate. This inference also occurs without the confounding factors of language sometimes associated with Francophone (e.g., Haiti, Martinique), Hispanophone (Cuba, Dominican Republic, Puerto Rico) and Néerlandophone Caribbean countries (e.g., Aruba, Curaçao).

Caribbean peoples have voluntarily migrated to various parts of the world for centuries (Alleyne, 2002; McCabe, 2011) largely due to being future oriented and seeking upward mobility. They have made concerted efforts to come to the US and other "first world" nations hoping for a better quality of life for themselves and subsequent generations (Benson, 2006; Foner, 2001; Hine-St. Hilaire, 2008; McCabe, 2011; Rogers, 2004). The Schomburg Center for Research and Black Culture (2005) notes, Caribbean Americans' growth at the turn of the twentieth century was due to "increasing economic hardship and disenchantment in the British West Indies and the simultaneous expansion of the U.S. economy with its relatively high wages and growing employment opportunities" ("Leaving the Caribbean," para. 1). These immigrants successfully became prominent persons in South Carolina and the Northeastern states including New York and Massachusetts during the height of racial divides and segregation (James, 1999).

Today, trends still reflect earlier waves of immigration in terms of influx and success. However, success comes at a cost. For example, although Caribbean Americans tend to have higher educational attainment and greater economic success than African Americans (Broman Torres, Canady, Neighbors, & Jackson, 2010; Model, 2008; Thomas, 2012), Caribbean Americans also tend to exhibit increasing rates of mental illness the longer they reside in the US (Williams et al., 2007). These health-related issues include high rates of stress, and high diagnosed rates of personality (Gibbs et al., 2013) and psychotic disorders (Gibbs et al., 2013; Oh et al., 2014; Williams, et al., 2007), mood disorders (Miranda, Siddique, Belin, & Kohn-Wood, 2005), panic disorder (Levine et al., 2013), and binge eating disorders (Taylor, Caldwell, Baser, Faison, & Jackson, 2007; Taylor et al., 2013). These issues are likely consequences of discrimination based on being a double minority in the US; i.e., being both Black and immigrants (Rumbaut, 1994). Numerous studies, including those aforementioned have indicated the impact of structural racism on Caribbean Americans the longer they reside in the US (Viruell-Fuentes, Miranda, & Abdulrahim, 2012). The longer they reside in the US the more likely they are to perceive racism as a cultural problem and have resulting coping issues with it. (Viruell-Fuentes, Miranda, & Abdulrahim, 2012)

The harsh realities of living as a Black immigrant in the US do not dissuade immigrants from migrating there. Instead, some, like Ferguson, enter the US in search of opportunities that may be unrealistic and experience obstacles that negatively affect their mental health (Baptiste, Hardy, & Lewis, 1997; Foner, 2001; Hine-St. Hilaire, 2008; Turner 1991). Many Caribbean Americans seek to attain a higher quality of life through educational and economic gains by any means necessary. This may include minimizing race and real health consequences, perhaps, resulting from race, for the sake of stability and status (Hine-St. Hilaire, 2008; Neighbors, Naji, & Jackson, 2007).

While some Caribbean Americans are very clear about race and racism in America- and its application to them as Blacks, some Caribbean Americans' decision not to place emphasis on race may be related to particular ideologies regarding the importance of it. The tendency to focus less on race as a "problem" may serve as a viable coping technique for Caribbean Americans to stay under the radar, *playing it cool* and gaining favor from Whites. Members of this community might attribute Ferguson's rage as *too much* attention to race. Thus, seeing race as a key issue when adjusting to life in the US may be deemed unnecessary and costly by the average Caribbean American.

Racial Climate, Socializations and Perspectives

> All black people are discriminated against… Ask anyone and they'll tell you stories that would curl your hair. But you can't take everything in life and say it is the product of racism. He [Ferguson] took all his failures in life and gave it a name and made it a cause. (Ferguson's (Caribbean American) Landlord, (McFadden, 2013, p. 1))

The US has traditionally reflected a complex system of racial categorization that sharply contrasts with the way race is conceptualized in some other parts of the world (Alleyne, 2002; Forsyth, Hall, & Carter, 2015; Hall, 2012). Washington (2004) defined two "fundamental principles" (e.g., *monothetic* and *polythetic)* of arbitrary race categorization throughout the world. Historically, the US would represent one region of the world to have held a *monothetic* system of race construction. That is, a system that primarily uses physical markers (i.e., skin tone and hair) for the purposes of maintaining racial exclusivity and "purity." This system maintains and adheres to strict social boundaries (e.g., marriage and schooling) for its citizens regarding resources and relationships. Monothetic systems encourage unequal sharing of resources between different races and "overt conflict characterized by continuous racial struggles over resources and violent discriminatory practices that are often reinforced by the state" (Washington, 2004, p. 52).

Most Caribbean immigrants, including Ferguson, would have been socialized under a *polythetic* racial categorization system. Polythetic systems are based on various defining criteria, such as ancestry, phenotype, and social class that take on varied weight when socio-racial categories are constructed. Each factor is considered equally important in defining racial categories. These systems are more permeable and applied so that resources (e.g., opportunity for social mobility, education, and work) are distributed liberally among its citizens (Washington, 2004).

Formative slavery institutions for US Blacks and Blacks from the British West Indies have led to these historically diverse racial socialization systems (Benson, 2006). These diverse conditions have likely affected the differing racial experiences of Black Caribbean Americans and African Americans to date. For instance, during the first migratory process to the US between the colonial period and the 1900s enslaved Africans of Caribbean descent had a "reputation for rebelliousness" (e.g., runaways, revolts). As a result, US slave owners and laws placed higher duties on them than Africans who came directly from the continent ("The Colonial Period to 1900," para. 2, Schomburg Center for Research and Black Culture, 2005). This "rebelliousness," was due to a slavery system with certain permissible freedoms, less direct contact with Whites, and a larger number of Africans than Whites (Sutton & Makiesky, 1975; Vickerman, 2001). Likewise, early US enslaved Africans of Caribbean descent were not intimidated by the US's hostile racial discrimination (James, 1999), likely a result of migrating from a culture where they had more leeway to see themselves as equal to Whites (Benson, 2006).

Variances in race constructions and subsequent socializations from the US and the West Indies influence the development of racial identity because they both happen within the racial climate.

Renegotiating a New Salient Black Identity

"This is the case of stereotyped victimization of a Black man and subsequent conspiracy to destroy him." (Ferguson, 1995).

Racial identity refers to a "sense of group or collective identity based on the individual's *perception* that he/she shares a common racial heritage with a particular racial group" (Helms, 1990, p. 3). "Sense of group or collective identity" for Blacks, given the history and nature of race relations in the United States, is integral to understanding the US conceptualization of a healthy racial identity (Helms, 1990). US racial categories have been used culturally to promote the idea of the inferiority of People of Color and the superiority of Whites through forms of privilege (e.g., access) and racism (e.g., racial discrimination and harassment) from its inception. Healthy "group" or "collective" racial identity for Blacks in the US entails not only racial group pride but also, self-awareness as a racially oppressed group in relation to Whites.

For People of Color migrating into the North American racial system, exploring racial identity within the United States' cultural context can be complicated due to cultural differences from the Immigrants of Color's previous country's racial climate (Alleyne, 2002; Bashi-Bobb, 2001; Benson, 2006; Waters, 1999). For Black immigrants, this level of complexity in racial identity research based on a US model is rarely considered. While it is possible for Black immigrants to understand the global implications of *colorism* and Blackness throughout the world (Alleyne, 2002; Rogers, 2004), attaching the same psychological meaning to the US' racial politics may prove challenging (Alleyne, 2002; Bashi-Bobb, 2001). As race became the dominant factor for culturally determining American social identity, other variations of group identification such as ethnicity, gender, or social class sometimes used to classify immigrants are lost. As a result, ethnically Black Caribbean immigrants can feel an increased loss and marginalization as they fold into established Black American communities (Bashi-Bobb, 2001; Bryce-Laporte, 1972). This loss, marginalization, and knowledge of negative social roles Blacks in the US often occupy, transforms into an ethnic group distinction; therefore, the distinction becomes not about Blacks in the US but a "Black American" issue. Thus, when discrimination becomes personalized as a group issue, it may bring about a desire to assert difference from instead of allegiance to, their Black American peers and Black American culture (Hine-St. Hilaire, 2008).

Some Caribbean Americans may hold biased or even ethnocentric attitudes about African Americans (Hall, 2012; Jackson & Cothran, 2003; Waters, 1994). These attitudes include perceiving African Americans as lazy, vociferous, unintelligent, having a 'chip' on their shoulder and being overly concerned with race while Caribbean Americans tend to perceive themselves as smart, loyal, hardworking, etc. (Jackson & Cothran, 2003). Varied racial group and ethnocentric attitudes held by Black immigrants have been theorized to relate to a specific type of ethnic group self-identification chosen by Caribbean American youth while in the US. Caribbean/immigrant (e.g., Jamaican), Caribbean American (Grenadian-American), or American (American/African American) identifications were found to relate to specific attitudes about African Americans (Waters, 1994). Waters (1994) found second-generation Caribbean Americans who identified with their parents' immigrant status denigrated African Americans and passively endorsed White ideals. Hall (2012) found in her 151 sample of 1.5 and second-generation Black West Indian youth/young adults, that Caribbean Americans can hold negative views of African Americans and not endorse the associated passive, color-blind ideals associated as Waters (1994) previously found. Hall (2012) also found that Caribbean Americans could hold pride in being Black and still harbor ethnocentric bias towards their Black American peers indicating that racial identity attitudes for this group is not the one dimensional "either or" but more complex "but, and."

PART II

Caribbean Americans and Mental Health

> ... He got very quiet, incredibly quiet. He didn't play his radio and he stopped praying for the first time in a very long time. "This kind of alarmed me," he went on. "Just before those two weeks, we did ask him to leave, because I got the feeling I just couldn't reason with him anymore. I got the feeling one day I was going to walk in and his door would be half open and I might see him swinging on a rope. (Ferguson's landlord, in McFadden, 1993, p. 3)

In the past, epidemiologic literature (coinciding with census data) that explored the physical and mental health of Communities of Color treated Blacks as a monolith (Gibbs et al., 2013). Recent changes in racial categories aimed at specifying ethnic differences have led to a plethora of new untapped data about the diverse Blacks in the US (Jackson et al., 2007).

Caribbean Americans have only recently surfaced in these studies with some studies tracking this growing populations' physical and mental health statistics. Several mental health concerns have been found among Black Caribbean Americans when comparisons have been made with African Americans and Non-Hispanic White peers (Gibbs et al., 2013; Levine et al., 2013). Thus, psychological diagnoses are likely connected to acculturating to being Black in the US. One notable outcome of this status is experiencing traumatic stress. Franklin-Jackson & Carter (2008) and Pieterse (2005) suggest that racism against Blacks creates race-related traumatic stress resulting in psychological and emotional injury (Carter, 2007). This specific type of stress has not only physical health consequences such as high blood pressure (Broman et al., 2010; Williams et al., 2004) for Blacks, but also mental health problems (Bryant, 2003; Williams et al., 2004). The results of the studies have been mixed. Some scholars contend that Caribbean Americans are less likely to be diagnosed with Major Depressive Disorder (MDD) than African Americans (Gibbs et al., 2013). This was contrary to Williams et al. (2007) study where Caribbean Americans were more likely to have a diagnosis of MDD. Closer observation of the data indicates generational status as the moderator for the varied results (Williams et al., 2007). Williams et al. (2007) noted mental health risks including MDD were influenced by differences in diversity between gender and generational status of Caribbean Americans. Caribbean American women had lower psychiatric risks when compared to African American women and Caribbean American men had higher risk compared to African American men. Overall, first generation Caribbean Americans had lower rates of psychiatric disorders compared to second or third-generation Caribbean Americans. The authors surmised what had been proposed from Hall & Carter's (2006) and confirmed by Williams et al.'s (2007) study of first through third generation Caribbean Americans indicated that increased exposure to a marginalized status could account for changes in mental health status for this population.

What is notable from the studies is that Caribbean Americans, when compared to African Americans were less likely to be diagnosed with social anxiety disorder and substance use disorder but, have a greater likelihood of being diagnosed with psychotic disorder than African Americans (Gibbs et al., 2013; Williams, 2007). In fact, it is highly likely that this diagnosis occurs after the migration experience (Williams et al., 2013). This theme has especially been documented at disproportionate rates in Europe, emerging since the 1960s (Maynard, Harding, & Minnis, 2007). Scholars have long suggested that this is due to misdiagnosis because of a lack of understanding of the culture. Newhill, (1990) notes the difficulties clinicians have distinguishing culturally acceptable behaviors from pathology. This is likely due to limited understanding of the culture from which the client comes (Johnson, Weller, Brown, & Pottinger, 2008).

Despite these broad outcomes, the participants included in the studies are only a small percentage of the actual Caribbean population. The National Survey of American Life research indicates that Caribbean Americans use of outpatient mental health services significantly less than other ethnic groups (Jackson et al., 2007) including Black Americans (Gibbs et al., 2013; Williams et al., 2007). Furthermore, individuals, who are primarily among second-generation Caribbean populations, who do seek counseling have been generally less satisfied with mental and health care services received (Jackson et al., 2007). The reasons for this are often linked to the clinical staff's cultural incompetence, ethnocentric stereotyping, or the clients' poor previous experiences with mental health system (Fiscella et al., 2000). Caribbean Americans have a different set of issues relating to acculturation/accommodation and tri-cultural issues (e.g., immigration, social class, race, ethnicity, gender, sexuality, racial and ethnic discrimination, etc.) (Hine-St. Hilaire, 2008), which often get overlooked or minimized by mental health clinicians.

The literature suggests that nativity and immigrant characteristics are correlated with psychological health (Bryant, 2003; Williams et al., 2007), use of formal mental health programs (Gibbs et al., 2013; Jackson et al., 2007), and satisfaction with them (Jackson et al., 2007). The combination of these factors can serve as impediments to seeking support from these Eurocentric institutions. Thus, having a greater understanding of the potential cultural issues regarding Caribbean American adjustments to the US is very important for mental health practitioners.

Therapeutic Issues

Caribbean Americans are a misunderstood population in the mental health profession making them vulnerable to inadequate treatment. Considered to experience what Bryce-Laporte (1972) notes a "double invisibility," Caribbean Americans have been specifically studied in US psychology only within the last few decades. There has been even less attention provided to studies within mental health and epidemiologic research (Jackson et al., 2007). It is imperative when working with this group that mental health clinicians understand core challenges that are experienced by Caribbean American communities. As the chapter discussed, Caribbean immigrants and their descendants are likely to experience cultural issues that maybe different from both larger mainstream White American culture as well as their African American peers. It is highly likely that issues of race are even more complex for this group due to what I note as *dual acculturation*, which can be defined as simultaneous acculturation to the mainstream US culture and the African American culture. Classic acculturation theory from which newer theories are derived have not accounted for this when describing classic models whether they be uni-dimensional (Gordon, 1964) or bi-dimensional (Berry 1992, 1997) models. This issue is only a few of the considerations of note for Caribbean Americans. Additional themes are as follows:

1. Lack of belief in mental illness and modern medicine

Caribbean Americans are reluctant to share their concerns with others outside their circle (Hine-St. Hiliare, 2008). This reluctance may be connected to several culturally-related preferences and beliefs. First is the preference for indigenous healing practices over Western medicine including traditional mental health counseling. Spiritual healers, clergywomen and clergymen are often consulted and confided in (Gopaul-McNicol, 1998; Sutherland, Moodley, & Chevannes, 2014). They have become a common reliable practice as indigenous spirituality practices have been handed down for generations and deemed very effective.

Secondly, there may be the stigma of mental illness in the community (Sutherland, Moodley, & Chevannes, 2014). Baptiste, Hardy, and Lewis (1997) note the prevailing cultural belief is that "crazy people" seek mental health services. "Craziness" is also believed to be genetically transmitted and not socially constructed. Therefore, pursuing therapy can result in family stigmatization (Hine-St. Hilaire, 2008). The social upkeep of the family unit can be important in smaller communities. Thus, not making family appear in a negative manner is important. Unfortunately, this reduces the likelihood of mentally ill persons getting the help needed, which may ultimately result in experiences of increased psychological issues.

Previous research has explored how ambivalence exists in religious and traditional practices. For example, Sutherland, Moodley, and Chevannes (2014) contend, "It is important to factor in the cultural practices of a people in any attempt to develop an efficacious health model" (p. 37). Any health model that is not cognizant of people's cultural beliefs will experience resistance in application. Thus, Sutherland, Moodley, and Chevannes (2014) support flexibility and suggest recognizing the appeal of indigenous healing traditions (e.g., herbal remedies, prayer, spiritual baths, etc.) for clients of Caribbean descent when working with them. These and other typical practices can be used to complement one's practice and may assist the effectiveness of the clinical work. Clinicians grounded in the common healing principles of "holism and mind-body sprit connection" can be found in the worldviews of many Caribbean Americans at home and abroad (Sutherland, Moodley, & Chevannes, 2014). Additionally, Short et al. (2010) note that flexibility with immigrants and refugees can have great therapeutic utility for these clients depending on their needs and particular acculturation background.

A third possible issue affecting reluctance to seek mental health assistance, at least in the US, may involve immigrants' legal status. If immigrants are undocumented, or even if they have legal documentation, they may also weigh the costs/benefit of seeking help. Fear of them or family members being discriminated against by detainment and/or deportation, thus may cost them care (Lipson & Dibble, 2005).

2. Economic priorities

In California, he [Ferguson] was remembered as brash, arrogant, disdainful of the menial jobs he found… (McFadden, 2013, p. 1).

Short et al. (2010) discuss the importance of exploring the psychological meaning of work and advancement for immigrants. This may be one of the best ways to build *credibility* (Sue & Zane, 1987) for this population, which may support clients in developing trust in the therapeutic alliance and process. This component of therapeutic exploration may be ignored or minimized by many clinicians who place a larger emphasis on other life roles. However, considering the historical importance for many Caribbean Americans of upward social mobility as the ultimate purpose of the migration (Gopaul-McNicol, 1998), and the adverse impact of immigration on family structure, ignoring or underestimating the efficacy of this type of exploration may be problematic.

3. Disconnection/disruption of family unit migration

Traveling for Caribbean communities was and mostly remains an integral part of several Caribbean countries' culture (Alleyne 2002) and can have both costs and benefits to the family unit amid the financial and other quality of life benefits often sought in the US (Bashi-Bobb, 2001; Hine-St. Hilaire, 2008). Characteristically, immigrants may arrive in a chain form, which means that the mother or father arrives before the children (Gopaul-McNicol, 1998; Turner, 1991) in order to create a foundation for other family members to come (Turner, 1991). This arrival pattern can be disruptive to the family unit and, as many dynamic theorists may posit, can adversely impact identity development for children (Gopaul-McNicol, 1998).

4. Discrepancy between expectations and realities of living in the US

Baptiste, Hardy, and Lewis (1997) discuss the misperceptions of the US that become clear for immigrants upon arrival to the US. Clients often recount tales of a fantastic US, based on family and friends' extravagant reports, only to feel bamboozled and disappointed once in the US. It is also quite likely that the media's glamorous portrayal of the US adds to the immigrants' lofty expectations about life there. Therefore, mental health clinicians should be sensitive to clients' narratives concerning themes of confusion, disappointment, and regret regarding their adjustment to US culture.

Assessing clients' social supports can be helpful in this case. The presence of supportive extended family members can be an asset to cultural adjustments to the US. Lincoln and Chae (2011) note, however, that while a family that provides emotional support can be a protective factor from Major Depressive Disorder (MDD) it can also be a significant stressor for a Caribbean American who experiences depression and can contribute to MDD. The authors state that negative interaction defined as "conflict, excessive demands and criticism" of the depressed person and a perceived unsupportive environment of Caribbean Americans can actually be a risk factor for those with MDD.

5. Disconnection related to understanding the culture

This theme is applicable to first- and second-generation Caribbean Americans. In 2009, 1.2 million Black children were either immigrants or had at least one Caribbean-born parent (McCabe, 2011). Thus, problems navigating the US culture could serve as a source of concern for families with multiple levels of acculturation.

Members of this population can feel marginalized during cultural transitions where they may find it challenging to fit one or both contexts. Despite this, there are some benefits. Hall (2012) and Hall and Carter (2006) noted that second-generation Caribbean Americans exhibit a level of sophistication in navigating several cultures, for example, mainstream culture, Black American and the culture of their parents. Their ability to perceive discrimination at higher rates than their parents (Hall & Carter, 2006) may help them make more sense of the pervasive role of discrimination and adjusting their own understanding to it (e.g., mistrust of Whites, or preparation for bias), thereby conceptualizing race in ways that would be consistent with US society. However, this ability and awareness also can create conflict between them and their first-generation parents (Baptiste, Hardy, & Lewis, 1997; Hine-St. Hilaire, 2008).

Essentially, these second-generation Caribbean Americans become pioneers due to not likely having a similar working model of racial socialization like their African American peers. They may become stressed from code switching or oscillating between their parent's cultural values, ideas of how to be Black and those associated with Black America (Hall, 2012); self-socializing themselves to the US context, especially if these protective socialization styles clash with their parents' beliefs and perceptions about race. Clinicians should be open to exploring these dynamics with second-generation Caribbean American clients. Culturally competent therapeutic exploration of these issues can assist the client in attaining greater understanding about the relationship between their acculturation experiences and their racial identity development.

6. Redefining and navigating race

Caribbean Americans may identify with Black individuals of diverse ethnicities. Caribbean Americans, who are, as previously stated, situated at the intersection of two different conceptions of group identity, race and ethnicity, negotiate these complex identities (Hall, 2012). Both race and ethnicity differ vastly and have important implications for identity development. However, although race and ethnicity are both important, race is the most important construct in the US. To develop a racial identity ego status one is socialized by his/her family/community, which leads one to evolve an orientation to a racial group. As discussed earlier, ethnocentric bias (Hall, 2012; Jackson & Cothran, 2003) and stereotypes may come up for Caribbean Americans along with racial pride (Hall, 2012). Exploring both pride and prejudice for Caribbean Americans about their own racial group in counseling may be challenging if the therapist does not understand the complexities of identity development for this population. Thus, counselors must be sensitive to the existence of Caribbean American clients' diverse views about "Blackness."

Global Considerations for Working With Caribbean Americans

In counseling the Caribbean American clients, several issues must be addressed. First, mental health clinicians should take into account the unique acculturation stories that multiple generations of Caribbean Americans may hold as a part of their 'collective unconscious,' including intergenerational trauma, and acculturation processes to the US culture and existing subcultures.

The first task of the therapist is to communicate understanding and acceptance of the Caribbean American clients and their system and presenting problems. The next task would be an exploration of one's attitudes, feelings and beliefs about Caribbean American clients. Misinformation and cultural differences are significant contributors to dissatisfaction of Caribbean American clients (Jackson et al., 2007). It is also best to learn the clients' culture from the client, as there is heterogeneity among the various Caribbean islands (Sutherland, Moodley, & Chevannes, 2014).

Readdressing Colin Ferguson

> In sum, let us enter a plea for *clinical* clinicians who can distinguish unconscious depression from conscious despair, paranoia from adaptive wariness, and who can tell the difference between a sick man and a sick nation. (Grier & Cobbs, 1968, p. 158)

Colin Ferguson never entered therapy although he had expressed signs of unrest. Several of the aforementioned concepts for working with Caribbeans outlined in this chapter would be applicable to Ferguson if he presented clinically. Three of the major factors can be lack of successful economic gains, race negotiation, and disinterest in mental health.

For instance, expectance of economic success correlated with coming to the US for most immigrants is paramount in Ferguson's case. It was something Ferguson constantly complained about and a catalyst to his complaints about institutionalized racism that he expressed experiencing. He took higher education courses for the goal of having better, more lucrative employment opportunities. To seek a better life yet not feeling successful at creating one can be difficult to accept.

Ferguson's disconnection with the US culture may have led to his subsequent challenges with navigating racial relations as a Black immigrant in the US. While they are many ways immigrants can find themselves feeling disconnected or even marginalized from the host culture, for a Black immigrant like Ferguson, how to negotiate race is key because it entails how to cope with the likelihood of racial discrimination. Paranoia and rage are viable coping responses to racism. However, Grier and Cobbs (1968) caution about the ways both paranoia and rage can fluctuate, if not contextualized and controlled. This is, quite possibly, what occurred for Ferguson.

Blacks socialized in the US can be considered "educated recipients," a term used by Grier and Cobbs (1968) to describe Blacks with formal education in integrated professional settings who may experience rage. They note:

> If these educated recipients of the White man's bounty find it hard to control their rage, what of the less fortunate kinsman who has less to protect, less to lose, and more scars to show for his journey in this land? (Grier & Cobbs, 1968, p. 207)

In Ferguson's situation and that of other immigrants, the education of "educated recipients" extends beyond formal education. It includes a specific type of cultural education necessary for managing American racism as a Black immigrant. Black immigrants specifically have to accommodate and integrate new racial information about being Black in the US, an often, overlooked component in acculturation discussions for Black immigrants (Hall, 2012). This *education* is likened to "street smarts." These *cultural street smarts* a Caribbean American often needs comes from gradual emersion in US culture and society as a Person of Color. In "losing his cool," it was likely Ferguson had not developed the competencies required to understand his three socialization perspectives (i.e., Caribbean Indian, Black American and White American) in ways that allowed him to succeed. What many believed to be his obsession with racism resulted in him becoming a novelty, an oddity to his Caribbean American and, he was stigmatized for it.

Finally, Ferguson was another novelty because he highlighted mental illness in his community. Persons in Ferguson's community (e.g., college professors, college disciplinary board, neighbors, landlord, etc.) admittedly experienced his decomposition, yet offered no support, effectively turning a 'blind eye.' While their actions suggested Ferguson should be self-reliant and illustrated their own lack of social responsibility, they were likely also informed by the stigma of mental illness (Gopaul-McNicol, 1998; Johnson, Weller, Williams, & Pottinger, 2008). Unfortunately, Ferguson was also unable to assess his mental health needs and bypassed any options for requesting help from others.

CONCLUSION

Caribbean Americans' influence has impacted American culture enough to now see signs of this on US Census forms. Yet, they are one of the most misunderstood groups, often overlooked regarding their specific mental health needs. Rarely are they explicitly targeted for outreach and psycho-education to improve their quality of life as double marginalized groups in the US. The high importance that Caribbean Americans place on success often creates a dilemma: they may be accomplished and yet have significant mental health problems that can go undiagnosed or therapeutically treated. Immigrants often feel they must present as being strong, unscathed, or resilient (Johnson, et al. 2008). This value can hold firm even in the midst of challenging experiences, which can include adapting US-based racial identity attitudes (Hall, 2012) to navigate the *Two Americas*. They likely can need additional support and may not seek it overwhelmingly due to stigma of mental health or the general desire to be self-sufficient, thus successful. Mental health clinicians working with Caribbean Americans can help relieve the stigma of seeking and receiving mental health treatment. They can do this by understanding and catering to the culture, creating programs to outreach and support Caribbean Americans.

REFERENCES

Alleyne, M. C. (2002). *The construction and representation of race and ethnicity in the Caribbean and the world.* Kingston, Jamaica: University of the West Indies.

Baptiste, D. A., Hardy, K .V., & Lewis, L. (1997). Family therapy with English Caribbean immigrant families in the United States: Issues of emigration, immigration, culture, and race. *Contemporary Family Therapy, 19*(3), 337–359.

Bashi Bobb, V. (2001). Neither ignorance nor bliss: Race, racism, and the West Indian immigrant experience. In H. Cordero-Guzmán, R. Smith, & R. Grosfoguel (Eds.),

Migration, transnationalism, and race in a changing New York (pp. 212–238). Philadelphia, PA: Temple University Press.

Benson, J. (2006). Exploring the racial identities of Black immigrants in the United States. *Sociological Forum, 21*(2), 219–247.

Berry, J. W. (1992). Acculturation and Adaptation in a New Society. *International Migration, 30*, 69–85. doi: 10.1111/j.1468-2435.1992.tb00776.x

Berry J. W. (1997). Immigration, acculturation, and adaptation. *Applied Psychology: An International Review, 46*, 5–68. doi: 10.1111/j.1464-0597.1997.tb01087.x

Boyd-Franklin, N. (2003). *Black families in therapy. Understanding the African American experience* (2nd ed.). New York, NY: Guilford Press.

Bryant, S. A. (2003). Making culture visible: An examination of birthplace and health status. *Health Care for Women International, 24*, 103–114.

Bryce-Laporte, R. S. (1972). Black immigrants: The experience of invisibility and inequality. *Journal of Black Studies, 3*, 29–56.

Broman, C. L., Torres, M., Canady, R. B., Neighbors, H. W., & Jackson, J. S (2010). Race and Ethnic Self-identification influences on physical and mental health statuses among Blacks. *Race and Social Problems, 2*, 81–91.

Carter, R. T. (2007). Racism and psychological and emotional injury: Recognizing and assessing race-based traumatic stress. *The Counseling Psychologist, 35*(1), 13–105.

Chae, D. H., Lincoln, K. D., & Jackson, J. S. (2011). Discrimination, attribution, and racial group identification: Implications for psychological distress among Black Americans in the National Survey of American Life (2001–2003). *American Journal of Orthopsychiatry, 81*(4), 498–506.

Fiscella K., Franks, P., Gold, M. R., & Clancy, C. M. (2000). Inequality in quality: Addressing socioeconomic, racial, and ethnic disparities in health care. *Journal of the American Medical Association, 283*(19), 2579–2584.

Foner, N. (2001). *Islands in the city: West Indian migration to New York*. Berkeley, CA: University of California Press.

Forsyth, J. M., Hall, S., & Carter, R. T. (2015). Racial identity among African Americans and Black West Indian Americans. *Professional Psychology, 46*, 124–131.

Gibbs, T. A., Okuda, M., Oquendo, M. A., Lawson, W. B., Wang, S., Thomas, Y. F., & Blanco, C. (2013). Mental health of African Americans and Caribbean Blacks in the United States: Results from the National Epidemiological survey on Alcohol Related Conditions. *American Journal of Public Health, 103*(2), 330–338. doi:10.2105/AJPH.2012.300891

Gopaul- McNicol, S. (1998). Caribbean families: Social and emotional problems. *Journal of Social Distress and the Homeless, 7*(1), 55–73.

Gordon M. (1964). *Assimilation in American life*. New York, NY: Oxford University Press.

Grant, B. F., Stinson, F. S., Hasin, D. S., Dawson, D. A., Chou S. P., & Anderson, K. (2004). Immigration and lifetime prevalence of DSM-IV psychiatric disorders among Mexican Americans and non-Hispanic Whites in the United States: Results from the National Epidemiologic Survey on Alcohol and Related Conditions. *Archives of General Psychiatry, 61*(12), 1226–33.

Grier, W., & Cobbs, P. (1968). *Black rage*. New York, NY: Bantam.

Hall, S. P. (2012). The role of racial socialization and ethnocentrism in the racial identity development of second-generation West Indian Americans. *Dissertation Abstracts International, Section B: The Sciences and Engineering, 68*(9–B), 6356.

Hall S. P., & Carter R. T. (2006). The relationship between racial identity and perceptions of racial discrimination in an Afro-Caribbean sample. *Journal of Black Psychology, 32*(2), 155–175.

Harrison, G., Owens, D., Holton, A., Neilson, D., & Boot, D. (1988). A prospective study of severe mental disorder in Afro-Caribbean patients. *Psychological Medicine, 18,* 643–657.

Helms, J. E. (1990). *Black and White racial identity: Theory, research, and practice.* Westport, CT: Greenwood.

Hine-St. Hilaire, D. (2008). Immigrant West Indian families and their struggles with racism in America. *Journal of Emotional Abuse, 6*(2–3), 47–60.

hooks, b. (1996). *Killing rage.* New York, NY: Henry Holt and Company.

Hutchinson, G., & Haasen, C. (2004) Migration and schizophrenia: The challenges for European psychiatry and implications for the future. *Social Psychiatry and Psychiatric Epidemiology, 39,* 350–357.

Jackson, J. S., Neighbors, H. W., Torres, M., Martin, L. A., Williams, D. R., & Baser, R. (2007). Use of mental health services and subjective satisfaction with treatment among Black Caribbean immigrants: Results from the National Survey of American Life. *American Journal of Public Health, 97*(1), 60–67.

Jackson, J. V., & Cothran, M. E. (2003). Black versus Black: The relationships among African, African American, and African Caribbean persons. *Journal of Black Studies, 33*(5), 576–604.

James, W. (1999). *Holding aloft the banner of Ethiopia: Caribbean radicalism in early Twentieth Century America.* New York, NY: Verso.

Johnson R., Weller P., Brown S., & Pottinger A. M. (2008). The application of traditional psychotherapy models in the Caribbean. In F. W. Hickling, B. K. Matthies, K. Morgan, & R. C. Gibson (Eds), *Perspectives in Caribbean Psychology* (pp. 537–557). Philadelphia, PA: Jessica Kingsley Publishers.

Kent, M. M. (2007). Immigration and America's Black population. *Population Bulletin, 92*(4), 1–16.

Kuby, R. (2012). *Investigation Discovery's 'Killer trials: Judgment day Long Island Railroad massacre'.* Retrieved from http://watchseries-online.li/2012/05/killer-trials-judgment-day-121-the-long-island-railroad-massacre

Levine, D., Siegel, J. A., Himle, R., Joseph T., Abelson, J. M., Matusko, N., Muroff, J., & Jackson, J. S. (2013). Panic disorder among African Americans, Caribbean blacks and non-Hispanic whites. *Social Psychiatry and Psychiatric Epidemiology, 48*(5), 711–723.

Lincoln, K. D., & Chae, D. H. (2011). Emotional support, negative interaction and major depressive disorder among African Americans and Caribbean Blacks: Findings from the National Survey of American Life. *Social Psychiatry Psychiatric Epidemiology, 47,* 361–372.

Link, B. C., & Phelan, J. (1995). Social conditions as fundamental causes of disease. *Journal of Health and Social Behavior, 35,* 80–94.

Logan, J. R., & Deane, G. (2003). *Black diversity in metropolitan America.* Lewis Mumford Center for Comparative Urban Regional Research. Albany, New York: Author.

Maynard, M. J., Harding, S., & Minnis, H. (2007). Psychological well-being in Black Caribbean, Black African and White adolescents in the UK medical research council DASH study. *Social Psychiatry Psychiatric Epidemiology, 42,* 759–769.

McCabe, K. (2011) *Caribbean immigrants in the United States.* Washington, D.C.: Migration Policy Institute. Retrieved from http://www.migrationinformation.org/US-focus/display.cfm?ID=834

McFadden, R. D. (1993). A tormented life—A special report. A long slide from privilege ends in slaughter on a train. *The New York Times.* Retrieved from http://www.nytimes.com/1993/12/12/nyregion/tormented-life-special-report-long-slide-privilege-ends-slaughter-train.html?pagewanted=all

McQuiston, J. T. (1995, February, 18). Jury finds Ferguson guilty of slayings on the L.I.R.R. *The New York Times.* Retrieved from http:// www.nytimes.com

Miranda, J., Siddique, J., Belin, T. R., & Kohn-Wood, L. (2005). Depression prevalence in disadvantaged young Black women: African and Caribbean immigrants compared to US-born African Americans. *Social Psychiatry and Psychiatry Epidemiology, 40,* 253–258.

Model, S. (*2008*). *West Indian immigrants: A Black success story?* New York, NY: RussellSage.

Neighbors, H., Naji, R., & Jackson, J. S. (2007). Race, ethnicity, John Henryism, and depressive symptoms: The national survey of American life adult reinterview. *Research in Human Development, 4*(1&2), 71–87.

Newhill, C. E. (1990). The role of culture in the development of paranoid symptomatology. *American Journal of Orthopsychiatry, 60*(2), 176–185.

Oh, H., Yang, L. H., Anglin, D. M., & DeVylder, J. E. (2014). Perceived discrimination and psychotic experiences across multiple ethnic groups in the United States. *Schizophrenia Research, 157*(1), 259–65.

Pieterse, A. L. (2005). The relationship between perceptions of racism, life stress, racial identity, and psychological functioning in Black men: An exploratory investigation. Ph.D. dissertation, Columbia University, United States—New York. Retrieved March 18, 2014, from *Dissertations & Theses: Full Text.* (Publication No. AAT 3182978).

Rogers, R. (2004). Race based coalitions among minority groups, Afro-Caribbean immigrants and African Americans in New York City. *Urban Affairs Review, 39*(3) 283–317.

Rumbaut, R. G. (1994). The crucible within: Ethnic identity, self-esteem and segmented assimilation among children of immigrants. *International Migration Review, 28,* 748–794.

Selten, J. P., Slaets, J. P. J., & Kahn, R. S. (1997). Schizophrenia in Surinamese and Dutch Antillean immigrants to the Netherlands: Evidence of an increased incidence. *Psychological Medicine, 27,* 807–811.

Sharpley, M., Hutchinson, G., McKenzie, K., & Murray, R. M. (2001). Understanding the excess of psychosis among the African-Caribbean population in England: review of current hypotheses. *British Journal of Psychiatry, 178* (suppl. 40), S60–S68.

Short, E., Suzuki, L., Prendes-Lintel, M., Prendes-Lintel Furr, G., Madabhushi, S., & Mapel, G. (2010). Counseling immigrants and refugees. In J. G. Ponterotto, J. M. Casas, L. A. Suzuki, & C. M. Alexander (Eds.), *Handbook of Multicultural Counseling* (3rd ed., pp 201–211). Thousand Oaks, CA: Sage.

Soto, J. A., Dawson-Andoh, N. A., & BeLue, R. (2011). The relationship between perceived discrimination and Generalized Anxiety Disorder among African Americans, Afro Caribbeans, and Non-Hispanic Whites. *Journal of Anxiety Disorders, 25*(2), 258–265.

Sue, D. W., & Sue, D. (2012). *Counseling the culturally diverse: Theory and practice* (6th ed.). New York, NY: Wiley.

Sue, S., & Zane, N. (1987). The role of culture and cultural techniques in psychotherapy: A critique and reformulation. *American Psychologist, 42*(1), 37–45.

Sutherland, P., Moodley, R., & Chevannes, B. (Eds.) (2014). *Caribbean healing traditions: Implications for health and mental health.* New York, NY: Routledge.

Sutton, C. R., & Makiesky, S. P. (1975). Migration and West Indian racial and ethnic consciousness. In H. I. Safa & B. M. Dutoit (Eds.), *Migration and development: Implications ethnic identity and political conflict.* Berlin, Germany: Mouton de Gruyter.

Taylor, J. Y., Caldwell, C., Bayser, R., Faison, N., & Jackson, J. (2007). Prevalence of eating disorders among Blacks in the National Survey of American Life. *International Journal of Eating Disorders, 40,* S10–S14.

Taylor, J. Y., Caldwell, C., Baser, R., Matusko, N., Faison, N., & Jackson, J. (2013). Classification and correlates of eating disorders among Blacks: Findings from the National Survey of American Life. *Journal of Health Care for the Poor and Underserved, 24*(1), 289–310.

The Schomburg Center for Research and Black Culture: African American Migration Experience. (2005). *Caribbean Migration.* Retrieved from http://www.inmotionaame.org/print.cfm?migration=10

Thomas, K. J. A. (2012). *A demographic profile of Black Caribbean immigrants in the United States.* Washington, DC: Migration Policy Institute.

Turner, J. E. (1991). Migrants and their therapists: A trans-context approach. *Family Process, 30,* 407–419.

Vickerman, M. (2001). Tweaking the monolith: The West Indian immigrant encounter with "blackness." In N. Foner (Ed.), *Islands in the city: West Indian migration to New York* (pp. 237–256). Berkley, CA: University of California Press.

Viruell-Fuentes, E. A., Miranda, P. Y., & Abdulrahim, S. (2012). More than culture: Structural racism, intersectionality theory, and immigrant health. *Social Science & Medicine,* 2099–2106.

Washington, S. L. (2004). *Principles of racial taxonomy.* Paper presented at the annual meeting of the American Sociological Association, San Francisco, CA. Retrieved from http://www.allacademic.com/meta/p110912_index.html

Waters, M. C. (1994). Ethnic and racial identities of second-generation Black immigrants in New York City. *International Migration Review, 28*(4 Special Issue: The new second generation), 795–820.

Waters, M. C. (1999). *Black identities: West Indian immigrant dreams and American realities.* Cambridge, MA: Harvard University Press.

Williams, D. R., Gonzalez, H. M., Neighbors, H. Randolph, N., & Abelson, J. M., Sweetman, J., & Jackson, J. S. (2013). Prevalence and distribution of major depressive disorder in African Americans, Caribbean Blacks, and Non-HispanicWhites. *Archives of General Psychiatry, 64*(3), 305–315.

Williams, D. R., Haile, R., Gonzalez, H. M., Neighbors, H. Baser, R., & Jackson, J. S. (2007). The mental health of Black Caribbean immigrants: Results from the National Survey of American Life. *American Journal of Public Health, 97*(1), 52–59.

Williams, D. R., Lavizzo-Mourey, R., & Warren, R. C. (2004). The concept of race and health status in America. *Public Health Reports, 109*(1), 26–41.

CHAPTER 2

AFRICANA WOMEN'S WAYS OF COPING WITH TRAUMATIC LIFE EVENTS

A Meta-Ethnography

Nyasha Grayman-Simpson, Jacqueline S. Mattis, and Nenelwa Tomi

This chapter presents results of a meta-ethnographic study of the coping strategies employed by Africana women in response to traumatic life events. Within the stress and coping literature, Traumatic Life Events (Kubany et al., 2000) are variably known as Negative Life Events (Garnefski, Kraaij, & Spinhoven, 2001), Stressful Life Events (Goodman, Corcoran, Turner, Yuan, & Green, 1998), and simply as Life Events (Gray, Litz, Hsu, & Lombardo, 2004). Consistent with the criteria set forth in the Diagnostic and Statistical Manual of Mental Disorders (5th ed.; *DSM–5*; American Psychiatric Association, 2013), this body of literature construes traumatic life events as discrete experiences that involve actual or threatened death or serious injury; or, a threat to the physical integrity of self and/ or others. Such events may include the death of a loved one, a physical assault, a sexual assault, a life-threatening accident, receiving a life-threatening/debilitating medical diagnosis, the sudden loss of shelter/dislocation, and/or the sudden loss of paid work/basic provisions.

Talking About Structural Inequalities in Everyday Life: New Politics of Race in Groups, Organizations, and Social Systems, pages 25–45.
Copyright © 2016 by Information Age Publishing
All rights of reproduction in any form reserved.

Interest in this work emerged out of the first author's reflections on her own coping with a traumatic life event-namely, the sudden death of her son, Isaiah in 2010. Her main strategies included: (1) reliance on religion and spirituality, (2) reliance on social support (especially from other Black women), and (3) reliance on adaptive characteristics of The Strong Black Woman archetype. The first author wondered if Black women situated across the African diaspora utilized these same coping strategies to make it through experiences of trauma. In other words, she wondered if the strategies reflected broader transnational Africana women's ways of coping.

Noted Black feminist thought scholar, Patricia Hills Collins (1991), suggests that theorizing Africana women's ways of coping with trauma requires first, searching our own experiences, and those of other Africana women, for themes we think important. Second, theorizing requires consultation with related established bodies of scholarship. The first author's subjective knowledge of the importance of religion/spirituality, Black women's support, and The Strong Black Woman archetype to Africana women's ways of coping is supported by knowledge derived from a well-respected body of scholarship. This work speaks to Africana people's shared ontological understanding of the universe; specifically, our spiritual/metaphysical orientation toward it (Mbiti, 1991; Myers, 1985; Nobles, 1972; Wade-Gayles, 1995). It also highlights our shared anti-Black colonial and imperial histories (Rodney, 1981), and Africana women's resulting relatively low political-economic-social positioning within global racial patriarchies (Collins, 2000). While previous scholars have discussed the influence of these forces on Black women's religious/spiritual, supportive, and archetypal ways of coping within an American context (see Goins, 2011; Mattis, 2002; Woods-Giscombé, 2010), the aforementioned ontological and social dynamics transcend nation-state boundaries. Thus, it is reasonable to suppose the utilization of similar coping strategies on a transnational scale. The chapter authors use meta-ethnography to interrogate the viability of the first author's supposition that religion/spirituality, support from other Black women, and reliance on the Strong Black Woman archetype represent prototypical Africana women's ways of coping with traumatic life events. In this way, we seek to innovate and complicate current conceptualizations of, and approaches to the study of the impact of racial-gender structural inequalities on our everyday lives.

METHODOLOGY

Meta-ethnography offers a systematic approach to synthesizing findings from existing qualitative research studies (Noblit & Hare, 1988). As a perspective, it "is a methodology born of the sociology of knowledge" (p. 5). It is value-explicit, comparative, and interpretive. IRB approval for this meta-ethnographic investigation has been granted by the first author's affiliated institution.

Noblit and Hare suggest a seven-step process to conducting meta-ethnography that includes: (1) Getting started; (2) Deciding what is relevant to the initial interest; (3) Reading the studies; (4) Determining how the studies are related; (5) Translating the studies into one another; (6) Synthesizing translations; and (7) Expressing the synthesis (1988). These phases "overlap and repeat as the synthesis proceeds" (p. 26). Our journey with this particular meta-ethnography took us through several complete cycles of this seven-step process.

Phase 1 of this process "involves identifying an intellectual interest that qualitative research might inform…that is worthy of the synthesis effort" (p. 26). We believe that we have already offered a compelling justification for this meta-ethnographic study of Africana women's coping with traumatic life events in the introduction. Thus, we will not take up space repeating our rationale here.

Phase 2 involves deciding which literature is relevant to the area of research interest. Recognizing that it is "difficult to know when one is being exhaustive, given that not all studies are published or publicly available" (p. 27), we did attempt to conduct a comprehensive search of the literature within the parameters that we set forth. The first parameter set concerned date of publication. In order to make the task of analyzing the data manageable, the review was restricted to studies published in 2000 or later. Second, publications had to be written in English. Third, the study had to focus on the phenomenological experiences of Africana women coping with traumatic life events, as subjectively narrated by Africana female study participants themselves. More than 20 search terms were entered into Academic Search Complete and Google Scholar. These terms included *Black Canadian Women Coping, Afro-Caribbean Women Coping, Sudanese Women Coping, Afro-European Women Coping, Afro-Latina Women Coping, LatiNegra Coping,* and *African American Women Coping.* The search led to a review of more than 1000 studies contained within approximately 200 pages of results. Studies deemed methodologically untrustworthy according to accepted criteria set forth by Lincoln and Guba (1986) were excluded from analysis. The remaining eligible pool of studies was analyzed until we felt that we had reached the point of saturation with respect to emergent themes of coping with traumatic life events (Morse, 1995). Ultimately, 31 studies inclusive of more than 1000 Africana women's voices from close to 20 Africana enclaves sufficiently captured the thematic trends present in Africana women's coping.

Repeated careful reading of the narrative accounts contained within each individual study is at the heart of Phase 3. Specifically, the first and third authors separately read and re-read narratives within individual studies for the purposes of generating preliminary types of coping codes. We compared, discussed, and integrated our separate lists to create one preliminary list of codes. Interestingly, although the first and third authors come from ethnically dissimilar backgrounds (i.e., the first author's family roots are in the U.S. South, Caribbean, and Canada, while the third author's family roots are in Tanzania), our codes were remarkably similar. The few instances of disagreement were easily resolved through brief discussion and consensus. In Phase 4, we replicated the process of Phase 3, this time looking for consistency in codes across studies.

Phase 5 involved translating the name of codes into language consistent with psychological discourse. During Phase 6, we synthesized the translations into superordinate themes for the purpose of creating a cogent new narrative that was greater than the sum of its parts. Getting to the final analysis required movement through several cycles of this process. Phase 7, the final phase of this process involved deciding how to express the results of the investigation. We chose to express our findings through the written word, in the form of this book chapter.

FINDINGS

Spirituality

Concerning the nature of spirituality, Black feminist writer, Gloria Wade-Gayles (2002) reminds us:

> ...spirituality, defies definition-a fact that speaks to its power as much as it reflects its mystery. Like the wind, it cannot be seen, and yet, like the wind, it is surely there, and we bear witness to its presence, its power. We cannot hold it in our hands and put it on a scale, but we feel the weight, the force, of its influence in our lives. We cannot hear it, but we hear ourselves speaking and singing and testifying because it moves, inspires, and directs us to do so. (p. 2)

And still, while spirituality defies simple definition, it is crucial to attend to the ways that Africana women attempt to define the phenomenon. With this aim in mind, the second author's qualitative study of spirituality proposes that Africana women envision spirituality as:

> ...an intimate relationship between God, the individual, and others...a journey of self-reflection, self-criticism, and self-awareness that culminates in a greater understanding of the relationship between self, God, and the larger community (including the community of ancestors). (Mattis, 2000, p. 118)

The importance of spiritual coping cannot be overstated. Without exception, it was discussed as a primary way of coping with traumatic life events among Africana women.

God Has a Greater Purpose and Plan for Us

Africana women believe that God is omnipotent, and as such, allows traumatic things to happen. Not for nefarious reasons or for their own sake, but always as part of a greater beneficent plan and purpose. For example, in response to being diagnosed with a mental illness, Joann, a Caribbean Canadian woman says:

> I try not to let umm make things bother me. I just believe that anything that happens in your life, any circumstances or any situations are all a part of the plan God have fah yuh. That's what I think. I mean that certain things that happen to you are a part

of the choices that you make but it's all a part of the divine plan that God has for you. (Jackson & Naidoo, 2012, p. 228)

Being personally connected to traumas that God allows to happen, makes us part of God's greater plan, and players in God's greater purpose. The traumatic event becomes special, and we become special beings with a specially defined purpose. In this way, there is great meaning attached to our suffering.

God Gives Us Strength and Power to Survive

Africana women also believe that God gives us the strength to survive; to continue to exist, despite our traumatic life experiences. Comfort, a Black American woman whose grandson was murdered notes:

I am not a weeping crying person, but it was a deep hurt, a deep hurt [*sic*], and I just think I needed what I depended on most of my life, a faith in God, being able to help us get through anything, and that is one of the worst things to try to get through. (Sharpe & Boyas, 2011, p. 862)

God Gives Us Strength and Power to Endure

Related, we believe that God gives us the strength to endure the pain until we are able to get to the place of survivorship. Kwenhangana, who witnessed the beating and rape of her sister during the Rwandan genocide, describes this divinely inspired endurance:

You know if Jesus went through all that, if he had the power to stop it and he didn't just to show me how difficult life is, who am I to quit? Who am I to quit? With that said, okay, I changed the whole situation. (Sherwood & Liebling-Kalifani, 2012, p. 100)

Humanistic psychologist, Abraham Maslow (1943) developed a theory suggesting that all humans are fundamentally motivated toward the realization of self-actualization. He went on to explain that self-actualization required first, the fulfillment of more basic human needs, including physiological, safety, belonging/love, respect/esteem, cognitive, and aesthetic needs. If we think about adaptive coping from a Maslowian needs perspective (Maslow, 1943), God's provision of strength and power to endure and survive meets our most basic physiological human needs.

God Gives Us Strength and Power to Surrender

In addition to providing us with strength and power to survive and endure, we believe that God gives us the strength to surrender to God's greater power. We turn troubles over to God, possessing a sense of assurance that everything will turn out alright. Illustrating these points, Beatrice, a Caribbean Canadian woman whose son was murdered, shares, "I felt, you know what, let God be in charge because I'm not in charge, He is. I just ask God, Lord you are in control, let your spirit abide in me because I can't do this alone" (Bailey, Hannays-King, Clarke, Lester, & Velasco, 2013, p. 345).

Our finding around Africana women's reliance on spiritual surrender to cope with traumatic life events mirrors second author, Mattis' finding unearthed within a qualitative study of African American women over a decade earlier (see Mattis, 2002). Consistent with Mattis' earlier interpretation of that finding, we again suggest that spiritual surrender among Africana women is not a passive, escapist coping response, as it has been construed within traditional psychodynamic psychological literature (see Freud, 1952). Rather, spiritual surrender among Africana women is a response requiring active confrontation of trauma-related problems; and, it is a response that seems to ultimately lead to a sense of personal empowerment.

God Gives Us Strength and Power to Transform Our Traumas

Representing the position that God provides us with the strength and power to transform our traumatic circumstances, Winnifred, a Black Nova Scotian survivor of intimate partner violence, articulates:

> I don't think that the Strong Black Woman is a myth...I think it's such a reality—I think Black women have been strong. Their spirituality is their key. I think that's the key to their strength...There's so many Black women in our communities going through abuse, that are enduring abuse from their husbands. Whether we feel that's right or not, but through their spirituality...I'm just going to pray this thing down. And pray this thing out. (Este & Bernard, 2006, para. 3)

Within this chapter, we discuss reliance on The Strong Black Woman archetype separate from spirituality. We see a heuristic value in doing so. However, Winnifred's comment reminds us that our conceptual separation of the two may not be phenomenologically meaningful.

God Gives Us Strength and Power to be Resilient and Transcend Adversity

Study findings further support that we, as Africana women, are of the opinion that spirituality is the birthplace of our resilience and post-traumatic growth. Specifically, we believe that spirituality provides us with strength to return to our pre-traumatic level of functioning, as well as the strength to embrace a new life with new perspectives, and new life skills. Fazila, a Sudanese woman dislocated as a consequence of civil war, delineates the relationship between spirituality and post-traumatic growth, thusly:

> Being a single mother with five children, life was full of ups and downs. It is hard to describe exactly how I was able to manage. But, it involved sacrifice, commit-

ment, and courage to accomplish my dream. Being a Christian, my faith played a great role in my life in many ways. We always pray as a family and cast all of our problems into the hands of the Lord. The hardship I overcame motivated me to be strong, struggle and never give up whatever the case might be, that was my motto. Survival was not a problem anymore because I have learnt to live with enough. With or without, life is the same. (Lenette, Brough, & Cox, 2013, p. 16)

Again, from a Maslowian perspective, post-traumatic growth is a higher-order human need that relies on the fulfillment of basic lower level needs like endurance and survival. Here, Fazila discusses the phenomenon of post-traumatic growth as happening in tandem with endurance and survival, which is consistent with this precept.

God Gives Us the Strength and Power to Serve Others

As we see, spiritual strength and power allow us to survive, endure, surrender, transform, rebound, and transcend. Additionally, findings suggest that it provides us with the strength to demonstrate communalistic love. We perform this love even in the midst of our own suffering. Such a love is consistent with the Afrocultural appreciation of the interconnectedness of beings (Mbiti, 1991); and, acting in accordance with this dimension of our cultural identity may serve to bring a sense of coherence in what is otherwise a time of great chaos. Lesley, a Caribbean Canadian woman whose son was murdered, reaffirms this standpoint when she offers:

He (God) has given me that desire to turn whatever evil into good. I'm trying to do what I can so another mother doesn't suffer, doesn't have to go through something like this...I tried to look past my pain and look for the opportunity in my struggle. (Bailey et al., 2013, p. 345)

God Provides Direct Emotional and Instrumental Support

In addition to providing us with strength and power to act, we as Africana women also know God as The Comforter, an ever-present direct source of emotional and instrumental support. We access this divine support through prayer, praise, meditation, and other forms of communion. Aaliya, a Kenyan American woman whose infant was diagnosed with autism, substantiates this claim:

At the age of 18 months our precious son was diagnosed with autism...The change was sudden...When we received the official diagnosis, it hit us like a thunderbolt! Every parent has dreams for their children and the report was devastating. It did not help that we were so far from family and we had no support system at all. We could only turn to God for solace and comfort. As I drove to a training the following day, I found myself singing, 'Baba wa mbinguni nyosha mkono wako, watu wauone walitukuze jina lako' (Kiswahili for 'Our Heavenly Father stretch Your Hand that people may see and praise Your name'). (Kinyua-Gathetu, 2013, p. 5)

Lesedi, a West African American survivor of intimate partner violence, further supports this sentiment:

> I prayed; I felt comfort in praying. At night I read the Bible where it said, 'that I will be with you, as you travel, when you are suffering, I am with you.' So that was comforting me, that God was with me. (Ting, 2010, p. 351)

Karen, a Black American woman who was dislocated during Hurricane Katrina, articulates God's provision of instrumental support to us in times of trouble:

> God was there. He blessed me. My home is safe. A tree could have fell on it or anything. And then when I got to the shelter, I was the first one to leave. You see the good Lord removed me from there before I was hurt. (Lawson & Thomas, 2007, p. 347)

God Sends Emotional and Instrumental Support Through Others

Africana women also know that God sends emotional and instrumental support via divinely selected others. Ingabire, a Rwandan woman survivor of genocide, talks about how God takes care of us emotionally by sending the right people into our lives at the right time:

My special thanks go to the family that cares for me like I am their own daughter and have wiped away my tears. I have always said to myself that this is the parent God has given me. (Krieger, 2011, p. 47)

In sum, Africana women, as we are transnationally situated, rely most heavily on spirituality to cope with the myriad of traumatic life events that we are forced to face. Spirituality, the heart of our deep culture structure (see Myers, 1985), addresses all of the needs most commonly discussed within the contemporary stress and coping literature. In response to traumatic life events, spirituality provides us with meaning and purpose. It offers pathways to survival, endurance, resilience, and growth. Spirituality enables us to be solution-focused, while simultaneously encouraging us to give up our desire for total control. It motivates us to love one another, and to receive love from one another. Spirituality is Africana women's conduit to this/and, complementary, harmonious ways of coping. It is important to keep this truth about the quality of our spiritual coping, along with spirituality's connection to The Strong Black Woman archetype in mind as we next consider the second most common prototypical Africana women's way of coping with traumatic life events.

The Strong Black Woman

The Strong Black Woman was first introduced into the scholarly community by Black American feminist writer, Michele Wallace (1978). In Part II of her seminal text, *Black macho and the myth of the superwoman*, Wallace offers the reader a cogent conceptualization of this mythological archetype:

From the intricate web of mythology which surrounds the black woman, a fundamental image emerges. It is of a woman of inordinate strength, with an ability for tolerating an unusual amount of misery and heavy, distasteful work. This woman does not have the same fears, weaknesses, and insecurities as other women, but believes herself to be and is, in fact, stronger emotionally than most men. Less of a women in that she is less "feminine" and helpless, she is really *more* [original emphasis] of a woman in that she is the embodiment of Mother Earth, the quintessential mother with infinite sexual, life-giving, and nurturing reserves. In other words, she is a superwoman.

Through the years this image has remained basically intact, unquestioned even by the occasional black woman writer or politician. In fact, if anything, time has served to reinforce it. Even now I can hear my reader thinking, *Of course she is stronger. Look what she's been through. She would have to be* [original emphasis]. Of course she's not like other women. Even for me, it continues to be difficult to let the myth go. Naturally black women want very much to believe it; in a way, it is all we have. (Wallace, 1978, p. 107)

In her ground-breaking study, Cheryl Woods-Giscombé empirically examined the meaning of The Strong Black Woman archetype among an ethnically and socially diverse community sample of Black American women (2010). Woods-Giscombé's research is the first to take an ethnographic data-driven approach to the conceptualization of The Strong Black Woman. To summarize her findings, the women specified that The Strong Black Woman is an innovation of Africana women's shared spiritual orientation (a sentiment previously expressed in this chapter by Winnifred), our cultural memory of, and contemporary experiences with structural racial and gender oppression, intergenerational transmission by our foremothers, and life lessons mastered through our own personal experiences of disappointment and mistreatment. These lessons reinforce our individual perceptions of the ongoing necessity of The Strong Black Woman performance. In other words, she is at the same time a spiritual, social, cultural, and personal creation.

Describing her qualities, the women in Woods-Giscombé's study say that she is communally-oriented, stoic, and independent and driven. Participants in Abrams, Maxwell, Pope, and Belgrave's 2014 qualitative study of The Strong Black Woman agree. So, how does this archetype help Africana women to cope with traumatic life events? Our findings suggest that when enacted she: (1) fosters our survival by distracting us from our suffering, and giving us the strength to ward off opportunistic physical and emotional attacks; (2) gives us strength to persevere through our suffering; (3) affords us respect; and (4) enables us to expand the boundaries of our known capabilities.

The Strong Black Woman Distracts Us From Our Own Suffering

As pointed out by Michele Wallace (1978), The Strong Black Woman is a relational paradox. In one sense, her care of others leads her to self-sacrifice; a veritable concern that is repeatedly raised by Black feminist scholars. In the same sense, her other-oriented nurturance is a positive character trait known to be negatively associated with psychological distress (Baumann, Cialdini, & Kendrick, 1981), and positively associated with subjective social, emotional, psychological, and spiritual well-being (Grayman-Simpson, 2012, 2013). The known connections between caretaking and subjective well-being, and caretaking and decreased reports of psychological distress may help to explain why Africana women continue to discuss nurturance of others as an adaptive means of coping with trauma. Being other-oriented helps us to survive. Addressing this point, Brenda, a Black American woman whose cousin was murdered, shares:

> I mean my primary concern was taking care of everybody else, to make sure everyone was okay, to make sure that everybody was able to go to the funeral, that his mother was okay (who was amazingly supportive of everybody else), but I don't know what I needed in terms of support, I don't know. (Sharpe & Boyas, 2011, p. 864)

Brenda's comment speaks to how helping others can take one's mind off of one's own negative feelings and distress. While the research shows that this is not a healthy long-term coping strategy, we do suggest that focusing on the needs of others in the immediate aftermath of a traumatic life event may offer some short-term survival benefit.

The Strong Black Woman Enables Us to Ward Off Opportunistic Attacks

Black feminist theoretical literature is replete with references to the stoicism associated with The Strong Black Woman, and the long-term dangers of following her guidance to restrict and suppress affect (see Beauboeuf-Lafontant, 2009, for an example). This same body of literature also highlights how Black women's bodies make them especially vulnerable to physical assault (see West, 2003, for an example). Again, while not a good long-term strategy, this meta-ethnography illuminates how we Africana women across the Diaspora invoke The Strong Black Woman, in the form of self-silencing and stoicism, in order to ward off opportunistic attacks. Bijoux, a Haitian woman dislocated by the earthquake in Haiti, and now living in the Dominican Republic, reminds us of this truth through her description of self- protection from physical attack after a sexual assault:

> I never said anything to the wife. She is Dominican and I was afraid to say anything because I thought she might hit me and she would think I was agreeing to it. I lasted

only 4 days in that job…I kept it in my heart…. (Petrozziello & Wooding, 2013, p. 193–194)

When Steebeth, a Trinidadian woman and survivor of community violence states, "…you try to look tough and in control so you would not appear to be a potential victim" (Adams, 2012, p. 293) we are reminded of the same.

Current and previous findings also remind us that not all opportunistic attacks against Africana women are of a physical nature. For example, the women in Woods-Giscombé's study discuss the threat of potential psychological attacks that must also be thwarted. Enacting The Strong Black Woman archetype in the form of self-silencing and stoicism, allows us Africana women to "put a shield around" ourselves (to borrow the language of one participant, Beatrice) in order to protect ourselves from emotional and psychological exploitation as we experience and attempt to manage our traumatically-induced fragile states. Speaking to this point, Naomi, a Caribbean Canadian woman whose son was murdered offers:

> When I first lost [my son] I would sit on the train or bus and cry and when people asked me, I would say I am ok…Shame kept me silent for a long time. As a black woman…I know the stigma and because of that I would never tell anyone how he died. I would not say he was shot…His death was not blamed on gang violence. But I was the one who was stigmatized. (Bailey et al., 2013, p. 347)

Similar to our findings with respect to the nature of Africana women's spiritual ways of coping, with The Strong Black Woman, we see seemingly opposing strategies at work. She simultaneously encourages connection and disconnection with others. Personal liabilities lay in both approaches if practiced to the extreme. But, as an initial means of coping, both appear to serve our basic survival needs.

The Strong Black Woman Gives Us Strength to Persevere Through Our Suffering

Continuing to speak to the ways in which The Strong Black Woman meets our basic survival and endurance needs, Neza, a Rwandan women who is a survivor of genocide-rape, articulates:

> Kwihangana simply means to withstand something you have experienced that hurts your heart. You withstand it to avoid committing suicide…You feel as if it were the end of life but you eventually realize you are not the only one who has suffered because there are other people with whom you share problems. This then makes you withstand and you no longer experience these feelings…. (Zraly & Nyirazinyoye, 2010, p. 1660)

More specific to this general point about the provision of strength to endure, The Strong Black Woman provides us with the fortitude to carry on in, and because of our roles as mothers. Aliyinza, a Ugandan woman who was diagnosed as HIV

Positive describes the maternal fortitude found among Africana women coping with traumatic life events:

> I have to be strong hearted just because of the responsibility ahead of me. I have very young children whom I have to care for, so if I fear, who will care for them? I have no choice but to be strong. (Medley, Kennedy, Lunyolo, & Sweat, 2009, p. 1748)

The Strong Black Woman Affords Us Respect

In her description of The Strong Black Woman, Wallace (1978) is sympathetic to our need to hold on to her, as she acknowledges that strength is one of few Africana women qualities that garners respect from within and outside of our community. Again, from a Maslowian perspective, this respect meets a basic human need that is valuable for its ability to move us further along the trajectory toward self-actualization (Maslow, 1943). Beverly, a Caribbean Canadian woman facing a mental illness diagnosis, illustrates how enacting the stoic and other-oriented nature associated with The Strong Black Woman can serve as a pathway to community respect:

> You feel like a burden. I'd listen to people, but when it comes to me people think that I am strong. I think that I am always the person that they would like to talk to. They think that I should be strong. I told them my story and they thought that they would never see me sad. They just thought I was always strong. I was telling a friend a story and I broke down and cried, she said, 'wow I never knew I'd see you cry' as if I am not human…People think I'm so strong 'Oh that will roll off you're back soon.' 'Oh she has everything on lock'…But I don't mind it. (Jackson & Naidoo, 2012, p. 231)

The Strong Black Woman Gives Us Strength to Transcend Our Known Capacities

Finally, The Strong Black Woman catalyzes transcendence of our previously known capacities. Mujjawimana, a Rwandan woman who survived genocide-rape, speaks to the phenomenon of Africana women stepping up and into new space as truth tellers. These spaces have been prepared for us by community foremothers. They model this tradition. Mujjawimana explains:

> Normally, our parents used to tell us what happened in the year 59…They said that in the 59 war my mother's family house was burnt down, and they were helped to flee by a Hutu man who was their neighbor…We used to ask her, 'but Mom is there a person who can kill another one like that, who can hunt you that way?' She told us that this is what happened. I couldn't believe it. But she told us because she survived. As for me now, I survived and I saw it. I feel I should tell, and as soon as I'm able to shout about it, I would tell anyone who doesn't know about it so that they know it, and it will not happen again. (Zraly & Nyirazinyoye, 2010, p. 1661)

Fatimah, a Sudanese woman dislocated by civil war also talks of transcending previously known capacities:

> Up to now I still wonder how I survived in a place where there was no safety, where anything could happen to you and your family any time, and you have no option. I still don't know how I am managing a family of five and how I am doing the triple job that is work, study, and family. (Lenette et al., 2013, p. 15)

Sisterhood

In addition to coping with traumatic life events through spirituality and The Strong Black Woman archetype, we also cope through sisterhood. Speaking on the power of sisterhood, Collins (2000) states, "In the comfort of daily conversations, through serious conversations and humor, African-American females as sisters and friends affirm one another's humanity, specialness, and right to exist" (p. 102). Black feminist scholar, Marnel Niles Goins (2011) goes on to say:

> Friendships between Black females represent an important homeplace. Collins (2000) argued that Black females can relate to each other in unique and significant ways; Black females often are supporters and listeners of other Black females. Friendships are necessary relationships for Black females because they affirm Black females' sense of self and nurture their spirit in an environment that often contradicts their experiences in the world. These friendship groups allow the females to speak with freedom, to strengthen their souls, and to tell stories that reinforce their identities, particularly in a society that magnifies their differences. (p. 532)

Africana women generally agree with their perspectives on the therapeutic effects sisterhood.

Sisters Offer Empathy and Love

Uwimana, a Rwandan woman who survived genocide-rape, and Miremba, a Ugandan woman who survived sexual abuse and physical assault on her job as a sex worker, suggest that Africana women's status as intimate knowers of each other's traumatic life experiences make them especially empathic and uniquely qualified to serve as co-bearers of burdens and companions in the healing journey:

> They've advised me not to hide it, because it happened to all of us, but you can't talk about it with someone who was not concerned, for them they think it's shameful. But when we talk about it, be it with my sister, be with it anyone else from the association or any other survivors outside of the association, we feel it's normal. (Zraly & Nyirazinyoye, 2010, p. 1661)

> When we sex workers meet together, we discuss many issues and advise one another. We comfort ourselves and come with good ideas, which can help us and this makes us feel like we are also human beings and relieves us from stress. (Scorgie et al., 2013, p. 10)

Sisters Permit Catharsis

Africana woman, by virtue of an assumed shared racial-gender experience, may present as ideal safe spaces for candid disclosure and conversation. As suggested by Uwimana, discernment about who to count as a sister is still required. But, having these safe spaces where we can candidly disclose and converse is especially crucial given our tendency toward emotional containment as Strong Black Women. The safe spaces may be occupied by biological and non-consanguineous sisters. Nola, a West African American survivor of intimate partner violence, speaks to this particular benefit of coping through sisterhood when she shares:

> No it was not hard to tell people. I tell people so that my heart can be open and lighter. I don't keep some thing in my heart; I was telling everyone. I told everything. I went to other women for advice. (Ting, 2010, p. 354)

Sisters Offer Guidance and Physical Safety

Finally, sisters counsel and protect us, as well as our families in the face of traumatic life events. Lerato, a South African woman who is a survivor of incest and was displaced from her home, describes:

> I was abused and became pregnant while looking for a job. I had no money to take care of the child and myself. So I met a lady who said that I should come with her to Park Station where you don't need money to rent a flat.... (Olufemi & Reeves, 2004, p. 75)

Rosita, a Trinidadian woman survivor of intimate partner violence, further substantiates this claim:

> She would talk to me. She would help me. It has times when he was hitting me and she was there, she would try and talk to him. She would call him and she would make him sit down and she would talk to him, all now. She would talk to the both of us, she would sit down and talk to us. She would take the kids. It has times when I had to run out of the house. It was by her I had to go. (Hadeed & El-Bassel, 2006, p. 749)

COMMUNITY SUPPORT, ACTIVE ADAPTATION, PASSIVE ACCEPTANCE, AND HOPE

Community Provides Us With Social, Emotional, and Instrumental Support

At the outset of this project, our focus was limited to the perceived connection between traumatic life happenings within the context of globalized racial patriarchies, and Africana women's necessary reliance on communal self-help. We did not consider the role that communal coping, more broadly construed, plays in

Africana women's adaptive functioning. The data forced us to expand our thinking. With less, but still significant frequency, Africana women discuss the importance of broader communal support to coping with traumatic life events. Ahok, a Sudanese woman dislocated as a consequence of civil war, and Mary, a Black American woman whose grandchild was murdered, highlight the importance of the broader community to Africana women's coping when they express:

> Yeah, like when I first came we met a group of Sudanese, we sometime got a meeting, discuss about our life issues here in Australia and how we can help our people back there in a refugee camp…Be together sometimes as a community, sharing life, forget about the difficulty, and thinking about the future…That's what we did to change the life a bit. So that you cannot thinking about the bad fact all the time, just think about the positive thinking so that you will change your life. (Murray, 2010, p. 38)

> The support that I did get was from my family, my children, my grandchildren… There is a sharing of grief or trouble and what not…it was a family pulling together and supporting each other…we were aware of each other's pain and I really believed we helped share it and that sharing helped carry me through and I believe it helped carry [the deceased's mother] through. (Sharpe & Boyas, 2011)

Active Adaptation to Reality Enables Us to Ward Off Opportunistic Attacks

In addition to coping with violent community spaces by acting tough once in them, we also protect ourselves by discerning when and where to enter these physically dangerous environments. Rhonda, a Trinidadian woman coping with community violence describes this ability:

> At night I tend to avoid having to walk up [Socaville's main road]. But in Trinidad generally, I try not to travel, even public transportation, after 9 pm. After 8:30, 9 o'clock, I not going anywhere unless I know someone is dropping me home in a car…Sometimes you want to go to church at night but if I know there isn't anybody to drop me home then I would rather stay home because I don't want to come out there sometime in the night and something happen to me. (Adams, 2012, p. 290)

While, Chantal, a Haitian woman who was dislocated by the earthquake in Haiti, adds:

> During a time I avoided crossing through Oche [Haiti and Dominican Republic border crossing area], because they hurt a woman there…they told us to turn back, that a woman had been killed in Oche…I did not go back through for one month because I was scared….(Petrozziello & Wooding, 2013, p. 190)

Passive Acceptance of Reality Helps Us to Endure and Persevere

A notable number of women in the study also suggested that we cope with traumatic life events through passive acceptance. Sharon, a Caribbean Canadian woman who faced the death of a loved one, elucidates the nature of this coping strategy among Africana women when she explains simply, "Certain things in life you have to accept, you know, that you have to live with—that you can't do anything about it" (Schreiber, Stern, & Wilson, 2000, p. 41).

Hiba, a Sudanese woman who survived civil war agrees:

> There's nothing you can do about it. Because...sometimes you get used to it, you get used to dead bodies and a lot of people dying. Then sometimes, then after sometime you think 'it is the nature' so you get used to it, you get used to the idea of people just dying like that. (Khawaja, White, Schweitzer, & Greenslade, 2008, p. 502)

Hope Keeps Us Optimistic

Finally, Africana women discuss holding on to hope as a way of coping with traumatic life events. To this point, Ashia, another Sudanese woman dislocated by civil war offers: "It was the hope that, you know, that you are not staying here [in Egypt], you are leaving for a better life," (Shakespeare-Finch & Wickham, 2009, p. 35). And, Kwenhangana, the Rwandan woman who witnessed her sister being beaten and raped during the genocide reminds us:

> There is a day...although you don't know when that better day is going to come but there is always hope that there's going to be a better day and my life is going to be a little bit better than how it is now. (Sherwood & Liebling-Kalifani, 2012, p. 99)

Addressing the critical need for connection between theory and praxis, the final section of this chapter speaks to the application of these findings to strengths-based counseling and psychological intervention from a Black feminist standpoint.

IMPLICATIONS FOR BLACK FEMINIST STRENGTHS-BASED COUNSELING AND PSYCHOLOGICAL INTERVENTIONS

"Ideally therapy is the art of self-healing, which enables the client to draw on personal resources to empower and enrich her life" (Boyd, 1990, p. 166). A Black feminist perspective on human functioning proposes that Africana women are the experts on our own lived experiences (Collins, 1991). Foundational to counseling psychological practice is a complementary strengths-based approach to intervention (Gelso & Woodhouse, 2003) that would suggest that Africana women are also hard-wired for healing, and are already in possession of the tools and strategies needed to endure, survive, rebound, and transcend our traumas. In sum, we already have everything that we need. Integrating the two, the main goals of an interventionist then becomes to: (1) develop knowledge of Africana women's lived experiences of traumatic life events; (2) honor these narratives through humanistic responding; (3) develop knowledge of our existing adaptive indigenous coping processes; and (4) support Africana women's ongoing utilization of adaptive indigenous coping processes.

Develop Knowledge of Africana Women's Lived Experiences of Traumatic Life Events

A Black feminist standpoint on trauma in the lives of Africana women acknowledges the roles of European and Arab imperialism, slavery and colonialism in sanctioning and institutionalizing the phenomenon of Africana women's trauma; of controlling images in the normalization of our traumas; and, of social institutions like mental healthcare and law enforcement in the minimization of our traumas (West, 2003). Efficacious interventionists understand this economic-political-social context within which our trauma is experienced, and they are knowledgeable of our lived experiences of trauma. Some of this knowledge may be derived from one's own lived experience, as in the case of the first author. Tapping into knowledge-of-self offers an excellent starting point of reference for the gathering of cultural understanding. However, it ought not to be our only point of reference. It is imperative that the interventionist, regardless of professional station, be willing to assume a posture of humility, embrace the role of student, and complete the homework required to become more knowledgeable (Boyd, 1990). This homework may involve speaking with other Africana women who have lived through trauma, and are in the practice of openly sharing their experiences. It may involve reading, listening to, witnessing, and analyzing Africana women's novels, music, dance, and other forms of artistic expression, as these are the traditional public spaces within which our stories of trauma get expertly told (Robinson, 1983). And, it certainly involves becoming a discerning consumer of the ethnographic research concerning Africana women's experiences of trauma.

Honor Africana Women's Trauma Narratives through Humanistic Responding

"Sometimes, simply listening carefully with empathy and care is enough to produce meaningful change" (Ivey, Ivey, & Zalaquett, 2010, p. 17). Findings from this study help to support this claim. In their interviews, Africana women discussed how a select circle of other Africana women offered safe spaces where they could relieve The Strong Black Woman of active duty, disclose their stories of trauma, experience catharsis, and receive guidance and assistance. Undoubtedly, these women were effective sources of support because they embodied basic interpersonal qualities known, through more than three decades of empirical research, to have therapeutic effects (Ivey, Ivey, & Zalaquett, 2010). They were engaged and warm, open and authentic, and affirming and encouraging. Enacting these qualities in our conversations and relations with Africana women affords opportunities to honor what we have gone through, and encourage therapeutic encounters.

Develop Knowledge of Africana Women's Existing Adaptive Indigenous Coping Processes

"...it is important for therapists to be aware of strengths that may be available to clients based on their membership in a particular cultural or other group" (Gelso & Woodhouse, 2003, p. 192). In addition to empathic listening, a Black feminist strengths-based counseling psychological approach to trauma intervention requires knowledge of adaptive indigenous coping strategies. Previous literature has addressed adaptive coping strategies among African Americans, generally (see Daly, Jennings, Beckett, & Leashore, 1995; Utsey, Adams, & Bolden, 2000 for examples), coping with racism and sexism among African American women, specifically (see Shorter-Gooden, 2004 for example), and Africana women's coping with particular traumas, such as male-perpetrated intimate partner violence (see Ting, 2010 for example). Yet, no other known study has attempted to integrate these investigations into a larger examination of Africana women's coping with trauma, as trauma is more inclusively construed. This study seeks to fill this knowledge gap in an effort to develop greater appreciation for the shared trials of Africana women around the world, and better serve the helping goals of interventionists from a strength-based perspective.

Support Ongoing Utilization of Adaptive Indigenous Coping Strategies

Finally, a Black feminist strengths-based counseling psychological approach to intervention with Africana women managing trauma involves reinforcement and encouragement of the utilization of adaptive indigenous coping practices. "... strengths are attended to and developed in a myriad of ways. The prototypical way, however, is that of...support and reinforcement..." (Gelso & Woodhouse, 2003, p. 174). We empathically bear witness to her story of trauma, listening for, questioning, and assessing her reliance on the coping strategies highlighted in this chapter. We encourage her to continue on a path of self-healing by standing in the gap as therapeutic sisters, gently reminding her that she is already in possession of everything that she needs to make it through. In sum, the heart of our work as interventionists coming from this perspective is to help the Africana woman to remember, develop, and apply her adaptive indigenous ways of coping in service of her own healing.

ACKNOWLEDGEMENT

The first author wishes to thank Dr. Aaronette White (1961–2012), Black feminist psychological scholar-warrior-activist. Your work and your spirit continue to inspire.

REFERENCES

Abrams, J. A., Maxwell, M., Pope, M., & Belgrave, F. Z. (2014). Carrying the world with the grace of a lady and the grit of a warrior: Deepening our understanding of the "Strong Black Woman" schema. *Psychology of Women Quarterly*. Advance online publication. doi: 10.1177/0361684314541418

Adams, E. B. (2012). "We are like prey": How people negotiate a violent community in Trinidad and Tobago. *Race and Justice, 2*(4), 274–303.

American Psychiatric Association. (2013). *Diagnostic and statistical manual of mental disorders* (5th ed.). Arlington, VA: American Psychiatric Publishing.

Bailey, A., Hannays-King, C., Clarke, J., Lester, E., & Velasco, D. (2013). Black mothers' cognitive process of finding meaning and building resilience after loss of a child to gun violence. *British Journal of Social Work, 43*(2), 336–354.

Baumann, D. J., Cialdini, R. B., & Kendrick, D. T. (1981). Altruism as hedonism: Helping and self-gratification as equivalent responses. *Journal of Personality and Social Psychology, 40*(6), 1039–1046.

Beauboeuf-Lafontant, T. (2009). *Behind the mask of the strong Black woman: Voice and the embodiment of a costly performance*. Philadelphia, PA: Temple University Press.

Boyd, J. A. (1990). Ethnic and cultural diversity: Keys to power. *Women & Therapy, 9*(1–2), 151–156.

Collins, P. H. (1991). *Black feminist thought: Knowledge, consciousness, and the politics of empowerment*. New York: Routledge.

Collins, P. H. (2000). *Black feminist thought: Knowledge, consciousness, and the politics of empowerment* (2nd ed.). New York: Routledge.

Daly, A., Jennings, J., Beckett, J. O., Leashore, B. R. (1995). Effective coping strategies of African Americans. *Social Work, 40*(2), 240–248.

Este, D., & Bernard, W. T. (2006). Spirituality among African Nova Scotians: A key to survival in Canadian society. *Critical Social Work, 7*(1).

Freud, S. (1952). *Totem and taboo: Some points of agreement between the mental lives of savages and neurotics*. New York, NY: Norton.

Garnefski, N., Kraaij, V., & Spinhoven, P. (2001). Negative life events, cognitive emotion regulation and emotional problems. *Personality and Individual Differences, 30*(8), 1311–1327.

Gelso, C. J., & Woodhouse, S. (2003). Toward a positive psychotherapy: Focus on human strength. In W. B. Wlash (Ed.), *Counseling Psychology and optimal human functioning* (pp. 171–197). Mahwah, NJ: Lawrence Earlbaum Associates.

Goins, M. N. (2011). Playing with dialectics: Black female friendship groups as a homeplace. *Communications Studies, 62*(5), 531–546.

Goodman, L. A., Corcoran, C., Turner, K., Yuan, N., & Green, B. L. (1998). Assessing traumatic event exposure: General issues and preliminary findings for the Stressful Life Events Screening Questionnaire. *Journal of Traumatic Stress, 11*(3), 521–542.

Gray, M. J., Litz, B. T., Hsu, J. L., & Lombardo, T. W. (2004). Psychometric properties of the life events checklist. *Assessment, 11*(4), 330–341.

Grayman-Simpson, N. (2012). Black community involvement and subjective well-being. *Journal of Pan African Studies, 5*(3), 26–42.

Grayman-Simpson, N. (2013). Doing good and feeling good among African Americans: Subjective religiosity, helping, and satisfaction. *Journal of Black Psychology, 39*(4), 411–427.

Hadeed, L. F., & El-Bassel, N. (2006). Social support among Afro-Trinidadian women experiencing intimate partner violence. *Violence Against Women, 12*(8), 740–760.

Ivey, A., Ivey, M., & Zalaquett, C. (2010). *Intentional interviewing and counseling: Facilitating client development in a multicultural world* (7th ed.). Belmont, CA: Brooks/ Cole.

Jackson, F. Z., & Naidoo, K. (2012). "Lemeh check see if meh mask on straight": Examining how Black women of Caribbean descent in Canada manage depression and construct womanhood through being strong. *Southern Journal of Canadian Studies, 5*(1–2), 223–24.

Khawaja, N. G., White, K. M., Schweitzer, R., & Greenslade, J. H. (2008). Difficulties and coping strategies of Sudanese refugees: A qualitative approach. *Transcultural Psychiatry, 45*(3), 489–512.

Kinyua-Gathetu, B. W. (2013). The challenges of "belonging": Personal experience and perception of counseling among African American women immigrants in the United States of America. *The Journal of Global Gender Studies, 1*(2), 1–61.

Krieger, L. (2011). *Narratives of resilience: Stories of survival among Rwandan women who endured the 1994 genocide.* (Unpublished master's thesis). Smith College School for Social Work.

Kubany, E. S., Haynes, S. N., Leisen, M. B., Owens, J. A., Kaplan, A. S., Watson, S. B., & Burns, K. (2000). Development and preliminary validation of a brief broad-spectrum measure of trauma exposure: The Traumatic Life Events Questionnaire. *Psychological Assessment, 12*(2), 210–224.

Lawson, E. J., & Thomas, C. (2007). Wading in the waters: Spirituality and older Black Katrina survivors. *Journal of Health Care for the Poor and Underserved, 18*(2), 341–354.

Lenette, C., Bough, M. K., & Cox, L. (2013). Everyday resilience: Narratives of single refugee women with children. *Qualitative Social Work, 12*(5), 637–53.

Lincoln, Y. S., & Guba, E. G. (1986). But is it rigorous?: Trustworthiness and authenticity in naturalistic observation. *New Directions for Program Evaluation, 30,* 73–84.

Maslow, A. H. (1943). A theory of human motivation. *Psychological Review, 50*(4), 370–396.

Mattis, J. S. (2000). African American women's definitions of religion and spirituality. *Journal of Black Psychology, 26*(1), 101–122.

Mattis, J. S. (2002). Religion and spirituality in the meaning-making and coping experiences of African American women: A qualitative analysis. *Psychology of Women Quarterly, 26*(4), 309–321.

Mbiti, J. S. (1991). *Introduction to African religion* (2nd ed.). Portsmouth, NH: Heinemann.

Medley, A. M., Kennedy, C. E., Lunyolo, S., & Sweat, M. D. (2009). Disclosure outcomes, coping strategies, and life changes among women living with HIV in Uganda. *Qualitative Health Research, 19*(12), 1744–1754.

Morse, J. M. (1995). The significance of saturation. *Qualitative Health Research, 5*(2), 147–149.

Murray, K. E. (2010). Sudanese perspectives on resettlement in Australia. *Journal of Pacific Rim Psychology, 4*(1), 30–43.

Myers, L. J. (1985). Transpersonal psychology: The role of the Afrocentric paradigm. *Journal of Black Psychology, 12*(1), 31–42.

Nobles, W. (1972). African philosophy: Foundations for Black Psychology. In R. L. Jones (Ed.), *Black psychology,* (pp. 18–32). New York, NY: Harper & Row Publishers.

Noblit, G. W., & Hare, R. D. (1988). *Meta-ethnography: Synthesizing qualitative studies.* Thousand Oaks, CA: Sage.

Olufemi, O., & Reeves, D. (2004). Lifeworld strategies of women who find themselves homeless in South Africa. *Planning Theory & Practice, 5*(1), 69–91.

Petrozziello, A. J., & Wooding, B. (2013). Borders, buscones, brothels, and bi-national markets: Haitian women negotiate how to get through. *Cultural Dynamics, 25*(2), 183–205.

Robinson, C. R. (1983). Black women: A tradition of self-reliant strength. *Women & Therapy, 2*(2–3), 135–144.

Rodney, W. (1981). *How Europe underdeveloped Africa.* Baltimore, MD: Black Classic Press.

Schreiber, R., Stern, P. N., & Wilson, C. (2000). Being strong: How Black West-Indian Canadian women manage depression and its stigma. *Journal of Nursing Scholarship, 32*(1), 39–45.

Scorgie, F., Casey, K., Harper, E., Richter, M., Nare, P., Maseko, S., & Cherisch, M. F. (2013). Human rights abuses and collective resilience among sex workers in four African countries: A qualitative study. *Globalization and Health, 9*(1), 33.

Shakespeare-Finch, J. E., & Wickham, K. (2009). Adaptation of Sudanese refugees in an Australian context: Investigating helps and hindrances. *International Migration, 48*(1), 23–46.

Sharpe, T. L., & Boyas, J. (2011). We fall down: African American experience of coping with the homicide of a loved one. *Journal of Black Studies, 42*(6), 855–873.

Sherwood, K., & Liebling-Kalifani, H. (2012). A grounded theory investigation into the experiences of African women refugees: Effects on resilience and identity and implications for service provision. *Journal of International Women's Studies, 13*(1), 86–108.

Shorter-Gooden, K. (2004). Multiple resistance strategies: How African American women cope with racism and sexism. *Journal of Black Psychology, 30*(3), 406–425.

Ting, L. (2010). Out of Africa: Coping strategies of African immigrant women survivors of intimate partner violence. *Health Care for Women International. 31*(4), 345–364.

Utsey, S. O., Adams, E. P., & Bolden, M. (2000). Development and initial validation of the Africultural Coping Systems Inventory. *Journal of Black Psychology, 26*(2), 194–215.

Wade-Gayles, G. (1995). *My soul is a witness: African-American women's spirituality.* Boston, MA: Beacon Press.

Wade-Gayles, G. (2002). *My soul is a witness: African-American women's spirituality.* Boston, MA: Beacon Press.

Wallace, M. (1978). *Black macho and the myth of the superwoman.* New York, NY: Verso.

West, C. M. (2003). *Violence in the lives of Black women: Battered, Black, and blue.* New York, NY: The Haworth Press, Inc.

Woods-Giscombé, C. L. (2010). Superwoman schema: African American women's views on stress, strength, and health. *Qualitative Health Research, 20*(5), 668–683.

Zraly, M., & Nyirazinyoye, L. (2010). Don't let the suffering make you fade away: An ethnographic study of resilience among survivors of genocide-rape in southern Rwanda. *Social Science & Medicine, 70*(10), 1656–1664.

CHAPTER 3

SYSTEMIC AND WORKPLACE MICROAGGRESSIONS AND THE WORKPLACE

Recommendations for Best Practices for Institutions and Organizations

Aisha M. B. Holder and Kevin L. Nadal

INTRODUCTION

Despite evidence of political and social progress in the United States (US), discriminatory attitudes and behaviors continue to persist in US society. While significant progress has been made in the civil rights movement and expressions of bias such as racial discrimination have diminished in terms of frequency and intensity since the 1960s (Dovidio & Gaertner, 2000; Sue & Sue 2007), discrimination continues to manifest in subtle and implicit ways, resulting in significant and deleterious outcomes for individuals, particularly those belonging to marginalized identity groups. Covert forms of discrimination have been described as *aversive racism* (Dovidio & Gaertner, 2000), *modern racism* (McConahay, 1986), *symbolic racism* (Sears, 1988), and *racial microaggressions* (Pierce et al., 1978;

Talking About Structural Inequalities in Everyday Life: New Politics of Race in Groups, Organizations, and Social Systems, pages 47–63.

47

Sue et al., 2007). These types of discrimination are more likely to be disguised, having evolved from conscious and blatant expressions of hatred and bigotry to more nebulous forms (Sue et al., 2007), making it more difficult to identify and to acknowledge these acts when they occur (Dovidio, Gaertner, Kawakami, & Hodson, 2002). Previous scholars have argued that blatant acts of discrimination can be easier to detect and respond to in some respects because the intentions of the perpetrators are clear versus subtle discrimination in which bias may be more difficult to prove (Sue, 2010).

Racial microaggressions, first proposed by psychiatrist Chester Pierce, have been defined as "brief and commonplace daily verbal, behavioral, and environmental indignities, whether intentional or unintentional, that communicate hostile, derogatory, negative racial slights and insults to the target person or group" (Sue et al., 2007, p. 273). Racial microaggressions are most similar to aversive racism in that they are more likely to be committed by well-intentioned individuals who believe they are not prejudiced, yet hold unconscious and less socially acceptable biases that can translate into discriminatory behavior (Sue, 2010). Initial scholarship on microaggressions has been from the perspective of race; however, members of historically devalued groups can be the targets of these experiences, including women and lesbian, gay, bisexual, transgender, and queer (LGBTQ) individuals (Capodilupo et al., 2010; Nadal et al., 2011; Sue, 2010).

A theoretical taxonomy of racial, gender, and sexual orientation microaggressions falls into three major categories: microassaults, microinsults, and microinvalidations (Sue, 2010). *Microassaults* are overt forms of discrimination manifested in verbal and nonverbal ways, by individuals who are consciously aware of the discriminatory act, yet who do not mean to intentionally hurt the recipient. Referring to women as "bitches" or gays as "fags" are examples of microassaults based on gender or sexual orientation; displaying a noose or using derogatory words like "spick" or "chink" are examples of microassaults based on race. People who tell racially charged jokes but then follow up with "I'm just kidding" may acknowledge that their insults may be controversial, but may insist that they are not racist can be considered a microassault. *Microinsults* are interpersonal or environmental encounters that convey insult and insensitivity and demean a person's race, gender, sexual orientation or identity. Unlike microassaults, perpetrators of microinsults are not consciously aware of their actions or how they convey hidden and insulting messages to the recipient. One example may include a Black man who is followed around a store while shopping because he is presumed to be a criminal. A male supervisor expressing surprise about his female director's keen mathematical abilities may appear harmless yet communicates the unconscious message that women are generally not good in mathematics. In both scenarios, the perpetrator of the microinsult may not recognize that his or her behavior was prejudiced or may rationalize the behavior in some other way that does not admit to any potential bias. Lastly, *microinvalidations* are statements that invalidate the thoughts, feelings and experiences of women, people of color, LGBTQ individuals, and other marginalized groups, often denying the unearned benefits accorded to certain groups because of privilege (Sue et al., 2007). For example, when a White person points to the election of Barack Obama as the first African-American US president as evidence that racism no longer exists in the US, she or he invalidates the role that race plays in shaping the daily experiences of people of color in this country. Similarly, a statement such as "I'm not homophobic, I have a gay friend," thus denying one's heterosexist biases and behaviors, is also an example of a microinvalidation.

Sue (2010) also developed a taxonomy of themes that outlined the ways in which microaggressive incidents occur based on race, gender, and sexual orientation. Some examples include *Ascription of Intelligence,* which involves assigning one's intelligence based on his or her identity group such as assuming that Asian Americans are inherently gifted in math and science and African Americans are intellectually inferior. *Assumption of Abnormality* asserts that there is something about one's identity group that is pathological and deviant. An example is when the sexual behavior of LGBTQ groups is viewed as abnormal. The *Sexual Objectification* theme includes statements that dehumanize women and refer to them as sexual objects. *Assumption of Criminality* relates to beliefs that people of color are dangerous, antisocial and likely to commit crimes and engage in violent behavior. Research has shown that the perception of criminality is less applicable to Asian Americans and more likely for African Americans and Latino/as (Sue, Bucceri, Lin, Nadal, & Torino, 2007; Sue, Capodilupo, & Holder, 2008). The *Myth of Meritocracy* theme refers to the belief that everyone has an equal opportunity to excel in this society without recognizing the influence that racial, gender, and sexual orientation privileges have in creating disparities in areas such as education, housing, and healthcare—all of which can impact one's personal and professional success. The theme *Second Class Citizen* communicates unconscious messages that certain groups are less worthy and deserving of discriminatory treatment (Sue, 2010). A telling example of this theme was shared on the Technology, Entertainment and Design (TED) website where Mellody Hobson, a Black female Princeton educated investment firm president, and aspiring senator Harold Ford, who is also African American, were mistaken for kitchen "help" by a receptionist when they arrived for a meeting with the editorial board of a major New York media company (Hobson, 2014).

Some authors have questioned the validity and impact of microaggressions claiming they are no different from the general interpersonal slights that all people experience at times, regardless of race (Schacht, 2008; Thomas, 2008). Ironically, this assertion represents yet another example of how the experiential realities of people of color and other identity groups are invalidated and attempted to be defined by privileged identity groups (Sue, 2010), thus undermining and limiting rights and opportunities for stigmatized groups (Ong, Burrow, Fuller-Rowell, Ja, & Sue, 2013). In recent years, there has been an increasing and compelling body of literature documenting the detrimental physical and psychological impact of cumulative and continuous exposure to microaggressions for individuals of marginalized identity groups (Frost & Meyer, 2009; Tummala-Narra, Alegria, & Chen, 2012; Utsey & Hook, 2007; William, Neighbors, & Jackson, 2003). Numerous studies have found that discrimination related to race, gender, and sexual orientation is associated with depression, anxiety-related symptoms, diminished psychological wellness and physical health. For instance, for African Americans, racism has been linked to hypertension (Brondolo, Rieppi, Kelly, & Gerin, 2003), substance abuse (Gibbons, Gerrard, Cleveland, Wills, & Brody, 2004) and high rates of morbidity (Clark, Anderson, Clark, & Williams, 1999). In a study conducted with Mexican adults, perceived discrimination predicted poorer general health and health outcomes (Flores et al., 2008). LGBTQ people who had more incidents of indirect discrimination experienced more health-related issues (Smith & Ingram, 2004).

Regarding studies that focus specifically on microaggressions, results have been similar, in that microaggressions have been found to predict negative mental and physical outcomes. For instance, one study found that when college students experience microaggressions, they also binge drink or develop other alcohol-related issues (Blume, Lovato, Thyken, & Denny, 2012). Smith, Hung, and Franklin (2011) revealed that African-American male college students who experienced racial microaggressions reported higher levels of mundane, extreme, and environmental stress, while Wang, Leu, and Shoda (2011) report that racial microaggressions led to negative emotional intensity for Asian Americans more than for White Americans. Nadal, Griffin, and colleagues (2014) found that the cumulative experiences of racial microaggressions were a predictor of poorer mental health, particularly depression and negative affect, and that White Americans experience significantly less racial microaggressions than African Americans, Asian Americans, Latina/o Americans, and multiracial people. Finally, Nadal, Wong, Griffin, and colleagues (2014) found that college students who experience microaggressions in school or workplace environments reported lower scores of self-esteem. Given all of these, it is evident that microaggressions are anything but harmless to stigmatized groups. While some individuals may perceive microaggressions as minor or inconsequential, these types of experiences are indeed consequential and require deeper acknowledgment and understanding of their impact.

SYSTEMIC MICROAGGRESSIONS

Microaggressions are not solely confined to verbal and nonverbal interpersonal encounters. These mechanisms also operate in systemic ways that permeate our educational, legislative, healthcare and employment institutions, just to name a few. Systemic microaggressions represent subtle forms of discrimination that are integrated into the structures of various systems (e.g., government, educational systems) (Nadal, 2013) resulting in disparate treatment and outcomes for marginalized communities. It can be argued that institutional or systemic microaggressions are more dangerous and insidious because they are more difficult to eradicate and can have a deep and profound impact on the quality of people's lives. This section will offer brief examples of the ways in which racial indignities manifest in US society.

In spite of the gains realized from the landmark United States Supreme Court case of *Brown vs. Board of Education* in 1954 to desegregate public schools, there still remains a significant achievement gap between youth of color and White students (Condron et al. 2013; McKown, 2013). A growing number of scholars point to the existence of systemic discrimination within the public education system as a factor in explaining these educational disparities (Billings-Ladson, 2013; Lopez, 2003; Noguera, Hurtado, & Fergus, 2012). For instance, while school curricula have evolved over the decades to be more inclusive and representative of diverse identity groups and cultures, their core principles still operate from White, middle class and Western perspectives. Culturally incongruent curricula have contributed to the disproportionate number of African American students in special education programs (Blanchett, 2006). The historical narratives and experiences of marginalized communities are limited and are often only recognized during cultural celebration months like Black History or LGBTQ Pride months. In the 2009 National School Climate Survey conducted by the Gay, Lesbian & Straight Education Network (GLSEN), findings revealed that less than one-fifth of the seven thousand students' surveys reported that neither LGBTQ history, people nor issues were included in their assigned readings (Kosciw et al., 2009). School curricula with positive representations of the LGBTQ community helped to promote an overall culture of inclusion as well as improve LGBTQ students' experiences and sense of connection to their school community (Kosciw et al., 2009). When students of marginalized identity groups are educated in environments that affirm their personhood and the contributions their communities have made to society, they in turn feel more valued and engaged as students, all of which are key drivers for academic success.

Disciplinary policies represent another area of disparity that leads to unequal treatment in public schools. In a report compiled by the US Department of Education Office for Civil Rights (2014), disproportionate high suspension and expulsion rates were found among students of color and those with disabilities. Across racial groups, these statistics were particularly alarming for Black students who are suspended and expelled at a rate three times higher than White students. Students with disabilities are more than twice as likely to receive an out-of-school suspension than students without disabilities. With no evidence suggesting that students of color or those with disabilities misbehave more than White students to a degree that would explain these disparities, one must consider the role discrimination plays in explaining these statistics. We know, for example, that African Americans, particularly men, are perceived to be more likely to break the laws and engage in criminal and deviant behavior (Sue, 2010; Sue et al., 2008). These implicit biased attitudes can influence how school disciplinary policies are implemented which have clearly led to findings of discrimination. When you consider that children who are suspended are more likely to be left behind a grade, drop out of school, and commit a crime as adults, it is clear how the consequences of suspensions can be devastating for students, parents and society as a whole (Children's Defense Fund, 2007).

Systemic microaggressions also persist in the US political system resulting in the disenfranchisement of historically marginalized groups. In June 2012, the US Supreme Court upheld the controversial Arizona anti-immigration law making it legal for police to determine the immigration status of anyone arrested or detained when there is "reasonable suspicion" they are not in the US legally (ACLU, 2012). Similar legislation has been passed in Georgia, Alabama, and South Carolina. These laws encourage racial profiling by making it legal to target people of color such as Latino/as perceived to be "foreign" based on their physical appearance and/or accent. Some claim that these fears of racial profiling are not justified since the law prohibits any such targeting. Yet, research shows that Latino/as have exceeded African Americans as a racial group most likely to encounter discrimination (Pew Research Center, 2010). Nier, Gaertner, Nier, and Dovodio (2011) found that store clerks were more likely to ask for documentation or identification when Latino/a patrons purchased an item with a check than when a White patron used the same method of payment. Many Latino/as and Asian American and Pacific Islanders are often viewed automatically as illegal immigrants and less American and treated as foreigners in their own land (Rivera, Forquer, & Rangel, 2010; Wu, 2002).

Legislative inequities have also impacted women in the failure to address the wage gap between men and women in the US. Women continue to earn only 77 cents for every dollar earned by men for full-time work (U.S. Census Bureau, 2009). The wage gap is even worse for women of color with African American women earning only approximately 64 cents and Latinas 54 cents for each dollar earned by a White male. Legislators have failed to address gender-based wage discrimination which could be addressed by passing laws like the Paycheck Fairness Act to help secure equal pay for all Americans by providing more transparency and accountability with regard to employers' wage practices. With women making up about half of the US workforce, wage discrimination based on sex not only compromises economic security for women but also has implications for families and the economy as a whole.

Lastly, systemic microaggressions are also exhibited by the close proximity of low-income or communities of color to environmentally hazardous facilities such as garbage and transportation depots, some of which are managed by government entities. In New York City, for example, neighborhoods in Northern Manhattan which have predominantly residents of color include six of Manhattan's eight diesel bus depots along with multiple highways and sewerage treatment facilities (Shepard, 2005/2006), some of which are located near housing, hospitals, and schools. It is not surprising that areas in Northern Manhattan have one of the highest death and disease rates from asthma in the country (Columbia Center for Children's Environmental Health, 2014). Similar patterns can be found in the South Bronx in New York City, another low-income community of color, where 30 percent of New York's City's waste and 70 percent of its sewage sludge are handled (Carter, 2007). In addition to these health hazards, research has shown that proximity to fossil fuel emission sources can result in developmental impairment, asthma, and cancer (Perera, 2008). These environmental systemic microaggressions represent gross discriminatory practices that maintain racial privilege at the expense of the health of marginalized groups (Randall, 2006–2007).

RACIAL MICROAGGRESSIONS IN THE WORKPLACE

With the implementation of an array of federal laws prohibiting blatant discrimination and biased attitudes becoming less socially acceptable, blatant racism in the workplace has become less prevalent. However, not unlike other settings, racism in the workplace has not disappeared but has transformed into subtle acts more difficult to identify. It is the very nature of racial microaggressions that poses certain challenges in combating these experiences in the workplace. First, they are often overlooked and ignored because they operate on an unconscious level (Stallworth, McPherson, & Rute 2001). Second, microaggressive acts may not necessarily be in violation of any laws which can compromise any efforts on the part of employees to seek legal action (Offerman et al., 2013). Lastly, the ambiguous nature of microaggressions makes it difficult to determine whether a transgression has occurred (Rowe, 1990).

The underrepresentation of people of color in positions of power and authority in various institutions represents a common microaggression in the workplace. People of color represent an important and growing source of talent in the workplace. Indeed, it is projected that by 2050, people of color will become a numerical majority in the US (Sue & Sue, 2007), earning undergraduate and graduate degrees in record numbers. Despite a staggering surge of highly educated employees of color in the workforce, the level of representation at senior levels remains meager. When examining senior leadership such as board membership among people of color at Fortune 500 companies, African Americans account for 7.4%, Asian Americans 2.5% and Latinos 3.3% (Catalyst, 2013). When you do find people of color in senior level positions they are often tracked in racialized positions (Thomas, 2001) such as diversity and community relations. It is not uncommon to see a few successful employees of color showcased to illustrate a company's commitment to diversity when in fact the majority of professionals of color tend to plateau at more junior and mid-management levels. Low people of color representation cues in the workplace can lead professionals of color to perceive threatening identity contingencies and to mistrust the setting (Purdie-Vaughns et al., 2008). The lack of racial representation in senior, key decision- making roles is not consistent with values of inclusion and meritocracy that many organizations promote. When senior management and board of directors are overwhelmingly

White, the unconscious message conveyed to people of color is that they do not belong and are less likely to succeed in these institutions.

Racial microaggressions can also operate interpersonally in the workplace, most notably in the form of stereotyping. One of the most prominent stereotypes for African Americans and Latinos is the assumption of being intellectually inferior. African Americans frequently report having to constantly prove their ability as well as observe the surprise of managers and colleagues who may have had initial assumptions about their competence (Driscoll, Burrow, & Torres, 2010). It is not uncommon for professionals of color to have White colleagues question their expertise along with their professional qualifications and credentials. The increased anxiety associated with refuting stereotypes may lead to diminished work performance and ironically confirm the negative perceptions others hold of them (Cheryan & Bodenhauser, 2000). In contrast, while Asian Americans are often associated with words like intelligent and hardworking they encounter stereotypes of being perceived as being unassertive and lacking gravitas—important attributes for succeeding in the executive suite. With the positive stereotype of being a "model minority," the expectation to demonstrate strong intellectual capacities may lead to increased psychological anxiety and the distress for disappointing one's race (Cocchiara & Quick, 2004). When mentors and sponsors have negative perceptions about an employee's potential based on his or her race, they are less likely to lend their social capital and influence to accelerate an employee of color's career. Research shows that White employees are more likely to be put on the fast track based on their perceived potential while professionals of color have to consistently demonstrate solid records of performance before being placed on the executive track (Thomas, 2001).

Exclusionary practices represent another form of discrimination in the workplace. Many professionals of color experience being excluded from work meetings, networking events, and social gatherings. People of color are more likely to experience job dissatisfaction and lower sense of well-being (Barak & Levin, 2002) when excluded in the workplace. Exclusionary environments contribute to feelings of invisibility whereby one's presence and contributions are perceived as less valuable and visible than that of a White person. Professionals of color are also less likely to have access to informal networks of influential mentors and sponsors (Bagati, 2008). While excellent job performance is considered a prerequisite for career success, it is not sufficient. Access to informal networks is critical in fostering career and professional development because it is where key organizational information is shared, new job assignments are discussed and work partnerships are cultivated.

The costs of racial microaggressions in the workplace are numerous for both employees and organizations. Racial microaggressions in the workplace contribute in creating barriers to advancement that preserve racial inequalities and segregation in the workplace. Terms such as glass or concrete ceilings illustrate the severity of the challenges employees of color face in the workplace where in some cases they are not able to see or breakthrough to higher levels of career success. In addition to career consequences such as limited or no employment and denied promotions, racial microaggressions also have critical physical health and psychological costs. Racial discrimination in the workplace has been associated with elevated blood pressure among African Americans (Din-Dzietham, Nembhard, Collins, & Davis, 2004). Racial discrimination in the workplace was found to positively predict an increased number of physical health issues among Filipino Americans (de Castro, Gee, & Takeuchi, 2008). The psychological consequences of racial discrimination in the workplace can include increased anxiety, paranoia, and depression (Root, 2003) and diminished productivity in the workplace (Rowe, 1990; Steele 1997). When you consider the impact of having one's expertise and credentials questioned, it is not surprising that exposure to racial discrimination in the workplace can contribute to lack of confidence and intrusive cognitions. It is clear that the impact of microaggressions in the workplace also has a deleterious impact on organizations. Employers can potentially be more vulnerable to legal action and financial consequences of discriminating against employees belonging to protected classes such as race and gender (Shih, Young, & Bucher, 2013). Also, discrimination in the workplace leads to lower job productivity, greater absenteeism, and higher levels of attrition (Jones, Ni, & Wilson, 2009; Madera, King, & Hebl, 2012). A culture of discrimination and exclusion can tarnish the reputational brand of an institution, making it more difficult to attract and develop the top talent needed to achieve financial success.

INTERSECTIONAL MICROAGGRESSIONS

In recent years, there has been an increase in literature that has focused on the ways that systemic discrimination negatively affects people with multiple oppressed statuses (Nadal, 2013; Sue, 2010). For instance, while women in general earn about 77 cents for every dollar that a man makes, African American women and Latina women earn even less, earning 70 and 60 cents for the same type of work as compared to men (National Committee on Pay Equity, 2012). Furthermore, one report found that 70% of anti-LGBT hate crime murder victims involved people of color (Dixon, Frazer, Mitchell-Brody, Mirzayi, & Slopen, 2010), while another study found that transgender women of color and of lower socioeconomic statuses are likely to be victimized by hate crimes more often than their White or non-transgender counterparts (Stotzer, 2008).

Given these experiences, it is important to recognize that individuals with multiple identities, particularly those from historically oppressed communities, may experience microaggressions as a result of many of their identities. Nadal (2013) defines intersectional microaggressions as subtle forms of discrimination that are encountered, based on many of their identities. While there has been a dearth of literature that has focused on intersectional microaggressions, there are a few studies that have demonstrated their existence and impact. First, Balsam and colleagues (2011) created the Lesbian, Gay, Bisexual, and Transgender People of Color Microaggressions Scale, with the aim of examining the types of microaggressive experiences that LGBTQ People of Color may encounter in their everyday lives. Utilizing an 18-item self-report scale, LGBTQ people of color would be able to quantify their experiences with (a) racism in LGBT communities, (b) heterosexism in communities of color, and (c) racism in dating and close relationships. Findings indicated that: (1) gay and bisexual men of color reported more microaggressions than gay and bisexual women, (2) lesbians and gay men reported more microaggressions than bisexual women and men, and (3) LGBTQ Asian Americans reported more microaggressions than LGBTQ African Americans and LGBTQ Latina/os. Regarding intersectional microaggressions, the researchers found that (a) LGBTQ men of color may perceive or experience more intersectional microaggressions than LGBTQ women of color, (b) lesbian and gay people of color may perceive or experience more intersectional microaggressions than bisexual people of color, and (c) Asian Americans may perceive or experience more intersectional microaggressions than African Americans or Latina/o people of color.

Nadal, Mazzula, and colleagues (2014) examined how Latina/os may experience microaggressions differently based on gender, education, and other variables. Their results indicated that Latina women reported higher incidents of microaggressions than Latino men, likely due to the racism and sexism that women of color may experience in their lives. They also found that Latina/os with less education reported more microaggressions in their everyday lives, which may be the result of the fewer privileges and their lack of access to resources. Nadal, Wong, Griffin and colleagues (2014) conducted a similar study and found that Asian Americans without Bachelor's degrees were more likely to be exoticized, while those with Bachelor's degrees were more likely to experience microinvalidations. It is important to acknowledge that while certain groups may encounter certain types of racial microaggressions, individuals' experiences may vary when other identities (e.g., gender, education, etc.) are taken into consideration.

RECOMMENDATIONS FOR BEST PRACTICES

Based on the prevalence and significance of microaggressions in the workplace, it is vital for organizations and institutions to identify and implement policies and practices that promote a culture of inclusion and meritocracy. The first step in this effort is to acknowledge the unique and significant challenges that historically stigmatized groups face in the workplace that can have a deleterious impact on physical and psychological well-being and create barriers to career advancement. Senior level management and human resources professionals need to recognize that experiences of microaggressions can exist and take a significant toll on employees.

If employers truly value creating inclusive work environments, it would be necessary for them to promote cultural competence in all of their professional interactions. For example, supervisors should have open discussions about the ways that the company aims to be inclusive and ways that language and behavior can be exclusive. Similarly, supervisors may want to model appropriate behavior and language, in order to represent a positive example for their employees. For instance, when supervisors use phrases like "people of color" instead of "minorities" or "LGBTQ people" instead of "homosexuals," they demonstrate that they have knowledge of how communities should be addressed. Similarly, when supervisors have open dialogues about racial and cultural inequities, they contribute in creating environments in which they demonstrate their willingness to discuss systemic oppression and discrimination. Indeed, leadership commitment to and demonstration of cultural competencies is imperative in shaping organizational culture.

Additionally, managing diversity should be a core competence used to assess management's performance. A supervisor's ability to effectively cultivate and maintain inclusive work cultures should be one of the criteria used to directly determine compensation and promotion decisions. Cultural competence is an integral part of leadership especially with the increasing competition and changes occurring in global markets and the critical need to attract and retain global talent in order to achieve business success.

While companies can tout a variety of initiatives as evidence of their commitment to inclusion, a best practice is to view these efforts as strategic core operating businesses (Rice, 2012) with a clear vision, adequate resources, and accountability. For instance, direct involvement of the Chief Executive Officer (CEO) and senior leadership team in cultivating inclusive work environments communicates the message that such goals are imperative and critical to business success.

Another consideration for addressing microaggressions and creating inclusive work cultures is for companies to utilize objective appraisal systems for determining employees' performance and promotion decisions. To date, companies heavily use performance evaluations to retain and develop talent. It is important for transparency and objectivity to be at the core of how employees are evaluated particularly given the evidence of negative bias of performance evaluations of minority managers (Kilian, Hukai, & McCarty, 2005). When vacancies are open, particularly in top ranks it is vital to have a diverse candidate slate to consider for the roles. This practice can be a viable approach for addressing the lack of diverse representation at senior levels in an institution. When senior management teams and board of directors are overwhelmingly White, there is a threat and devaluation of one's social group identity (Purdie-Vaughns et al., 2008).

Organizations have an opportunity and responsibility to create and implement formal training opportunities to enhance employee awareness of the distinctive experiences of stigmatized groups because of their intersecting identities. It may be necessary for the concept of microaggressions to be introduced into multicultural competence training models in all workplace settings and other institutions (Nadal, Griffin, & Wong, 2011). These efforts can educate employees about how subtle discrimination can lead to exclusionary practices in the workplace. Additionally, employees can learn how their unconscious and unintentional biases may negatively influence their professional relationships.

It is important for organizations to create and implement policies in which microaggressions are addressed appropriately when they occur. One of the complications with microaggressions that occur in workplace settings is that there are a numerous amount of variables that may impact the ways that they manifest and how individuals react to them. First, because of power dynamics between supervisors and supervisees, it may be challenging for a recipient of a microaggression to confront their perpetrator because he or she might be concerned about the ramifications that may occur (Nadal, 2013) such as job termination or limited career advancement. Second, because microaggressions are so subtle and innocuous, it can be arduous for an individual to "prove" that they were discriminated against, particularly if they need to provide validation to Human Resources or other legal powers (Nadal, 2013). Organizations have an opportunity and responsibility to be vigilant in identifying any exclusionary practices in their business operations and institute a no tolerance policy for discrimination and send a message that violation of such a policy will result in serious corrective action.

REFERENCES

American Civil Liberties Union. (2012). *Arizona's SB 1070*. Retrieved from https://www.aclu.org/arizonas-sb-1070

Bagati, D. (2008). *Women of Color in U.S. securities firms: Women of Color in professional services series*. Retrieved from Catalyst website: http://www.catalyst.org/file/237/woc_finance_with_cover.pdf

Balsam, K. F., Molina, Y., Beadnell, B., Simoni, J., & Walters, K. (2011). Measuring multiple minority stress: The LGBT people of color microaggressions scale. *Cultural Diversity and Ethnic Minority Psychology, 17*(2), 163–174. http://dx.doi.org/10.1037/a0023244

Barak, M. E., & Levin, A. C. (2002). Outside of the corporate mainstream and excluded from the work community: A study of diversity, job satisfaction, and well-being. *Community, Work, & Family, 5,* 133–157. doi:10.1080/13668800220146346

Billings-Ladson, G. (2013). "Stakes is high": Educating new century students. *The Journal of Negro Education, 82*(2), 105–110.

Blanchett, W. J. (2006). Disproportionate representation of African American students in special education: Acknowledging the role of white privilege and racism. *Educational Researcher, 35,* 24–28. doi: 10.3102/0013189X035006024

Blume, A. W., Lovato, L. V., Thyken, B. N., & Denny, N. (2012). The relationship of microaggressions with alcohol use and anxiety among ethnic minority college students in a historically White institution. *Cultural Diversity and Ethnic Minority Psychology, 18*(1), 45–54. doi: 10.1037/a0025457

Brondolo, E., Rieppi, R., Kelly, K. P., & Gerin, W. (2003). Perceived racism and blood pressure: A review of the literature and conceptual and methodological critique. *Annals of Behavioral Medicine, 25,* 55–65. doi:10.1207/S15324796ABM2501_08

Capodilupo, C. M., Nadal, K. L., Corman, L., Hamit, S., Lyons, O., & Weinberg, A. (2010). The manifestation of gender microaggressions. In D. W. Sue (Ed.), *Microaggres-*

sions and marginality: Manifestation, dynamics, and impact (pp. 193–216). New York, NY: Wiley & Sons.

Carter, M. (2007, October). *Sustainable South Bronx: A model for environmental justice.* Lecture conducted from New Economies Institute, Great Barrington, MA.

Catalyst. (2013). *Missing Pieces: Women and minorities on Fortune 500 boards—2012 Alliance for board diversity census.* Retrieved from http://www.catalyst.org/knowledge/missing-pieces-women-and-minorities-fortune-500-boards–012-alliance-board-diversity

Cheryan, S., & Bodenhausen, G. V. (2000). When positive stereotypes threaten intellectual performance: The psychological hazards of model minority status. *Psychological Science, 11,* 399–402. doi: 10.1111/1467-9280.00277

Children's Defense Fund. (2007). A report of the Children's Defense Fund: *America's Cradle to Prison Pipeline.* Retrieved from Children's Defense Fund website: http://www.childrensdefense.org/child-research-data-publications/data/cradle-prison-pipeline-report-2007-full-lowres.pdf

Clark, R., Anderson, N. B., Clark, V. R., & Williams, D. R. (1999). Racism as a stressor for African Americans. *American Psychologist, 54,* 805–816. doi:10.1037/0003-066X.54.10.805

Cocchiara, F. K., & Quick, J. C. (2004). The negative effects of positive stereotypes: ethnicity-related stressors and implications on organizational health. *Journal of Organizational Behavior, 25,* 781–785.

Columbia Center for Children's Environmental Health. (2014). *Asthma.* Retrieved from http://ccceh.org/our-research/research-studies/asthma

Condron, D. J., Tope, D., Steidl, C. R., & Freeman, K. J. (2013). *The Sociological Quarterly, 54,* 130–157.

de Castro, A. B., Gee, G. C., & Takeuchi, D. T. (2008). Workplace discrimination and health among Filipinos in the United States. *American Journal of Public Health, 98,* 520–526. doi: 10.2105/AJPH.2007.110163

Din-Dzietham, R., Nembhard, W. N., Collins, R., & Davis, S. K. (2004). Perceived stress following race-based discrimination at work is associated with hypertension in African Americans: The metro Atlanta heart disease study, 1999–2001. *Social Science and Medicine, 58,* 449–461. doi:10.1016/S0277-9536(03)00211-9

Dixon, E., Frazer, S., Mitchell-Brody, M., Mirzayi, C., & Slopen, M. (2010). *Hate violence against lesbian, gay, bisexual, transgender, queer, and HIV-affected communities in the United States in 2010: A report from the National Coalition of Anti-Violence Programs.* New York, NY: National Coalition of Anti-Violence Programs.

Dovidio, J. F., & Gaertner, S. L. (2000). Aversive racism and selective decisions: 1989–1999. *Psychological Science, 11,* 315–319.

Dovidio, J. F., Gaertner, S. L., Kawakami, K., & Hodson, G. (2002). Why can't we all just get along? Interpersonal biases and interracial distrust. *Cultural Diversity and Ethnic Minority Psychology, 8,* 88–102. doi:10.1037/1099-9809.8.2.88

Driscoll, M. W., Burrow, A. L., & Torres, L. (2010). Racial microaggressions and psychological functioning among highly achieving African Americans: A mixed methods approach. *Journal of Social and Clinical Psychology, 29,* 1074–1099. doi: 10.1521/jscp.2010.29.10.1074

Flores, E., Tschann, J. M., Dimas, J. M., Bachen, E. A. Pasch, L. A., & de Groat (2008). Perceived discrimination, perceived stress, and mental and physical health among

Mexican-origin adults. *Hispanic Journal of Behavioral Sciences, 30*, 401–424. doi: 10.1177/0739986308323056

Frost, D. M., & Meyer, H. H. (2009). Internalized homophobia and relationship quality among lesbians, gay men, and bisexuals. *Journal of Counseling Psychology, 56*, 97–109.

Gibbons, F., Gerrard, M., Cleveland, M. J., Wills, T. A., & Brody, G. (2004). Perceived discrimination and substance use in African American parents and their children: A panel study. *Journal of Personality and Social Psychology, 86(4)*, 517–529. doi: 10.1037/0022-3514.86.4.517

Hobson, M. (2014, March). *Mellody Hobson: Color blind or color brave.* [Video file]. Retrieved from http://www.ted.com/talks/mellody_hobson_color_blind_or_color_brave/transcript?language=en#t-93027

Jones, J. R., Ni, J., & Wilson, D. C. (2009). Comparative effects of race/ethnicity and employee engagement on withdrawal behavior. *Journal of Managerial Issues, 21*, 195–215.

Kilian, C. M., Hukai, D., & McCarty, C. E. (2005). Building diversity in the pipeline to corporate leadership. *Journal of Management Development, 24*, 155–168. doi: http://dx.doi.org/10.1108/02621710510579518-168

Kosciw, J. G., Greytak, E. A., Diaz, E. M., & Bartkiewicz, M. J. (2010). *The 2009 National School Climate Survey: The experiences of lesbian, gay, bisexual and transgender youth in our nation's schools.* New York, NY: GLSEN.

Lopez, N. (2003). *Hopeful girls, troubled boys: Race and gender disparity in urban education.* New York, NY: Routledge.

Madera, J. M., King, E. B., & Hebl, M. R. (2012). Bringing social identity to work: The influence of manifestation and suppression on perceived discrimination, job satisfaction, and turnover intentions. *Cultural Diversity and Ethnic Minority Psychology, 18*, 165–170. doi: 10.1037/a0027724

McConahay, J. B. (1986). Modern racism, ambivalence, and the modern racism scale. In J. F. Dovidio & S. L. Gaertner (Eds.), *Prejudice, discrimination, and racism* (pp. 91–126). Orlando, FL: Academic Press.

McKown, C. (July/August 2013). Social equity theory and racial-ethnic achievement gaps. *Child Development, 84*(4), 1120–1136

Nadal, K. L. (2013). *That's so gay! Microaggressions and the lesbian, gay, bisexual, and transgender community.* Washington, DC: American Psychological Association.

Nadal, K. L., Griffin, K., & Wong, Y. (2011). Gender, racial, and sexual orientation microaggressions in the workplace: Impacts on women leaders. In M. A. Paludi & B. Coates (Eds.). *Women as transformational leaders: From grassroots to global interests, Volume 1: Cultural and organizational stereotypes, prejudice, and discrimination* (pp. 1–26). Santa Barbara, CA: Praeger.

Nadal, K. L., Griffin, K. E., Wong, Y., Hamit, S., & Rasmus, M. (2014). Racial microaggressions and mental health: Counseling clients of color. *Journal of Counseling and Development, 92*(1), 57–66.

Nadal, K. L., Issa, M., Leon, J., Meterko, V., Wideman, M., & Wong, Y. (2011). Sexual orientation microaggressions: "Death by a thousand cuts" for lesbian, gay, and bisexual youth. *Journal of LGBT Youth, 8*, 1–26.

Nadal, K. L., Mazzula, S. L., Rivera, D. P., & Fuji-Doe, W. (2014). Microaggressions and Latina/o Americans: An Analysis of Nativity, Gender, and Ethnicity. *Journal of Latina/o Psychology, 2*(2), 67–78.

Nadal, K. L., Wong, Y., Griffin, K. E., Davidoff, K., & Sriken, J. (2014). The adverse impact of racial microaggressions on college students' self-esteem. *Journal of College Student Development, 55*(4), 462–474.

National Committee on Pay Equity. (2012). *Wage gap statistically unchanged and still stagnant.* Retrieved from http://www.pay-equity.org/index.html

Nier, J. A., Gartner, S., L., Nier, C. L., & Dovodio, J. F. (2011). Can racial profiling be avoided under Arizona immigration law? Lessons learned from subtle bias research and anti-discrimination law. *Analyses of Social Issues and Public Policy, 12*, 5–20. doi: 10.1111/j.1530-2415.2011.01248.x

Noguera, P., Hurtado, A., & Fergus, E. (Eds.). (2012). *Invisible no more: Understanding the disenfranchisement of Latino men and boys.* New York: Routledge.

Offermann, L. R., Basford, T. E., Graebner, R. DeGraaf, S. B., & Jaffer, S. (2013). Slights, snubs, and slurs: Leader equity and microaggressions. *Equality, Diversity, and Inclusion: An International Journal, 32(4)*, 374–393.

Ong, A. D., Burrow, A. L., Fuller-Rowell, T. E., Ja, N. M., & Sue, D. W. (2013). Racial microaggressions and daily well-being among Asian Americans. *Journal of Counseling Psychology, 60*(2), 188–199. doi: 10.1037/a0031736

Perera, F. P. (2008). Children are likely to suffer most from our fossil fuel addiction *Environmental Health Perspective, 116*(8), 987–990. doi: 10.1289/ehp.11173

Pew Research Center. (2010). *A year after Obama's election Blacks upbeat about Black progress, prospects.* Retrieved from Pew Social Trends website, http://www.pewsocialtrends.org/files/2010/10/blacks-upbeat-about-black-progress-prospects.pdf

Pierce, C., Carew, J., Pierce-Gonzalez, D., & Willis, D. (1978). An experiment in racism: TV commercials. In C. Pierce (Ed.), *Television and education* (pp. 62–88). Beverly Hills, CA: Sage.

Purdie-Vaughns, V., Davis, P. G., Steele, C. M., & Ditlmann, R. (2008). Social identity contingencies: How diversity cues signal threat or safety for african americans in mainstream institutions. *Journal of Personality and Social Psychology, 94*, 615–630. doi:10.1037/0022-3514.94.4.615

Randall, V. R. (2006–007). Eliminating racial discrimination in health care: A call for state health care anti-discrimination law. *Depaul Journal of Health Care Law, 10*, 1–26.

Rice, J. (2012). Why make diversity so hard to achieve? *Harvard Business Review, 90*, 40–41.

Rivera, D. P., Forquer, E. E., & Rangel, R. (2010). Microaggressions and the life experience of Latina/o Americans. In D. W. Sue (Ed.) *Microaggressions and marginality: Manifestation, dynamics, and impact* (pp. 59–83), New York, NY: Wiley.

Root, M. P. P. (2003). Racial and ethnic origins of harassment in the workplace. In D. B. Pope Davis, H. L. K. Coleman, W. M. Liu, & R. L. Toporek (Eds.), *Handbook of multicultural competencies in counseling and psychology* (pp. 478–492). Thousand Oaks, CA: Sage.

Rowe, M. P. (1990). Barriers to equality: The power of subtle discrimination to maintain unequal opportunity. *Employee Responsibilities and Rights Journal, 3*, 153–163.

Sears, D. O. (1988). Symbolic racism. In P. A. Katz & D. A. Taylor (Eds.), *Eliminating racism: Profiles in controversy* (pp. 53–84). New York, NY: Plenum.

Schacht, T. E. (2008). A broader view of racial microaggression in psychotherapy. *American Psychologist, 63*, 273. doi:10.1037/0003-066X.63.4.273

Shepard, P. (Winter 2005/2006). Breathe at your own risk: Transit justice in west Harlem. *Race, Recovery, and the Environment*, 51–53. Retrieved from http://reimaginerpe. org/files/16.Peggy.Shepard.pdf

Shih, M., Young, M. J., & Bucher, A. (2013). Working to reduce the effects of discrimination: Identity management strategies in organizations. *American Psychologist, 68*, 145–157.

Smith, W. A., Hung, M., & Franklin, J. D. (2011). Racial battle fatigue and the "Mis"Education of Black Men: Racial microaggressions, societal problems, and environmental stress. *Journal of Negro Education, 80*(1), 63–82.

Smith, N. G., & Ingram, K. M., (2004). Workplace heterosexism and adjustment among lesbian, gay, and bisexual individuals: The role of unsupportive social interactions. *Journal of Counseling Psychology, 51(1)*, 57–67. doi: 10.1037/0022-0167.51.1.57

Stallworth, L. E., McPherson, T., & Rute, L. (2001). Discrimination in the workplace: How mediation can help. *Dispute Resolution Journal, 56*(1), 35–44, 83–7.

Steele, C. (1997). A threat in the air: How stereotypes shape intellectual identity and performance. *American Psychologist, 52*, 613–629. doi: 10.1037/0003-066X.52.6.613

Stotzer, R. L. (2008). Gender identity and hate crimes: Violence against transgender people in Los Angeles County. *Sexuality Research and Social Policy, 5*, 43–52.

Sue, D. W. (2010). *Microaggressions in everyday life: Race, gender, and sexual orientation.* Hoboken, NJ: John Wiley & Sons.

Sue, D. W., Bucceri, J., Lin, A. I., Nadal, K. L., & Torino, G. C. (2007). Racial microaggressions and the Asian Americans experience. *Cultural Diversity and Ethnic Minority Psychology, 13*, 72–81.

Sue, D. W., Capodilupo, C. M., & Holder, A. M. B. (2008). Racial microaggressions in the life experiences of Black Americans. *Professional Psychology: Research and Practice, 39*, 329–336. doi:10.1037/0735-7028.39.3.329

Sue, D. W., Capodilupo, C. M., Torino, G. C., Buccieri, J. M., Holder, A. M. B., & Esquilin, M. E. (2007). Racial microaggressions in everyday life: Implications for clinical practice. *American Psychologist, 62*, 271–286. doi:10.1037/0003-066X.62.4.271

Sue, D. W., & Sue, D. (2007). *Counseling the culturally diverse: Theory and practice* (5th ed.). Hoboken, NJ: Wiley.

Thomas, D. A. (2001). The truth about mentoring minorities: Race matters. *Harvard Business Review, 79*, 99–107.

Thomas, K. R. (2008). Macrononsense in multiculturalism. *American Psychologist, 64*, 274–275. doi:10.1037/0003-066X.63.4.274

Tummala-Narra, P., Alegria, M., & Chen, C. A. (2012). Perceived discrimination, acculturative stress, and depression among South Asians: Mixed findings. *Asian American Journal of Psychology, 3*, 3–16. doi: 10.1037/a0024661

U.S. Census Bureau. (2009). *Men's and women's earnings from states and metropolitan statistical areas: 2009* (Publication No: ACSBR/09–3). Retrieved from http://www. census.gov/content/dam/Census/library/publications/2010/acs/acsbr09-3.pdf

U.S. Department of Education Office for Civil Rights. (2014). *Civil rights data collection of data snapshot: School discipline.* Retrieved from United States Department of Education website: http://www2.ed.gov/about/offices/list/ocr/docs/crdc-discipline-snapshot.pdf

Utsey, S. O., & Hook, J. N. (2007). Heart rate variability as a physiological moderator of the relationship between race-related stress and psychological distress in African Americans. *Cultural Diversity Ethnic Minority Psychology, 13*(3), 250–253. doi: 10.1037/1099-9809.13.3.250

Wang, J., Leu, J., & Shoda, Y. (2011). When the seemingly innocuous "stings": Racial microaggressions and their emotional consequences. *Personality and Social Psychology Bulletin, 37*(12), 1666–1678. doi: 10.1177/0146167211416130

Williams, D. R., Neighbors, H. W., & Jackson, J. S. (2003). Racial/ethnic discrimination and health: Findings from community studies. *American Journal of Public Health, 93*(2), 200–208.

Wu, F. (2002). *Yellow: Race in America beyond Black and White*. New York, NY: Basic Books.

CHAPTER 4

THE IMPACT OF MICROAGGRESSIONS AND STRUCTURAL INEQUALITIES ON THE WELL-BEING OF LATINA/O AMERICAN COMMUNITIES

David P. Rivera, Rebecca Rangel Campón, and Krista Herbert

INTRODUCTION

Latina/o Americans are one of the fastest growing and largest ethnic groups in the United States (US) (U.S. Census Bureau, 2011). Roughly 53 million people living in the US are Hispanic or Latina/o, which constitutes 17% of the nation's population (Brown & Patten, 2014). Of this number, 35.5% are first-generation (i.e., born outside of the US). Among the 40 million documented immigrants living in the US, about 28% immigrate from Mexico, 7.8% from Central American, and 6.7% from South America. More specifically, large numbers of Latinas/os are immigrating to the US from Mexico, followed by El Salvador, Cuba, Dominican Republic, Guatemala, Columbia, Honduras, Ecuador, Peru, Nicaragua, Venezuela, Argentina, Panama, Chile, Cost Rica, Bolivia, Uruguay, and Paraguay. These

Talking About Structural Inequalities in Everyday Life: New Politics of Race in Groups, Organizations, and Social Systems, pages 65–83.
Copyright © 2016 by Information Age Publishing
All rights of reproduction in any form reserved.

figures do not include Puerto Ricans, who are considered US citizens and comprise roughly 9% of the US population (U.S. Census Bureau, 2011).

Despite Latina/o Americans comprising a significant proportion of the US population, their story is nuanced, complicated, and contradictory at best. For example, older generations of Latinas/os tout themselves as being among the first non-indigenous citizens of the present day US and are likely to identify as culturally American, while newer generations are likely to identify as being bicultural or more culturally aligned with their country of origin (Marotta & Garcia, 2003). The contributions of Latina/o Americans are honored and celebrated, such as through the appointment of Justice Sonia Sotomayor to the US Supreme Court. Conversely, the seemingly never-ending contentious debate over immigration reform has put a spotlight on Latinas/os, whether documented or undocumented, and contributes to the numerous ways this group is adversely treated on a daily basis (Rivera, Forquer, & Rangel, 2010). For example, Arizona sheriff Joe Arpaio was prosecuted due to a violation of civil and constitutional rights against Latinas/os (Wian & Martinez, 2012). Determined to rid the US of undocumented immigrants, Arpaio's tactics appeared to target all Latinas/os and included pulling over drivers and passengers during county traffic stops. Not only did Arpaio harass Latinas/os for proof of immigration documentation, but even when individuals possessed a valid documentation they were still arrested.

While Latina/o Americans are on the verge of reaching a critical mass population wise, there continues to exist a relatively consistent degree of inequalities and disparities in access to and participation in the vast majority of social institutions in the US. Despite being the largest growing ethnic minority group in the US, Latinas/os are still considered second-class citizens and are overrepresented among the unemployed and poor (Sue & Sue, 2012). Latinas/os also experience a significant discrepancy in income and housing when compared to White Americans. These experiences of social inequalities not only impact their education and work, but also significantly affect their ability to receive adequate and appropriate medical and mental health services. Furthermore, the lack of cultural understanding of Latinas/os among professional and laypersons further contributes to these disparities. Latinas/os' cultural beliefs, such as their strong ties and responsibility towards their families, strong Catholic religious affiliations, and traditional sex role beliefs can conflict with the individualistic and independent society of the US (Sue & Sue, 2012). For many Latinas/os, discrimination in their everyday lives has been considered to be the most important issue that they face (Sue & Sue, 2012). Not only does discrimination affect Latinas/os role in society, but it also affects their ability to succeed and achieve optimum quality of life. In order to help make sense of the various social inequalities that are experienced by Latina/o Americans, this chapter will focus on interpersonal and structural barriers that influence the well-being of Latina/o Americans.

MICROAGGRESSIONS & INTERPERSONAL BARRIERS

Interpersonal barriers that Latinas/os report experiencing on a daily basis come in the form of microaggressions (Nadal, Mazzula, Rivera, & Fujii-Doe, 2014; Rivera et al., 2010). Microaggressions, originally conceptualized in the context of interracial interactions, are defined as "brief and commonplace daily verbal, behavioral, and environmental indignities, whether intentional or unintentional, that communicate hostile, derogatory, or negative racial slights and insults to the target person or group" (Sue et al., 2007, p. 273). Latinas/os report experiencing a variety of microaggressions on the interpersonal level that include having their intelligence questioned, being ignored or denied services in social settings, having their cultural values pathologized, receiving adverse treatment for speaking Spanish, and being treated like perpetual foreigners to name a few (Rivera et al., 2010). An example of a microaggression is found in the seemingly innocuous question "Where are you from?" This question seems harmless because it is a question that is frequently asked upon first meeting someone. However, it becomes microaggressive when the inquirer is not satisfied with the first answer and proceeds to question the individual further about their geographic origin. The implicit message conveyed from this line of inquiry is that the individual in question is not originally from the US. Furthermore, the microaggressive encounter is typically inspired by a stereotype internalized by the enactor that is informed by prejudicial beliefs about where people with physical (e.g., darker skin) and verbal characteristics (e.g., Spanish language, accent, etc.) similar to the aggressed individual are from. Microaggressions also manifest environmentally via the draconian legal measures proposed and taken in regards to immigration reform, as well as the underrepresentation of Latinas/os in managerial and professional occupations and overrepresentation in service related occupations (U.S. Department of Labor, 2008).

These interpersonal and environmental microaggressions (i.e., subtle, covert insults and invalidations embedded in public and private spaces, such as in the media) are correlated with compromises in well-being for Latinas/os (Nadal, Griffin, Wong, Hamit, & Rasmus, 2014; Rivera, 2012). For example, microaggressions were significantly correlated with compromised mental health such that Latinas/os who reported higher levels of microaggressions also reported compromises in mental health indicators, such as higher levels of anxiety and depression and poorer behavioral control and positive affect (Nadal et al., 2014; Rivera, 2012). Additionally, microaggressions have been linked with poorer general physical health as assessed by a global self-rating of physical health (Rivera, Molina, & Watkins, 2012). It has been suggested that a global self-rating of physical health can provide accurate information about mortality and health status (Idler & Benyamini, 1997). Although still in a nascent stage of development, microaggression and health-related outcomes research is beginning to provide support for the detrimental impact of these interactions.

In addition to this individual-level impact, microaggressions are also believed to play a role in creating and maintaining institutional- and societal-level inequalities (Sue, 2010). People of Color, including Latinas/os, describe the workplace as hostile and unwelcoming (Rivera et al., 2010; Sue, Lin, & Rivera, 2009). This hostility manifests in the form of interpersonal and environmental microaggressions that influence the movement of people through the social institutions we as citizens navigate on a daily basis. In effect, these hostile interactions help to maintain two vastly different pathways used to navigate daily life; one pathway that supports, validates, and encourages movement of the social majority through institutions (e.g., healthcare, education, workplace, etc.), and one pathway that opposes, invalidates, and discourages movement of the socially marginalized through these same institutions. Healthcare is one such institution where these different pathways operate to benefit some and harm others. The following sections will discuss the issues and structural inequalities that impact the healthcare of Latina/o Americans.

The following example illustrates the complexity of how microaggressions in the context of a racist system contribute to the above-mentioned structural inequalities. There is a long history of individuals being discrimination against until they have been forced out, to live with others "like themselves." The location of where one resides impacts many aspects of one's social life (Massey, 2004; Williams & Collins, 2001). For instance, the location of an individual's residence is a large determinant of which school they attend, what jobs are accessible to them, the type and quality of public benefits accessible to them, and what stores and other commercial resources are accessible near their residence. These social, educational and health resources, influenced by where the individual lives, in turn impact their quality of education, future careers, health and quality of life, as well as defining their lifestyle (Marger, 2006).

Taking accessibility to schools as an example, the results from the Education Trust Study demonstrate that clear inequities exist in state and local distribution of education dollars to districts with the highest student of color enrollments (Orlofsky, 2002). According to data collected between 1999–2000, 22 of the 47 states studied sent substantially less money per student to school districts that have the greatest number of student of color enrollment. One example is that of New York State which provides an additional $1,339 per student in state revenue to districts with the *fewest* student of color enrollments when compared to districts with the highest number of minority students. Thus, for New York, its districts with the highest populations of color have significantly *less* money allocated per student then its districts with the fewest students of color. Nationally, districts with the greatest number of poor students receive $966 less per student than districts with lower poverty rates. Hence, these statistics demonstrate the reality for individuals of color who statistically are more likely to live in poverty (U.S. Department of Health and Human Services, 2001) will have less access to quality education. Their districts (determined by where they live) have less funding to obtain the most qualified teachers and provide additional instructional time, resources and equipment that has shown to make a difference in education (Orlofsky, 2002). These overwhelming statistics represent the serious consequences of oppression that render people powerless and dependent. In this way, people of color may find themselves at a disadvantage and targets for daily microaggressions, thus feeling the weight of their social status in their everyday lives.

STRUCTURAL INEQUALITIES FOR LATINAS/OS IN EVERYDAY LIFE

Access to Quality Healthcare:

According to the National Healthcare Disparities Report (U.S. Department of Health & Human Services, 2013), disparities related to race, ethnicity, and socio-economic status still pervade the American healthcare system and are observed across a number of dimensions including, effectiveness of care for common clinical conditions, effectiveness of care across the lifespan, patient safety, timeliness, patient centeredness, efficiency, health system infrastructure, and access to healthcare. Analyses of these dimensions reveal significant disparities in healthcare for Blacks, Asians, American Indians, Alaska Natives, Native Hawaiians/Pacific Islanders, and Latinas/os when compared to their White counterparts. For example, Latinas/os experienced no significant change in the majority of indicators used to assess these dimensions, and experienced an increase in disparities for three of the indicators. In sum, these statistics demonstrate limited progress in the elimination of healthcare disparities and that significant gaps in quality and access persist.

Additionally, factors such as cost of care, lack of sufficient insurance for mental health services, social stigma, fragmented organization of services, and mistrust all present significant barriers to treatment. Economic and geographic factors also significantly influence mental health. Poverty is a risk factor for poor mental health as well as a result of poor mental health. Additionally, many people who reside in rural and remote areas with mental illnesses have less adequate access to care, more limited availability of skilled care providers, lower family incomes, and greater societal stigma for seeking mental health treatment than those residing in urban areas (NHDR, 2013).

In terms of access to healthcare, a logical issue to explore is that of insurance. Latinas/os are more likely to suffer from chronic conditions such as high blood pressure, arthritis, neck and back pain, diabetes, obesity, hypertension, heart disease, and comorbid substance abuse and other mental health disorders (Ai, Appel, Huang, & Lee, 2012; U.S. Department of Health & Human Services, 2009). Despite this obvious need for access to quality healthcare, Latinas/os are overrepresented among the uninsured (Betancourt, Green, Carrillo, & Ananeh-Firempong, 2003). As a result, Latinas/os are more likely to delay care for their chronic conditions and less likely to seek mental healthcare than any other ethnic group (Ai et al., 2012). Questions remain as to why Latinas/os lack health insurance, in addition to their underutilization of medical and mental health services.

There are several issues that may account for the lack health insurance coverage for Latinas/os, including quality of employment opportunities and access to public resources. For many Americans, health insurance coverage benefits comes with full-time employment opportunities; however, Latina/o Americans are less likely to be offered these healthcare benefits from employers (Weinick, Jacobs, Cacari Stone, Ortega, & Burstin, 2004). Although Latinas/os constitute a large portion of the labor force a disproportionate number have little or no access to public or private health insurance. Even those who qualify for public assistance coverage, such as Medicaid, find it extremely difficult to find quality providers who are willing to accept this type of insurance (Valdez, Giachello, Rodriguez-Trias, Gomez, & de la Rocha, 1993).

Additionally, many Latinas/os are employed at low-wage salaries and are less likely to be offered health insurance or be able to afford insurance on their own. Research has shown that regardless of the type of work, amount of hours worked, or size of the employer, Latinas/os are less likely to have employer-sponsored health insurance compared to White Americans (Weinick et al., 2004). For example, in every type of industry, from small firms and public administration to agricultural work, Latinas/os are significantly less likely to receive healthcare benefits from the employer (Brown, Ojeda, Wyn, & Levan, 2000). This inequality of health insurance for Latina/o Americans serves as a structural barrier to their access and utilization of healthcare, and also affects access to preventative care, high usage of emergency departments, and difficulty obtaining prescription medications (Betancourt et al., 2003).

Despite the fact that the high-uninsured rates hinder Latinas/os from receiving physical and mental healthcare, even the insured have significant barriers that prevent them from receiving adequate care. Racial and ethnic disparities in the access and utilization of healthcare, and in the diagnosing and treatment of various conditions exist even when researchers control for factors such as insurance status, income, age, condition, socioeconomic status and site of care (Betancourt et al., 2003). Microaggressions, bias, discrimination, and prejudice on the part of healthcare providers can significantly contribute to the variation in healthcare for Latinas/os. For example, many Latinas/os may experience maltreatment, be neglected or ignored, or not provided quality treatment from one or more providers that hinders their trust and desire to go back.

Many Latina/o Americans have reported that they feel racism and discrimination exists within the healthcare system, which impacts their willingness to go to a facility, the quality of care they receive, and satisfaction with their care (Chen, Fryer, Philips, Wilson, & Pathman, 2005). Latinas/os report that they receive substandard quality of care that often occurs when the healthcare provider is not Latina/o. Research has found that when Latinas/os perceive racism to exist in the healthcare system, they not only prefer a physician and mental health provider who is also Latina/o, but have also reported higher levels of satisfaction with the care, higher quality of care, and feel more comfortable and confident in a physician who is Latina/o because of factors such as shared cultural beliefs, social experiences, language, and how they treat the patient (Betancourt et al., 2003; Chen et al., 2005).

For example, patients' of color and low to middle socioeconomic status were associated with physicians' perception of patient intelligence, their perception of their ability to connect to and relate to the patient, and their beliefs about the patient's engagement in risky behaviors and adherence to medical advice (van Ryn & Burke, 2000). In addition to these perceptions, the race, ethnicity, and socioeconomic status of the patient are related to the physician's perception of the patient's personality, role demands, and abilities. The physician's perceptions of the patient directly impacts how they treat the patient, on both a personal and professional level, in addition to the decreased likelihood of patients of color continuing to get quality medical care.

Latinas/os without health insurance are often required to utilize public health services, which are often underfunded, understaffed, and antiquated in their design. These facilities rarely reflect the cultural or social concerns of the communities where they are located and too few providers locate their facilities in Latina/o communities (Valdez, et al., 1993). Some of the justified criticisms of healthcare provision Latinas/os consistently report include language problems/lack of interpreter services, long waits at the physician' office and to make appointments, limited clinical office hours, and the lack of culturally (and linguistically) appropriate physical and mental health resources (Betancourt et al., 2003; Flores, Abreu, Olivar, & Kastner, 1998; Valdez et al., 1993). For many Latinas/os, these factors are associated with dissatisfaction of care, and lower quality of care. When these cultural and linguistic barriers exist, they negatively impact communication and trust between patient and physician, thus causing poorer health outcomes and less comprehension and compliance with medical advice.

The structural inequalities that exist in the medical and mental health community go beyond that of the healthcare provider's bias and discrimination of Latinas/os, but are also reflected on a societal level. The nation's leaders in healthcare and the healthcare workforce do not reflect the racial and ethnic composition of the general population, which affects the utilization and availability of healthcare for Latinas/os (Betancourt et al., 2003). African Americans, Latinas/os, and Native Americans are substantially underrepresented in the health professions. The absence of diversity in the healthcare system causes structural policies, procedures, and delivery systems to be poorly designed to serve diverse patient populations. Furthermore, the lack of culturally competent medical and mental health professions not only discourages Latinas/os and people of color from utilizing various services, but also significantly impacts the quality of services they receive. People of color in the healthcare professions are more likely to organize policies, procedures and healthcare delivery systems that meet the needs of people of color (Betancourt et al., 2003). Additionally, the lack of community outreach programs for Latinas/os creates significant barriers to receiving adequate care. This failure to provide education and target programs and services for Latinos significantly limits the services available for them, in addition to quality service available (Valdez et al., 1993). Without culturally competent physicians, mental health professionals, policies, and procedures, the healthcare of Latina/o Americans is severely compromised, thus preventing many Latinas/os from receiving necessary healthcare.

Interpersonal and Institutionalized Discrimination

According to the American Psychiatric Association (2006), "racism and racial discrimination are two of the factors leading to mental healthcare disparities" and encourages that those in the mental health field "should be mindful of the existence and impact of racism and racial discrimination in the lives of patients and their families, in clinical encounters, and in the development of mental health services" (Resolution Against Racism and Racial Discrimination and Their Adverse Impacts on Mental Health). For many Latinas/or, instances of racism and racial discrimination are daily occurrences (Pérez, Fortuna, & Alegría, 2008). Understanding the occurrences and impact of racism and racial discrimination among Latinas/os is vital to assessment, diagnosis, and treatment for Latinas/os, as these factors may significantly influence their worldview, symptoms, self-esteem, and ethnic identity. Evidence has found a significant relationship between racial discrimination and mental health disorders (e.g., Bhui, Stansfeld, McKenzie, Karlsen, Nazroo, & Weich, 2005; Gee, Spencer, Chen, Yip, & Takeuchi, 2007; Karlsen, Nazroo, McKenzie, Bhui, & Weich, 2005). For example, evidence suggests a relationship between perceived discrimination and psychopathology for Latina/o Americans (Chou, Asnaani, & Hofmann, 2012). More specifically, Latina/o participants who reported instances of perceived discrimination were more likely to report symptoms of panic disorder, agoraphobia, and depression. Other researchers have found that instances of racial discrimination have been association with poor self-assessed mental health for Latina/o Americans (see Araújo, & Borrell, 2006, for a literature review).

Despite the mounting evidence suggesting the negative implications of racism and racial discrimination on mental health for Latinas/os, few researchers have attempted to understand why these relationships exist. Gaining an understanding of the causal nature of these experiences could be vital when developing interventions for Latinas/os to help them cope with and respond to instances of discrimination. In their attempt to explore the causal relationship between discrimination and mental health problems, Pascoe and Smart Richman (2009) conducted a meta-analysis of over 134 articles and proposed a perceived discrimination-stress response model based on the results. The proposed model conceptualizes discrimination as a social stressor that could have a direct impact on the physical and mental health of Latinas/os and people of color. This study suggested that this relationship could be partially mediated by the individual's response to stress, such as negative emotions and psychological responses. The more occurrences of discrimination an individual perceives, the more likely this negative stress response becomes activated, potentially leading to a constant negative emotional state. Furthermore, the authors propose that health risk behaviors (such as drinking and substance use) could manifest as possible coping mechanisms, which could further impact mental health. In fact, Carter and Forsyth (2010) asked participants to describe significant moments of racial discrimination throughout their lifetime and found that about half of the participants reported feeling stressed 2 months to 1 year or long after the discriminatory event. They also found that more than half of the participants described events that occurred between 5 and 10 years prior to the study, suggesting that the memory and stress of those events are carried with the individual for a significant portion of their lives.

These racial disparities in healthcare are compounded by a lack of culturally and linguistically competent providers. In fact, lack of culturally competent healthcare providers and stereotypes perpetuated by healthcare providers may lead to underutilization of services. In 2009, the federally designated mental health professional shortage areas were estimated to be 3,291, an increase from 1,669. An analysis of data from the National Institute of Mental Health's (NIMH) Collaborative Psychiatric Epidemiology Surveys Initiative (CPES) investigated what types of care were used, to assess the extent the care used was consistent with the American Psychiatric Association (APA) *Guidelines for the Treatments of Patients with Major Depressive Disorder,* and how insurance, education and household income influenced rates of care (González, Vega, Williams, Tarraf, West, & Neighbors, 2010). Findings indicated that overall 51 percent of those individuals meeting criteria for major depression during the prior year received some kind of treatment with only 21 percent receiving care that was consistent with APA *Guidelines.* Noteworthy was the finding that prevalence and severity of major depression was similar among the five studied racial/ethnic groups-Mexican Americans, Puerto Ricans, Caribbean Blacks, African Americans and non-Latina/o Whites. Moreover, when compared to non-Latina/o Whites (54% received care), African Americans (40% received care) and Mexican Americans (34% received care) with major depression were least likely to receive any care or care consistent with the *Guidelines.* The authors concluded that there were distinctive differences in mental healthcare usage between Mexican Americans and other Latina/o subgroups that had not been previously reported and indicated that future research exploring the extent to which patients' perceived experiences of discrimination might affect their access and utilization of mental healthcare.

If such a need for mental health services is present, why is there such an underutilization of services rate and high early termination rates? In addressing this question, researchers utilized a grounded theory method to understand the dynamics of the early termination from the Latina/o client's perspective (Bein, Torres, & Kurilla, 2000). The sample consisted of twenty Latina/o clients who attended no more than four sessions in a Latina/o focused or non-Latina/o focused outpatient settings. From the data, the authors developed the central concept of the "repelled Latina/o client" in which it was determined that the clients presented themselves as motivated to receive counseling, but some adverse condition, behavior, or demand from the service provider caused them to react by staying away from the service provider. This study found that there were four distinct overarching reasons for early termination from the Latina/o client's perspective: service denial, institutional demands, cultural dissonance, and incompetence. It is possible that the Latina/o clients experienced their treatment provider as culturally biased in overt and covert ways, which created cultural impasses that encouraged the clients to prematurely terminate services.

Many studies have examined racial and ethnic discrimination and how it impacts quality of care. Equally as important to study is how microaggressions on a daily basis impact Latinas/os ability to receive quality healthcare. For example, Latinas/os spirituality and religiosity at times is not respected, as indicated by a roll of the eyes or slight joke from the healthcare provider or staff. Studies have shown that Latinas/os in particular tend to somaticize their symptoms that may stem from mental illness, among other distinct differences on how symptomology is manifested (Falicov, 1998). When providers fail to take into consideration the various ways that psychopathology manifests, they might write off the somatic pain as something "in their head" without doing further physical studies that they may have done on a non-Latina/o. This type of "health" stereotype is dangerous and can lead to improper care and diagnosis. Further, it consistently dismisses and treats the Latina/o individual as a second-class citizen. Understanding the cultural needs of Latinas/os in the US will help address the issues of engaging Latinas/os in treatment, early termination, and underutilization of services as well as educating providers in acknowledging their own biases.

Mental health services for marginalized populations usually lack sensitivity to cross-cultural issues, particularly in assessment and treatment. The cultural values for people of color may be ignored by mental health professionals who are not familiar with the cultural worldviews, lifestyles, values, norms, and histories of various racial and ethnic groups (Sue & Sue, 2012). This lack of culturally sensitive therapy not only can lead to mistrust of mental health services, but also misunderstandings in cultural values and beliefs, misinterpretation of experiences of people of color, and mental health needs being left unmet. Traditional individualistic methods of Western psychotherapy treatment based on verbal therapy and introspection may not match the needs and cultural values of clients of Latina/o descent.

For instance, the traditional Western views of psychotherapy place value and emphasis on the individual and independence, while many Latinas/os highly value the family unit (*familismo*) and have a strong identification, attachment, loyalty and respect for their family (Ayón, Marsiglia, & Bermudez-Parsai, 2010; Sue & Sue, 2012). Numerous studies have indicated that Latinas/os rely on family members for their main source of help when experiencing problems and mental health issues and often do not seek help until familial resources have been exhausted (Griner & Smith, 2006; Sue & Sue, 2012). The family provides such strong support, comfort, trust, empathy, and feelings of safety for many Latinas/os. In addition, many Latino families feel that it is a sign of weakness to experience mental illness and some Latinas/os have reported that their family may be stigmatized and feel ashamed and fear social criticism (Rastogi, Massey-Hastings, & Wieling, 2012). In fact, stigma from one's family and fears that their family will be stigmatized has been found to be a significant barrier to mental health treatment for many Latinas/os (Ayón et al., 2010). Thus, Latinas/os may be reluctant to share their problems and mental health issues with people outside of their family, especially mental health professionals. Many mental health professionals may try to encourage therapeutic techniques that promote the well-being and success of the individual, while neglecting take into account the client's cultural values and consider the consequences these techniques may cause for a Latina/o client. Furthermore, the Latina/o population may not respond well to this Westernized style of linear language and more elaborated verbal expression.

Additionally, some Latinas/os tend to explain psychological symptoms as being caused by supernatural phenomena and tend to somaticize psychological symptoms (Marquez & Ramierz Garcia, 2013; Ruiz, 2002). These alternative views of mental illness may actually be perceived as psychological symptoms rather than cultural views and beliefs. Furthermore, Latinas/os have traditionally used song, dance, rituals, theatre, poetry, and art as a means of emotional expression (Ciornai, 1983). As such, community healers such as a pastors, priests, curanderos, espiritistas, santerios, and shamans have been utilized by Latinas/os for spiritual and mental healing whom in turn use expressive modes of healing. Understanding Latinas/os cultural beliefs and norms is not only vital for therapeutic success, but also important in minimizing the barriers for mental health service utilization among the Latina/o community. Research has found that targeting and altering interventions that match clients' cultural, especially for Latinas/os, has been found to be four times more effective than traditional Western interventions (Griner & Smith, 2006).

Immigration Issues

Many immigrants encounter structural barriers during the process of entering and acculturating to the US. Specifically, Latina/o immigrants face significant challenges when seeking medical and mental healthcare. For many, they not only have to learn and become familiar with the US healthcare system, but they also face language barriers, stigma and bias, and acculturation issues (Weinick et al., 2004). For many immigrant Latinas/os, language barriers have the greatest impact on receiving healthcare. Due to the lack of Spanish speaking medical and mental health professionals, many immigrants have extreme difficulty in comprehending the education and treatment plans provided by healthcare professionals (Timmins,

2002). This can lead to poor patient satisfaction, as Latinas/os may feel judged for not speaking the native language, misunderstood, and even misdiagnosed, and also leads to poor treatment compliance (Timmins, 2002). Latina/o immigrants who experience stigma are less likely to want to be in treatment for medical and mental health disorders and underuse services in the future (Nadeem, Lange, Edge, Fongwa, Belin, & Miranda, 2007).

It can be very difficult to navigate a new culture, especially when the individual does not know the primary language. Ramos-Sanchez, Atkinson, and Fraga (1999) note that the "preoccupation of English subordinate clients on producing grammatically correct speech may interfere with the clients' emotional expression" (p. 126). This is an example of the client not only struggling to try to figure out how they are feeling, but also having to search for words in a second language to express and explain how they feel. This can be very taxing for any individual and can cause the healthcare provider to inaccurately interpret a language barrier as a sign of an uncooperative, negative, or repressed relational style (Sue & Sue, 2012). Thus, what may be expressed in body language as stress from the psychological and sometimes physical exertion of speaking in a second language might be perceived as symptoms of anxiety or other forms of psychopathology. Sue and Sue (2012) caution the practitioner that the problem may be linguistic and not psychological when working with people of color: "Euro-American society places such high premium of one's use of English, it is a short step to conclude that minorities are inferior, lack of awareness, or lack conceptual thinking powers" (p. 119). As such, bilingual clients not only have to worry about being understood verbally, they may also encounter misdiagnosis.

The language barrier causes feelings of discomfort in many Latina/o immigrants and instills a feeling of mistrust in the healthcare professions due to the stigma and bias they perceive. Most healthcare facilities are not adequately prepared to address language barriers, forcing family members or friends to stand in as the interpreter (Timmins, 2002). This is not only unethical, but also can impact the accuracy of information being transferred (Timmins, 2002). This lack of culturally competent care for Latina/o immigrants directly impacts their satisfaction with care, the quality of care they receive, and negatively affects the patient/healthcare provider relationship (Documet & Sharma, 2004). Many Latina/o immigrants have reported receiving substandard care due to their race, ethnicity, and because of language barriers. These negative experiences can cause Latinas/os to avoid using medical and mental health facilities in the future. When attempting to receive mental healthcare, many Latina/o immigrants were unaware of the mental health services available to them (Shattell, Hamilton, Starr, Jenkins, & Hinderliter, 2008). When they did seek services, many Latina/os felt misunderstood and as if they could not trust the mental health professional. Additionally, many felt that the mental health practitioner misdiagnosed them and misunderstood their needs.

Unfortunately, political and economic barriers exist in healthcare systems and inhibit the provision of culturally appropriate bilingual or interpretation services for monolingual Latinas/os. Most hospitals have protocols that interpretation services are required to be offered, but many times this is overlooked or the patient responds to English "enough" that the staff person believes that they are fluent and do not offer services. Other times providers are in a rush, are not familiar with the protocol, or do not feel it is important and do not provide an interpreter when it is appropriate and necessary for the provision of quality healthcare services.

Nonetheless, studies have shown that a therapist's ability to converse in the clients' preferred language may demonstrate a greater cultural sensitivity and thus affords them higher credibility (Ramos-Sanchez et al., 1999). Only 1% of US psychologist practitioners identify as Latina/o (Dingfelder, 2005), and obviously such a small number cannot keep up with the amount of individuals who prefer services with bicultural, bilingual psychologists. Nevertheless, these bilingual psychologists require the assistance of the field in order to preserve an ethical standard in their services. Very little is offered in terms of assistance for bilingual practitioners in providing services in Spanish. Biever et al. (2002) comment that "psychologists with conversational proficiency in Spanish have very few resources or guidance in making the transition from social to professional levels of Spanish proficiency" (p. 330). Furthermore, there is a lack of adequate training for bilingual therapists in the realm of psychology courses taught in Spanish in U.S. institutions. This lack of training opportunities presents an additional structural barrier to Spanish-speaking Latinas/os receiving culturally competent care.

In addition to language barriers, many Latina/o immigrants face employment and health insurance difficulties that impact their ability to seek healthcare. Many Latina/o immigrants are forced to work low-wage jobs due to their current legal status, skill level, or language barriers that exist (Shattell et al., 2008). Many governmental policies and changes in welfare reforms and Medicaid eligibility have impacted Latinas/os ability to receive public welfare funds or even employer benefits (Brown et al., 2000). For example, legal immigrants who came to the US after 1996 are not eligible for Medicaid for five years, and are reluctant to apply for it when they are eligible because they fear it will impact their citizenship or they will be forced to repay medical costs in the future (Brown et al., 2000). This is an example of how governmental policies can serve as structural barriers to healthcare.

RECOMMENDATIONS

Specific awareness surrounding the needs of Latinas/os in the US must be studied in order to become more multiculturally competent in the healthcare fields. When discussing treatment plans with Latina/o clients there are several cultural factors to consider. However, one must keep in mind that each individual may experience these factors differently. The Latina/o population is a very large, diverse group of individuals that represent a wide variety of ethnic, racial, political, socioeconomic, and religious backgrounds, for example. It is for this reason that we must be cognizant of these differences and be careful not to over generalize without first seeing the individual in their specific context. Nevertheless, there are some cultural beliefs, values, and practices that generally speak to the Latina/o population at large. Factors like level of acculturation, socioeconomic status, and ethnic background must be considered in determining applicability to Latina/o individuals. There are various culture-specific values that potentially impact a Latina/o individual's beliefs, thoughts, and behaviors.

The Latina/o culture is generally collectivistic and values interdependence. It is focused on the community and society at large and values group goals versus individual goals. It is seen as quite different from the American individualistic culture of independence, autonomy, and valuing the individual's goal over the group's goals. Latina/o clients may have familial or community responsibilities and/or obligations that precede their individual mental health that can potentially be misconstrued by a non-culturally sensitive clinician as reluctance or resistance to treatment. Therefore, when working with a Latina/o client it is important to assess the level that they adhere to collectivistic versus individualistic worldviews and consider how this might impact the therapeutic alliance. All these factors must be considered when treating Latinas/os/as. Again, it is in this area that microaggressions arise due to cultural misunderstandings, lack of knowledge, or insufficient multicultural training.

Understanding the various ways that Latina/o clients may conceptualize their illness is another vital aspect of the culture that is helpful in preventing microaggressions or in the very least informing a provider. The extent to which cultural differences are prevalent in today's society is made obvious throughout the *Diagnostic and Statistical Manual of Mental Disorders* (DSM–5; American Psychiatric Association, 2013) concerning culture's influence on the manifestation of mental issues. The DSM–5 describes several culture-bound syndromes that may be more familiar to clients more so than the conventional psychotherapy disorders. More specifically, these syndromes help the clinician differentiate between folk illnesses (from the client's perspective) versus mainstream psychotherapy labels such as anxiety or mood disorders. This assists in the clinician's attempt to be more culturally sensitive to the Latina/o client's experiences.

Religious and spiritual beliefs have also been found to be pertinent in the lives of Latinas/os in terms of intersecting with how they cope with physical and mental illness. The uses of natural healers who use herbs, oils, incense, massages, and 'homework' assignments as well as practice divination are common in some Latina/o communities. For example, *curanderismo* is an indigenous method that Latina/o individuals may go to heal folk illnesses such as *susto* or *mal de ojo*. *Curanderos, brujos,* and *espiritistas* (all known as folk healers) are reassuring and confident in their ability to diagnose and cure whatever ails the individual. Similarly, *santeros* (usually found in Cuba, Puerto Rico and other Caribbean countries) are very practical and try to solve the concrete problems presented to them. They too act as healers, diviners, and carry out rituals using special herbs, candles, potions, incense, and other ritual objects.

One last area of consideration is another form of coping with stress and aversive experiences through that of somatization (medically unexplained physical symptoms). These symptoms commonly point to emotional distress and seem to be observed more frequently in women and older individuals, those in developing nations, in lower socioeconomic statuses and lower education (Falicov, 1998). The presence of somatization may represent the integration of mind and body within the Latina/o culture. By asking Latina/o clients if they can speculate or guess about the emotional reasons for their physical ailments, they might ultimately uncover the meaning behind the somatizations. Moreover, as previously stated it is important to also honor and respect the Latina/o clients' beliefs and traditional theories regarding their health and healing practices.

The aforementioned underscore the value of understanding the Latina/o culture's concepts surrounding illness and healing in being able to be more effective in treating this population. Moreover, different clients within different cultures have preferred ways of expressing themselves. Healthcare providers are therefore challenged in helping clients and patients discover what works best for them at a particular time and place in their lives. By tapping into the various nuances of their culture, clinicians and researchers alike can promote a better understanding of their Latina/o clients' cultural backgrounds and thus a better understanding of the client as an individual. It is important to note that the creative arts works as a universal language, one that has found itself in almost every culture, in song, dance, visual art, storytelling, or poetry, and can be a powerful intervention.

CONCLUSION

Latina/o Americans represent a diverse culture that is more heterogeneous than homogenous. As such, one chapter can only speak to a handful of the significant issues and experiences that influence the well-being of this group. Despite the heterogeneity that exists within this group, Latinas/os consistently report that they experience microaggressions and other structural barriers in their daily lives. These microaggressions come in the form of individual and environmental interactions that insult and invalidate the lived experiences of Latinas/os, as well as help maintain the structural barriers that prevent Latinas/os from accessing and participating in social institutions. As discussed in this chapter, an area salient to the well-being of all Latinas/os is access to adequate and culturally responsive healthcare. It is difficult to negate the existence of a connection between the lack of access to healthcare and the health-related disparities that exist for Latina/o Americans. In order to foster a healthier sense of well-being within Latina/o American communities, the interpersonal and structural barriers that maintain a healthcare system that neglects the needs of Latina/o Americans must be addressed at the individual, institutional, and societal levels.

REFERENCES

Ai, A. L., Appel, H. B., Huang, B., & Lee, K. (2012). Overall health and healthcare utilization among Latino American women in the United States. *Journal of Women's Health, 21*(8), 878–885.

American Psychiatric Association. (2006). *Position statement: Resolution against racism and racial discrimination and their adverse impacts on mental health.* Retrieved March 25, 2014 from http://www.socialworkgatherings.com/Resolution%20 Against%20Racism%20APA.pdf

American Psychiatric Association. (2013). *Diagnostic and Statistical manual of mental disorders: DSM 5.* Arlington, VA: American Psychiatric Association.

Araújo, B. Y., & Borrell, L. N. (2006). Understanding the link between discrimination, mental health outcomes, and life chances among Latinos. *Hispanic Journal of Behavioral Science, 28*(2), 245–266.

Ayón, C., Marsiglia, F. F., & Bermudez-Parsai, M. (2010). Latino family mental health: Exploring the role of discrimination and familismo. *Journal of Community Psychology, 38*(6), 742–756

Bein, A., Torres, S., & Kurilla, V. (2000). Service delivery issues in early termination of Latino clients. *Journal of Human Behavior in the Social Environment, 3,* 43–59.

Betancourt, J. R., Green, A. R., Carrillo, J. E., & Ananeh-Firempong, O. A. (2003). Defining cultural competence: A practical framework for addressing racial/ethnic disparities in health and healthcare. *Public Health Reports, 188,* 293–302

Biever, J. L., Castano, M. T., de las Fuentes, C., Gonzalez, C., Servin-Lopez, S., Sprowls, C., et al. (2002). The role of language in training psychologists to work with Hispanic clients. *Professional Psychology: Research and Practice, 33,* 330–336.

Bhui, K., Stansfeld, S., McKenzie, K., Karlsen, S., Nazroo, J., & Weich, S. (2005). Racial/ethnic discrimination and common mental disorders among workers: Findings from the Empiric Study of Ethnic Minority Groups in the United Kingdom. *American Journal of Public Health, 95*(3), 496–501.

Brown, R. E., Ojeda, V. D., Wyn, R., & Levan, R. (2000). *Racial and ethnic disparities in access to health insurance and healthcare.* UCLA: UCLA Center for Health Policy Research. Retrieved from: https://escholarship.org/uc/item/4sf0p1st

Brown, A., & Patten, E. (2014). *Statistical portrait of the foreign-born population in the United States, 2012.* Pew Research Center, Washington, D.C. Retrieved from http://www.pewhispanic.org/2014/04/29/statistical-portrait-of-the-foreign-born-population-in-the-united-states-2012/#population-by-nativity-and-citizenship-status-2000-and-2012.

Carter, R. T., & Forsyth, J. (2010). Reactions to racial discrimination: emotional stress & help-seeking behaviors. *Psychological Trauma: Theory, Research, Practice, and Policy, 2*(3), 183–191.

Chen, F. M., Fryer Jr., G. E., Philips Jr., R. L., Wilson, E., & Pathman, D. E. (2005). Patients' beliefs about racism, preferences for physician race, and satisfaction with care. *Annals of Family Medicine, 3*(2), 138–43.

Chou, T., Asnaani, A., & Hofmann, S. G. (2012). Perception of racial discrimination and psychopathology across three U.S. ethnic minority groups. *Cultural Diversity and Ethnic Minority Psychology, 18*(1), 74–81.

Ciornai, S. (1983). Art therapy with working class Latino women. *The Arts in Psychotherapy, 10*(2), 63–76.

Dingfelder, S. F. (2005). Closing the gap for Latino patients. *Monitor on Psychology, 36,* 56–61.

Documet, P. L., & Sharma, R. K. (2004). Latinos' healthcare access: Financial and cultural barriers. *Journal of Immigrant Health, 6*(1), 5–13.

Falicov, C. J. (1998). *Latino families in therapy: A guide to multicultural practice.* New York, NY: Guilford.

Flores, G., Abreu, M., Olivar, M.A., & Kastner, B. (1998). Access barriers to health care for Latino children. *Archives of Pediatric and Adolescent Medicine, 152,* 1119–1125.

Gee, G. C., Spencer, M., Chen, J., Yip, T., & Takeuchi, D. T. (2007). The association between self-reported racial discrimination and 12-month DSM-IV mental disorders among Asian Americans. *Social Science & Medicine, 64*(10), 1984–1996.

González, H. M., Vega, W. A., Williams, D. R., Tarraf, W., West, B. T., & Neighbors, H. W. (2010). Depression care in the United States: Too little for too few. *Archives of General Psychiatry, 67*(1), 37–46.

Griner, D., & Smith, T. B. (2006). Culturally adapted mental health interventions: A meta-analytic review. *Psychotherapy: Theory, Research, Practice, and Training, 43*(4), 531–548.

Idler, E. L., & Benyamini, Y. (1997). Self-rated health and mortality: A review of twenty-seven community studies. *Journal of Health and Social Behavior, 38,* 21–37.

Karlsen, S., Nazroo, J. Y., Mckenzie, K., Bhui, K., & Weich, S. (2005). Racism, psychosis and common mental disorder among ethnic minority groups in England. *Psychological Medicine, 35*(12), 1795–1803.

Marger, M. N. (2006). *Race and ethnic relations: American and global perspectives.* Belmont, CA: Thompson Learning, Inc.

Marotta, S. A., & Garcia, J. A. (2003). Latinos in the United States in 2000. *Hispanic Journal of Behavioral Sciences, 25,* 13–34.

Marquez, J. A., & Ramíerz García, J. I. (2013). Family caregivers' narratives of mental health treatment usage processes by their Latino adult relatives with serious and persistent mental illness. *Journal of Family Psychology, 27*(3), 398–408.

Massey, D. (2004). Geographies of responsibility. *Geografiska Annaler: Series B, Human Geography, 86*(1), 5–18.

Nadal, K. L., Griffin, K. E., Wong, Y., Hamit, S., & Rasmus, M. (2014). The impact of racial microaggressions on mental health: Counseling implications for clients of color. *Journal of Counseling & Development, 92*(1), 57–66.

Nadal, K. L., Mazzula, S. L., Rivera, D. P., & Fujii-Doe, W. (2014). Microaggressions and Latina/o Americans: An analysis of nativity, gender, and ethnicity. *Journal of Latina/o Psychology, 2*(2), 67–78.

Nadeem, E., Lange, J. M., Edge, D., Fongwa, M., Belin, T., & Miranda, J. (2007). Does stigma keep poor young immigrant and U.S.-born Black and Latina women from seeking mental healthcare? *Psychiatric Services, 58*(12), 1547–1554.

Page, D., & Shepherd, H. (2008). The sociology of discrimination: Racial discrimination in employment, housing, credit, and consumer markets. *Annual Review in Sociology, 34,* 181–209.

Orlofsky, G. F. (2002). *The funding gap: Low-income and minority students receive fewer dollars.* Washington, DC: The Education Trust.

Pascoe, E. A., & Smart Richman, L. (2009). Perceived discrimination and health: A meta-analytic review. *Psychological Bulletin, 135*(4),531–554.

Pérez, D. J., Fortuna, L., & Alegría, M. (2008). Prevalence and correlates of everyday discrimination among U.S. Latinos. *Journal of Community Psychology, 36*(4), 421–433.

Ramos-Sánchez, L., Atkinson, D. R., & Fraga, E. (1999). Mexican Americans' bilingual ability, counselor bilingualism cues, counselor ethnicity, and perceive counselor credibility. *Journal of Counseling Psychology, 46,* 125–131.

Rastogi, M., Massey-Hastings, N., & Wieling, E. (2012). Barriers to seeking mental health services in the Latino/a community: A qualitative analysis. *Journal of Systemic Therapies, 31*(3), 1–17.

Rivera, D. P. (2012). *Microaggressions and health outcomes for Latina/o Americans: Understanding the influences of external characteristics and psychological resources* (Doctoral dissertation, Columbia University, New York, NY).

Rivera, D.P., Forquer, E. E., & Rangel, R. (2010). Microaggressions and the life experience of Latina/o Americans. In D. W. Sue (Ed.), *Microaggressions and marginality: Manifestations, dynamics, and impact* (pp. 59–84). New York, NY: Wiley & Sons.

Rivera, D. P., Molina, K., & Watkins, N. L. (2012, February). Microaggressions, generational status, and health outcomes for Latina/o Americans. Kevin L. Nadal (Chair) symposium entitled *The impact of racial microaggressions on physical and mental health: A review of quantitative research.* Paper presented at the 29th Annual Winter Roundtable on Cultural Psychology & Education, New York, NY.

Ruiz, P. (2002). Hispanic access to health/mental health services. *Psychiatric Quarterly, 73*(2), 85–19.

Shattell, M. M., Hamilton, D., Starr, S. S., Jenkins, C. J., & Hinderliter, N. A. (2008). Mental health service needs of a Latino population: A community-based participatory research project. *Issues in Mental Health Nursing, 29,* 351–370.

Sue, D. W. (2010). *Microaggressions in everyday life: Race, gender, and sexual orientation.* Hoboken, NJ: John Wiley & Sons.

Sue, D. W., Capodilupo, C. M., Torino, G. C., Bucceri, J. M., Holder, A. M. B., Nadal, K. L., & Esquilin, M. (2007). Racial microaggressions in everyday life: Implications for clinical practice. *American Psychologist, 62,* 271–286.

Sue, D. W., Lin, A. I., & Rivera, D. P. (2009). Racial microaggressions in the workplace. In J. L. Chin (Ed.), *Diversity in mind and in action, Volume 2: Disparities and competence* (pp. 157–172). Westport, CT: Greenwood.

Sue, D. W., & Sue, D. (2012). *Counseling the culturally diverse: Theory and practice* (6th ed.). New York, NY: John Wiley & Sons.

Timmins, C. (2002). The Impact of language barriers on the healthcare of Latinos in the United States: A review of the literature and guidelines. *Journal of Midwifery & Women's Health, 47*(2), 80–96.

U.S. Census Bureau. (2011). *Hispanic heritage month 2011.* Retrieved on March 25, 2014 from https://www.census.gov/newsroom/releases/archives/facts_for_features_special_editions/cb11-ff18.html

U.S. Department of Health and Human Services. (2001). *Mental health: culture, race, and ethnicity. A supplement to mental health: A report of the surgeon general.* Rockville, MD: U.S. Department of Health and Human Services, Substance Abuse and Mental Health Services Administration, Center for Mental Health Services.

U.S. Department of Health and Human Services. (2009). *Office of Minority Health*. Retrieved from http://www.omhrc.gov/templates/browse.aspx?lvl=1&lvlID=2

U.S. Department of Health and Human Services. (2013). *National healthcare disparities report*. Retrieved on February 9, 2015, from http://www.ahrq.gov/research/findings/nhqrdr/nhdr13/2013nhdr.pdf.

U.S. Department of Labor, Bureau of Labor Statistics. (2008). *Household data annual averages*. Retrieved on April 16, 2009, from ftp://ftp.bls.gov/pub/special.requests/lf/aat11.txt.

Valdez, R. B., Giachello, A., Rodriguez-Trias, H., Gomez, P., & de la Rocha, C. (1993). Improving access to healthcare in Latino communities. *Public Health Reports, 108*(5), 534–539.

van Ryn, M., & Burke, J. (2000). The effect of patient race and socioeconomic status on physicians' perceptions of patients. *Social Science & Medicine, 50,* 813–828.

Weinick, R. M., Jacobs, E. A., Cacari Stone, L., Ortega, A. N., & Burstin, H. (2004). Hispanic healthcare disparities: Challenging the myth of a monolithic Hispanic population. *Medical Care, 42*(4), 313–320.

Wian, C., & Martinez, M. (2012, July 20). *Arizona sheriff faces civil trial in alleged targeting of Latinos*. CNN. Retrieved from http://www.cnn.com/2012/07/19/justice/arizona-arpaio-trial/

Williams, D. R., & Collins, C. (2001). Racial residential segregation: A fundamental cause of racial disparities in health. *Public Health Reports, 116*(5), 404.

CHAPTER 5

HIDDEN IN PLAIN SIGHT

Structural Inequalities and (In)visible Violence in the Lives of African American Women

Carolyn M. West

...it is easier to talk about violence as an individual pathology than it is to think about violence as a product of systemic inequalities that act on and through individuals in ways we don't yet fully understand
—Jones (2004, p. 23)

Intimate partner violence (IPV) is all too common in the United States (US). According to the National Intimate Partner and Sexual Violence Survey (NISVS), 32.9% of women and 28.1% of men have been victims of physical violence (Breiding, Chen, & Black, 2014). Defining IPV can be complex; however, a comprehensive definition includes physical aggression, ranging from less injurious violence, such as slapping and shoving, to more lethal forms of violence, including beatings and assaults with weapons. Sexual violence can include forced or drug-facilitated attempted or completed rape in the form of oral, vaginal, or anal penetration as well as reproductive coercion (e.g., pressuring a woman to become pregnant). Other frequently reported forms of violence include stalking and psy-

Talking About Structural Inequalities in Everyday Life: New Politics of Race in Groups, Organizations, and Social Systems, pages 85–102.

chological aggression, in the forms of name calling or threats (Breiding et al., 2014).

Victimization can involve men, women, and transgender individuals of every racial/ethnic background, socioeconomic status, age and sexual orientation (West, 2012). Yet, researchers have consistently documented gender, race, and social class differences in the rates of victimization. For example, more women than men reported having been raped (9.4% vs. 2.2%), severely physically assaulted (24.3% vs. 13.8%), or stalked (10.7 vs. 2.1%) by an intimate partner during the course of their lifetime (Breiding et al., 2014). When compared to their White and Latino/a counterparts, African Americans[1], whether as individuals or couples, consistently reported higher rates of overall, severe, mutual, and recurrent past year and lifetime physical IPV victimization and perpetration (see West, 2012; West, in press for a review). Finally, when compared to their more economically advantaged counterparts, women who earned less than $25,000 and women who experienced food and housing insecurity reported higher rates of intimate partner rape, physical violence, and stalking (Breiding et al., 2014).

Taken together, a demographic profile of the most vulnerable group emerges: African American women who are young, single or divorced, impoverished, and live in rental property that is located in urban areas (Rennison & Welchans, 2000). In the general population, nearly 4 out of 10 Black women (43%) have been raped, physically abused, or stalked in their lifetime. This prevalence rate translates into an estimated 6,349,000 victims (Breiding et al., 2014).

Despite their vulnerability, African American women's experience with violence is "hidden in plain sight" (Collins, 1998, p. 920) and, ironically, so hypervisible and pervasive that it has become "obscured, routinized, and thereby legitimated" (Collins, 1998, p. 926). More simply put, Black women are the target of so much violence that their victimization has become normalized, such that it is no longer visible or as I prefer to call it: (in)visible. The purpose of this chapter is to explain this paradox. First, I will review the research on IPV in the lives of Black women. By contextualizing Black women's use of violence, I will make the gendered nature of IPV more evident. There is rich demographic diversity among Black women. In order to make these subpopulations more visible, I will use intersectional analyses that considers the victims' social location in terms of age, socioeconomic class, ethnicity, and sexual orientation. The focus on individual acts of visible physical aggression renders other forms of violence invisible. Accordingly, in the third section, I will highlight the similarities and parallels between various forms of coercive control that are perpetrated by intimate partners and by agents of the state and service providers. Next, I will explore how structural risk factors, including poverty and concentrated neighborhood disadvantage, contribute to higher rates of IPV in the lives of Black women. To conclude, I will discuss how the criminal justice system and the economic system can better serve this marginalized population.

OVERVIEW OF INTIMATE PARTNER VIOLENCE

High rates of victimization and perpetration have been documented among African American women in general population studies. The lifetime prevalence rate of IPV was 26.3% in the National Violence Against Women Survey (NVAWS) (Tjaden & Thoennes, 2000) and even higher, at 40.9%, in the more recently conducted National Intimate Partner Sexual Violence Survey (NISVS) (Breiding et al., 2014). Ideally, both IPV victimization and perpetration should be measured in couples over time. This was accomplished in the National Longitudinal Couples Survey (NLCS) by interviewing both male and female partners in 1995 and 2000. The rate of male-to-female partner violence (MFPV) among Black couples was 23%. The most common forms of violence was pushing, slapping, and hitting with something (Caetano, Cunradi, Clark, & Schafer, 2000). At follow-up, these violent couples continued to experience both minor (15%) and severe (4%) MFPV (Caetano, Field, Ramisetty-Mikler, & Lipsky, 2009).

African American women actually reported higher rates of female-to-male partner violence (FMPV) than MFPV (30% vs. 23%). Almost one-third of Black wives used minor or moderate physical aggression against their husbands, such as throwing something; pushing, shoving, and grabbing; and hitting with something (Caetano et al., 2000). However, mutual, also referred to as bidirectional violence, was the most frequently reported pattern of relationship violence, with 61% of couples acknowledging that both partners had used physical aggression. One-third of Black couples who reported bidirectional partner violence described it as severe, defined as beat up, choked, raped or threatened with a weapon. Five years later, 17% of Black couples continued to engage in mutual violence and 11% of these couples progressed into severe IPV (Caetano, Raimisetty-Mikler, & Field, 2005).

Interestingly, some Black women did not deny their use of violence. In fact, they were more willing to identify themselves as perpetrators than Black men were willing to identify themselves as victims (Caetano, Schafer, Field, & Nelson, 2002). Other African American women, sometimes proudly and unapologetically, used aggression as a form of self-defense, in retaliation for past abuse, or to pre-empt future abuse. One battered Black woman described her role in a mutually abusive relationship: "I was a spirited co-combatant" (Potter, 2008, p. 133).

Although not to minimize Black women's use of violence, these gender patterns must be contextualized. First, the Conflict Tactics Scale (CTS) has been the most frequently used measure of overall, minor, and severe rates of physical aggression[2] (Straus & Gelles, 1990). When compared to Black men and women of other ethnic groups, African American women were overrepresented among victims of nonfatal strangulation (Thomas, Joshi, & Sorenson, 2014) and intimate partner femicide (Glass, Laughon, Campbell, Block, Hanson, Sharps, & Taliaferro, 2008). The CTS does not measure these two serious forms of gender-based violence. Thus, rendering them invisible.

Second, mutuality of violence does not mean that women's and men's violent acts are equivalent. While both members of the couple may use violence, when contextualized, it is evident that frequency and severity of assaults are seldom equal. These relationships may be better characterized as *bidirectional asymmetrical violence* (Temple, Weston, & Marshall, 2005). To illustrate, Janay Palmer and her fiancée, now husband, Ray Rice, a running back for the National Football League's (NFL's) Baltimore Ravens, was described as having "little more than a very minor physical altercation." However, in later video footage, Rice could be seen dragging her limp body from an Atlantic City casino elevator after he had allegedly knocked her unconscious (Boylorn, 2014). Although both partners used violence, at least in the case, the woman sustained more serious injuries.

Finally, women's use of physical aggression typically occurred in the context of their own victimization (Potter, 2008). Thus, these women may be more appropriately characterized as *Abused Aggressors* (Swan & Snow, 2003). Despite their violent behavior, these women seldom felt a sense of control, independence, or power within their relationships; rather, they reported symptoms of depression, anxiety, and posttraumatic stress (Swan & Snow, 2003). Beyond the mental health consequences, a disproportionate number of Black abused aggressors become victim-defendants after they use violence against abusive partners (West, 2007). Consider the case of Marissa Alexander, a Florida mother of three. She was arrested after firing a "warning shot" at Rico Grey, her abusive husband, who had beaten, choked, and punched her, causing injuries that required hospitalization (Lee, 2012).

In conclusion, Black women reported high rates of both victimization and perpetration, and even higher rates of mutual violence in national studies (West, 2007). However, it is too simplistic to conclude that men and women's use of IPV is equivalent. Three factors have led to the misperception that men and women are equally combative: the failure to include more comprehensive measures of IPV, the failure to acknowledge bidirectional asymmetrical violence, and the failure to consider motives, injury, and the consequences that are associated with IPV.

INTERSECTIONALITY

Although there is rich demographic diversity among Black women, it has been obscured in national samples. In order to make these subpopulations more visible, Black feminists have called for intersectional analyses that considers the victims' social location in terms of age, socioeconomic class, ethnicity, and sexual orientation (Crenshaw, 2012; Potter, 2008). For example, special attention should be paid to the unique forms of violence that Black women experience across the age spectrum. Black adolescent girls, particularly those who are poor, are at risk for dating violence in their intimate relationships, family violence in their homes, and sexual harassment in their schools or neighborhoods (Kennedy, 2008; Tonnesen, 2013). At the other end of the age continuum, older African American women are at risk for financial abuse from their adult children and for physical and emotional abuse from their husbands (Paranjape, Corbie-Smith, Thompson, & Kaslow, 2009).

There also are variations in the violence that Black women experience across social class and ethnicity. Much of the research in this area has focused on impoverished Black women; yet, their middle-class peers also face challenges. Revealing that they were victims of IPV could jeopardize the status and reputation of professional Black women and their partners. Moreover, their disclosure of abuse or request for services may be met with skepticism because they appear to be financially secure (Bent-Goodley, 2014; Potter, 2008). In addition, the prevalence rates and risk factors that are associated with IPV differ between US born African American women and second-generation or immigrant African and Caribbean women. A growing body of literature has sought to make these populations more visible (Lacey, West, Matusko, & Jackson, in press).

Finally, there is a dearth of research that investigates how the intersection of racism, sexism, and homophobia converge to increase the risk of physical and sexual IPV in the lives of Black lesbians and bisexual women (Hill, Woodson, Ferguson, & Parks, 2012; Richie, 2012). Although reliable official statistics are nonexistent, the website Transgender Day of Remembrance gave details of 170 violent deaths in the US between 2000 and 2012. A disproportionate number of these victims were African American transgender women. When their gender identity was discovered, perpetrators, including strangers, acquaintances, and intimate partners shot, suffocated, strangled, and sexually mutilated these women (Pilkington, 2014).

To conclude, the experiences of battered Black women can be best understood in relation to their multiple social locations and range of diverse identities. This requires intersectional analyses that considers where victims are located within the hierarchies of age, social class, ethnic, sexual orientation identities (Potter, 2008).

COERCIVE CONTROL

Definitions

It is time to move beyond single measures, such as the CTS, which oversimplify violence by reducing it to individual acts of aggression that cause physical injury and contributes to the presumption that IPV is mutual combat. Instead, IPV is better characterized as a form of *coercive control*. More explicitly, *coercion*, has been defined as "the use of force or threats to compel or dispel a particular response" (Stark, 2007, p. 228) and *control* has been characterized as "structural forms of deprivation, exploitation, and commands that compel obedience indirectly by monopolizing vital resources, dictating preferred choices, micro-regulating a partner's behavior, limiting her options, and depriving her of supports needed to exercise independent judgment" (Stark, 2007, p. 229).

As illustrated in the Power and Control Wheel, coercive control tactics used by batterers include isolation, emotional abuse, sexual abuse, using children, intimidation, and physical violence (Pence & Paymer, 1993). More recently, a Multicultural Power and Control Wheel has been created to reflect how IPV is shaped by intersecting identities (e.g., race, social class, and sexual orientation) and various systems of oppression (e.g., racism, classism, and heterosexism) in the lives of marginalized women (Chavis & Hill, 2009).

In order to capture the full range of violence that is experienced by Black women, these models need to include a discussion of institutionalized and structural violence. African American women are visibility battered by their intimate partners and invisibly battered by *institutional racism*, which are unfair polices and discriminatory practices of particular institutions that have a disparate impact on people of color (Kupenda, 2009). Similar to the (in)visibility of interpersonal violence in the lives of Black women, structural racism is so damaging and insidious because it is omnipresent. To give a more concrete example, Johnnie Tillmon, a welfare rights advocate, described the welfare system as "a super-sexist marriage" in that "you trade in *a* man for *the* man." In the Black vernacular tradition, "the man" is:

> …not a singular person but rather to a broad array of racist practices that have clearly discernible structural effects even though their origins may be difficult to locate. This intangible quality of "the man" makes racialized power appear simultaneously as all pervasive and difficult to confront. "The man" is both everywhere and nowhere specifically. (Kandaswamy, 2010, p. 253)

Relatedly, *structural racism* is the cumulative and compounding effects of an array of societal factors including the history, culture, ideology, and interactions of institutions and policies that systematically privilege White people and disadvantage people of color (James, Johnson, Raghavan, Lemos, Barakett, & Woolis, 2003).

In the next section, I will highlight the similarities and parallels between various forms of coercive control, as identified by the Power and Control Wheel (Pence & Paymer, 1993), that are perpetrated by intimate partners and by agent of the state and service providers. In particular, I will discuss physical aggression, rape and reproductive coercion, psychological aggression, economic abuse, isolation, and stalking. Although each form of violence will be discussed individually, they are all inextricably connected.

Types of Violence

Physical Aggression. Nonfatal strangulation, which has been reported by 40% of African American women (Glass et al., 2008), is a unique form of physical aggression, which can be used, sometimes just once, to immobilize and terrorize the victim. It is a potentially lethal, but invisible form of violence, in that there is seldom immediate external evidence. Bruising and swelling may not appear until days later, especially on darker complexions. Strangulation seems to be triggered by the perpetrator's jealousy and accusations of infidelity, the victim's attempt to terminate the relationship, or her failure to comply with his demands. Immediate and lasting fear are the primary post-event reactions to strangulation (Thomas et al., 2014).

African American women also are subjected to various forms of physical aggression by state agents. For example, according to Richie (2012), they include: "excessive use of force by police officers toward women during an arrest, physical abuse while in the custody of state agencies, and battering by public employees upon whom women depend for protection and resources, including child welfare workers, employees in public assistance offices, and drug treatment counselors" (p. 48). A less overt aspect of direct physical assaults of Black women by state agencies, is how the state's lack of response to acts of male violence leaves Black women vulnerable to further victimization. Consider the case of Deanna Cook, a 32-year old Black women in Dallas, who made repeated calls to the police reporting her drug-addicted, ex-husband for stalking, attempted murder, and domestic violence. On her final 11-minute 911 recording, she could be heard pleading for the dispatcher to send help as he strangulated and drown her in the bathtub. Officers arrived nearly an hour later, found nothing amiss, and left (Eiserer, 2013).

Rape and Reproductive Coercion. Perpetrators use sexual violence to injure and control their victims. Approximately 1 in 5 Black women (22%) has been raped during their lifetime (Black et al., 2011). Among Black couples, the overall rate of male-to-female sexual assault (MFSA) was 23.2%, which most commonly involved pressuring the partner (without the use of physical force) to engage in sexual intercourse, often without a condom. Although categorized as "minor," sexual coercion frequently occurred in conjunction with psychological abuse and physical violence (Ramisetty-Mikler, Caetano, & McGrath, 2007). Perpetrators also used reproductive coercion (25.9%) and birth control sabotage (27%), which were associated with high rates of unintended pregnancy (49.9%) among Black women (Miller, Decker, McCauley, Tancredi, Levenson, Waldman, et al., 2010). In addition to gaining access to the victim through joint custody arrangements, perpetrators were motivated by the restrictions that they perceived that children would place on a woman's economic and social future. For example, one Black battered woman felt imprisoned because "He would say that I couldn't do anything with two kids" and, in reference to future partners, "Let's see if they want you now knocked up" (Potter, 2008, p. 98).

Similar to abusive intimate partners, institutions deny and minimize the pervasive sexual assaults that are perpetrated against African American girls and women. For example, school personnel and Title IX policies, that are required to address gender-based violence in academic settings, do not adequately protect Black elementary and high school girls from sexual harassment. For example, boys' sexual advances may be perceived as flirtatious, or even as gender appropriate, while girls who use physical aggression in self-defense, self-protection, or retaliation are punished (suspended or expelled from school under "Zero Tolerance Polices") (Tonnesen, 2013).

Regarding reproductive coercion, *family caps* or *child exclusion* policies prevent Black women on welfare from receiving additional financial assistance if they have another child. Without additional economic resources, it can be difficult, or impossible, for victims to escape from their abusers (Flavin, 2007). The medical community has a long legacy of reproductive coercion. Between 1929 and 1974, under the authority of the Eugenics Board of North Carolina, an estimated 7,600 people, many of them poor Black women, were sterilized by force or uniformed consent. Deemed "promiscuous" and "feebleminded," medical providers preformed a *"Mississippi appendectomy"* (involuntary sterilization and hysterectomy) (Flavin, 2007), on 14-year-old Elaine Riddick, who was raped and impregnated by a neighbor. Now 57 years old, Riddick, in her lawsuit said, "I was raped twice, once by the perpetrator and once by the state of North Carolina" (James, 2012).

Psychological Aggression. Perpetrators maintain control by bombarding the victim with severe psychological, verbal, and emotional abuse. In the NCLS, 36.7% of Black women had been called fat or ugly, had been accused of being a lousy lover, had their property destroyed, or had been threatened (Ramisetty-Mikler et al., 2007). Although it is less visible than physical violence, emotional abuse can be pervasive, severe, and can leave lasting emotional harm. In reflection, one participant said: "That verbal abuse is hard. You can fight off a fist; you just block it or run away. But when you hear that stuff, I don't forget it" (Potter, 2008, p. 96).

Importantly, "Psychological violence occurs when other forms of structural violence become accepted, promoted and integrated into the collective psyche often forming stereotypes about particular groups" (James et al., 2003, p. 132). For example, cultural representations that depict Black women as aggressive, domineering, and violent can be a form of institutional psychological aggression, which is subsequently internalized by service providers, and directed toward Black battered women when they seek help. For instance, domestic violence shelter workers may engage in various forms of *microaggression,* or subtle racial invalidations or insults (Nnawulezi & Sullivan, in press).

Economic Abuse. Batterers can directly and indirectly interfere in the economic livelihood of their victims. First, they can create disfiguring or disabling injuries, which prevent the woman from seeking employment. Another method is to sabotage the victim's aspirations and achievements: get her expelled from job training programs by stalking her at work or fail to provide reliable childcare. In addition, the long term consequences of battering can include physical, mental, and emotional damage that can impair a woman's ability to prepare for, obtain, and maintain family supporting employment. Furthermore, battering and its consequences may make it difficult for currently or formerly battered woman to focus on specific job duties, plan for the future, manage fear, perform in high pressure settings, respond appropriately to criticism, avoid depression, and conform to the professional culture or their organization (Kandaswamy, 2010).

When they seek assistance for social service agencies, the economic abuse may continue. For example, the Personal Responsibility and Work Opportunity Reconciliation Act (PRWORA), or welfare reform, requires recipients to meet strict work requirements. Rather than being offered job training programs and educational opportunities, battered Black women were compelled, with the loss of benefits, to work in low-paying service jobs, mostly as day care workers, home health care aids, and cashiers. Without economic resources, they remained entrapped in abusive relationships (Davis, 2004).

Isolation. Isolation is a particularly powerful form of coercive control. Among Black couples who exhibited mutual violence, male abusers were more prone to restrict their partners' use of the car, telephone, or her access to family and friends. Male perpetrators also prevented the female partner from leaving the house, seeking medical care, or obtaining employment. Despite their use of violence, when Black women attempted to use this form of coercive control, they used fewer controlling acts, and were less successful in controlling their partner's behavior (Swan & Snow, 2002).

The criminal legal system, also referred to as the *prison nation* or *prison industrial complex* (Richie, 2012, p. 3) because of its pervasive reach, is one of the most powerful forms of structural isolation and segregation. Recall the case of Marissa Alexander, the victim-defendant who was described above. After a jury deliberated for 12 minutes, the judged sentenced her to a lengthy prison sentence because "under the state's 10-20-life law, a conviction for aggravated assault where a firearm has been discharged carries a minimum and maximum sentence of 20 years without regarding any extenuating or mitigating circumstances that may be present, such as those in this case." Jacksonville congresswoman Corrine Brown described the sentencing as a product of "institutional racism" (CNN Wire Staff, 2012). In 2013, an appeals court overturned her conviction. At retrial, the prosecutor threatened her with 60 years in prison if convicted again (20 years, to be served consecutively, for 3 counts of aggravated assault with a deadly weapon). In November 2014, Alexander agreed to a plea bargain that included time served for the three years she had already spent incarcerated, an additional 65 days in jail, and two years house arrest (Law, 2015).

Stalking. Perpetrators stalk their victims with repeated harassing or threatening behaviors, such as following a victim, appearing at her home or workplace, making harassing phone calls, leaving written messages or objects, or vandalizing her property. According to the NISVS, 14.6% of Black women have been stalked by an intimate partner in their lifetimes (Black et al., 2011). What's more, poor Black women who lived in urban areas reported that their whereabouts were monitored by their abuser's relatives and associates, which is referred to as "third party stalking" (Tamborra, 2012).

Increasingly, "third party policing" is used as a method to monitor and control the behavior of Black battered women. That is, "The police began convincing and coercing community actors (landlords, business owners) to assume some responsibility for correcting misconduct" (p. 117), For example, after repeated 911 calls to report serious IPV, Milwaukee police deemed the tenant and property, which were often located in distressed Black urban areas, to be a "nuisance." Police then asked landlords to use some form of "abatement" strategy, which generally consisted of an eviction. Thus, the victim had two undesirable choices, both which could further embolden the abuser. If she doesn't report the abuse, he maintains power and control over the victim. If she calls the police, she faces eviction and possible homelessness, which can propel her into a cycle of residential instability, poverty, and greater dependency on the abuser (Desmond & Valdez, 2012).

To conclude, after reflecting on her personal and family history of IPV, Kupenda (2009) concluded that "in many ways, the condition of Blacks in America is analogous to the condition of a battered wife in an abusive relationship" (p. 35). In this section, I highlighted the similarities and parallels between various forms of coercive control that are perpetrated by intimate partners and by agents of the state and service providers. It is clear, that Black battered women are frequently battered by institutions that should service them.

STRUCTURAL RISK FACTORS

There are two structural risk factors that have consistently predicted higher rates of IPV among African Americans. In particular, couples who reported higher rates of poverty (Cunradi, Caetano, & Schafer, 2002) and who lived in neighborhoods that were characterized by concentrated neighborhood disadvantage and economic distress experienced rates of IPV (Pinchevsky & Wright, 2012). The purpose of this section is to explore the pathways by which these structural risk factors contribute to higher rates of IPV in the lives of Black women.

Poverty

Annual household income had the greatest relative influence on the probability of partner violence, with lower incomes being associated with higher rates of IPV. Specifically, Black couples who reported MFPV and FMPV had significantly lower mean annual incomes than nonviolent couples (approximately $22,838 vs. $32,685, respectively) (Cunradi et al., 2002). The pathways between economic marginalization and higher rates of partner violence is complex. According to social structural theory "those from lower SES strata may have had greater exposure to childhood violence, have higher rates of depression, experience more alcohol-related problems, have poorer coping mechanisms, and more commonly endorse the use of physical aggression as a tactic in marital disputes" (Cunradi et al., 2002, p. 386).

Poverty can shape gender roles and relationships between African American men and women. Due to systematic discrimination in the labor market, African American men experience high rates of unemployment and poverty. Meanwhile, incarceration has banished Black men from the community in staggering numbers and when, or if they return given the length of mandatory minimum sentences, they are often unemployable, have limited education and works skills, and may suffer from higher rates of mental health problems (Crenshaw, 2012). As a result, there is a gender ratio imbalance in the Black community where there are more single Black women and fewer marriageable Black men. In response, some Black women stay with abusive partners to avoid loneliness (Bent-Goodley, 2014). Other Black women stay in abusive relationships because they feel a cultural or religious mandate to emotionally support men who are "endangered" by structural challenges: "He's just upset because he doesn't have a job and he's doing drugs and that's very stressful on him...Soon as he cleans himself up and get a job, everything will be fine" (Potter, 2008, p. 108).

In addition, poverty also can contribute to conflicts around gender roles norms. Black women have historically made substantial contributions to the economic well-being of their households and may be less likely to tolerate violent partners without retaliating or engaging in defensive violence, thereby increasing rates of mutual violence (Caetano et al., 2005). In contrast, when they are unable to fulfill these traditional gender roles, "interpersonal conflicts arise between black males and black females because many black males are aware of their role failures and are inclined to counterattack any perceived challenge to their manhood with violence" (Hampton & Gelles, 1994, p. 115). These conflicts can escalate to femicide. Black women were more likely to be murdered during the course of an argument with an intimate partner (Violence Policy Center, 2012) and more likely to be murdered by unemployed partners (Campbell, et al., 2003).

Concentrated Neighborhood Disadvantage

Concentrated neighborhood disadvantage has not been uniformly measured across studies. It has been assessed by the percentage of residents who lived below the poverty line or received public assistance, unemployment rates, and numbers of vacant homes. Regardless of the measure used or the population that was surveyed, couples who lived in the most resource-limited neighborhoods reported the highest rates of IPV (Pinchevsky & Wright, 2012). Accordingly in the NCLS, nearly half (47%) of the Black couples in the sample resided in impoverished neighborhoods and those residents were at a threefold risk for MFPV and twofold increase for FMPV compared to Black couples who did not reside in poor areas (Cunradi, Caetano, Clark, & Schafer, 2000). Thus, it appears that individual economic distress in the form of low household income and residence in economically resource-limited neighborhoods work in tandem to increase women's risk for inflicting and sustaining IPV.

There are several pathways between economically distressed neighborhoods and IPV. First, living in these environments can expose residents to various forms of violence, which can spill over into their intimate relationships. Among low-income Black women (Stueve & O'Donnell, 2008) and Black men (Reed, Silverman, Ickovics, Gupta, Welles, Santana, & Raj, 2010), IPV perpetration and victimization have been linked to microaggressions in the form of perceived racial discrimination in their community (e.g., being unfairly stopped and frisked by police or followed by store clerks, called insulting names or physically attacked because of skin color or race).

Exposure to community violence in any role (witness, victim, or perpetrator) has been associated with higher rates of intimate partner abuse. For example, community violence was correlated with emotional dating victimization among young Black urban women (Stueve & O'Donnell, 2008). Black men were more likely to batter their girlfriends if they had been involved in street violence, had a history of gang involvement, or perceived that there was a "great deal" of violence in their neighborhood (Reed, Silverman, Welles, Santana, Missmer, & Raj, 2009). All these forms of violence can converge in the lives of victims. For example, exposure to community violence (e.g., getting beaten up in the neighborhood) was associated with witnessing adult-on-adult family violence, being the victim of physical abuse by a parent or adult caregiver, and being the victim of dating violence. Kennedy (2008) concluded that "these higher rates of cumulative exposure to violence can be attributed, in part, to structural issues facing African Americans living in urban settings which shape life opportunities and may influence intimate partner relationships and family dynamics" (p. 38).

Finally, when faced with extreme, persistent, economic and social inequalities, individuals are more likely to use and abuse drugs or alcohol. General population studies have provided substantial evidence that alcohol-related dependence indicators (e.g., withdrawal symptoms and alcohol tolerance), alcohol-related social problems (e.g., job loss, legal problems), and greater mean male and female alcohol consumption were especially strong predictors of IPV among African American couples, independent of who in the couple reports the problem. As the density of alcohol outlets increases in the community, so does the risk of MFPV, particularly among couples who report alcohol-related problems (McKinney, Caetano, Harris, & Ebama, 2009).

CHANGING SOCIAL STRUCTURES

Rather than individual-level solutions, there is an urgent need to changing the social systems that contribute to elevated rates of IPV against African American women. Indeed, these structural changes should also reduce all forms of violence perpetrated against them. The purpose of this section is to discuss how the criminal justice system and the economic system can better serve this marginalized population.

Criminal Legal System

Black women and their communities have historically been "overpoliced and underprotected" (Crenshaw, 2012, p. 1420). The criminal legal system can begin to listen to the voices of battered Black women. They have clearly articulated their needs. For example, Black women expressed a desire for alternatives to incarceration: mandated counseling, anger management, or substance abuse treatment. In some cases, incarceration was too brief to provide meaningful safety. They also were concerned about their interactions with court personnel—they wanted them to file paperwork in a timely fashion, follow-up when abusers missed their court appearance, and keep victims updated on their partner's probation and incarceration status. They wanted court personnel to be "nice" and "friendly" rather than hostile and dismissive, and to connect them with local resources that could help (e.g., domestic violence shelters, information on child support). In short, victims wanted to feel like they had a voice in the process (Bell, Perez, Goodman, & Dutton, 2011).

In addition, the courts and police can take more care when investigating cases of what appear to be mutual violence. Black women are more likely to be arrested themselves for behavior that may be consistent with self-defense, but are interpreted through the lens of stereotypes as overly aggressive. Mandatory arrests and sentencing laws have had a devastating economic and emotional impact on Black victim-defendants. To name a few, they may be denied access to victim assistance programs, welfare benefits, crime victim compensation, and employment opportunities in childcare, teaching, and education (West, 2007). Finally, easy access to guns can facilitate, escalate, and amplify anger and conflict, which makes nonfatal violence into a homicide (Violence Policy Center, 2012). When possible, they can increase the safety of victims, particularly Black women, by removing guns from these violent homes.

Economic System

Access to financial resources is a key component to helping Black women escape poverty, resource-limited neighborhoods, and abusive partners. According to statistics that were compiled by the African American Policy Forum (2013), African American women had the highest unemployment rate among women nationwide. When Black women are employed, they earn less than other racial groups. What's more, single Black women have the lowest net worth among all racial and gender groups, only 100.00! Coker (2000) has suggested that every effort to combat gender-based violence be subjected to the "material resource test":

> Domestic violence laws and policies may directly provide women with material resources such as housing, food, clothing, or money, or they may increase resources indirectly through the availability of services such as job training, childcare, and transportation...We should always prefer assessment that is informed by the circumstances of those women who are in the greatest need. In most circumstances this

will be poor women of color who are sandwiched by their heightened vulnerability to battering, on the one hand, and their heightened vulnerability to intrusive state control, on the other. (p. 1011)

In addition, raising the minimum wage to a living wage, helping women make the transition from welfare-to-work, and investing resources in economically resource-limited neighborhoods could be other important structural changes.

To conclude, Black women's intimate partner violence, and its devastating impact on the larger African American community, will remain (in)visible until there is a substantive policy-focused and data-driven public discourse on this topic. Perhaps, it is time for battered women's organizations, civil rights groups, anti-poverty organizations, survivors, and other stake holders to form coalitions, across their ideological and political spectrums. Together, they must act as institutional reformers to address all the forms of violence in the lives of Black women that remain "hidden in plain sight."

NOTES

1. African American and Black will be used interchangeably.
2. In the Conflict Tactics Scale (CTS) minor aggression has been defined as pushed, slapped, and hit with an object. Severe violence or wife battering has been defined as kicked, bit, hit with fist; hit or tried to hit other with an object; beat up the other; choked other; threatened with knife or gun; used knife or fired a gun. The "overall" violence rate was any form of relationship aggression, regardless of level of severity (Straus & Gelles, 1990).

REFERENCES

African American Policy Forum. (2013). *Did you know? The plight of Black girls & women in America.* Retrieved from: http://aapf.org/2014/02/did-you-know-plight-of-black-women/

Bell, M. E., Perez, S., Goodman, L. A., & Dutton, M. A. (2011). Battered women's perceptions of civil and criminal court helpfulness: The role of court outcome and process. *Violence Against Women, 17*, 71–88.

Bent-Goodley, T. B. (2014). An exploration of African American women's perception of the intersection of domestic violence and HIV/AIDS. *Journal of HIV/AIDS & Social Services, 13*, 97–116.

Black, M. C., Basile, K. C., Breiding, M. J., Smith, S. G., Walters, M. L., Merrick, M. T., et al. (2011). *The National Intimate Partner and Sexual Violence Survey (NISVS): 2010 summary report.* Atlanta, GA: National Center for Injury Prevention and Control, Centers for Disease Control and Prevention. Retrieved from: http://www.cdc.gov/violenceprevention/pdf/nisvs_report2010-a.pdf

Boylorn, R. (2014, August 1). *The blame game: Black women, shame an victim blaming* [Web log post]. Retrieved from http://www.crunkfeministcollective.com/2014/08/01/the-blame-game-black-women-shame-and-victim-blaming/

Breiding, M. J., Chen, J., & Black, M. C. (2014). *Intimate partner violence in the United States—2010.* Atlanta GA: National Center for Injury Prevention and Control, Centers for Disease Control and Prevention. Retrieved from http://www.cdc.gov/violenceprevention/pdf/cdc_nisvs_ipv_report_2013_v17_single_a.pdf

Caetano, R., Cunradi, C. B., Clark, C. L., & Schafer, J. (2000). Intimate partner violence and drinking patterns among White, Black, and Hispanic couples in the U.S. *Journal of Substance Abuse, 11,* 123–138.

Caetano, R., Field, C., Ramisetty-Mikler, S., & Lipsky, S. (2009). Agreement on reporting of physical, psychological, and sexual violence among White, Black, and Hispanic couples in the United States. *Journal of Interpersonal Violence, 24,* 1318–1337.

Caetano, R., Ramisetty-Mikler, S., & Field, C. A. (2005). Unidirectional and bidirectional intimate partner violence among White, Black, and Hispanic couples in the United States. *Violence and Victims, 20,* 393–404.

Caetano, R., Schafer, J., Field, C., & Nelson, S. M. (2002). Agreement on reports of intimate partner violence among White, Black, and Hispanic couples in the United States. *Journal of Interpersonal Violence, 17,* 1308–1322.

Campbell, J. C., Webster, D., Koziol-McLain, J., Block, C., Campbell, D., Curry, M. A., et al. (2003). Risk factors for femicide in abusive relationships: Results from a multisite case control study. *American Journal of Public Health, 93,* 1089–1097.

Chavis, A. Z., & Hill, M. S. (2009). Integrating multiple intersecting identities: A multicultural conceptualization of the Power and Control Wheel. *Women & Therapy, 32,* 121–149.

CNN Wire Staff. (2012, May 11). *Florida woman sentenced to 20 years in controversial warning shot case.* Retrieved from: http://www.cnn.com/2012/05/11/justice/florida-stand-ground-sentencing/

Coker, D. (2000). Shifting power for battered women: Law, material resources, and poor women of color. *U.C. Davis Law Review, 33,* 1009.

Collins, P. H. (1998). The tie that binds: Race, gender, and US violence. *Ethnic and Racial Studies, 21,* 917–938.

Crenshaw, K. W. (2012). From private violence to mass incarceration: Thinking intersectionally about women, race, and social control. *UCLA Law Review, 59,* 1418–1472.

Cunradi, C. B., Caetano, R., Clark, C., & Schafer, J. (2000). Neighborhood poverty as a predictor of intimate partner violence among White, Black, and Hispanic couples in the United States: A multilevel analysis. *Annals of Epidemiology, 10,* 297–308.

Cunradi, C. B., Caetano, R., & Schafer, J. (2002). Socioeconomic predictors of intimate partner violence among White, Black, and Hispanic couples in the United States. *Journal of Family Violence, 17,* 377–389.

Davis, D. (2004). Manufacturing mammies: The burden of service work and welfare reform among battered Black women. *Anthropolgica, 46,* 273–288.

Desmond, M., & Valdez, N. (2012). Unpolicing the urban poor: Consequences of third-party policing for inner-city women. *American Sociological Review, 78,* 117–141.

Eiserer, T. (March 6, 2013). 911 tape reveals horrific last minutes for murdered Dallas woman. *Dallas Morning News.* Retrieved from http://www.dallasnews.com/news/crime/headlines/20130306-dallas-911-tape-reveals-horrific-last-minutes-for-woman-murdered-while-begging-for-help.ece

Flavin, J. (2007). Slavery's legacy in contemporary attempts to regulate Black women's reproduction. In M. Bosworth & J. Flavin (Eds.), *Race, gender, and punishment:*

From colonialism to the war on terror (pp. 95–14). New Brunswick, NJ: Rutgers University Press.

Glass, N., Laughon, K., Campbell, J., Block, C. R., Hanson, G., Sharps, P. W., & Taliaferro, E. (2008). Non-fatal strangulation is an important risk factor for homicide of women. *The Journal of Emergency Medicine, 35*, 329–335.

Hampton, R. L., & Gelles, R. J. (1994). Violence toward Black women in a nationally representative sample of Black families. *Journal of Comparative Family Studies, 24*, 105–119.

Hill, N. A., Woodson, K. M., Ferguson, A. D., & Parks, C. W. (2012). Intimate partner abuse among African American lesbians: Prevalence, risk factors, theory, and resilience. *Journal of Family Violence, 27*, 401–413.

James, S.D. (2012, Jan. 10). N.C. to compensate victims of sterilization in 20th century eugenics program. *ABC News.* Retrieved from: http://abcnews.go.com/Health/WomensHealth/north-carolina-compensate-victims-eugenics-program-sterilized/story?id=15328707

James, S. E., Johnson, J., Raghavan, C., Lemos, T., Barakett, M., & Woolis, D. (2003). The violent matrix: A study of structural, interpersonal, and intrapersonal violence among a sample of poor women. *American Journal of Community Psychology, 31*, 129–141.

Jones, N. (2004). A bad relationship: Violence in the lives of incarcerated Black women. *Souls, 6*, 16–23.

Kandaswamy, P. (2010). "You trade in a man for the man": Domestic violence and the U.S. welfare state. *American Quarterly, 62*, 253–277.

Kennedy, A. C. (2008). An ecological approach to examining cumulative violence exposure among urban, African American adolescents. *Child and Adolescent Social Work Journal, 25*, 25–41.

Kupenda, A. M. (2009). The state as batterer: Learning from family law to address America's family-like racial dysfunction. *University of Florida Journal of Law & Public Policy, 20*, 33–64.

Lacey, K. K., West, C. M., Matusko, N., & Jackson J. S. (in press). Prevalence and factors associated with severe intimate partner violence among U.S. Black women: A comparison of African American and Caribbean Blacks. *Violence Against Women.*

Law, V. (January 29, 2015). *Why is Marissa Alexander still being punished for fighting back?* Retrieved from http://www.thenation.com/article/196361/why-marissa-alexander-still-being-punished-fighting-back

Lee, T. (2012, May 10). *Marissa Alexander, Mom facing 20 years, shot at abusive husband in anger, prosecutor says.* [Web log post]. Retrieved from http://www.huffingtonpost.com/2012/05/09/marissa-alexander-prosecutor_n_1504428.html

McKinney, C. M., Caetano, R., Harris, T. R., & Ebama, M. S. (2009). Alcohol availability and intimate partner violence among U.S. couples. *Alcoholism: Clinical and Experimental Research, 33*, 169–176.

Miller, E., Decker, M. R., McCauley, H. L., Tancredi, D. J., Levenson, R. R., Waldman, J., et al. (2010). Pregnancy coercion, intimate partner violence and unintended pregnancy. *Contraception, 81*, 316–322.

Nnawulezi, N. A., & Sullivan, C. M. (in press). Oppression within safe spaces: Exploring racial microaggressions within domestic violence shelters. *Journal of Black Psychology.*

Paranjape, A., Corbie-Smith, G., Thompson, N., & Kaslow, N. J. (2009). When older African American women are affected by violence in the home. *Violence Against Women, 15,* 977–990.

Pence, E., & Paymer, M. (1993). *Education groups for men who batter: The Duluth model.* New York, NY: Springer.

Pilkington, E. (2014, August 1). Fear and violence in transgender Baltimore: "It's scary trusting anyone." *The Guardian.* Retrieved from http://www.theguardian.com/world/2014/aug/01/murder-transgender-women-baltimore-heighten-fears-mia-henderson

Pinchevsky, G. M., & Wright, E. M. (2012). The impact of neighborhoods on intimate partner violence and victimization. *Trauma, Violence, and Abuse, 13,* 112–132.

Potter, H. (2008). *Battle cries: Black women and intimate partner abuse.* New York, NY: University Press.

Ramisetty-Mikler, S., Caetano, R., & McGrath, C. (2007). Sexual aggression among White, Black, and Hispanic couples in the U.S.: Alcohol use, physical assault, and psychological aggression as its correlates. *The American Journal of Drug and Alcohol Abuse, 33,* 31–43.

Reed, E., Silverman, J. G., Ickovics, J. R., Gupta, J., Welles, S. L., Santana, M. C., & Raj, A. (2010). Experiences of racial discrimination and relation to violence perpetration and gang involvement among sample of urban African American men. *Journal of Immigrant Minority Health, 12,* 319–326.

Reed, E., Silverman, J. G., Welles, S. L., Santana, M. C., Missmer, S. A., & Raj, A. (2009). Associations between perceptions and involvement in neighborhood violence and intimate partner violence perpetration among urban, African American men. *Journal of Community Health, 34,* 328–335.

Rennison, C. M., & Welchans, S. (2000). *Criminal victimization 1999: Changes 1998–9 with trends 1993–9.* Washington, DC: U.S. Department of Justice, Bureau of Justice Statistics.

Richie, B. E. (2012). *Arrested justice: Black women, violence, and America's prison nation.* New York, NY: University Press.

Stark, E. (2007). *Coercive control: How men entrap women in personal life.* New York, NY: Oxford University Press.

Straus, M. A., & Gelles, R. J. (1990). *Physical violence in American families: Risk factors and adaptations to violence in 8,145 families.* New Brunswick, NJ: Transaction Books.

Stueve, A., & O'Donnell, L. (2008). Urban young women's experiences of discrimination and community violence and intimate partner violence. *Journal of Urban Health, 85,* 386–401.

Swan, S. C., & Snow, D. L. (2002). A typology of women's use of violence in intimate relationships. *Violence Against Women, 8,* 286–319.

Swan, S. C., & Snow, D. L. (2003). Behavioral and psychological differences of among abused women who use violence in intimate relationships. *Violence Against Women, 8,* 286–319.

Tamborra, T. L. (2012). Poor, urban, battered women who are stalked. How can we include their experiences? *Feminist Criminology, 7,* 112–129.

Temple, J. R., Weston, R., & Marshall, L. L. (2005). Physical and mental health outcomes of women in nonviolent, unilaterally violent, and mutually violent relationships. *Violence and Victims, 20,* 335–359.

Thomas, K. A., Joshi, M., & Sorenson, S. B. (2014). "Do you know what it feels like to drown?" Strangulation as coercive control in intimate relationships. *Psychology of Women Quarterly, 38,* 124–137.

Tjaden, P., & Thonnes, N. (2000). *Extent, nature, and consequences of intimate partner violence: Findings from the National Violence Against Women Survey.* Washington, DC: National Institute of Justice/Centers for Disease Control and Prevention. Retrieved from https://www.ncjrs.gov/pdffiles1/nij/181867.pdf

Tonnesen, S. C. (2013). "Hit it and quit it": Response to Black girls' victimization in school. *Berkeley Journal of Gender, Law & Justice,* Winter, 1–29.

Violence Policy Center. (2012). *When men murder women: An analysis of 2010 homicide data.* Retrieved from https://www.vpc.org/studies/wmmw2012.pdf

West, C. M. (2007). "Sorry, we have to take you in": Black battered women arrested for domestic violence. *Journal of Aggression, Maltreatment, & Trauma,* 15, 95–121.

West, C. M. (2012). Partner abuse in ethnic minority and gay, lesbian, bisexual, and transgender populations. *Partner Abuse, 3,* 336–357.

West, C. M. (in press). Living in a web of trauma: An ecological examination of violence among African Americans. C. A. Cuevas & C. M. Rennison (Eds.), *Handbook on the Psychology of Violence.* Wiley-Blackwell.

CHAPTER 6

TIPPING THE SCALE

Implementation of The Project SisterCircle Intervention to Facilitate Youth Coping with the Effects of Structural Inequalities

Wendi S. Williams and Janee Nesbitt

Structural inequalities create instances of economic and social disparities that shape the lives of persons of color and youth globally (Williams, Dhami, & Moody, 2014). Due to the lack of access to social and political capital, which is perpetuated through engagement in inadequate educational/social systems and disenfranchisement from the political process and decisions that affect their lives, young people's environments and development are negatively shaped. For instance, while articulated as setting educational standards for "struggling schools," the Bush Administration's version of the No Child Left Behind education policy rendered the learning communities of poor youth of color in the United States (US) to high stakes testing and academic environments rife with pressure and anxiety (Lacey & Cornell, 2013). Adolescents, on the precipice of independence, are in a unique position because their sense of identity and future planning is vulnerable to social inequities, which have the potential to shape their psychological and physical health and development. This chapter will consider the impact of structural inequalities on the growth and development of adolescent girls of color.

Talking About Structural Inequalities in Everyday Life: New Politics of Race in Groups, Organizations, and Social Systems, pages 103–120.

A particular focus on Black/African and Latina descent girls' educational and health outcomes is considered, primarily for their social, cultural, and political positionality. Black/African and Latina girls carry a significant portion of the public health burden for negative sexual and mental health outcomes. More specifically, relevant to adolescent Black/African and Latina descent adolescent girls, in addition to health-related structural inequalities, Forhan (2008) reported that 1 in 4 carries a sexually transmitted infection (STI), a likely consequence of poor sexual decision-making at early sexual debut among adolescent girls with low self-esteem (Ethier et al., 2006). Further, Latina and Black/African girls are at increased risk for engaging in unprotected sexual encounters and resultant teenaged pregnancy (Karpati et al. 2004), which are exacerbated by a sequelae of secondary mental health (e.g., depression, anxiety, and substance abuse) (Collins et al., 2010) and social (e.g., financial, domestic violence, and parenting challenges) consequences (Walton et al., 2011) associated with parenting at a young age. Indicative of the disproportionate health burden among Black/African and Latina girls, these are mere indicators of the effects of the systemic inequities that shape their lives with the potential to be perpetuated over time.

We begin the chapter with a definition of structural inequalities and narrow in on the life experiences of adolescent Black/African and Latina girls. We then focus on the role of intervention programming to support pro-social coping among this population, with a specific focus on localized, grass-roots, university-community collaborations. One such intervention program, Project SisterCircle (PSC), is presented. The underlying rationale of this intervention is to address the socio-emotional needs of adolescent Black/African and Latina middle school girls in an urban context by interrupting negative social and health trajectories. Thus, we envision interventions, such as PSC, implemented at the developmental stage of adolescence for girls of color in under-resourced urban social contexts, as "tipping the scale" of social and resources imbalance in favor of their health and well-being.

STRUCTURAL INEQUALITIES

Youth and social justice scholars have initiated a discussion of the social and cultural inequities in which young people of color are tasked to make meaning of their lives (Cohen, 2010; Lopez, 2012). Set up against the backdrop of historic/political movements for justice and equity (e.g., Civil Rights, Black Power, Women's movement, etc.), youth voice and perspective strengthens an analysis of youth experiences. Cohen (2010) suggests the specific needs and experiences of young people are more accurately described by them, rather than academics and older adults who are removed from their direct experience. She asserts that faced with the political realities and social contexts of a particular point and time, youth recognize their agency to avail them of the choices, positive or negative, available to them. It is the contention of these authors that the choices available to youth are structured by social and political decisions and policies of which they are not in control nor have voice in their authorship, and at times do not align with their best interest.

Structural inequalities are the condition wherein groups of people, based on their racial, gender, socio-economic status, and other social/cultural groupings and statuses are treated unequally in comparison to members of other groups with access to infrastructural resources necessary for all (Hare, 1987). We argue that the unequal status of children and adolescents to participate in the political life of the society that shapes their access to critical resources and power justifies the inclusion of age as a determinant of how inequality is structured. Structural inequalities are embedded in institutions (e.g., political, education, healthcare, legal system, etc.) making it difficult for individuals with limited resources to access or take advantage of opportunity. Consequently, a person's ability to obtain skills and abilities are targeted by structural inequalities, and the inequalities position them such that they are not able to actualize their full potential (Hare, 1987). For example, Cohen (2010) articulates the inspiration for her book, her nephew Terry, who while loved, adored and provided for, was not able to respond to the hopes and expectations of his family, but rather had been incarcerated and fathered a number of children for whom he was not prepared to parent. She holds up the fact of his sincerity, and willingness to take responsibility for his actions alongside these other aspects of his life to suggest: (1) simplistic analysis of his situation is ineffective for conceptualizing and intervening with Terry, and (2) to highlight that youth make choices. Those choices occur within a matrix of power and privilege from which they are disenfranchised.

An essential aspect of the workings of structural inequalities is that they are often invisible to both individuals with and without sufficient access to resources. Consequently, these dynamics can foster a sense of blame and internalization of blame on youth, therefore permitting those that lack access to take responsibility for it and those that are privileged to be oblivious to their role and responsibility for equalizing these power, privilege and access differentials (Lopez, Gurin, & Nagda, 1998). Continuing in this vein, current researchers deem the self-blame by persons in unequal systems as a function of internalized oppression which may manifest due to their race (Bailey, Williams, & Favors, 2014), gender and/ or sexuality (Szymanski & Henrichs-Beck, 2014), as their own "personal efforts, traits and abilities" (Lopez et al., 1998) are seen as the reason for their lack of opportunity or ability to capitalize on it. Thus, educational inequalities and awareness of the social structures and polices that organize one's life in inequitable ways has the potential to make them vulnerable for internalizing the effects of limited access as an attribute of their personal being. Taking Cohen's nephew's situation as an example, it could be useful to inquire about how social policies have shaped his life? Did these policies and consequent allocation for material and social resources unduly create inadequate structures at critical junctures in his life? Whether intended or not, structural inequalities shape the life choices and health outcomes for youth, such that even those in the best of circumstances are at risk for failing to achieve their own personal potential.

Based on the articulation of a faculty logic about racial deficiencies evidenced by biology, social structures and culture, the larger society has sought to provide explanation to justify the disproportionate numbers of non-White, poor persons, and women in the lower rungs of the social hierarchy (Conyers, 2002; Hare, 1987). Known as the "deficit hypothesis" (Kyrk, 1953), it has been suggested that the social and cultural deficiencies legitimize the lower social positioning and accomplishments of women and people of color compared to White men. Obviously missing from this analysis is a more nuanced consideration of what Cohen (2010) describes as the balance between structural inequities and individual agency. Thus, the need for persistent vigilance against simplistic and/or stereotyped analysis attempting to be descriptive of complex social and cultural phenomena is necessary to adequately interpret and intervene on these circumstances and their effect on youth.

UNEQUAL CHILDHOODS

In 2003, sociologist Annette Lareau focused the social sciences on the effect of childhood access and background to resources on the life experiences and outcomes of African and European American children reared in affluent and poor home and community environments. The effect of access and absence of resources on the lives of young people has been characterized in their exposure to and utility of the social and cultural capital needed to overcome challenging circumstances. Black/African and Latina descent adolescent girls in resource poor urban communities are vulnerable to the effects of the structural inequalities that shape the availability of resources to them and their families (Williams et al., 2014). Further, it is the contention of the authors that the inequality they experience is structured around gender and race and is mediated by social class stratifications.

Nearly 50 years ago then, assistant secretary of labor, Daniel Patrick Moynihan (1965) wrote *The Negro Family: The Case for National Action*, which was characterized largely for articulating the challenges facing Black families as a function of their being "female-headed" and not conforming to the "traditional," "nuclear" family structure indicated as the norm. Thus, the behavior of Black/African descent persons, their relationships and the ways they have constructed family and community were pathologized, rather than considered reasonable responses to inadequate community infrastructure and a history of disenfranchisement from the social, political and economic systems of the US. In the vacuum of a critical analysis of the Moynihan report, scholars have attempted to delineate the instances of disproportionate under-attainment by members of the Black/African descent community. One example includes Hare's (1987) "class-plus" analysis which purports the additive effect of race, to enhance the unfair burden Black/African Americans face in a hierarchically organized capitalist society. Hare specifically highlights the impact of poverty and its effect on "conditions of deprivation" (i.e., impoverished conditions and single-parent households), which may increase familial instability and turmoil and lead to an increase in negative childhood experiences for Black/African youth (e.g., becoming victims of child abuse, inadequate nutrition, poor health care, exposure to drugs and crime, and material deprivation).

Certainly an attempt to make meaning of the Black family experience in the US through an evaluation of its health within a capitalist economic system, Hare's writings do fall short of comprehensively considering attributes of the Black family, and by extension Black/African youth's development. A failure to address the systemic forces, within which Black/African and Latino/a youth are placed, de-contextualizes their behavioral responses from socio-cultural and environmental conditions that require specific response for survival. Critical to the consideration of the development of Black/African and Latin descent youth is a comprehensive view of the socio-cultural context in which they are developing and the historical factors that shape their current living conditions. This includes appreciation of the ways their families have adapted their structure and functioning to adjust to the structurally unequal conditions and the ways this shapes their development. For example, Belgrave and Allison (2010) address the important role of extended family and kinship relationships to buttress all forms of family in Black communities. While mindful these dynamics may not operate in the same ways for all Black families, the dependence on close relationships outside the nuclear family structure has preserved the connection between family members and maintained stability for youth whose parents were not able to care for them since the times of enslavement (Belgrave & Allison, 2010, p. 133). Therefore, the alternate forms of family construction has the potential to minimize the stress related to rearing children in structurally unequal context, as well as placing additional supportive adults in the lives of youth.

Considered within a comprehensive historic and systemic review, it remains the case that the circumstances of poor Black/African descent children in urban communities have not changed much from nearly three decades ago. Youth of color are subject to the effects of race and gender inequality due to their mothers' limited earning potential (Reid, Adelman, & Jaret, 2007). Due to racial, gender and class structural inequalities, some African and Latin descent youth are likely to develop in homes in which these dynamics shape the earning potential of a parent/guardian, thus inheriting a context of poverty and lack of access (Chau, 2009). In their study of differential earning among women in US metropolitan areas, Reid and colleagues found that women of color and White women were unequally distributed in occupations and industries affected by trends in global cities toward more producer, higher wage earning services (White women), rather than lower wage earning consumer service positions typically held by women of color (Reid et al., 2007, p. 141). Additionally, they found patterns of immigration also affected all women's earnings, such that hiring immigrant workers depressed the earning potential of "native-born minority workers" (i.e., African

Americans). Given the overcrowding and mixed cultures/ethnicities present in urban communities, it is possible these effects may be a source of tension between racial/ethnic groups in the lower end of the social hierarchy, with implications for youth relationships, as specific youth may be perceived as competitors for critical familial resources within their communities. In addition to the expected effects of structural inequalities on the educational experiences of youth of color (Wilson, 2011), other effects include poor health outcomes and elevated instances of community violence, which are characteristic of under-resourced urban communities (Lee, 2005; Miller, 2008). The current eruption of violence in Chicago which began over the 2014 Fourth of July holiday and has continued, is one example, so intense it has exhausted the law enforcement resources of the city imploring the federal government to intervene (Curry, 2014). With 60 children shot, and nine killed, this current outcropping of violence is seen as taking a specifically dreadful toll. Thus, poor youth of color, particularly of Black/African and Latin descent, have the potential to experience a foreboding anxiety relative to competition for limited resources which, due to structural inequalities specifically impacting communities of color, may contribute to psychosocial and environmental stressors with the potential to erupt into community and/or race-based violence.

To be a girl. Absent from Hare's (1987) early formulation was an articulation of the gendered experiences of Black/African descent persons. Further, lacking from most formulations relative to the experiences of women and girls of color is a discussion of Latinas. As the impacts of structural inequalities on members of urban communities are revealed, more about the effects on the psychology of Black/African and Latina girls is needed. Specific focus on their transition from child (e.g., little girl) to adolescent, and the corresponding shifts in identity, concept of self in relation and individualized, within family and community, continues to be an area of developing discourse. One approach has been informed by the intersectionality literature put forth by sociologist and Black feminist scholar Patricia Hill Collins (2000) and legal scholar Kimberlé Crenshaw (1989). In their work, both have articulated the multiple organizing societal structures, "matrices of domination," that shape the lives Black/African women and, by extension, girls. As explained by Williams et al. (2014), "In opposition to reductionist perspectives wherein injustice is seen as the result of singular 'isms,' an intersectional analysis conveys the understanding that oppressions work together to create different types of injustices with specific effects on life experiences," such that an interactive and dynamic process creates varying experiences of oppression and privilege by different people in different points in time (pp. 3–4). Collins' (2000) formulation holds the perspective of Black/African women and girls in the foreground and thus has served as a model for organizing conceptualization relative to the intersection of race, social class, gender and other social systems of hierarchal organization that shape the lives of women of color, generally. The literature focused on the dynamics of intersectionality among Latinas has largely centered on the experiences of educated, high-status women (Nielsen, 2013; Ramirez, 2013) and those that are economically disadvantaged (Bermúdez, Stinson, Zak-Hunter, & Abrams, 2011; Bowie & Dopwell, 2013), failing to provide an analysis for the ways these intersections may have made impact on the women in their adolescence or the daughters they rear. Additionally, it is notable that much of this work is particularly recent having occurred within the last five years and thus certainly speaks to a dearth of focus by which to conceptualize life experiences of Latina adolescent girls.

Though the intersectionality theorization provides a framework by which to conceptualize the organization of systems of domination on the lives of women and girls of color, further articulation of the relational aspects of female-hood within African/Black or Latina cultural experiences is needed. Specifically, the ways in which gender differentially shapes inter-relations within communities of color and families and directly influences girls' sense of self is important to examine in an analysis of the psychology of adolescent girls of color. Girls' (and women's) sense of self-in-relation is a critical aspect of how meaning is made about their identity. Carol Gilligan's (1982) framework outlining the relational aspects of female socialization highlights the dependence of girls and women for feedback from their culture, environment and other women/girls to communicate whether they are behaving appropriately and belong. While scholars have espoused the critical role women can play in the mental health and healing of one another (Short & Williams, 2014; Williams, Frame, & Green, 1999), this dependence can be counter-intuitive when relational dynamics carry the dysfunction of gendered and racial internalized oppression (Bailey, Williams, & Favors, 2014; King & Ferguson, 1996). Dellasega (2005) has suggested the dynamics of middle school girls' friendship and enemy determination behavior ("mean girls" or relational aggression), remains a practice among their aged-up counterparts. We suggest that these dynamics, similar to Hare's (1987) "class-plus" analysis, are shaped by race and gender dynamics in urban contexts and are a manifestation of competitive social relations in the face of limited material and social coping resources.

HEALTH AND DEVELOPMENT OUTCOMES

The current chapter takes the position that there is an effect on mental health and well-being for adolescent Black/African and Latina girls shaped by structural inequalities due to their lesser positioning in the hierarchical organization of the larger society. Whether consciously aware of the overarching forces at play or merely mindful of the restrictions of their localized context, people from disenfranchised groups are likely to adhere to the dominant ideology of "meritocracy" and "just deserts for proportional efforts" despite incongruence of these ideas in their lived realities (Lopez et al., 1998). Further, as women and girls of color are devalued in structurally unequal contexts (Ehrlich, 2009), their physical health and safety are vulnerable (Anderson, 2009). It is the contention of these authors that poor, Black/African and Latina girls in under-resourced, urban communities are also at risk for internalizing the inequities of the society as indicative of their self-worth and consequently may result in maladaptive coping with the potential to threaten healthy development and well-being (Williams et al., 2014). As a result of operating in life and relationship from a position of lower self-worth/ esteem, they may be at risk for failing to negotiate experiences and context in their best interest. One example relative to sexual health includes unsafe sexual practices and encounters and particularly negotiating the use of condoms. Studies have shown that girls, fearing potential loss of favor with their sexual partner are at greater risk to forego condom use no matter the known associated sexual health risk (Boyer, Tschann, & Shafter, 1999; Ethier et al., 2006).

Adolescent girls' exposure to neighborhood and community violence (Miller, 2008), including gendered violence by perpetrators they know, who have raped and committed intimate partner violence against them (Miller, 2008; Teitelman, Ratcliffe, Morales-Aleman, & Sullivan, 2008), and ethnoviolence by strangers, based on their ethnic/racial and/or gender group membership (Ehrlich, 2009; Helms, Nicolas, & Green, 2012), can result in maladaptive coping. Further, seeking support within familial and community context that are at times dysfunctional and are plagued by trans-generational transmission of internalized racial and/or gender oppression and trauma (Boyd-Franklin, 1991; Degruy-Leary, 2005) and childhood abuse (sexual, battering and neglect) (Boyd-Franklin, 1991) has the potential to put girls at risk for gendered violence within their homes and by persons for whom they have trusted. The fact of violation by someone who they expect trust and protection has the potential to place girls at increased risk for complex relational trauma and its mental health complications. Experiences of this sort can lead some youth to seek support and comfort outside of the home and typically in the context of sexual risks and/or drug/alcohol abuse as a means to cope with a sense of lowered self-worth and inadequate social, cultural and/or familial support (Ethier et al., 2006). Thus, addressing the injury to girls' self-esteem and safety is critical to buttressing the effects of societal stressors/pressures on their home and community lives.

While researchers have considered the protective effects of the "village" it takes to raise a child (Homonoff, Martin, Rimpas, & Henderson, 1994), specificity of that community and protective aspects have been highlighted. For example, Browning, Burrington, Leventhal, & Brooks-Gunn (2008), identified the concept of "collective efficacy" in communities to support healthy, prosocial development among adolescents. Collective efficacy, the combined influence of intergenerational closure, social cohesion and informal social control orientations toward local youth was found to be negatively associated with sexual risk defined as early sexual debut and multiple partners in this study. Further, as the youth matured, Browning et al. (2008) found that the community/family outside the home had more of an impact or, "regulatory effect" for curbing adolescent sexual risk behavior. These findings suggest the important role of supportive and caring adult relationships for healthy youth development in risk context. Poor youth of color, due to the social inequalities that shape their lives, are at particular risk and thus require intervention to address the potential gaps in family and community support.

PROJECT SISTERCIRCLE: INTERVENTION

Project SisterCircle (PSC) is one intervention type with the focus on relationship development and health as a means to support Black/African and Latina adolescent girls' transition through adolescence. The work of Browning et al. (2008) highlights the importance of trusted, supportive adults outside the home on whom adolescents can depend and rely to encourage healthy decision-making. Project SisterCircle (PSC), a psychosocial spiritual intervention for adolescent Black/African and Latina girls in an urban setting was developed to address the issue of sexual risk vulnerability (SRV), a term coined by the first author to describe the "tendency to put oneself at risk for the potential negative consequences of unsafe sexual encounters" (Williams, Karlin, & Wallace, 2012). The negative consequences of sexual behavior were conceptualized as both physical and psychological and with the potential to have an effect over the short- (e.g., emotional, situational) and long-term (e.g., sexually transmitted infections, teen parenting, etc.). Deemed evidence of stress coping in high-risk, under-resourced urban communities, SRV is the target risk attitude and behavior indicative of psychological distress among girls of color in urban context and was the specific focus of the PSC intervention.

In the following, a description of the PSC intervention components is presented. A focus on the elements of the intervention and their potential to support youth adjustment to structural inequalities is presented. PSC consists of both process and activity-based components.

PROCESS COMPONENTS

Set-up. As structural inequalities in the lives of adolescent, poor Black/African and Latina girls place them in subordinate positions within their families and communities, the Project SisterCircle (PSC) program intended to off-set this positionality, not only in interpersonal interactions with the girls, but also the programmatic structures. The room set-up consisted of moving tables and/or desks to the periphery of the room and placing yoga mats in a circular formation with the head or top of the mat facing the center of the circle and radiating outward. This positioning equalized power of all girls and group facilitators, as all persons sit on the yoga mats, on the floor, and engage the elements of the program together. During the beginning sessions of the program the facilitators took a primary role in setting up the room and the yoga mats, it is expected that as group cohesion emerged, the girls would begin to take up their authority of the space by structuring the room themselves.

Set-up also includes creating a mood or tone that supports the relaxation and trust of the participants. At the session start, "spiritually-focused" music, songs espousing messages of personal empowerment, faith in better outcomes and peace of mind, were played. This music is meant to facilitate the girls' transition from the school day to the girl-centered focus of the group. Brown (2011) suggests school settings are contentious environments for Black/African adolescent girls as their needs and expectations for their futures are subjugated for other priorities. Similarly, adolescent Latinas are also sent overt and covert messages about being a "good girl" and performing well in school; however, to do so, within the boundaries of male dominance and authority that undermine their sense of self-worth (Gallegos-Castillo, 2006). Consequently, creating a structural context in the group that privileged the girls' agenda is a critical element of the program.

Group rules and cultural norms. Structural inequalities place persons on the lower rungs of the social hierarchy in futile competition with one another for limited resources. The effect of this positionality shapes the relationships among persons within marginalized and oppressed groups with the potential to create dysfunctional dynamics in groups of persons with shared experiences (McCloud, 2011). The "frenemy," one who is simultaneously friend and enemy, is a relationship dynamic that many girls are engaged with deleterious effects for their ability to form healthy, supportive and satisfying relationships with women in adulthood (Dellasega, 2005). Recognizing these dynamics and their potential to negatively shape the development of the group, Project SisterCircle enacted an intentional approach to develop genuine trust and respect among the girls and the group process to support stable group cohesion. To this end, a series of team building activities were implemented to build closeness among the girls, establish appropriate boundaries and define sisterhood. As preliminary focus group data indicated conflict and fighting among girls was largely due to gossip, misunderstandings, and norms of ephemeral inclusion/exclusion in smaller groups or cliques, the intervention sought to establish norms of respect and the importance of keeping each member's confidence. For example, one activity, "The Group Oath," in which the girls engaged the process of making a promise to the group and themselves, highlights concepts such as trust and commitment to the group. The girls created an oath that was written by them on poster print paper, signed, and posted during each session as a reminder of the norms that guide their relationship and the group process. In this way, the group cultural norm engendered the expectations for interactions among the girls that ran counter to the divisive processes characteristic of societal expectation.

Group Facilitators. Black/African and Latina girls' positionality in the social hierarchy causes them to enact and articulate power in the ways that are available to them. For example, Schippers' (2008) work describing a mentor program for poor, Black/African girls in an urban setting suggests that the girls exacted their power in the choice of their mentors. Specifically, the Black/African college student mentors were coveted, and became an indication of power and value in that setting. Though in the larger social context, Blackness and femaleness are not prioritized, within the program the girls had the power to set the standards of priority and preference, placing their gender and race identifications on top. The Project SisterCircle intervention recruited women, counselor-trainees and undergraduate psychology students that mirrored the racial/ethnic and cultural experiences of the girls with whom they worked. Having themselves been reared as girls of color in urban context, the facilitators were able to occupy a space of recognition that supported their work with the girls. The intervention adopted a use-of-self model in which the facilitators were engaged in the parallel process of development through their work with the girls (Baldwin, 2000). Thus, the training of facilitators focused on their personal experiences as young girls of color in urban context and how these dynamics may come to bear on their facilitation.

There are a number of dynamics within communities of color that shape relationships among women and the training of facilitators aimed to make the women aware of these in order that they mindfully engage their relationships with the girls and one another. Some examples include comparisons and self-valuations based on skin color (e.g., light or dark complexion), hair texture, facial features, and body shape and size, and the relationship of these to their self-esteem and relations with other women. Histories of colonization shape Black/African women and girls' perceptions of themselves (Williams, 1996) and dynamics within their families (Boyd-Franklin, 1991). Unfortunately, this has caused the development of internalized racial and gender oppression as observed through relationships with oneself and others and is transmitted across generations. As the facilitator training for the intervention prioritized a process of identity awareness and development, the facilitators were positioned to engage in psychologically healthy and potentially corrective ways with the girls. The potential to challenge a rather significant manifestation of structural inequalities exemplified in the social relations among women and girls of color is perhaps the most significant aspect of this intervention and indicative of the importance of shaping process and culture for the health and wellness of participants in group work.

ACTIVITY-BASED COMPONENTS

Centering exercise. The ability to determine one's environment is not likely permitted by those functioning in the lower levels of social hierarchy. Girls of color are no exception. With little to no authority over what occurs in their home and school environments, they are likely to feel a constant sense of disempowerment. Thus, providing girls the opportunity to set the tone and take some authority over their circumstances was a critical aspect of PSC. Each session began with a series of activities to facilitate the girls' transition from their school day to the group. The girls and facilitators led the group through stretching, affirmations and check-in with each member. Two to three light intensity yoga-type stretches and affirmations selected from Iyanla Vanzant's (1999) "Don't give it away," a self-help book for adolescent girls, oriented the girls to the culture and process of the group. After the girl-led recitation of the affirmation, each girl and facilitator "checked in," stating her "high" (accomplishments/good experiences) and "low" (challenges) since the previous group meeting. It was expected and confirmed through qualitative data analysis of the program's outcomes that these practices, particularly the check-in, provided a shared/equalized space in which program participants were able to cathartically release their experience of stress within the supportive environment of the group.

Group discussion. The 16 sessions of the PSC curriculum utilized the SCRR (Self Collective Root Responsibility, Sankofa Community Empowerment, Inc., 2001) dialogue organization framework. This framework structures the discussion of each topic in the curriculum guiding the girls to consider the relationship of the topic to the self (her individual experiences with a topic area), collective (effect and relationship to others), root (possible causes of the issue/topic); and responsibility (consideration of how she may become active in addressing the issue). The curriculum posed questions the facilitators used to prompt the girls through each stage of the SCRR framework. Taking the perspective that the girls would need to address the social inequities that shaped the experiences of access and deprivation in their lives, this discussion framework began the process of engaging their proclivity toward social action to address concerns that affect them and others girls.

Project Work. The project work aspect of PSC was the girls' response to an identified problem, issue or concern they believed was significant for them and other girls. The "Legacy Project," created through the program and presented at the end was intended to raise awareness of relevant issues about girls in their community and through awareness engender change. One characteristic of social inequalities is the lack of power of members disenfranchised by their position in the social hierarchy. Through continued dialogue, girls in PSC are in the practice of connecting the relationship of life issues and challenges to their interpersonal and intrapersonal experiences. Development of and work on the Legacy Project positioned the girls to name, address, and build awareness about the effect of large scale social systems on their lives. The PSC program sought to foster a sense of purposive action to address the areas which directly impacted the girls' lives. For example, one year the girls developed an anti-gossiping and anti-violence skit highlighting the effect of gossip on girls' friendships and demonstrating ways to resolve conflict. Given what is known about girls' competition and divisive friendship/relationship dynamics, their work on this issue, dramatizing the process of in/out group member selection, and gossiping behaviors, made them and others aware and thus in a position to address the issue in their relationships with one another.

Journaling/Closing. At the end of each session, the girls wrote for approximately 5–7 minutes in their journals and closed out the session in a ritualized activity call the "Gratitude Circle." Convening these aspects at the end of the session gave the girls an opportunity to digest the experiences of the day and reflect on the impact of the members and the facilitators. The program sought to cultivate a sense of sisterhood among the participants, to prompt connection and healthy relationship within the program and outside the bounds of the group meetings. Therefore, cultivating healthy and positive emotional experiences with girls in the group was considered one localized way to counter social and environmental challenges that place them at risk and alleviate their vulnerability to the effects of structural inequalities on their lives.

RESEARCH AND PRACTICE IMPLICATIONS

Given the interdependence of research findings to relevant development and implementation of interventions for Black/African and Latina adolescent girls in urban communities, implications for research and practice are discussed concurrently. As there is a dearth of research on the experiences of Latina adolescent girls, as well as a primary focus on risk and deficits of Black/African girls and their communities, it is critical that researchers and practitioners partner to highlight the work within these communities and among these girls that is effective and descriptive of their resilience. Williams (2014) articulates relative to Black/African descent women and girls that a paradigmatic shift from deficit and deficiency hypotheses to consideration of the elements that contribute to the health and resilience needs to be considered. This reasoning is extended to Latina girls underscoring the importance of making their experience central to intervention and research in order that their intersectionalities might be more comprehensively considered. Specifically, the localized work of the Project SisterCircle intervention within communities in Brooklyn, NY may highlight points of inquiry and implications for practice in areas that researchers and practitioners may consider developing further. One point consists of the area of intersectionality. As indicated in this chapter, the writings of Crenshaw and Collins inform this work and are inspired by the experiences of Black/African women and have been broadened to conceptualize the experiences of Black/African girls. We argue an intersectional analysis of experience relative to Latinas and girls in particular is needed to more fully develop and implement intervention appropriate for them. Furthermore, we contend the failure to do so may exemplify the impact of structural inequalities based on their specific positionality in the fields of psychology and education.

The work with adolescent Black/African descent and Latina girls through Project SisterCircle also provides some sense of the effect of the girls' positionality on the socio-emotional and academic/career development. Williams et al. (2014) suggest a negative impact on adolescent girls' sense of self when developing in under-resourced communities as they are at increased risk for internalizing the "context of interlocking gendered, racialized, and class-based systems of oppression" and thus may in fact be at increased need for intervention to counter their absorptions of these environmental messages. Further, while anecdotal experiences from working with the girls suggest their vulnerability, limited work has been done to outline the relationship between the ways their social and cultural context may create conditions of risk and resilience as they seek to cope with increased stress in these situations (Williams, 2014; Williams et al., 2014). Rather, a focus on the risk experiences of Black/African boys often supersedes a discourse of the varied needs of all urban youth of color coming of age in restricted context (Brown, 2011). Recognizing the specific challenges to Black/African adolescent boy's mental health and education, the current work underscores the significance of racialized and gendered experiences to shape the health and development of all youth in the dire circumstances they face in under-resourced, urban contexts.

Project SisterCircle consisted of grass-roots outreach between a university researcher and local schools in her community. As many universities stand adjacent to poor communities of color, it is important to consider the ways the knowledge and resources within the university community may be widened to benefit surrounding communities. Furthermore, the proximity of universities to communities in which students are preparing to work and engage within, creates a pipeline of relevant knowledge and information to inform practices most effective for these communities (Officer, Grim, Medina, Bringle, & Foreman, 2013). As the need for intervention is immediate and necessary, development and implementation of effective programs is critical. Further, as we consider the ways to improve upon these interventions, continuous feedback to practices in higher education context, particularly relative to teacher and educational leadership preparation in addition to practitioners whose work centers on youth development and mental health/well-being and family engagement in educational settings is indicated. Models of university-community collaborations which amplify the voices of communities to shape education of developing professionals have proven quite effective (Matusov & Smith, 2011). Further, collaborations that are sustainable and thus further contribute to the development of communities and of the academic programs have the potential for long term growth and development of relevance in both contexts.

As indicated above, Project SisterCircle is considered a grass-roots intervention. As the research climate of evidence-based practice and translational intervention driven by large, governmental research grant programs shapes the development of youth intervention programming across our nation's communities, it is critical that practitioners and researchers remain cognizant of the unique attributes of their communities and context which may make a "one-size-fits all" approach to intervention inappropriate and thus ineffective to the nuances of specific communities. Failure to consider the specific needs of youth in particular context has the potential of applying essentialism to the unique aspects of each youth's intersectional experience and the shared aspects that may or may not generalize to young people in other communities. One example is the work of Ozer, Wanis, & Bazell (2010) in which the researchers examined the adaptations health teachers made to empirically-supported substance abuse and violence prevention programs in two urban school districts. They found that the teachers' adaptations to the curriculum did not interfere with the program's goals and perhaps the relevance of these adaptations to the students and teacher stakeholders may have supported study outcomes. Thus, stakeholder buy-in may create pathways to cater the intervention to their context and support program sustainability and consistency of pro-social youth development interventions throughout the school and beyond its boundaries. Further, as researchers have found school-based, youth development programming difficult to maintain beyond the conclusion of research funding (Lyon, Frazier, Mehta, Atkins, & Weisbach, 2011), stakeholder investment is likely critical to sustaining positive programmatic effects for the schools and the communities in which they are held. Rather than the current top-down model of research funding which directs localized efforts, programming, perhaps described as "small batch," may provide important insights regarding what is effective in specific communities and thus off-set the impact of structural inequalities which shape the funding mechanism and consequent access and implementation of interventions within urban, under-resourced communities dependent on external funding for programming implementation and youth/community change.

CONCLUSION

Structural inequalities shape the lives of Black/African and Latin descent adolescent girls in under-resourced urban contexts and thus place them at risk for socio-emotional coping with the potential to exacerbate the effect of these inequities on their lives. The current chapter examined the role of structural inequalities to affect the socio-emotional and health risk and vulnerability of adolescent girls and the need for intervention programming to counter the effect of an unequal system. Specifically, Project SisterCircle, a small scale, psycho-social spiritual intervention implemented in middle schools in Brooklyn, NY was presented as a means to "tip the scale" in order to address the effects of large-scale structural inequalities on Black/African and Latina adolescent girls' health and well-being.

REFERENCES

Anderson, K. L. (2009). Gendering coercive control. *Violence against women, 15*(12), 1444–1457. doi. 10.1177/1077801209346837.

Bailey, T. M., Williams, W. S., & Favors, B. (2014). African Americans. In E. J. R. David (Ed.), *Internalized oppression: The psychology of marginalized groups* (pp. 138–162). New York, NY: Springer.

Baldwin, M. (2000). *The use of self in therapy.* Binghamton, NY: The Haworth Press.

Belgrave, F., & Allison, K. W. (2010). *African American psychology: From Africa to America.* Thousand Oaks, CA: Sage.

Bermúdez, J. M., Stinson, M. A., Zak-Hunter, L., & Abrams, B. (2011). Mejor sola que mal acompañada: Strengths and challenges of Mexican-origin mothers parenting alone. *Journal of Divorce & Remarriage, 52*(8), 622–641. doi. 10.1080/10502556.2011.619939

Bowie, S. L., & Dopwell, D. M. (2013). Metastressors as barriers to self-sufficiency among TANF-reliant African Americans and Latina women. *Affilia: Journal of Women & Social Work, 28*(2), 177–193. doi. 10.1177/0886109913484693

Boyer, C. B., Tschann, J. M., & Shafter, M. (1999). Predictors of risk for sexually transmitted diseases in 9th grade urban high school students. *Journal of Adolescent Research, 14*(4), 448–465.

Boyd-Franklin, N. (1991). Recurrent themes in the treatment of African American women in group psychotherapy. *Women & Therapy, 11*(2), 25–40. doi: 10.1300/J015V11N02_04

Brown, A. (2011). Descendants of 'Ruth': Black girls coping through the 'Black Male Crisis.' *The Urban Review, 43*(5), 597–619. doi: 10.1007/s11256-010-0162-x

Browning, C. R., Burrington, L. A., Leventhal, T., & Brooks-Gunn, J. O. (2008). Neighborhood structural inequality, collective efficacy, and sexual risk behavior among urban youth. *Journal of Health and Social Behavior, 49*, 269–285.

Chau, M. (2009). *Low-income children in the United States: National and state trend data, 1998–2008.* National Center for Children in Poverty. Retrieved from http://nccp.org/publications/pub_907.html.

Cohen, C. (2010). *Democracy remixed: Black youth and the future of American politics.* New York, NY: Oxford University Press.

Collins, P. H. (2000). *Black feminist thought: Knowledge, consciousness and the politics of empowerment.* New York, NY: Routledge.

Collins, M. H., Kelch-Oliver, K., Johnson, K., Wellkom, J. Kottke, M. S., & Oyeshiku, C. (2010). Clinically significant depressive symptoms in African American adolescent females in an urban reproductive health clinic. *Journal of Clinical Psychology in Medical Settings, 17*, 175–182. doi: 10.1007/s10880-010-9200-9

Conyers, J. E. (2002). Racial inequality: Emphasis on explanations. *Western Journal of Black Studies, 26*(4), 249–254.

Crenshaw, K. (1989). Demarginalizing the intersection of race and sex: A Black feminist critique of antidiscrimination doctrine, feminist theory and antiracist politics. *University of Chicago Legal Forum*, 139–167.

Curry, C. (2014, July 21). *This is the toll Chicago's gun violence has taken on the city's kids.* Retrieved July 26, 2014 from http://abcnews.go.com/US/chicagos-gun-violence-taking-terrible-toll-citys-youth/story?id=24646710.

Degruy-Leary, J. (2005). *Post traumatic slave syndrome: America's legacy of enduring injury and healing.* Milwaukee, OR: Uptone Press.

Dellasega, C. (2005). *Mean girls grown up: Adult women who are still queen bees, middle bees and afraid to bees.* Hoboken, NJ: John Wiley & Sons.

Ehrlich, H. J. (2009). *Hate crimes and ethnoviolence: The history, current affairs and future of discrimination in America.* Boulder, CO: Westview Press.

Ethier, K. A., Kershaw, T. S., Lewis., J. B., Milan, S., Niccolai, L. M., & Ickovics, J. R. (2006). Self-esteem, emotional distress and sexual behavior among adolescent females: Inter-relationship and temporal effects. *Journal of Adolescent Health, 38*(3), 268–274. doi: 10.1016/j.jadohealth.2004.12.010

Forhan, S. E. (2008, March). *Prevalence of sexually transmitted infections and bacterial vaginosis among female adolescents in the United States: Data from the National Health and Nutritional Examination Survey (NHANES) 2003–2004.* Report presented at the National STD Conference, Chicago, IL.

Gallegos-Castillo, A. (2006). La casa: Negotiating family cultural practices, constructing identities. In J. Denner & B. L. Guzman (Eds.), *Latina girls: Voices of adolescent strength in the United States* (pp. 44–58). New York, NY: New York University.

Gilligan, C. (1982). *In another voice: Psychological theory and women's development.* Cambridge, MA: Harvard University Press.

Hare, B. R. (1987). Structural inequality and the endangered status of Black youth. *Journal of Negro Education, 56*(1), 100–110.

Helms, J. E., Nicolas, G., & Green, C. (2012). Racism and ethnoviolence: Enhancing professional and research training. *Traumatology, 18,* 65–74. doi. 10.1177/1534765610396728

Homonoff, E., Martin, J., Rimpas, D., & Henderson, M. (1994). It takes a village to raise a child: A model of training for prevention of youth abuse of alcohol and other drugs. *Child & Adolescent Social Work Journal, 11*(1), 53–61. doi. 10.1007/BF01876103

Karpati, A., Kerker, B., Mostashari, F., Singh T., Hajat, A., Thorpe, L., Bassett, M., Henning, K., & Frieden, T. (2004). *Health disparities in New York City.* New York, NY: New York City Department of Health and Mental Hygiene.

King, T. C., & Ferguson, S. A. (1996). Clinical analysis of chronic dependency and help-giving in African American female friendships. *Smith College Studies in Social Work, 66*(2), 163–183.

Kyrk, H. (1953). *The family in the American economy.* Chicago, IL: University of Chicago Press.

Lacey, A., & Cornell, D. (2013). The impact of teasing and bullying on schoolwide academic performance. *Journal of Applied School Psychology, 29*(3), 262–283.

Lareau, A. (2003). *Unequal childhoods: Class, race and family life.* Berkeley, CA: University of California Press.

Lee, C. C. (2005). Urban school counselors: Context, characteristics and competencies. *Professional School Counseling, 8,* 184–188.

Lopez, G. E., Gurin, P., & Nagda, B.A. (1998). Understanding structural causes for group inequalities. *International Society of Political Psychology, 19*(2), 305–329.

Lopez, N. (2012). *Hopeful girls, troubled boys: Race and gender disparity in urban education* (2nd ed.). New York, NY: Routledge.

Lyon, A. R., Frazier, S. L., Mehta, T., Atkins, M. S., & Weisbach, J. (2011). Easier said than done: Intervention sustainability in an urban after-school program. *Administration and Policy in Mental Health and Mental Health Services Research, 38*(6), 504–517. doi. 10.1007/s10488-011-0339-y

Matusov, E., & Smith, M. P. (2011). An ecological model of inter-institutional sustainability of an after-school program: The La Red Mágica community-university partnership in Delaware. *Outlines: Critical Practice Studies, 13*(1), 19–45.

McCloud, M. T. (2011, March). *Crabs in a Barrel Syndrome: Will it ever end? Don't crawl over and compete; instead, celebrate each other.* Retrieved from http://www.psychologytoday.com/blog/black-womens-health-and-happiness/201103/crabs-in-barrel-syndrome-will-it-ever-end

Miller, J. (2008). *Getting played: African American girls, urban inequality, and gendered violence.* New York, NY: New York University Press.

Moynihan, D. P. (1965). *The Negro family: The case for national action.* United States Department of Labor. Retrieved July 26, 2014 from http://www.dol.gov/dol/aboutdol/history/webid-meynihan.htm.

Nielsen, C. (2013). Wise Latina: Framing Sonia Sotomayor in the general-market and Latina/o-oriented prestige press. *Howard Journal of Communications, 24*(2), 117–133. doi. 10.1080/10646175.2013.776418

Officer, S. D. H., Grim, J., Medina, M. A., Bringle, R. G., & Foreman, A. (2013). Strengthening community schools through university partnerships. *Peabody Journal of Education, 88*(5), 564–577. doi. 10.1080/0161956X.2013.835152

Ozer, E. J., Wanis, M. G., & Bazell, N. (2010). Diffusion of school-based prevention programs in two urban districts: Adaptations, rationales, and suggestions for change. *Prevention Science, 11*(1), 42–55. doi. 10.1007/s11121-009-0148-7

Ramirez, E. (2013). Examining Latinos/as' graduate school choice process: An intersectionality perspective. *Journal of Hispanic Higher Education, 12*(1), 23–36. doi. 10.1177/1538192712452147

Reid, L. W., Adelman, R. M., & Jaret, C. (2007). Women, race, and ethnicity: Exploring earnings differentials in metropolitan America. *City & Community, 6*(2), 137–156.

Sankofa Community Empowerment, Inc. (2001). *The SCRR Model.* Retrieved from Sankofa Community Empowerment, Inc. website, http://www.sankofaempowerment.org/

Schippers, M. (2008). Doing difference/doing power: Negotiations of race and gender in a mentoring program. *Symbolic Interaction, 31*(1), 77–98. doi: 10.1525/si.2008.31.1.77

Short, E. L., & Williams, W. S. (2014). From the inside out: Group work with women of color. *The Journal for Specialists in Group Work, 39*, 71–91.

Szymanski, D. M., & Henrichs-Beck, C. (2014). Exploring sexual minority women's experiences of external and internalized heterosexism and sexism and their links to coping and distress. *Sex Roles, 70,* 28–42. doi. 10.1007/s11199-013-0329-5

Teitelman, A. M., Ratcliffe, S. J., Morales-Aleman, M. M., & Sullivan, C. (2008). Sexual relationship power, intimate partner violence and condom use among minority urban girls. *Journal of Interpersonal Violence, 23*(12), 1694–1712. doi: 10.1177/0886260508314331

Vanzant, I. (1999). *Don't give it away.* New York, NY: Fireside.

Walton, M. A., Resko, S., Whitesude, L., Chermack, S. T., Zimmerman, M., & Cunningham, R. M. (2011). Sexual risk behaviors among teens at an urban emergency department: Relationship with violent behaviors and substance use. *Journal of Adolescent Health, 48,* 303–305. doi: 10.1016/j.jadohealth.2010.07.005

Williams, A. L. (1996). Skin color in psychotherapy. In P. Foster, M. Moskowitz, & R. A. Javier (Eds.), *Reaching across boundaries of culture and class: Widening the scope of psychotherapy* (pp. 211–224). Northvale, NJ: J. Aronson, Inc.

Williams, C. B., Frame, M. W., & Green, E. (1999). Counseling groups for African American women: A focus on spirituality. *Journal for Specialists in Group Work, 24,* 260–273.

Williams, W. S. (2014). Women and girls of African descent. In C. Z. Enns, J. K. Rice, & R. L. Nutt, (Eds.), *Psychological practice with diverse groups of women* (pp. 53–80). Washington, DC: American Psychological Association.

Williams, W. S., Dhami, A. K., & Moody, A. (2014). The social injustice of stress: Identity intersectionality and well-being among urban Black/African and Latina adolescent girls. In C. V. Johnson, H. Friedman, J. Diaz, B. Nastasi, & Z. Franco (Eds.), *Praeger handbook for social justice and psychology*, (Chapter 3). Westport, CT: Praeger.

Williams, W. S., Karlin, T., & Wallace, D. (2012). Project SisterCircle: Risk, intersectionality and intervening in urban schools. *Journal of School Counseling, 10,* 1–35.

Wilson, W. J. (2011, Spring). Being poor, Black and American: The impact of political, economic and cultural forces. *American Educator,* 10–25.

CHAPTER 7

ETHNOVIOLENCE AS STRUCTURAL INEQUALITY

Media Representations of Black/African Descent Women

Wendi S. Williams, Ellen L. Short, and Dianne Ghiraj

ETHNOVIOLENCE AS STRUCTURAL INEQUALITY: THE CASE OF BLACK/AFRICAN WOMEN

At the annual meeting for the American Psychological Association (APA) in 2011, Dr. Janet Helms, an African American psychologist, racial identity scholar, researcher, and educator laid the foundation for her conceptualization of Black/African descent women as victims of ethnoviolence and its resultant trauma. During a symposium examining ways Black/African descent women cope with trauma and demonstrate their resilience, Helms introduced the concept of ethnoviolence alongside racism as manifestations of specific gendered and racial/ethnically-based forms of violence which impact the psychological and physical health of Black/African descent women. Building on the work of Dr. Helms' conceptualization of ethnoviolence that has been discussed at conferences (2011a, 2011b) and examined in formative research (Helms, Nicolas, & Green, 2012), the

Talking About Structural Inequalities in Everyday Life: New Politics of Race in Groups, Organizations, and Social Systems, pages 121–138.

121

notion of intersecting racism and sexism to inform a specialized violence, ethnoviolence, experienced by Black/African descent women is a logical next step in conceptualizing the determinants of stress and trauma for Black/African descent women. Further, the relative absence of this domain in the psychological literature may in fact underscore the failure to recognize and acknowledge the impact and perpetuate ethnoviolent dynamics toward Black/African descent women.

The current chapter presents ethnoviolence and resultant trauma on Black/African descent women as a manifestation of structural inequalities that are gendered, racialized, and inconsistently informed by social class designations and respectability politics. Respectability politics, the social rules and expectations which confirm an individual's social acceptance and credibility, are enacted by Black/African descent women to elevate their social status but fails to protect them from racial and gendered aggression (Williams, 2014). The authors suggest that Black/African descent women's social and political positionalities serve to justify their victimization by perpetrators of ethnoviolence, and their experience of secondary adversities to the traumatic ethnoviolent event on the part of systems and processes which provide inadequate intervention and support. The chapter considers forms of ethnoviolence to which Black/African descent women are exposed, with a focus on macro and micro-level aggressions evident through media representations, and health implications and outcomes related to these exposures. We begin with a definition of ethnoviolence and discuss its relation to structural inequalities which inform the experiences and treatment of Black/African descent women in societal contexts.

ETHNOVIOLENCE AS EXPRESSION
OF STRUCTURAL INEQUALITY

A consideration of structural inequalities necessitates an analysis of societal organization which designates a hierarchy of groups. In other words, such an analysis would indicate which group(s) have been, "chosen to absorb an unfair share of an unfair burden in a structurally unfair system" (Hare, 1987, p. 102). Black/African descent women, bearing dual, marginalized identities, are positioned to carry undue burdens in the current social and political hierarchies (Harnois, 2010). Intersecting gender and racial identities are organized by systems of hierarchy and social organization that place Black/African descent persons and women in secondary and less valued social positions (Collins, 2008). Further, viewed through the lens of one's socio-economic status, nationality, ability status, sexual orientation, and age, Black/African descent women are placed in continuously shifting roles and positions that while dynamic, never position them more favorably than White men —their diametric and privileged opposite.

Howard Ehrlich and colleagues at The Prejudice Institute/Center for the Applied Study of Prejudice and Ethnoviolence are leaders in the field and study of ethnoviolence and have taken an interdisciplinary approach to define and identify instances of ethnoviolence. The work extends across 10 action research projects culminating in studies of the social and psychological effects of victimization; the nature of violent attitudes and behavior; the nature of prejudice, conflict, and ethnoviolence as they are played out in college campus and workplace settings; and the role of the news media in communicating prejudice ("Who we are," 2014). Thus, considering the effects of race-based violence has facilitated the development of a definition of ethnoviolence.

Ehrlich (2009) defines ethnoviolence as exposure to violence due to one's ethnic and/or racial background and/or gender. It is deemed a primary form of social intimidation and control informed by hierarchical dynamics and systems of domination operating within the society. Ehrlich and colleagues have delineated the following aspects of ethnoviolence, providing a more nuanced view of the etiology of this targeted violence (Ehrlich, 2009).

1. Race (skin color) is the major target of ethnoviolence, followed by gender (female), with White males least likely to be targeted.
2. Ethnoviolence is a natural outcropping of a cultural context of hate toward specific groups.
3. Attitudes toward specific groups are supportive of social interactions and conflict between groups in order to maintain the agenda and priorities of elite groups.

Helms, Nicholas, and Green (2012) define ethnoviolence as:

> violence or intimidation directed at members of ethnic groups that have been marginalized and stigmatized by the dominant or host culture because of their inability or unwillingness to assimilate threatens the dominant group's entitlement to society or community resources. (p. 67)

As Helms et al. (2012) does not implicate gender, Ehrlich (2009) suggests skin color and female gender are particularly targeted, and thus underscore the detrimental effect of Black/African descent women's positionality for making them especially vulnerable. Further, as Helms and colleagues indicate ones' "inability or unwillingness to assimilate" as a threat to the dominant group's sense of entitlement, the justification for the structural inequalities is defended through attacking them. Thus, Black/African descent women's existence, and perhaps developed, healthy sense of self and racial and gender identities, while an indicator of psychological wellness, may place them at risk for ethnoviolent acts by those offended and/or threatened by them.

WORTHY VICTIMS

Ehrlich (2009) purports it is the protection and maintenance of the status quo in which Whites and men are deemed deserving recipients of access to the majority of the societal resources that underlies the rationale for ethnoviolent acts. For example, in the 1997 film "Rosewood" directed by John Singleton (Peters & Singleton, 1997), poor White male members of the town Rosewood expressed outrage that a Black family whose home they were setting on fire had a piano. For them, their act of arson was further fueled and justified by the fact that this Black family had a symbol of middle-class status, a piano, in their home while their own living conditions left much to be desired. Cultural values and beliefs regarding merit and worth are espoused by societal institutions, such as media, academic discourse, political campaigns, religious institutions and so forth which socialize individuals to believe one's access and opportunity are only the result of their effort (Lopez, Gurin, & Nagda, 1998). Thus, there are likely to be usual and what Ehrlich (2009) describes as "worthy" victims designated as such because their demonization reaffirms the racial/ethnic and gender status quos and forwards the elite agenda which communicates:

1. The worthiness of Whites and men to be granted access and resources disproportionate to their contribution and/or representation.
2. Women and Persons of Color are NOT to be granted access and resources, which is out of proportion to their contribution and/or representation.
3. Threats to the status quo will result in ethnoviolent acts meant to control, or "keep one in one's place"—preserve the order.

Ehrlich (2009) indicates that most acts of ethnoviolence are not reported and therefore are not measured against the standards of hate crime legislation. Denial of the significance of the event, rationalization that the perpetrator did not mean to offend or commit the act, or that the incident is a usual aspect of life in a racist and sexist society are some of the reasons that victims of ethnoviolence offer for not reporting these actions(Ehrlich, 2009, p. 21). Helms et al. (2012) suggests failure to report may also be a manifestation of the trauma response and highlights the work of Bryant-Davis and Ocampo (2005). Drawing connections between women's internalizing symptoms and silence in response to sexual trauma and gendered-violence as a parallel to reactions to ethnoviolence among victims, Bryant-Davis and Ocampo (2005) suggests that both race-based and sexual trauma/gendered violence have the potential to initiate a set of "cognitive, emotional and physiological sequelae and affect victims' ability to maintain healthy relationships" and also result in somatic complaints (p. 487). Denial, numbing, and self-blame are self-preserving defense mechanisms employed to manage the processing of traumatic events (van der Kolk, McFarlane, & Weisaeth, 2006), and may explain individual and group level avoidance responses to trauma.

A discussion of Ehrlich's (2009) concept of "worthy" victims relative to Black/African descent women is incomplete without a discussion of the ways stereotypes, respectability and intersectionality shape perceptions of Black/African descent women. Collins (2005, 2008) indicated that controlling stereotypes shape the ways Black/African descent women perceive themselves and the ways others see and respond to them. These stereotypes are deemed controlling because they are not defined by Black/African descent women, and have been carried over from socio-historical and -political contexts in which the enslavement and sexual exploitation of Black/African descent women and their children toward the economic development of the White majority needed to be legitimized. The effect on the psychology of Black women is dramatically portrayed in Toni Morrison's (2004) *Beloved,* in which the main character Sethe, in an attempt to interrupt the cycle of sexual and labor exploitation of herself and children, kills them rather than return to the plantation from which they fled. In what can only be described as a desperate measure, Morrison makes clear the height of the stakes for a woman to claim her freedom and that of her children. Contemporary demeaning portrayals of Black/African descent women in the media suggest a continued campaign to interfere with their right to self-definition and determination. Historically, Black/African descent women attempted to counter these stereotypes through the authority of religious institutions and the Black men that ran them through engaging in the politics of respectability to differentiate themselves from poor, uneducated and non-religion affiliated Black/African descent women (Higginbotham, 1993). Williams' (2014) description provides some context for these politics.

> Characterized by guidelines for cleanliness of person and property, temperance, thrift, polite manners, and sexual purity, these politics held promise for African Americans as a way to gain access to the middle class through Black/African women's labor in the home. Black/African women's ability to demonstrate these tenets in their homes and through their families permitted potential access to the "cult of true womanhood." (p. 56)

These politics and their social class implications are likely the difference between who can respectably indicate they have been wronged. Helms et al. (2012) indicated persons that report instances of ethnoviolence may be perceived as unreliable reporters of their experience either because their way of being conforms to racial stereotypes or because they do not conform to expected stereotypes (p. 67). Deemed untrustworthy reporters of their experience, it is likely that they will not only be re-victimized, but direct and indirect witnesses may become co-victims due to vicarious traumatization, and the failure of response interventionists to adequately and appropriately respond to the victim (Ehrlich, 2009, p. 26). Contemporary and historic examples illustrate this dynamic. Whether it be Kanye West's post-Katrina declaration that, "George Bush does not care about Black people" (Shockroc1, 2006) or the Civil Rights community's determination that Claudette Colvin, an African American teen that became pregnant and had been arrested, was unsuitable to be the face of the Montgomery bus boycott (Adler, 2009), the ripple effects of vicarious traumatization of those deemed worthy of their trauma are evident.

ETHNOVIOLENCE: FORMS, EXPRESSIONS & RESPONSE

Ehrlich (2009) describes violence in the form of physical, psychological and/or verbal assault which primarily targets persons due to their race/ethnic and gender group identifications as ethnoviolence. Helms et al. (2012) explicitly indicates that psychological injury can be caused by:

a. direct cataclysmic racial or ethnic cultural events (hate crimes and other cataclysmic events such as natural disasters/human conditions that are exacerbated by racism or ethnoviolence).
b. vicarious or witnessed cataclysmic events, and
c. racial and cultural microaggressions. (p. 67)

They suggest persons of color (i.e., ALANA; African Americans, Asian/Pacific Islander Americans, Latinas/Latinos, Native Americans and related immigrant groups) are more likely to experience post-traumatic stress disorder (PTSD) symptomology, hyper-vigilance for or avoidance of racialized stimuli and/threats (i.e., microaggressions) in their environments, repetitive/intrusive recall of ethnoviolent events/acts, etc. Moreover, in various studies of The Prejudice Institute, Ehrlich (2009) reported that people who were physically and psychologically assaulted for reasons related to prejudice were more traumatized than victims of non-prejudice or race-related crime.

There are a number of contexts in which Black/African descent women's status as "worthy" victims lends them to continual exposure to ethnoviolent acts (Ehrlich, 2009). We examine the psychological and physical health consequences of this exposure. As their bodies have been deemed "contested areas for Black/African women and girls as they strive to define their femaleness" and because historically their labor and sex have been used for the economic gain of those with power over them (Williams, 2014), the instances of ethnoviolence and assault which occur in media portrayals in which the Black body is put to work legitimizes such treatment.

ETHNOVIOLENCE IN MIXED MEDIA REPRESENTATIONS OF BLACK/AFRICAN WOMEN

In keeping with Ehrlich's (2009) concept of Black/African descent women as "worthy" victims, particularly in the realm of maintenance of the dominant culture's racial/ethnic and gender status quos, this section will focus on ethnoviolence and media representations of Black/African descent women. We believe that media representations of Black/African descent women that send denigrating messages or exclude them can be categorized as ethnoviolence in the form of microaggressions, specifically, microassaults, which are "blatant, verbal, nonverbal, or environmental attacks intended to convey discriminatory or biased sentiments" (Sue & Sue, 2013, p. 155). Examples of this, which will be presented in this section, would be ethnoviolent media representations that exclude, blame and/or unfairly place judgment upon Black/African descent women.

Although historically there have been and currently are very positive images of Black/African descent women in mixed media, images of Black/African descent women in print, on television, in films, in art, and in online/virtual formats have often reinforced racist, sexist stereotypes. For instance, images of Black/African descent women in print media can reflect what hooks (1992) describes as a "postmodern analyses of fashion" in magazines that embody a cultural shift enabling bodies of Black women to be represented in certain domains of the "beautiful" where they were once denied entry. This representation, however, can be problematic, particularly if the goal is to simply show that the magazine is racially inclusive and not to show the beauty of Black skin and Black bodies (p. 71). hooks (1992) also suggests that models with darker skin complexions often appear in photographs where their features are distorted, while biracial women with lighter skin complexions tend to appear in sexualized images. Additionally, more recent printed images of Black/African descent women of all complexions have occasionally been altered to show them with lighter skin tones, which are indicative of a dominant culture's standard of beauty that continues to apply to women with brown skin (Owens, 2013; Wilson, 2014).

As with print media, television and film images of Black/African descent women often focus on evaluative aspects of their attractiveness, promoting objectified constructions of them that are embedded within colonized socio-historical and political contexts. These images are often in close proximity to the White, Euro-American beauty aesthetic and images of femininity or in direct opposition to them. For example, Black male actors and comedians frequently depict Black women on television and in film; well-known media personalities, such as Tyler Perry, Martin Lawrence, Jamie Foxx, Eddie Murphy, the late Flip Wilson, and, more recently, the comedic duo, Jordan Peele and Keegan-Michael Key of Keele & Peele, have all played Black women. These stereotyped characterizations often present distorted, grotesque images of femininity and depict Black women as angry, aggressive, violent, loud, sexually undesirable and physically unattractive, particularly in heterosexual contexts. Collins (2005) wrote that, "Through this act of cross-dressing, Black women can be depicted as ugly women who closely resemble men (big, Black, and short hair) and because they are aggressive like men, become stigmatized as 'bitches'" (p. 125).

Reality shows depicting Black/African descent women have also been cited as "reinforcing harmful racial stereotypes," and for providing a foundation for continued disrespect of Black women (Abrams, 2013). Overtly sexualized images of Black/African descent women in rap music videos have also been critiqued (e.g., Sharley-Whiting, 2008); the use of Black women's bodies in this context, according to Collins, provides a gender subtext regarding the process of objectification that positions men and women differently; African American men, as the stars of the music videos portray versions of manhood, while African American women are objectified in ways that render them anonymous, "quasi naked" and acceptable only as backdrop within "the Black male-controlled" universe of the videos (p. 130). Collins cites the use of hair extensions/weaves, colored contact lenses, dyed blond hair, silicone breast implants and other forms of cosmetic surgery, to be examples of African American women's attempts to "objectify" their bodies in order to become more desirable to Black men. Consistent with this assessment, the authors of this chapter view this type of behavior as an example of the worthy victimhood (Erlich, 2009) of Black/African descent women *and* males to value and embody White, Euro-American standards of beauty. In this regard, it is important to be aware of the phenomenon of worthiness as one that impacts both genders.

Black/African descent women are frequently victims of public, societal microaggressions related to their physical appearance and beauty, and, unfortunately, examples of these types of environmental microaggressions continue to emerge with regularity, particularly in virtual/online contexts. We highlight three instances for their level of aggression and assault, as well as to exemplify the unchallenged acceptance of such an ethnoviolent stance, even by those one might assume would be more sensitive to these dynamics. One example debuted on Martin Luther King, Jr. Day in 2014 in the form of a photograph posted on the Internet by a White male, described as a Norwegian millionaire, which consisted of a polyvinyl sculpture of a contorted Black woman, dressed in what appears to be a sadomasochistic costume, with a large afro, lying on her back; with thighs crushed against her chest supporting a cushioned seat, and with her legs and feet encased in black high-heeled boots facing straight in the air. Seated comfortably upon the "chair" was the artist's White girlfriend, looking straight into the camera. The intense reaction to the photograph and the accusations of racism prompted swift denials of racist intent by the creator, commentary by artists of color around the world, and posts from anti-racist activists about the meaning of this newest form of societal microaggression perpetrated against Black/African descent women (Dauphin, 2014; Mallika, 2014).

Another example of a virtual environmental microaggression that was connected to an historical female figure of Black/African descent, was the three-minute parody clip, entitled, "Harriet Tubman Sex Tape," created and posted online by African American Def Jam/All Def Digital mogul Russell Simmons, in which actors depicting Harriet Tubman and her slave master engaged in sexual relations that were secretly being recorded by Tubman for the purposes of "blackmailing" her master. The intense backlash that immediately followed the release of this clip caused Simmons to remove it and publicly apologize. In a Huffington Post interview, he expressed "surprise" at the controversy and identified his lack of understanding of the underlying historical, socio-political and gendered implications as the reason for producing the clip (Huff Post, Pop Culture, 2013). This example showed that even heroic, cherished and iconic women of Black/African descent are not immune from microaggressive, ethnoviolent representations of their identities as women of color.

Finally, yet another example of this type of disturbing artistic imagery was the international controversy over the "racist cake" displayed in Sweden as part of a 2012 World Art Day celebration. Circulation of the images via the Internet showed the supposed likeness of a naked Black/African descent female body, with a bloated abdomen and skeletal head in blackface, complete with audio effects of screams from the artist emitted each time the cake was cut into with a large knife by smiling guests of the "celebration," including the Swedish Prime Minister of Culture, caused a great deal of heated discussion. The cake, which was created by a self-identified Afro-Swedish male artist whose art presents stereotypical images of people of African descent, engendered discussions about the creation and use of art in politicized contexts, in this case, to symbolize blackface, female genital circumcision/mutilation, race and indifference to it, and whether an artist's race and gender lends more or less credibility to this type of subversive artwork (Burton, 2012). However, what may be lost in the ongoing discussion of artistic license regarding these examples is the continued presentation and use of the Black/African descent female body in questionable, subjugated and highly disturbing ways, and the impact that images like this may have, psychologically and emotionally, upon women of Black/African descent and other Women of Color.

hooks (1995), contends, in "Art on My Mind. Visual Politics," that the Black/African descent female body has been exploited artistically, through imagery that often reflects colonized, Euro-American or White supremacist contexts that perpetuate the acceptance of distorted, subjugated, racist and sexist depictions of Black female identity (pp. 95–96). According to hooks, Black/African descent women in Western culture are often depicted in colonized contexts as down to earth, practical, creatures of the mundane, transparent and completely lacking in complexity. She also writes, that "within racist sexist iconography, black females are most often represented as mammies, whores, or sluts; "Caretakers whose bodies and beings are empty vessels to be filled with the needs of others" (p. 97). These denigrated, distorted racist and sexist media images and representations are examples at societal levels of ethnoviolence that victimizes Black/African descent women in visual and artistic contexts. The authors of this chapter contend that it can be traumatic to be frequently assaulted by these images. Further we suggest that the stresses connected to the continued devaluation of Black beauty and the lack of recognition of White supremacist contexts that insist on defining Black bodies in denigrated ways may have detrimental consequences for Black/African descent women and girls.

THE OPPOSITIONAL GAZE

In response to the continued potentially damaging impact of mixed media images, hooks (1995) attests that when Black people are confronted with these images, they often "resist" them and "divert our gaze, much in the same way that we might shield a blow to the body." She further indicates:

> We learn to look at the images of blackness that abound in the popular cultural imagination with suspicion and mistrust, with the understanding that there may be nothing present in those images that is familiar to us, complex, or profound. Our eyes

grow accustomed to images that reflect nothing of ourselves worth seeing close-up. As a survival strategy, aware black folks often cultivate a constructive disregard for the power of the image. Some of us just dismiss it. (p. 96)

This tendency to frequently dismiss and/or cultivate a "constructive disregard" for disturbing and/or exclusionary images has been defined as the *oppositional gaze*. According to hooks (1995), the oppositional gaze represents Black/African descent women's "longing to look at blackness in ways that resist and go beyond stereotype"; to engage in the "practice of freedom in everyday life and that includes artistic freedom," which "is always a liberatory act that begins with freedom" (p. 97).

We concur with hooks' (1995) definition of the oppositional gaze as a survival strategy, and traumatic stress response (e.g., numbing) for Black people confronted with ethnoviolent imagery passed off as artistic expression. In the context of this chapter, we further define the oppositional gaze as a culturally adaptive, resilient method of coping with ethnoviolent trauma employed by Black/African descent women as a culturally-based form of self-expression, often in defiance of the repeated instances of ethnoviolence perpetrated by colonized media representations, such as, but certainly not limited to those mentioned in this chapter. Additionally, adaptive behaviors of resisting stereotypes among Black/African descent women and girls must be viewed and interpreted by researchers and practitioners in the field of psychology as being embedded within cultural contexts of ethnicity, social class, education, age, religious affiliation, sexual orientation, and geography. It is imperative that counselors, therapists, and other practitioners recognize and honor the importance of these cultural contexts and developmental identity statuses among Black/African descent women and girls when working with this population (Sue & Sue, 2013).

MEDIA REPRESENTATIONS: EXCLUSION, INCLUSION, AND INVISIBILITY

Ethnoviolence in media related contexts is often indicative of the *exclusion* of Black/African descent women in mixed media as well as the continued, tragic, lack of focus and attention provided to adult women, adolescents, young girls, and even female toddlers and infants who are victims of crimes, including murder, assaults (e.g., rape, domestic violence, sexual abuse and other forms of physical attacks), and those individuals who have been reported as missing by their family members and loved ones. The Black and Missing Foundation, Inc. (BAM FI), which was created in 2008 in response to the lack of media attention and awareness of missing persons of color is an example of a pro-active, much needed response to this issue (Black & Missing Foundation, Inc., 2014) as was the TV One series, "Find Our Missing" (CNN in America, 2012). In addition to being an environmental microaggression because it sends messages that Black/African descent females are devalued in life and death by society, this form of exclusion also falls under the category of direct and vicarious cataclysmic events. Witnessing the experiences of identity-group others' encounters with severe racism or ethnoviolence, that are both life-threatening or murderous assaults and ignored, can be traumatizing for the observer because the fact of being excluded from the social systems' safety efforts reinforces the sense of the observer's vulnerability (Helms et al., 2012).

Moody, Dorries, and Blackwell (2008), authors of the "Invisible Damsel: Differences in How National Media Outlets Framed the Coverage of Missing Black and White Women in the mid–2000s," states that one of the results of the news media's choices of which missing women to cover and publicize (e.g., White, young, upper-middle class women), is characterized as the gatekeepers' agenda, which affects views about the inherent value of people, which is transmitted to the public. The authors link this perspective with feminist theory and male dominant gatekeeping behavior to explore whether race makes a difference in how reporters cover stories of missing women.

A very recent example of this in an international context was the initial lack of coverage of the more than 200 missing Nigerian school girls between the ages of 15 to 18, who were violently kidnapped from their school by an extremist Muslim group called Boko Haram (Kristof, 2014). The President of Nigeria faced harsh criticism in the media for what was perceived to be a slow governmental and military response to the kidnappings (CNN World, 2014), but the international reaction to this event was also slow. *New York Times* columnist Nicolas Kristof cited the attack as part of a "global backlash against girls' education by extremists." Although this tragic event has now received a great deal of media coverage, the crimes committed against the girls, their families and communities remains unresolved and is a stark reminder of the complexities of media representation of Black/African descent women and girls on a global level.

When Black/African descent women *are* the focus of media coverage regarding crime, they are often further victimized by dehumanizing, judgmental stories that invalidate their right to be viewed sympathetically, empathically, and humanely. Examples of these strident negative characterizations can be found in crime-related media coverage of cisgendered and transgendered Black/African descent women and Women of Color that focus on the victims' physical appearance and behavior, particularly in sexist/misogynistic contexts (Johnson, 2012). The trauma of exposure to distorted and dehumanizing media representations can adversely affect the family and loved ones of the victims, and, as discussed by Helms et al. (2012), may function as traumatic catalysts and serve as exacerbating stressors in the types of commonly referenced trauma related situations that occur in familial and generational contexts. Additionally, in cases of crimes that result in death, the processes of a family's grief and bereavement, which is often embedded within cultural contexts, may be adversely impacted, unacknowledged and disenfranchised due to stigmas associated with the loss, which can also have negative consequences generationally (Doka, 2002, as cited in Werner-Lin & Moro, 2004). Traumas of this type may also "trigger emotional reactions that mirror those of PTSD" in clients seeking mental health services or those who are already in counseling (p. 66). We concur with Helms et al. (2012) regarding the importance of trauma practitioners and researchers to become trained in focusing on their role in providing supportive assessment environments when race and racism or culture or ethnoviolence are the focus of clients' trauma. Moreover, we believe that training practitioners and researchers will necessitate redefining trauma (e.g., what is considered to be traumatic in cultural contexts), for example, by utilizing research conducted by Helms et al. regarding ethnoviolence experienced by Black/African descent women, ALANA populations, and its relationship to PTSD, as well as what is currently known about the adverse impact of microaggressions on clients of color (Sue, Capodilupo, Torino, Bucceri, Holder, Nadal, & Esquilin, 2007; Sue & Sue 2013).

HEALTH OUTCOMES

The relationship between experiences of racism and health related effects among Black/African descent women are gaining a significant amount of attention (hooks, 2005; Jackson & Greene, 2000; White, 1994; Wyatt, 1998). The toxicity coming from race-based treatment can cause significant emotional reactions and stress (Jones et al., 2007). Research has shown a positive correlation between racial discrimination and negative health outcomes among Black/African descent women and men (Klonoff, 2014). Direct effects of racial discrimination can result in abnormal fasting glucose levels, hypertension, and physical illnesses (Butler et al., 2002; Dolezsar et al., 2014; Klonoff, 2014; Kwate et al., 2003). Helms et al.'s (2012) research on racism and ethnoviolence as trauma explores how race-related stress mirrors symptoms of PTSD. Scholars have linked an increase in diabetes and heart disease as a growing crisis facing the African American community that is intensified by psychological and physiological responses to exposure to racism (Utsey et al., 2008). Black/African descent women are at an especially higher risk of developing psychological symptoms such as depression and anxiety, due to stressful life events (Pieterse et al., 2013). Pieterse et al. (2013) conducted research based on how Black/African descent women perceived racism relating to their mental health. For example, Pieterse et al. (2013) found that racism-related stress did not predict psychological well-being; rather, it was the frequency of racist occurrences that accounted for psychological distress.

In another study, findings indicated that Black patients often feel that White doctors may not take them seriously and may diagnose them based on stereotypical beliefs, which often leads to mistrust in the health care system (Bradby, 2010). Because of these common microaggressive encounters, Black/African descent women tend to be reluctant in seeking medical care, which unfortunately, leads to an increase in health-related issues (Bradby, 2010). For example, Peek et al. (2013) conducted research based on the experiences of African Americans and their physicians in shared-decision making. Peek et al. (2013) suggests that African Americans are less likely to trust their doctors and less likely to engage in shared-decision making than non-Hispanic Whites, which leads to the dispro-portionate results in their health outcomes. Peek et al. (2013) further states that African Americans likely relate mistrust to "historical legacy of unethical experi-mentation within the United States, a segregated and under-sourced health care system, and prior experiences of overt racism" (p. 2). Peek et al. (2013) states that trust in physicians is based on interpersonal/relationship aspects and medical skills/technical competence. Many participants in their study felt that physicians communicate with them in a condescending way based on their doctor's tone of voice and mannerism (Peek et al., 2013). Some participants in this study felt that White physicians do not understand what it is to be Black and indicate that they are concerned that White doctors may be "experimenting" on them as they did in the Tuskegee syphilis experiment (Peek et al., 2013). Peek et al. (2013) suggests that doctors become trained in both interpersonal skills and cultural competence in order to effectively communicate with African American patients.

In another study conducted by Wagner et al. (2011), Black/African descent women believed that racism indirectly affected their emotions and health. They reported that food choices and portions were consumed as coping strategies for negative emotions relating to racism. Many Black/African descent women report being angry in situations where they are exposed to racism and in turn tend to in-ternalize the anger, only to find out that these negative emotions would resurface repeatedly when they were once again exposed to racial stressors (Wagner et al., 2011). Black/African descent women have also been found to internalize racism because they are usually dismissed by society and are not taken seriously for their reactions to microaggressive encounters. Wagner et al. (2011) concluded that be-cause of negative moods and emotions relating to racism, Black/African descent women often develop poor diabetes self-management and control.

Further, with respect to mental health, Black/African descent women are re-luctant to seek mental health services for fear of being misunderstood and mis-judged (Carter et al., 2011). For example, Carter and colleagues have found that "discrimination and racism are a source of psychological distress and trauma" (p. 2) and that mental health practitioners often do not incorporate racial/ethnic issues in diagnoses (Carter et al., 2011). The Diagnostic and Statistical Manual of Mental Disorders V (DSM V) (American Psychiatric Association, 2013) does not take into consideration race-related stress as criteria when diagnosing PTSD, although Black/African descent women often experience the same emotional dis-tress as someone with a PTSD diagnosis. According to the American Psychiatric Association (2013), in order to be diagnosed with PTSD, a person must experi-ence symptoms following "exposure to actual or threatened death, serious injury, or sexual violence" (p. 271). Given that racial discrimination may not involve actual threat to life, patients who experience racism as a form of PTSD, are often overlooked and misdiagnosed (Carter et al., 2011). Additionally, because racist incidents are often minimized by mental health professionals, victims typically experience heightened anxieties associated with PTSD (e.g., hyper-arousal and hyper-vigilance) (Carter et al., 2011).

Although racial discrimination continues to affect individuals, mental health professionals fail to provide clear and effective ways to support or treat these issues. Carter et al. (2011) conducted a study using the Race-Based Traumatic Stress Symptom Scale (RBTSSS), which measures the impact of psychological and emotional stress reactions to racism. The scale was used to measure the presence of race-based emotional reactions to a specific encounter. Carter et al. (2011) believed that this measure would be useful to both mental health professionals and individuals experiencing racism in various ways:

1. Such a measure could be used to facilitate awareness and recognition on the part of professionals and their clients of how particular memorable race-based event(s) might be related to psychological reactions.
2. To help targets of racism understand the emotional impact of systematic, covert, subtle, and subconscious forms of racial discrimination.
3. And to serve as a psychiatric and psychological assessment tool that can be used to determine how a person may have been harmed by a particular encounter with racism and racial discrimination.

In their study, Carter et al. (2011) found the measure to be useful in detecting the impact of specific race-based trauma on individuals which led to individuals' awareness of the impact of racism. They also proposed that the RBTSSS is promising in assisting professionals in understanding the effects of specific race-based encounters when counseling individuals. They believe that the RBTSSS should be implemented more often, both in research and in direct counseling as a guide to understand how experiences of racism affect Black/African descent clients. Consistent with the focus of this chapter, the authors suggest that the RBTSSS measure would be efficacious for assessment of race-based trauma related to microaggressive media representations of Black/African descent women.

New empirical data supporting the impact of health-related issues resulting from racism found that African American men who reported high levels of racial discrimination and who internalized anti-black mindsets were are at higher risk of aging more rapidly (Chae et al., 2014). The study found that African American men who experienced racial discrimination had shorter telomeres; having shorter telomeres results in a greater risk of diabetes, dementia, stroke and heart disease. Additional research needs to be conducted to assess the aging process of Black/African descent women who are exposed to racial discrimination. As previously discussed, Black/African descent women are already at a higher risk of developing diabetes and heart disease due to exposure of racism and gender discriminations.

In conclusion, Black/African descent women who are exposed to daily microaggressions, which may include verbal and non-verbal assaults, insults, as well as environmental microaggressions, for example, media representations that denigrate, re-victimize or exclude, are at higher risk for health-related complications.

Some women tend to internalize these incidents while others choose to ignore them; both modes of coping can lead to higher risk of physical and mental health concerns such as stress, diabetes, and heart disease. Research has shown poor coping strategies relative to experiences of racism indicating the need for more research on adaptive coping in response to race-based traumatic stress. Mental health professionals also need to be trained to properly assess and diagnose Black/African descent women who have been exposed to race-related trauma in order to more competently serve this population.

CONCLUSION

In this chapter, the authors explored the ethnoviolent treatment of Black/African descent women in the media as a focal point to articulate structural inequalities which negatively shape their psychological and physical health. Deconstructing the effects of media and artistic portrayals on the lives of Black/African descent women and girls engenders ethnoviolent trauma coping with consequences for their mental health and the development of preventable stress-related disease (e.g., heart disease and diabetes). Work with Black/African descent women and girls must consider the impact of implicit messaging about worth and value communicated to them that renders them excluded and invisible in contexts where their visibility would make them safe. The authors highlight the relationship between health and race-related stress coping and underscore the importance of relevant assessment and intervention to appropriately and effectively intervene with clients to facilitate adjustment to a society organized around inequities that place them at risk.

REFERENCES

Abrams, S. L. (2013, June 5). *From 'Julie to 'Nene': The impact of reality TV on Black women.* Retrieved March 11, 2014 from http://thegrio.com/2013/06/05-from-julia-to-nene-the-impact-of-reality-tv-on-black-women.

Adler, M. (2009, March 15). *Before Rosa Parks, there was Claudette Colvin.* Retrieved from http://www.npr.org/templates/story/story.php?storyId=101719889.

American Psychiatric Association. (2013). *Diagnostic and statistical manual of mental disorder* (5th ed.). Washington, DC: American Psychiatric Association.

Black & Missing Foundation. (n. d.) Retrieved June 17, 2014, from http://www.blackand-missinginc.com/cdad/about.htm.

Bradby, H. (2010). What do we mean by 'racism'? Conceptualizing the range of what we call racism in health care settings: A commentary on Peek et al. *Social Science and Medicine, 71,* 10–12. doi. 10.1016/j.socscimed.2010.03.020

Bryant-Davis, T., & Ocampo, C. (2005). Racist incident based trauma. *The Counseling Psychologist, 33,* 479–500. doi. 10.1177/0011000005276465

Burton, N. K. (2012, April 17). *'N—ger cake' flap: Hottentot venus 2.0. When will people learn that blatant racism and sexism aren't funny?* [Web log post]. Retrieved March 15, 2014 from http://www.theroot.com/articles/.../swedish_racist_cake_hottentot_venus_20.html.

Butler, C., Tull, E. S., Chambers, E. C., & Taylor, J. (2002). Internalized racism, body fat distribution, and abnormal fasting glucose among African-Caribbean women in Dominica, West Indies. *Journal of the National Medical Association, 94,* (3), 143–148.

Carter, R. T., Mazzula, S., Rodolfo, V., Vasquez, R., Hall, S., Smith, S., Barket-Sant, S., Bazelais, K., Forsyth, J., & Williams, B. (2011). Initial development of the Race-Based Traumatic Stress Symptom Scale: Assessing the emotional impact of racism. *Psychological Trauma: Theory, Research, Practice, and Policy, 5* (1), 1–9. doi. 10.1037/a0025911

Chae, D. H., Nuru-Jeter, A. M., Adler, N. E., Brody, G. H., Lin, J., Blackburn, E. H., & Epel, E. S. (2014). Discrimination, racial bias, and telomere length in African American men. *American Journal of Preventive Medicine, 46*(2), 103–111.doi:10.1016/j. amepre.2013.10.020

CNN in America. (2012, January 19). *TV one's 'Find our Missing' premiere draws new tips.* Retrieved June 18, 2014 from http://cnn.com/2012/01/19/tv-ones-find-our-missing-premiere-draws-new-tips/.

CNN World. (2014, May 10). *Amnesty: Nigeria warned of Boko Haram raid at girls school failed to act.* Retrieved June 18 from http://www.cnn.com/2014/05/09/world/africa/nigeria-abducted-girls/.

Collins, P. H. (2005). *Black sexual politics: African Americans, gender, and the new racism.* New York, NY: Routledge.

Collins, P. H. (2008). *Black feminist thought* (2nd ed.). New York, NY: Routledge.

Doka, K. (Ed.) (2002). *Disenfranchised grief: New directions, challenges, and strategies for practice.* Champaign, IL: Research Press.

Dolezsar, C. M., McGrath, J. J., Herzig, J. M. J., & Miller, S. B. (2014). Perceived racial discrimination and hyptertenson: A comprehensive systemic review. *Health Psychology, 33*(1), 20–34. doi. 10.1037/a0033718

Dauphin, N. (2014, January 23). *Thoughts on the "Black Woman Chair" scandal.* [Web log post]. Retrieved February 3, 2014 from http://www.huffingtonpost.com/tag/black-woman-chair.

Ehrlich, H. J. (2009). *Hate crimes and ethnoviolence: The history, current affairs and future of discrimination in America.* Boulder, CO: Westview Press.

Hare, B. R. (1987). Structural inequality and the endangered status of Black youth. *The Journal of Negro Education, 56*(1), 100–110.

Harnois, C. E. (2010). Race, gender and the Black woman's standpoint: An empirical investigation of standpoint theory. *Sociological Forum, 25*(1), 65–85.

Helms, J. E. (2011a, August). *Symposium: Trauma, coping, and resilience in Black women, racism and ethnoviolence as trauma.* Presented at the annual convention of the APA, Washington, DC.

Helms, J. E. (2011b, October). *Ethnoviolence and Black women.* Keynote address presented at the 11th Annual Diversity Challenge, sponsored by the Institute for the Study and Promotion of Race and Culture, Boston College, Chestnut Hill, MA.

Helms, J. E., Nicolas, G., & Green, C. (2012). Racism and ethnoviolence: Enhancing professional and research training. *Traumatology, 18,* 65–74. doi. 10.1177/1534765610396728

Higginbotham, E. (1993). *Righteous discontent: The women's movement in the Black Baptist church, 1880–1920.* Cambridge, MA: Harvard University Press.

hooks, b. (1992). *Black looks. Race and representation.* Boston, MA: South End Press.

hooks, b. (1995). *Art on my mind. Visual politics.* New York, NY: The New Press.

hooks, b. (2005). *Sisters of the yam: Black women and self-recovery.* New York, NY: South End Press.

Huff Post Pop Culture. (Posted 2013, August 20; Updated 2013, August 27). *Russell Simmons talks 'Harriet Tubman sex tape' backlash & all def digital launch.* Retrieved June 14, 2014 from http://www.huffingtonpost.com/2013/08/20/russell-simmons-harriet-tubman-sex-tape-backlash-all-def-digital-launch_n_3783281.html.

Jackson. L. C., & Greene, B. (Eds.). (2000). *Psychotherapy with African American women: Innovations in psychodynamic perspectives and practice.* New York, NY: Guilford Press.

Johnson, K. (2012, May 16). *No respect paid. The New York Times' anti-trans coverage and why there's hope for the future.* [Social Commentary]. Retrieved March 14, 2014 from http://bitchmagazine.org/post/speak-out-against-anti-trans-victim-blaming.

Jones, H. L., Cross Jr, W. E., & DeFour, D. C. (2007). Race-related stress, racial identity attitudes, mental health among Black women. *Journal of Black Psychology, 33,* 208–231. doi. 10.1177/0095798407299517

Klonoff, E. A. (2014). Introduction to the special section on discrimination. *Health Psychology, 33,* (1), 1–2. doi. 10/1037/hea0000070

Kristof, N. (2014, May 3). 'Bring back our girls.' *The New York Times Sunday Review,* Op-Ed Columnist. Retrieved June, 17, 2014, from http://www.nytimes.com/2014/05/04/opinion/sunday/kristof-bring-back-our-girls.html.

Kwate, N. O., Valdimarsdottir, H. B., Guevarra, J. S., & Bovbjerg, D. H. (2003). Experiences of racist events are associated with negative health consequences for African American women. *Journal of the National Medical Association, 95*(6), 450–460.

Lopez G. E., Gurin, P., & Nagda, B. A. (1998). Education and understanding structural causes for group inequalities. *Political Psychology, 19*(2), 305–329.

Mallika, R. (2014, January 24). *Artist offers bizarre defense for his racist chair sculpture* [Web log post]. Retrieved February 3, 2014 from http://www.huffingtonpost.com/tag/black-woman-chair.

Moody, M., Dorries, B., & Blackwell, H. (2008). *The invisible damsel: Differences in how national media outlets framed the coverage of missing black and white women in the mid–2000s.* Retrieved March 11, 2014 from http://citation.allacademic.com/metap232099_index.html.

Morrison, T. M. (2004). *Beloved.* New York, NY: Knopf Doubleday Publishing Group.

Owens, E. (2013, February 14). *Beyonce, colorism, and why all of this needs to end in 2013.* [Web log post]. Retrieved March 11, 2014 from http://www.huffingtonpost.com/earnet-owens/beyonce-colorism-and-why-_b2687029.html.

Peek, M. E., Gorawara-Bhat, R., Quinn, M. T., Odoms-Young, A., Wilson, S. C., & Chin, M. H. (2013). Patient trust in physicians and decion-making among African Americans with diabetes. *Health Communication, 28*(6), 616–623. doi. 10.1080/10410236.2012.710873

Peters, J. (Producer), & Singleton, J. (Director) (1997). *Rosewood* [Motion Picture]. United States: Warner Brothers.

Pieterse, A. L., Carter, R. T., & Ray, K. V. (2013). Racism-related stress, general life stress, and psychological functioning among Black American women. *Journal of Multicultural Counseling and Development, 41,* 36–46.

Sharley-Whiting, T. D. (2008). *Pimp's up, ho's down: Hip hop's hold on young black women*. New York, NY: NYU Press.

Shockroc1. (2006, April 16). *Bush doesn't care about Black people*. Retrieved from https://www.youtube.com/watch?v=zIUzLpO1kxI&feature=youtu.be.

Sue, D. W., Capodilupo, C. M., Torino, G. C., Bucceri, J. M., Holder, A. M. B., Nadal, K., & Esquilin, M. (2007). Racial microaggressions in everyday life. Implications for clinical practice. *American Psychologist, 62*(4), 271–286.

Sue, D. W., & Sue, D. (2013). *Counseling the culturally diverse: Theory and practice* (6th ed.). Hoboken, NJ: Wiley.

Utsey, S. O., Hook, J., Stanard, P. M., & Giesbrecht, N. (2008). Cultural, sociofamilial, and psychological resources that inhibit psychological distress in African American exposed to stressful life events and race-related stress. *Journal of Counseling Psychology, 55*, 49–62. doi. 10.1037/0022-0167.55.1.49

van der Kolk, B. A., McFarlane, A. C., & Weisaeth, L. (2006). *Traumatic stress: The effects of overwhelming experience on mind, body, and society.* New York, NY: Guilford Press.

Wagner, J. A., Osborn, C. Y., Mandenhall, E. A., Budris, L. M., Belay, S., & Tennen, H. A. (2011). Beliefs about racism and health among African American women and diabetes: A qualitative study. *Journal of the National Medical Association, 103*(3), 224–232.

Werner-Lin, A., & Moro, T. (2004). Unacknowledged and stigmatized losses. In F. Walsh & M. McGoldrick (Eds.), *Living beyond loss. Death in the family* (2nd ed., pp. 247–71). New York, NY: Norton.

White, E. C. (Ed.). (1994). *The Black women's health book: Speaking for ourselves* (2nd ed.). Berkeley, CA: Seal Press.

Who we are. (2014). Retrieved February 15, 2014, from http://www.prejudiceinstitute.com/whoweare.html

Williams, W. S. (2014). Women and girls of African descent. In C. Z. Enns, J. K. Rice, & R. L. Nutt (Eds.), *Psychological practice with diverse groups of women*. Washington, DC: American Psychological Association.

Wilson, J. (2014, January 16). *Vanity Fair accused of lightening Lupita Nyong'o's skin color, do you agree?* [Web log post]. Retrieved March 11, 2014 from http://www.huffingtonpost.com/2014/01/16/vanity-fair-lupita-nyongo-skin-lightening_n_4608954.html.

Wyatt, G. (1998). *Stolen women: Reclaiming our sexuality, taking back our lives*. New York, NY: Wiley.

CHAPTER 8

"BLACK LIVES MATTER"

Structural Violence, Agency, and Resiliency in Black Transgender Women's Communities

Leo Wilton and Ellen L. Short

I have come to believe over and over again that what is most important to me must be spoken, made verbal and shared, even at the risk of having it bruised or misunderstood. That the speaking profits me, beyond any other effect.

—-Audre Lorde (*Sister Outsider,* 1984)

It wasn't until I was a young adult that I realized that my life would be very different from what I had imagined. I had no idea that I would face brutal violence and structural oppression simply for existing. I had no idea that I could be legally denied access to medical care, housing and employment... I thought the fight for Black folk to obtain civil rights in this country happened over 45 years ago. What I realized is that fight was not for the liberation of the Black Trans Woman.

—-Lourdes Ashley Hunter (*Huffpost Black Voices,* 2015)

Talking About Structural Inequalities in Everyday Life: New Politics of Race in Groups, Organizations, and Social Systems, pages 139–164.
Copyright © 2016 by Information Age Publishing

139

It is not a woman's duty to disclose that she's trans to every person she meets. This is not safe for a myriad of reasons. We must shift the burden of coming out from trans women, and accusing them of hiding or lying, and focus on why it is unsafe for women to be trans.
—-Janet Mock (*Redefining Realness: My Path to Womanhood, Identity, Love, & So Much More*, 2014)

INTRODUCTION

Islan Nettles, a 21-year-old Black transgender[1] woman, was murdered adjacent to a police precinct on the streets of Harlem on August 17, 2013. According to media reports, while walking with two other Black transgender women friends, Nettles was stridently attacked by James Dixon, a 24-year-old Black man, who was accompanied by a group of male cisgendered[2] friends (Murphy, 2014). Before the events that occurred, the group of young Black men engaged in verbal sexual harassment in the form of jeering and taunting Nettles and her friends, initially identifying them as cisgendered women. After the young men recognized that Nettles and her friends were Black transgender women, homo(trans)phobic comments were made by them to the group of women. Thereafter, media accounts noted that Dixon "punched Nettles in the face, causing Nettles' head to hit the pavement so hard that she incurred a serious brain injury that left her unconscious… Dixon allegedly continued to punch Nettles even while she lay on the ground motionless" (Eromosele, 2015). Nettles was taken to Harlem Hospital where, in a coma, she was placed on life support, and died a few days later as a result of the brain trauma. The activism of Dolores Nettles, the mother of Islan Nettles, her family, and Black transgender women's (LGBT) communities through the Trans

FIGURE 8.1. This Photo Illustrates the Community Organizing and Mobilization That Occurred in Response to the Hate Crime and Murder of Islan Nettles.

Women of Color Collective[3] along with other supporters addressed the egregious hate crime that was committed against Nettles—an aspiring and talented fashion designer—including the legal structural barriers involving the mishandling and long delays of the legal case of Nettles, which resulted in the indictment of Dixon (Kellaway, 2015).

Tiffany Gooden, a 19-year-old Black transgender woman, was murdered as the result of being stabbed several times and found in an abandoned building on the west side of Chicago on August 14, 2012 (Jenkin, 2012). One of the residents in the Chicago neighborhood commented, "They said it was a male dressed like a female that they found in the house." It is important to note this description of Gooden did not portray her as an individual, nor as a person, but as an "it," who was "a male dressed like a female." This description denied Gooden's humanity and her choice to express her gender identity in a way that was meaningful to her in life and in death. Moreover, Gooden's body was found a few blocks away from where one of her friends, Paige Clay, a 23-year-old, Black transgender woman, was murdered by a gunshot wound to the face and found in an alley a few months earlier on April 16, 2012. Clay, an "'outgoing and determined' young woman, who had experienced gender-based violence, was recognized for her involvement in the house ball community[4] in Chicago (Kostek, 2013). There have been no arrests or charges in the cases of Paige and Clay and there is a void in information about the circumstances of their murders, which illustrates the persistent erasure, silencing, and invisibility related to the enactment of violence against Black transgender women's communities. In the 2012 article published on The Root entitled, "Transgender Deaths: Where is the Outcry?" the executive director of National Coalition of Justice, Sharon Lettman-Hicks cited a level of indifference and inaction towards violence perpetrated towards trans women. The article cited that Black and civil rights communities were "shamefully silent when victims of violence were [B]lack and transgender." The article identified the Trans People of Color Coalition, a national social-justice organization promoting the interests of transgender people of color as urging civil rights and community leaders to join their appeal to "consciousness and action" and to the Department of Justice to establish a task force to investigate the systemic murders of multiple transgender women of color who they cited as being "attacked for living their truth" (McLeod, 2012).

The murders of Islan Nettles, Tiffany Gooden, and Paige Clay are part of a larger, ongoing, and systemic problem of racialized and gendered violence perpetrated against women who are Black and transgender. This chapter will examine multi-layered structural inequalities embedded in acts of violence for Black transgender women. The domains of stigma, marginalization, and structural inequalities will be explored from an intersectional conceptual framework. A specific emphasis will be placed on contemporary contexts of violence directed against Black transgender women's communities. Another salient component of the chapter will explore how Black transgender women's communities respond to violence and enact a sense of agency and resiliency in addressing this understudied domain.

THE CONTEXT OF BLACK LIVES MATTER

"Our lives begin to end the day we become silent about things that matter."
Martin Luther King, Jr.

There has been an evolving public discourse about structural violence embedded in Black communities that emerged based on the case of Trayvon Martin, a 17-year-old, Black cisgendered male high school student who was racially profiled and murdered by George Zimmerman in Florida while walking home from the store in the evening on February 26, 2012; Zimmerman was not indicted in the killing of Martin (Alvarez, 2015). The Trayvon Martin case received (inter) national media attention involving ongoing protests and outcry in Black communities, which culminated into the Black Lives Matter Movement. Founded in 2012 by Alicia Garza, Patrisse Cullors, and Opal Tometi, three Black queer women, the Black Lives Matter movement—a call to action that affirms Black communities and addresses structural violence—engages the salience of social justice and human rights implications in the lives of Black people (Black Lives Matter, n. d.). Following the Trayvon Martin case, several occurrences of the murders of Black cisgendered men have been the focus of public discourse in the construction of this ideological framework, such as Eric Garner, John Crawford III, Walter Scott, and Freddie Gray, Jr. On July 17, 2014, Eric Garner, a 43-year-old, Black cisgendered man was placed in an illegal choke-hold by New York City police for allegedly selling "loosies" (i.e., individual cigarettes), which resulted in him indicating "I can't breathe" and subsequently dying on the street in Staten Island (Goodman & Baker, 2014). His death was classified as a homicide. John Crawford III, a 22-year-old, Black cisgendered male was shot and killed by Sean Williams, a White police officer, while handling a toy BB gun in a Walmart store in Dayton, Ohio on August 5, 2014 (Connolly, 2015). Michael Brown, an 18-year-old, Black cisgendered man was killed by White police officers for allegedly taking cigarillos in a convenience store in Ferguson, Missouri (Buchanan et al., 2014). Walter Scott, a 50-year-old Black cisgendered man, who was unarmed, was shot in the back by a White police officer while he was running away after a routine traffic stop for a non-working brake light in North Charleston, South Carolina on April 4, 2015 (Glinder & Santora, 2015). Freddie Gray, Jr., a 25-year-old, Black cisgendered man was arrested by the Baltimore Police Department for allegedly concealing a switchblade. Gray, Jr., while in police custody in a police van, died due to spinal cord injuries (Pérez-Peña, 2015).

According to the Black Lives Matter Movement, "When we say Black Lives Matter, we are broadening the conversation around state violence to include all of the ways in which Black people are intentionally left powerless at the hands of the state. We are talking about the ways in which Black lives are deprived of our basic human rights and dignity....How Black women bearing the burden of relentless assault of our children and our families is state violence. How Black queer and trans folks bear a unique burden from a hetero-patriarchal society that disposes us like garbage and simultaneously fetishizes us and profits off of us, and that is state violence..." (Black Lives Matter, n. d.). Nonetheless, one of the contradictions related to how the Black Lives Matter movement was created from an intersectional ideological framework by three Black queer women has involved the anchoring of this grassroots human rights intervention in a hetero-normative, male-centered discourse that places gendered analyses on the periphery. One glaring example of this erasure is the ongoing void and neglect in public discourse about structural violence embedded in Black communities pertaining to Black cisgendered women who experience gender-based violence (Richie, 2012).

Recent egregious illustrations of how Black cisgendered women have experienced multiple forms of violence include the cases of Rekia Boyd, Ersula Ore, and Chalena Cooks. In 2012, Rekia Boyd, a 22-year-old, Black cisgendered woman, was shot in the head and killed by Dante Servin, a White detective, who fired several shots with an unregistered gun into a large group of people while he was off duty, in Chicago. Servin inaccurately assumed that one of the people walking in the group of Black folks had a gun when, in actuality, was a cellphone. Although Servin was charged with involuntary manslaughter, he was acquitted of these charges (Schmadeke & Gorner, 2015). In 2014, Ersula Ore, an English professor at Arizona State University, a Black cisgendered woman, was subjected to excessive force by Stewart Ferrin, a White cisgendered male university police officer for "jay-walking" during the evening. Ore reported that she walked across the middle of the street due to construction. She was confronted by Ferrin and following a discrepancy between them was thrown to the ground and arrested by him, with some of her clothing being unveiled in public. Arizona State University initially supported Ferrin's actions but he later resigned from his position based on the University's intent to terminate his employment due to policy violations (Blinder, 2015). In 2015, Charlena Cooks, a Black pregnant woman, was wrestled to the ground by White police officers following a disagreement with a White woman regarding parking. When confronted by the police and asked for her name, Cooks only provided a first name and was subjected to this severe physical violence (Goodman, 2015).

Furthermore, these pervasive acts of police-related violence have been experienced by Black cisgendered girls. For example, Dajerria Becton, a 15-year-old Black girl, while at a graduation pool party in Texas, was violently thrown to the ground, placed faced-down with a knee in her back, and her braids being forcefully pulled by Eric Casebolt, a White cisgendered male corporal police officer on June 5, 2015; this extreme act of aggression and dehumanization was accompanied by Casebolt wielding his gun at other Black youth (Cole-Frowe & Fausset, 2015). The police indicated that community members in the majority White province of McKinney reported [inaccurately] that youth did not have permission to use the pool following an alleged altercation between White parents and some Black youth (Gross, 2015). These cases highlight how Black cisgendered women and girls have been disproportionately impacted by numerous acts of violence including but not limited to sexual assault (e.g., rape), intimate-partner, and police-related violence and are one of the least protected groups from these horrific assaults (Richie, 2012).

The marginalization of gendered analyses in the public formulation of the Black Lives Matter movement can be linked to that of Black transgender women, who have experienced multiple forms of exclusion embedded in structural disenfranchisement and subordination based on the intersection of race, gender, and class domains. For example, Kimberlé Crenshaw (2014) notes that "These [inequalities] are sometimes framed as distinctive and mutually exclusive axes of power, for example racism is distinct from patriarchy which is in turn distinct from class oppression. In fact, the systems often overlap and cross each other, creating complex intersections at which two, three, or four of these axes meet" (p. 17). The ongoing killing of Black transgender women, as will be further described later, is connected to structural violence in the form of legal, political, economic, health, and educational disenfranchisement, for example, as illustrated in the cases of Nettles, Gooden, and Clay. According to Master and Sherouse (2015), "These [murders] occur at the intersection of racism, transphobia, misogyny and homophobia—forms of discrimination that work together to force transgender people of color into poverty; deny them employment, housing, access to health care and fair treatment from law enforcement..." Therefore, the critical role of understanding multi-layered processes embedded in power relationships based on structural subordination is pivotal to addressing micro-level processes that occur in the everyday lived experiences of Black transgender women's communities.

EXPERIENCES OF VIOLENCE FOR BLACK TRANSGENDER WOMEN

Black transgender women experience increasing disproportionate rates of violence in the United States (US) (Graham et al., 2014). According to a national report on hate violence from the National Coalition of Anti-Violence Programs (NCAVP) (2015), which documented the experiences of lesbian, gay, bisexual, transgender, queer, and HIV-affected communities, Blacks represented the highest rate of hate violence with homicides (60%) as compared to Latino/as (15%) and Whites (15%). The NCAVP report also showed that 55% of the hate violence-related homicides were transgender women, with 50% representing transgender women of color (NCAVP, 2015), and the majority of these cases were Black transgender women (O. Ahmed, personal communication, June 8, 2015). Notably, transgender women of color reported elevated rates of police-related violence, including physical violence, as compared to White cisgendered individuals (NCAVP, 2015).

Furthermore, Grant et al. (2011) conducted a national survey, *Injustice at Every Turn: A Report of the National Transgender Discrimination Survey*, on the discrimination experiences of transgender communities in the US (n=6,436). Importantly, related to police-related violence, findings indicated that Black transgender individuals (n=290) reported the highest rates (38%) of police harassment and assault as compared to other racial/ethnic groups (the data presented in this report was not disaggregated by gender identity for Black respondents). Grant et al. (2011) also observed higher percentages of Black transgender respondents with a household income of less than $10,000 per year (38.0%) and a history of homelessness (41.0%), which is indicative of living below the federal poverty level. The survey respondents with a history of homelessness reported being denied access to shelters (40.0%) and experiencing harassment (61.0%), physical assault (32.0%), and sexual assault (31.0%) within the shelters. Earlier work on discrimination in Black LGBT communities demonstrated that the most common bias reported by survey respondents at Black pride events related to racial and ethnic identity (53%), followed by sexual orientation (42%) (Battle et al. 2002); Black transgender individuals indicated that bias related to gender identity (e.g., transgender) was the most common bias type (58%). Moreover, the overall sample noted that the most important issues experienced by Black LGBT communities related to HIV/AIDS (64.0%), hate crime violence (42.0%), and marriage/domestic partnerships (30.0%); however, Black transgender individuals reported that job discrimination/lack of jobs (45.0%) and HIV/AIDS (45.0%), followed by hate crimes (35.0%) and drugs (33.0) were their primary concerns. Taken together, these findings highlight the severe and pervasive impact of violence for Black transgender women's communities. These acts of violence are highly invisible in national media coverage, policy considerations, and structural prevention interventions (Grant et al., 2011; NCAVP, 2015). These findings must be situated within multi-layered forms of structural violence and disenfranchisement embedded in social, economic, legal, political, and educational systems. These acts of violence also occur within the context of intersectional frameworks of institutional racism, poverty, (trans) homophobia, and sexism.

STIGMA, MARGINALIZATION, AND STRUCTURAL INEQUALITIES

A critical component for interrogating and addressing violence for Black transgender women's communities involves the development and application of theoretical frameworks that are nested within culturally relevant conceptualizations. A critical analytic framework for violence research—based on theory, methodologies, and praxis—incorporates a connection to the intersection of racial, gender, sexuality, and social class politics (Cohen, 2004). In this context, a fundamental dimension of this work calls for a paradigm shift that links violence within interdisciplinary and intersectional frameworks that coalesce with socio-structural factors that are relevant to the life experiences of Black transgender women. Notably, the concepts of stigma, marginalization, and structural inequalities provide a theoretical framework to examine the multi-layered manifestations of structural violence, as located in the everyday, lived experiences of Black transgender women.

The overarching theoretical construct of marginalization, as articulated by (Cohen, 1999), can be applied to violence. Building on the work of Cohen (1999), these fundamental ideas provide a theoretical framework for addressing asymmetrical power relationships (i.e., power inequalities) in Black communities, including those that incorporate socio-historical and –political experiences of "exclusion and marginalization" based on race/ethnicity, gender, sexuality, and social class, for example. Moreover, according to Cohen (1999), a major component of these critical analyses pertain to the duality of examining macro (e.g., external processes) and micro (e.g., internal processes) structures that have an impact on Black communities in relation to articulations of violence. For example, macro level processes relate marginalization associated with larger social structures (e.g., structural inequalities based on legal, political, economic, and educational structures such as institutionalized racism) and micro level processes relate to "secondary marginalization" within Black communities (e.g., based on gender and sexuality) (Cohen, 1999). Therefore, the integration of transformative discourses in addressing structural domains that provide intersectional analyses serve as fundamental interventions in the work on violence. As such, this scholarly work must be at the center of the discourse through incorporating critical, innovative, and transformative analyses that interrogate and challenge hegemonic, Eurocentric, patriarchal, and hetero-normative discourses that pathologize Black transgender women's communities.

Building on intersectional theoretical approaches, an integral component to the study of violence in Black transgender women's communities is the incorporation and application of epistemological/theoretical frameworks and methodologies based on cultural studies (e.g., African Diaspora Studies), gender studies, queer/lesbian/gay/bisexual studies, and sexuality studies. One of the objectives in utilizing the scholarly work of these areas in the study of violence relates to the development of epistemological/theoretical frameworks that provide the basis for incorporating the socio-historical, -political, -economic, and –cultural contexts that have been integral in Black transgender women's communities. As such, theoretical and methodological approaches based on these scholarly areas work to juxtapose theory and practice that is grounded in culturally relevant conceptualizations, which are fundamental to the lived experiences of Black transgender women's communities. These areas provide a critical approach to the work on violence that engage a critique at macro- and micro-levels with respect to the sociopolitical processes that influence structural inequalities in Black transgender women's communities. This paradigm shift has the promise of providing opportunities to engage rigorous dialogues regarding the centrality of social justice perspectives as well as the interrogation of knowledge to incorporate intersectional approaches within the domain of violence.

MULTI-LAYERED STRUCTURAL INEQUALITIES
FOR BLACK TRANSGENDER WOMEN

It is beyond the scope of this chapter to examine the multitude of structural in-equalities that impact Black transgender women's communities. This section will consider some of the core structural barriers for Black transgender women that intersect with structural violence. The framing of this section of the chapter is situated based on the work of Farmer et al. (2006) and Kleinman (2000). Farmer et al. (2006) contend that "Structural violence...describes social structures—economic, political, legal, religious, and cultural—that stop individuals, groups, and societies from reaching their full potential...Structural violence is often embedded in longstanding 'ubiquitous social structures, normalized by stable institutions and regular experience'" (p. 1686).

Education. Issues related to access to education for Black transgender women are critical (Brockenbrough, 2015; Graham et al., 2014). Grant et al. (2011) contends that harassment, discrimination, and violence influence educational inequities for transgender communities, which were observed to varying degrees for Black transgender individuals including women. For example, Black transgender individuals reported that they were forced to leave school based on harassment (21.0%) or financial reasons due to transition (21.0%); Black transgender individuals also had the lowest rates of educational attainment in terms of college (17.0%) or advanced degrees (9.0%) as well as the highest rate of not receiving a high school degree (15.0%) as compared to other races/ethnicities. Grant et al. (2011) noted that "People of color were especially vulnerable to lower educational attainment and lower income, which may be in part due to the fact that people of color were more likely to report having expressed their gender identity or gender non-conforming at school because of the compounding effects of racism" (p. 46). Furthermore, research has shown that Black LGBT youth experience multiple forms of marginalization which have an impact on their educational outcomes (Brockenbrough 2015). Some of the major educational barriers for Black transgender (Male-to-Female) youth include bullying, harassment, emotional/physical/sexual abuse and violence, non-affirming school systems (e.g., invalidation of gender identities through mis-gendering practices, barriers to accessing optimal sexual health including school health programs), as well as biases related to transitioning (e.g., gender identity and/or expression) and "coming out" (e.g., gender and/or sexual identities) (Koken et al., 2009; Raspberry et al., 2014; Rice et al., 2013). These barriers are often compounded with higher mental health inequities (e.g., depression, suicidality), engagement in commercial sex work (e.g., survival sex), homelessness, incarceration, foster care, substance use, and HIV/STIs (Rowan et al., 2014). The negotiation of racial, gender, and sexual identities juxtaposed with experiences of micro-aggressions and invalidations embedded in structural racism and (trans)homophobia have worked as relevant culturally specific psychosocial issues for Black transgender (Male-to-Female) youth (Hightow-Weidman et al., 2011). A significant part of this work relates to the negotiation of relationships with significant others including family, friends, and sexual partners.

Employment. Black transgender women experience significant obstacles to employment. The National Transgender Discrimination Survey Report's key findings regarding employment were that the rate of unemployment was double for the survey respondents compared to the general population (Grant et al., 2011). The survey also showed that the rates for people of color were up to four times the national unemployment rate. Additional findings were that the pervasiveness of workplace discrimination was elevated based on race for Black, Latino/a, American Indian and multiracial respondents, at times resulting in two or three times the rates of various negative outcomes. Some of the major factors involving employment issues were related to outness at work and employment discrimination, which included discrimination in hiring, promotions, under-employment, and unemployment. Workplace abuse was pervasive with 90 percent of the respondents reporting experiences of direct mistreatment and discrimination; 50 percent of the sample reported harassment (Black respondents reported 44%), 7 percent of the overall sample reported physical assaults (Black respondents reported 14%), and 6 percent reported sexual assaults at work (Black respondents reported 14%). Grant et al. (2011) also observed a relationship between workplace harassment that resulted in unemployment and engagement in underground work (e.g., commercial sex work). These data connect to issues of vulnerability and exploitation regarding employment for Black transgender women.

Grant et al. (2011) cited other workplace challenges for transgender respondents, including being forced to present in the wrong gender, denied access to gender identity appropriate restroom accommodations, having been asked inappropriate questions, experiences with deliberate misuse of pronouns regarding their gender identity, and breaches of confidentiality (e.g., supervisors/coworkers inappropriately sharing information about the respondent's gender identity). Respondents also reported attempting to hide or delay their gender transition in order to avoid discriminatory actions, workplace abuse, and to maintain employment; they also reported family members (e.g., their spouses/partners or children) experiencing workplace discrimination via association with them. In categories where race was reported, some percentages were higher than average, as compared to the overall sample.

The survey's data for underground work for income showed 53% of Black respondents engaging in this type of work in comparison to the overall sample (16%), possibly as a result of educational barriers and abuse as well as employment discrimination. Data for participation in underground work by gender identity/expression showed 19% for any underground economy, 15% for sex work, and 8% for drug sales, respectively for MTF participants. Categories for sex work showed the highest percentages for Black respondents at 44% in comparison to an overall sample of 11%. MTF respondents were more likely to have engaged in sex work (15%) as opposed to FTM respondents (7%). The survey also included a category related to respondents whose experiences of improved workplace treatment and performance was connected to their having completely transitioned to their preferred gender identity (Grant et al., 2011).

Based on this report, there is a clear and disturbing relationship between gender identity and expression in the workplace and bias, mistreatment, and abuse. The authors' recommendations for employment linked the lack of workplace protections to a continuum of discrimination and abuse against transgender individuals and called for legislative and executive branches of government, corporations and other employers, as well as labor, for profit and not-for-profit organizations to enact laws that prohibit discrimination based on gender identity or expression (Grant et al., 2011).

Legal. There are numerous major legal barriers for Black transgender women, which often involve the establishment of legal status including legal changes vis-à-vis name or gender identity (Grant et al., 2011). This may include identity documents such as identification cards, driver licenses, birth certificates, passports, social security, educational transcripts, as well as tax and voting documents, etc. Legal status also impacts a multitude of factors, including access to education, housing, employment, health care, as well as parenting and child custody (e.g., parental rights, adoption) (Currah, Juang, & Minter, 2006). These legal structural barriers are rooted within racialized and gendered systems of domination and exclusion based on socio-historical and –political contexts for Black transgender women's communities. Moreover, President Barrack Obama, the first US president to refer to transgender communities in a State of the Union address, initiated reforms related to legal protections for LGBT communities (e.g., executive order focused on federal workplace discrimination, hate crimes legislation based on sexual and gender identity) (Obama, 2015). In this context, one of the major dilemmas experienced by Black transgender women's communities relates to legal disenfranchisement involving the persistent violation of their civil and human rights. These exclusionary practices based on gender identity and expression are evidenced by recent national survey findings of Black transgender individuals which indicate the experience of substantial challenges in accessing government and legal services (e.g., court systems with judges, legal officials, etc.) often enacted in the form of disrespect, harassment, and physical violence (Grant et al, 2011). These acts of violence in connection with legal disenfranchisement reinforce stigma, marginalization, and structural inequalities for Black transgender women's communities, which often facilitate unequal access to services. These multi-layered processes are embedded in power relationships based on structural disenfranchisement, which simultaneously, influence and reinforce routine occurrences of stigma for Black transgender women's communities.

Incarceration. Black transgender women experience disproportionate incarceration rates and over-representation in the criminal justice system as a result of discrimination and racialized and gendered targeting (Reisner, Bailey, & Sevelius, 2014). Current data indicate that approximately one in six transgender individuals has a history of incarceration, with about half of Black transgender people being incarcerated over the course of a lifetime (Grant et al., 2011). Grant et al. (2011) found that transgender people of color, based on interactions with the police, reported higher rates (29–38%) of police-related harassment due to bias as compared to the overall sample (22%). For example, Black (47.0%) and Latino/a (47.0%) transgender individuals reported the highest rates of disrespectful treatment by the police. Black transgender individuals had the highest rates of police harassment (38.0%) and police assault (15.0%) as compared to other race/ethnicities. Black transgender individuals reported the highest rates of arrest/jailed due to bias (41.0%) and jailed for other reasons (47.0%) than other races/ethnicities. Black transgender individuals typically indicated greater lengths of incarceration (e.g., six months to a year, one to three years, three to five years, five to 10 years, and 10 or more years) as compared to the overall sample; Black transgender individuals also had the lowest rates of being incarcerated for under six months than the overall sample (47.0% versus 81.0%, respectively). Black (30.0%) and Native American (36.0%) transgender individuals reported the highest rates of denial of hormone treatments while in jail/prison than the overall sample (17.0%). Furthermore, as Black transgender women have high disproportionate incarceration rates, housing issues are critical considerations in that federal/state prisons and local jails do not adhere to federal guidelines (e.g., being housed based on birth sex rather than gender identity such as in men's facilities), placing them at increased vulnerability for emotional, physical, and sexual violence by prison staff or other prisoners. The recent case of Ashley Diamond, a Black transgender woman incarcerated in a Georgia prison is an example of the challenges that transgender women face in prisons/jails in which prison officials view them as males and house them in men's facilities. Diamond filed a federal lawsuit in protest of the psychological and physical/sexual violence she experienced while incarcerated that lead her to attempt to commit suicide several times; she had also been deprived of hormone treatments, which she had taken for 17 years prior to her arrest. The lawsuit, filed by Diamond's lawyers at the Southern Poverty Law Center against Georgia corrections officials, resulted in a US District Court judge denying her request to be transferred to a lower-security prison. The lawsuit, however, brought much needed public attention to the refusal of prisons to provide hormone therapy to Black transgender women in prison. As a result, Georgia agreed to provide "constitutionally and appropriate medical and mental health treatment" and started Diamond on hormone therapy (Sontag, 2015). Despite this mixed victory and the courage Diamond displayed, the violent and traumatic experiences she and other Black transgender women who are incarcerated continue to endure is unconscionable and must be eradicated.

Health. Structural barriers for the health of Black transgender women involve several areas such as access to health care and insurance, health care discrimination, access to health and wellness services (e.g., sexual health), provider cultural competencies, and medical/surgical transition. HIV/STIs (sexually transmitted infections) is a major health care issue for Black transgender women. Black transgender women constitute the highest proportion of new HIV infections among transgender women (Centers for Disease Control and Prevention [CDC], 2015). Herbst et al. (2008) conducted a systematic review of HIV prevalence and risk behaviors for transgender individuals in the US and found that Black transgender women demonstrated increased HIV infection rates (e.g., 56.3% tested HIV positive and 30.8% self-reported an HIV positive status). Studies also have reported that transgender women have experienced health-related risks, including HIV risk behavior, through the administration of non-prescribed hormones (e.g., liquid subcutaneous silicon injections) by non-medical providers as a method to feminize their physical appearance (e.g., face, breasts, thighs, buttocks) (Lawrence, 2007). Epidemiologic research has shown that socio-structural factors have contributed to disproportionate HIV/STI rates among Black transgender women: elevated HIV/STI prevalence within sexual networks, acute HIV infection, irregular HIV testing patterns, undiagnosed and untreated HIV/STI infections, higher viral load, lower CD4 counts, lower income and inadequate access to health care and treatment (e.g., HIV antiretroviral medications) (CDC, 2015).

Mental Health. The fifth edition of the Diagnostic and Statistical Manual of Mental Disorders (DSM–5) categorizes transgender identity under the diagnostic identifier of *gender dysphoria*. The DSM–5 considers this to be a more descriptive diagnosis than the DSM-IV term *gender identity disorder*; dysphoria is defined as a clinical problem, as opposed to an individual's identity. Gender dysphoria "refers to the distress that may accompany the incongruence between one's experienced or expressed gender and one's assigned gender." The DSM–5 further states, "Although not all individuals will experience distress as a result of such incongruence, many are distressed if the desired physical interventions by means of hormones and/or surgery are not available" (American Psychiatric Association, 2013, p. 451). The revised DSM–5 diagnosis, while potentially less pathologizing than previous psychiatric diagnoses, must be moderated by other salient variables. Chapman et al. (2012) and Morgan and Stevens (2012) cited the importance of cultural competencies for clinicians who provide health care for transgender individuals as a critical but often neglected or absent component of health care professional education (as cited in Belluardo-Crosby & Lillis, 2012). Belluardo-Crosby and Lillis also cite Nemoto, Bodeker, and Iwamoto (2011) in their assessment that the "knowledge of and experience with transgender persons informs a diagnostician's perspective" in providing "gender-sensitive care." They state, however, "The vast majority of clinicians have never had clinical exposure to the assessment, diagnosis, and treatment of a transgender person." The authors, in citing the importance of context in making diagnostic decisions, identify transphobia as common in healthcare settings (Belluardo-Crosby & Lillis, 2012, p. 583). In light of what Graham et al. (2014) describes as the very limited amount of information about the health and well-being of transgender communities of color, mental health practitioners must be diligent in their efforts to become more competent regarding providing gender-sensitive care to Black transgender women clients.

Given the vulnerability of Black transgender women to transphobia, rejection and racism in multiple life contexts, it is imperative that mental health practitioners provide strong, empathic support for clients. In identifying clinical and advocacy implications for their study of resilience of transgender individuals of color, Singh and McKleroy (2011) recommend trauma work that is transgender-positive and responsive to this population's "multiple social locations." Additionally, they recommend that practitioners conduct extensive self-assessment, interrogating their potential biases, degree of knowledge, awareness and skills regarding working with transgender clients of color, "to ensure there is no harm done to clients who already experience intense societal discrimination and lack of understanding" (p. 40). Singh and McKleroy also advocate for the creation of safe environments for transgender people of color that have transgender-positive information that explicitly states a commitment to addressing the impact of systemic oppressions. Moreover, the authors advise that "all paperwork should reflect transgender-inclusive and collaborative approaches to treatment," for example, multiple gender boxes and/or spaces for clients to write their gender identity (American Psychological Association, 2008, as cited in Singh & McKleroy, 2011); practitioners' offices should also have gender neutral bathrooms. Finally, they advocate for practitioners to "actively seek out opportunities to increase access to health care and transgender-affirmative employment for transgender people of color, while also advocating for a reduction of societal stigma and violence towards them" (p. 41).

Assessment and diagnosis of depression when treating transgender clients is important due to their experiences with being stigmatized, discriminated against, and abused. Nuttbrock et al. (2011) conducted a quantitative study using the Life Chart Interview on a sample of 571 transgender women from the New York metropolitan area. The age range for the participants was from 19 to 59 years with 26.8 percent identifying as non-Hispanic Black. The study's findings replicated other descriptive studies that indicate the significance of gender identity conflict/affirmation for the emotional well-being of transgender women. Specifically, Nuttbrock et al. found that gender identity conflict stemming from disclosures of transgender identity in different types of relationships was a very strong risk factor for major depression and gender identity affirmation stemming from the same type of disclosures in these relationships was, in contrast, a protective factor against major depression.

In addition to assessing, diagnosing and treating depression, another important component of gender-sensitive care is the prevention and assessment of suicidality among Black LGBT client populations, specifically transgender and gender non-conforming clients. According to data gathered by The Williams Institute in collaboration with the American Foundation for Suicide Prevention, the National Transgender Discrimination Survey (NTDS) reported the prevalence of suicide attempts for transgender respondents at 41 percent (41%), which greatly exceeds 4.6 percent (4.6%) of the overall US population reporting a lifetime suicide attempt. This percentage is also higher than LGB adults who have reported suicide attempts. The Williams Institute survey cited interrelated risk factors that appear to be strongly correlated to suicidal behavior among transgender and gender nonconforming adults: rejection, discrimination, victimization, and violence related to anti-transgender bias and serious mental health conditions. The Discussion section of the survey cited respondents who reported experiencing stressors related to anti-transgender bias as well as those reporting having a mental health condition that substantially affected a major life activity, showed a markedly high prevalence of lifetime suicide attempts (Hass, Rodgers, & Herman, 2014). Given the history of biased clinical judgment in DSM diagnoses of populations of color, for example, African Americans (Neighbors, Trierweiler, Ford, & Muroff, 2003), the likelihood that ethnocentric, transphobic biases among mental healthcare professionals providing services to Black transgender women may result in incompetent, harmful, and pathologizing health care service delivery is quite high.

An additional barrier to providing competent, gender-sensitive mental health care to Black transgender women is their mistrust of health professionals who may focus inappropriately on the client's transgender identity as problematic as opposed to presenting problems related to their overall mental health and well-being (Samuelson, 2014). This mistrust is adaptive and has historical roots in the abuses and atrocities committed against Black people in the US by the medical and psychiatric communities, and therefore should be viewed in a social justice context that espouses an embedded, ecological perspective of counseling and psychology for Black transgender women's communities (Sue & Sue, 2013). Austin and Craig (2015) advocate the application of a new model of therapy for transgendered populations: Transgender-Affirming Cognitive Behavioral Therapy (TA-CBT), which they believe would be efficacious for use with transgender individuals experiencing depression, anxiety, and/or suicidality. An integral component of this model is a focus on helping transgender clients overcome reticence or distrust of therapy by creating a trans-affirmative culture at the start of the therapeutic relationship. Psychoeducation for clients about the adverse impact of transphobia, minority stress, and systemic and cultural/societal embeddedness regarding their multiple identities is embodied in the application of techniques to assist them in challenging transphobic negative self-beliefs (e.g., that can result in depression, hopelessness and suicidality), and encouraging trans-affirming social connectedness. A focus on resilience is also a part of the model. Thus, TA-CBT's emphasis on what Austin and Craig describe as a "culturally affirming worldview (e.g., a trans-affirmative approach)" to clinical practice is an example of a therapy/counseling that may be well suited for Black transgender women clients (p. 7).

Media. In June of 2014, an issue of *Time* magazine, entitled, "The Transgender Tipping Point: America's Next Civil Rights Frontier," featured the actress Laverne Cox on its cover. Cox, a self-described "proud African American transgender woman," is one of the stars of the Netflix program "Orange is the New Black" (Steinmetz, 2014, p. 38). In 2014, Janet Mock (2014), an American writer, transgender rights activist and author, published her autobiography, entitled, *Redefining Realness: My Path to Womanhood, Identity, Love & So Much More* in which she shared her personal narrative. In recent years, both Cox and Mock have become prominent in popular culture as successful, talented, activist transgender women of color. Prior to their ascendance, the likelihood of the public seeing depictions of transgender women of color, for example, on television was relegated to characters from television dramas, like the "Law and Order" series in which they frequently played commercial sex workers and/or victims of gender-based violence. Transgender individuals have also been depicted in films in similar contexts as marginalized, victimized and vulnerable and/or psychologically disordered and dangerous.

In keeping with the theme of emerging transgender narratives in the media, a non-fictionalized later-in-life White male to female transitioning has been that of Caitlyn Jenner, formerly Bruce Jenner, whose debut on the cover of *Vanity Fair* and televised processes of coming out in an interview with Diane Sawyer on "20/20" and the reality television series "Keeping Up with the Kardashians," has dominated multi-media outlets (Bissinger, 2015; Dooley et al., 2015). White transgender women have historically had visible pioneers and role models including, what may have been the first publicly heralded transgender woman, Christine Jorgensen (Hadjimatheou, 2012; Steinmetz, 2014). Transgender women of color now have their own role models—Laverne Cox and Janet Mock (among others) who actively use their privilege and public platforms to provide solidarity with and support for transgender individuals who continue to struggle with stigma and invisibility in multiple socio-structural contexts. However, as Caitlyn Jenner has received considerable media visibility, the lives and voices of Black transgender women, especially those articulating the importance of addressing the normalization of violence experienced in their communities, continues to be marginalized.

The public and media continue to grapple with engaging in discourse about Black transgender women that is de-stigmatized, accurate, and contextual. For example, there is the challenge of deconstructing long-held binary thinking about gender (e.g., that there is only female and male, absent the fluidity of gender identity). Gender identity and sexual identity are often inaccurately defined as the same constructs. There is also a lack of knowledge about the importance of avoiding mis-gendering transgender individuals through the use of appropriate terminology, gender neutral-pronouns, etc.

Public expressions of transphobia and the shaming of men who are attracted to Black transgender women continues to be problematic, as evidenced by the ridicule projected upon these men in the media for any type of interaction and relationship they may engage in with Black transgender women. In an online essay entitled, "Essays by Janet Mock: How society shames men dating trans women & how this affects our lives," Mock (2013) identifies this type of public and private shaming and attacking of the men's sexuality as evidence of the "pervasive, anti-trans woman ideology"… "that trans women are shameful, that trans women are not worthy of being seen and that trans women must remain a secret—invisible and disposable" (Mock, 2013). Mock further states that the impact of this phenomenon "directly affects trans women" and girls; it adversely affects the way they look at themselves, amplifies their body-image issues, self-esteem and overall sense of self-efficacy. The pervasiveness of this ideology and its connection to the invisibility and disposability of Black transgender women can be linked to similar ideologies about Black cisgendered women and are embedded in sociostructural dynamics related to sexism, racism, and patriarchal gender stereotypes.

Another problematic aspect of the treatment of Black transgender women involves the fixation that the public has with genitalia, which is often narrowly (and mistakenly) viewed as the overriding symbol of gender identity for all transgender individuals, as opposed to having a focus on the psychological, emotional processes of gender identity development and/or issues related to their overall well-being. An example of this is an interview conducted by Katie Couric on her talk show with guests Laverne Cox and transgender model Carmen Carrera, in which a discussion of issues of trans justice was repeatedly deflected by Couric in favor of her desire to focus on the women's genitalia, purportedly in an effort to "educate" others who might not be "familiar with transgenders." Cox responded to Couric's invasive questions by stating that the problem with the preoccupation with transition and surgery for transgender individuals is that it objectifies them and does not allow them to deal with their "real lived experiences," which include being targets of violence, discrimination, unemployment, and homicide. Cox also discussed the murder of Islan Nettles and stated, "By focusing on bodies we don't focus on the lived realities of that oppression and that discrimination" (McDonough, 2014). The opening paragraphs of this chapter contained dehumanizing descriptions of young Black transgender women who were brutally attacked and murdered; it is the pervasiveness of these types of transphobic attitudes, ideologies, projections, and structural inequities that perpetuates the victimization and dehumanization of Black transgender women.

MOVING BEYOND IMPOSED STRUCTURAL BOUNDARIES: BLACK TRANSGENDER WOMEN'S COMMUNITIES, AGENCY AND RESILIENCY

"Every breath that a Black Trans Woman Takes is an Act of Revolution"
Lourdes Ashley Hunter (2015)

It is imperative to focus not only on Black transgender women's experiences of structural violence but also on their agency and resiliency in the face of what can be overwhelming odds for their survival. This section will explore how Black transgender women's communities respond to structural violence and enact a sense of agency and resiliency (e.g., moving beyond structural inequalities and embracing/engaging activism).

Cece McDonald, who was incarcerated in 2011 due to having stabbed an assailant in self-defense during a violent attack, after much advocacy on the part of her supporters who established the "Free Cece" campaign via social media in the US and globally, was released in 2014. She is now continuing her work as an advocate for transgender populations and is the subject of a documentary, *Free Cece*, which was co-produced by Laverne Cox (Erdely, 2014). Cece McDonald is the living embodiment of agency and resilience as a Black transgender woman.

The story of Eisha Love, a 26-year-old Black transgender woman closely resembles Cece McDonald's story; as of September 2014, she was incarcerated in Chicago's Cook Country Department of Corrections awaiting trial for having defended her life from an attack deemed to have been an alleged hate crime in August of 2014. Her advocacy campaign, "Stop the Unjust Arrests of TWOC (Transgender Women of Color), #FreeEisha," challenges what seems to be an inevitability for Black transgender women who dare to defend themselves against gender-based violence: self-defense is murder when you're a Black transgender woman (Vincent, 2014). Eisha Love's story is yet another example of agency and resilience.

Monica Jones, a Black transgender woman activist who was found guilty in April 2014 of "manifesting" intent to solicit an act of prostitution succeeded, with the support of Laverne Cox, the American Civil Liberties Union (ACLU) and others in getting a superior court judge to reverse her conviction. The activism expressed by Jones and her supporters drew attention to the targeting of trans women for arrest by the Phoenix, Arizona police and police departments across the country. Jones believes that her vacated conviction is important but that it is also a "small win" in the larger fight for justice (Strangio, 2015). Her belief is indicative of the importance of engaging acts of activism and agency as integral to the deconstruction of systemic oppression against Black transgender women's communities. Consistent with Monica Jones' victory, the previously mentioned activism of Ashley Diamond, regarding her lawsuit for herself and the right of all incarcerated transgender individuals to receive hormone therapy while in prisons/jails, is yet another example of resilience in the face of oppressive institutional treatment (Sontag, 2015).

In addition to the above examples of agency and resilience among Black transgender women, there is the power of the Internet and social media, which can serve to unite transgender individuals and create "robust communities of support" (Steinmetz, 2014, p. 44) in global contexts. Online websites that focus on Black transgender pride, for example, like the National Black Justice Coalition's website, entitled, "Black, Trans and Proud," provides affirming narratives of "trans trailblazers," including Black transgender women who are role models in the transgender community (National Black Justice Coalition, n. d.). The website "I AM: Trans People Speak," provides images and videotaped narratives of

Black transgender individuals in an effort to empower transgender people and communities by the sharing of lived experiences (I AM: Trans People Speak, n. d.). Social media can also serve as a tool to educate the general public about Black transgender women, as well as their challenges regarding experiences of discrimination and abuse. There is also the potential for political advocacy for civil rights in multiple domains for Black transgender women in a similar context as the progress that has been made for LGB populations.

In a critical review of the literature concerning resilience among Black LGBT individuals, Follins, Walker, and Lewis (2014) cited the recent emergence of research that focuses on Black transgender women's resilience through their connection to "members of their racial community and personal traits that facilitate the development of resilience" (Singh, Hays, & Watson, 2011, as cited in Follins, et al., 2014; Singh & McKleroy, 2011). In their article entitled, "'Just getting out of bed is a revolutionary act': The resilience of transgender people of color who have survived traumatic life events," Singh and McKleroy (2011) presented a qualitative, phenomenological study of the lived experience of resilience for transgender people of color (MTF and FTM; 6 African American) who have survived trauma that engendered a model of resilience encompassing: (1) pride in one's gender and ethnic/racial identity, (2) recognizing and negotiating gender and racial/ethnic oppression, (3) navigating relationships with family of origin, (4) accessing health care and financial resources, (5) connecting with an activist transgender community of color, and, (6) cultivating spirituality and hope for the future (pp. 37–39). Based on the findings of their study, the authors provided relevant, explicit clinical implications for mental health providers working with transgender clients of color (see the previous section of this chapter under the subheading for Mental Health).

In another study, Singh, Hays, and Watson (2011) conducted a phenomenological inquiry exploring the lived experiences of resilience of 21 transgender individuals (11 self-identified as MTF and Black or of African heritage). Their findings revealed five common themes across all participants: (1) evolving a self-generated definition of self, (2) embracing self-worth, (3) awareness of oppression, 4) connection with a supportive community, and, (5) cultivating hope for the future. Variant themes of the importance of engaging in social activism and being a positive role model for others were also identified as influencing resilience among the participants of the study (pp. 23–24).

Thus, emerging research in counseling and psychology concerning agency and resilience points to the importance of self-efficacy and empowerment, awareness of racial/ethnic identity and oppression, connectedness to social support networks of family, activist transgender communities of color, and spirituality, as well as access to health care and financial resources, as salient factors for the overall well being of Black transgender women. Follins et al. (2014), in stating that opportunities for future research are "rich and plentiful," cite the importance of continuing to conduct research that, while not dismissing the very challenging lived experi-

FIGURE 8.2.   This Photo Captures the Community Organizing of the Trans Women of Color Collective at a Rally in Harlem That Recognized the One-Year Anniversary of the Murder of Islan Nettles.

ences of many Black LGBT individuals, focuses on the strengths and resiliency of these communities, particularly in light of "their continued ability to thrive in the face of institutional and individual racism, sexism, transphobia, biphobia, homophobia, as well as racialized sexual orientation and gender identity health disparities" (p. 20).

Finally, consistent with the aforementioned necessity for Black transgender women to have a connection with activist transgender communities of color, The Trans Women of Color Collective (TWOCC) is an example of a collective, organized effort to foster agency and resilience in the transgender and gender non-conforming communities. According to their website, TWOCC focuses on "Creating revolutionary change by uplifting the narratives, leadership and lived experiences of trans people of color" (TWOCC, n.d.). Moreover, the organization identifies its mission as creating safe spaces for trans and gender non-conforming people of color to have greater knowledge of and access to self-care, education, empowerment, and to celebrate community and strategize (TWOCC, n.d.). TOWCC's commitment to creating revolutionary change by continued activism and support of transgender and gender non-conforming people of color, is evidence of the ever-evolving fight for civil rights in the 21st century.

CONCLUSIONS

This chapter opened with quotes from Audre Lorde, Lourdes Ashley Hunter, and Janet Mock juxtaposed with a critical discussion of the murders of Islan Nettles, Tiffany Gooden, and Paige Clay, as well as profiles of Black transgender women who exhibited agency and resiliency. Each of these narratives engages a dialectical conversation about the salience of transcending imposed boundaries through challenging structural violence embedded in Black transgender women's communities. The murders of Black transgender women is connected to structural violence in the form of legal, political, economic, health, and educational disenfranchisement. In this context, the aim of this chapter was to explore multilayered structural inequalities embedded in acts of violence for Black transgender women. A critical analytic framework for addressing violence for Black transgender women's communities involves the integration of intersectional theoretical frameworks that are reflective of the everyday, lived experiences of Black transgender women. Furthermore, the centrality of Black transgender women's agency and resiliency in addressing structural violence is critical to challenging silencing, erasure, and marginalization of their experiences.

NOTES

1. Transgender is an umbrella term that describes a multitude of gendered identities and experiences.
2. Cisgender/ed is a term that describes individuals who identify with the gender that they were assigned at birth.
3. The Trans Women of Color Collective (TWOCC), facilitated by transgender women of color, is a national organizing collective, with the objective of engaging empowerment within transgender women of color communities along with their allies. The purpose of the TWCC is to develop "safe spaces for trans and gender non-conforming people of color" based on these principles: self-care, educate, empower, celebrate community, and strategize (TWOCC, n. d.).
4. House ball communities have been conceptualized as a network or group of individuals that are connected through houses, which serve as familial, cultural, and supportive systems (e.g., fictive kin) for men who have sex with men (MSM) and transgender women of color (Bailey, 2013).

REFERENCES

Alvarez, L. (2015, February 24). U.S. won't file charges in Trayvon Martin killing. *New York Times*. Retrieved from http://www.nytimes.com/2015/02/25/us/justice-dept-wont-charge-george-zimmerman-in-trayvon-martin-killing.html?_r=0

American Psychiatric Association. (2013). *Diagnostic and statistical manual of mental disorders* (5th ed.). Arlington, VA: American Psychiatric Publishing.

Austin, A., & Craig, S. L. (2015). Transgender affirmative cognitive behavioral therapy: Clinical considerations and applications. *Professional Psychology: Research and Practice, 46*, 21–29.

Bailey, M. M. (2013). *Butch queens up in pumps: Gender, performance, and ballroom culture in Detroit.* Ann Arbor, MI: University of Michigan Press.

Battle, J., Cohen, C. J., Warren, D., Fergerson, G., & Audam, S. (2002). *Say it loud: I'm Black and I'm proud; Black pride survey 2000.* New York, NY: The Policy Institute of the National Gay and Lesbian Task Force.

Belluardo-Crosby, M., & Lillis, P. J. (2012). Issues of diagnosis and care for the transgenderpatient: Is the DSM–5 on point? *Issues in Mental Health Nursing, 33*, 583–590.

Bissinger, B. (2015, July). Introducing Caitlyn Jenner. [Web log post] *VF Hollywood.* Retrieved from http://www.vanityfair.com/hollywood/2015/06/caitlyn-jenner-bruce-cover-annie-leibovitz

Black Lives Matter. (n. d.). *Black Lives Matter: Not a moment, a movement.* Retrieved from http://blacklivesmatter.com/

Blinder, R., (2015, February 17). Arizona State University police officer resigns after caught on video slamming professor to the ground for jaywalking. *New York Times.* Retrieved from http://www.nydailynews.com/news/national/asu-resigns-throwing-jaywalking-prof-ground-article-1.2118181

Brockenbrough, E. (2015). Queer of color agency in educational contexts: Analytic frameworks from a queer of color critique. *Educational Studies, 51*, 28–44.

Buchanan, L., Fessenden, F., Lai, K. K. R., Park, H., Parlapiano, A. Tse, A., et al. (2014). *What happened in Ferguson?* Retrieved from http://www.nytimes.com/interactive/2014/08/13/us/ferguson-missouri-town-under-siege-after-police-shooting.html

Centers for Disease Control and Prevention. (2015). *HIV surveillance report, 2013, 25,* 1–82. Retrieved from http://www.cdc.gov/hiv/pdf/g-l/hiv_surveillance_report_vol_25.pdf

Chapman, R., Wadrop, J., Freeman, P., Zappia, T., Watkins, R., & Shields, L. (2012). A descriptive study of the experiences of lesbian, gay and transgender parents accessing health services for their children. *Journal of Clinical Nursing, 21*, 1128–1135.

Cohen, C. (1999). *The boundaries of Blackness: AIDS and the breakdown of Black politics.* Chicago, IL: University of Chicago Press.

Cohen, C. (2004). Deviance as resistance: A new research agenda for the study of Black politics. *Du Bois Review, 1*, 27–45.

Cole-Frowe, C., & Fausset, R., (2015, June 8). *Jarring image of police's use of force at Texas pool party.* Retrieved from http://www.nytimes.com/2015/06/09/us/mckinney-tex-pool-party-dispute-leads-to-police-officer-suspension.html

Connolly, N. D. B. (2015, May 1). Black culture is not the problem. *New York Times.* Retrieved from http://www.nytimes.com/2015/05/01/opinion/black-culture-is-not-the-problem.html

Crenshaw, K. (2014). The structural and political dimensions of intersectional oppression. In P. R. Grzanka (Ed.), *Intersectionality: A foundations and frontiers reader* (pp. 16–21). Boulder, CO: Westview Press.

Currah, P., Juang, R. M., & Minter, S. P. (2006). *Transgender rights.* Minneapolis, MN: University of Minnesota Press.

Dooley, S., Dawson, M., Zak, L., Ng, C., Effron, L., & Keneally, M. (2015, April 24). *Bruce Jenner: 'I'm a woman.'* [Web log post]. Retrieved from http://abcnews. go.com/Entertainment/bruce-jenner-im-woman/story?id=30570350

Erdely, S. R. (2014, July 30). The transgender crucible. *Rolling Stone.* Retrieved from rollingstone.com

Eromosele, D. (2015, March 4). NYC man indicted for fatally beating transgender woman. *THE ROOT.* Retrieved from http://www.theroot.com/articles/news/2015/03/james_ dixon_is_indicted_for_fatally_beating_transgender_woman_islan_nettles.html.

Farmer, P., Nizeye, B., Stulac, S., & Keshavjee, S. (2006). Structural violence and clinical medicine. *PLOS ONE, 3,* e449. Retrieved from http://www. plosmedicine.org/article/fetchObject.action?uri=info:doi/10.1371/journal. pmed.0030449&representation=PDF

Follins, L. D., Walker, J. J., & Lewis, M. K. (2014). Resilience in Black lesbian, gay, bisexual, and transgender individuals: A critical review of the literature. *Journal of Gay & Lesbian Mental Health, 18,* 190–212.

Glinder, A., & Santora, M. (2015, April 8). Officer who killed Walter Scott is fired, and police chief denounces shooting. *The New York Times.* Retrieved from http://www. nytimes.com/2015/04/09/us/walter-scott-shooting-video-stopped-case-from-being-swept-under-rug-family-says.html

Goodman, A. (2015, May 29). *Barstow, CA police slam 8-month pregnant women to ground for failing to provide last name.* Retrieved from http://www.democracynow. org/2015/5/29/headlines/video_barstow_ca_police_slam_8_month_pregnant_ woman_to_ground_for_failing_to_provide_last_name

Goodman, J. P.., & Baker, A. (2014, December 3). Wave of protests after grand jury doesn't indict officer in Eric Garner chokehold case. *New York Times.* Retrieved from http:// www.nytimes.com/2014/12/04/nyregion/grand-jury-said-to-bring-no-charges-in-staten-island-chokehold-death-of-eric-garner.html

Graham, L., Crissman, H. P., Tocco, J., Lopez, W. D., Snow, R. C., & Padilla, M. (2014). Navigating community institutions: Black transgender women's experiences in schools, the criminal justice system, and churches. *Sexuality Research and Social Policy, 11,* 274–287.

Grant, J. M., Mottet, L. A., Tanis, J., Harrison, H., Herman, J. L., & Keisling, M. (2011). *Injustice at every turn: A report of the national transgender discrimination survey.* Washington, D.C.: National Center for Transgender Equality and National Gay and Lesbian Task Force. Retrieved on 1/11/16 from http://www.endtransdiscrimination. org

Gross, K. (2015, June 10). We must make police brutality against Black women an is-sue in 2016. *THE ROOT.* Retrieved from http://www.theroot.com/articles/poli-tics/2015/06/we_must_make_police_brutality_against_black_women_an_issue_ in_2016.html

Haas, A. P., Rodgers, P. L., & Herman, J. L. (2014, January). *Suicide attempts among transgender and gender non-conforming adults: Findings of the National Trans-gender Discrimination Survey.* Retrieved from http://williamsinstitute.law.ucla.edu/ research/suicide-attempts-among-transgender-and-gender-non-conforming-adults/.

Hadjimatheou, C. (2012, November 30). Christine Jorgensen: 60 years of sex change ops. *BBC News Magazine.* Retrieved from http://www.bbc.com/news/maga-zine-20544095.

Herbst, J. H., Jacobs, E. D., Finlayson, T. J., McKleroy, V. S., Neumann, M. S., Crepaz, N., & HIV/AIDS Prevention Research Synthesis Team. (2008). Estimating HIV prevalence and risk behaviors of transgender persons in the United States: A systematic review. *AIDS & Behavior, 12*, 1–17.

Hightow-Weidman, L. B., Phillips, G. II, Jones, K. C., Outlaw, A. Y., Fields, S. D., Smith, J. C., & YMSM of Color SPNS Initiative Study Group. (2011). Racial and sexual identity-related maltreatment among minority YMSM: Prevalence, perceptions, and the association with emotional distress. *AIDS Patient Care & STDs, 25*, S39–S45.

Hunter, L. A. (2015, February 6). Every breath a Black trans woman takes is an act of revolution. *Huffpost Black Voices*. Retrieved from http://www.huffingtonpost.com/lourdes-ashley-hunter/every-breath-a-black-tran_b_6631124.html.

I AM: Trans people speak. (n. d.). [Web log post]. Retrieved from http://www.transpeople-speak.org

Jenkin, M. (2012, August 17). Trans teen stabbed to death in Chicago. *Gay Star News*. Retrieved from http://www.gaystarnews.com/article/trans-teen-stabbed-death-chicago170812.

Kellaway, M. (2015, March 4). *Suspect indicted in beating death of N.Y. Trans woman Islan Nettles*. Retrieved from http://www.advocate.com/politics/transgender/2015/03/04/suspect-indicted-beating-death-ny-trans-woman-islan-nettles

Kleinman, A. (2000). The violences of everyday life: The multiple forms of dynamics of social violence. In V. Das, A. Kleinman, M. Ramphele, & P. Reynolds (Eds.)., *Violence and subjectivity* (pp. 226–241). Berkeley, CA: University of California Press.

Koken, J. A., Bimbi, D. S., & Parsons, J. T. (2009). Experiences of familial acceptance-rejection among transwomen of color. *Journal of Family Psychology, 23*, 853–860.

Kostek, J. (2013, January 7). Trans Woman who thrived in ball scene murdered on west side. *DNAinfo*. Retrieved from http://www.dnainfo.com/chicago/20130107/west-garfield-park/transgendered-woman-murdered-on-west-side.

Lawrence, A. A., (2007). Transgender health concerns. In I. H. Meyer & M. E. Northridge (Eds.), *The health of sexual minorities: Public health perspectives on lesbian, gay, bisexual, and transgender populations* (pp. 473–585). New York, NY: Springer Press.

Lorde, A. (1984). *The transformation of silence into language and action. Sister outsider: Essays & Speeches*. Freedom, CA: The Crossing Press.

Master, S., & Sherouse, B. (2015, January 30). As Black transgender women continue to die, it's time for a call to action. *THE ROOT*. Retrieved from http://www.theroot.com/articles/culture/2015/01/time_to_stop_end_the_violence_against_transgender_people.html

McDonough, K. (2014, January 7). Laverne Cox flawlessly shuts down Katie Couric's invasivequestions about transgender people. *Salon* [Web log post]. Retrieved from http://www.salon.com

McLeod, K. (2012, September 1). *Transgender deaths: Where is the outcry*. Retrieved from: http://www.theroot.com/articles/culture/2012/09/transgender_women_killings_advocates_urge_doj_to_investigate.html

Mock, J. (2013, September 12). Essays by Janet Mock: How society shames men dating Trans Women & how this affects our lives. [Web log post]. Retrieved from http://janetmock.com/2013/09/12/men-who-date-attracted-to-trans-women-stigma/

Mock, J. (2014). *Redefining realness: My path to womanhood, identity, love & so much more*. New York, NY: Atria Books.

Morgan, S. W., & Stevens, P. E. (2012). Transgender identity development as represented by a group of transgendered adults. *Issues in Mental Health Nursing, 33,* 301–308.

Murphy, T. (2014, March 4). Who cares about Islan Nettles? *Huffpost Gay Voices*. Retrieved from http://www.huffingtonpost.com/2014/03/06/islan-nettles-trans_n_4913663. html.

National Black Justice Coalition (NBJC). (n. d.). *Black, trans and proud* [Web log post]. Retrieved from http://nbjc.org/black-trans-and-proud

National Coalition of Anti-Violence Programs. (2015). *Lesbian, gay, bisexual, transgender, queer, and HIV-affected hate violence in 2014*. New York, NY: New York City Gay and Lesbian Anti-Violence Project.

Neighbors, H. W., Trierweiler, S. J., Ford, B. C., & Muroff, J. R. (2003). Racial differences in DSM diagnosis using a semi-structured instrument: The importance of clinical judgment in the diagnosis of African Americans. *Journal of Health and Social Behavior, 43,* 237–256.

Nemoto, T., Bodeker, B., & Iwamoto, M. (2011). Social support, exposure to violence and transphobia, and correlates of depression among male-to-female transgender women with a history of sex work. *American Journal of Public Health, 101,* 1980–1988.

Nuttbrock, L., Bockting, W., Rosenblum, A., Mason, M., Macri, M., & Becker, J. (2011). Gender identity conflict/affirmation and major depression across the life course of transgender women. *International Journal of Transgenderism, 13,* 91–103.

Obama, B. (2015). *Remarks by the President in State of the Union Address*. Washington, D.C.: White House. Retrieved from https://www.whitehouse.gov/the-press-office/2015/01/20/remarks-president-state-union-address-january-20-2015

Pérez-Peña, R. (2015, May 21). *Six Baltimore officers indicated in death of Freddie Gray*. Retrieved from http://www.nytimes.com/2015/05/22/us/six-baltimore-officers-indicted-in-death-of-freddie-gray.html?gwh=D12E9F365FE903DBD37E148FE3318 C78&gwt=pay

Raspberry, C. N., Morris, E., Lesesne, C. A., Kroupa, E., Topete, P., Carver, L. H., & Robin, L. (2014). Communicating with school nurses about sexual orientation and sexual health: Perspectives of teen young me who have sex with men. *Journal of School Nursing*, [Epub ahead of print].

Reisner, S. L., Bailey, Z., & Sevelius, J. (2014). Racial/ethnic disparities in history of incarceration, experiences of victimization, and associated health indicators among transgender women in the U.S. *Women's Health, 54,* 750–767.

Rice, E., Barman-Adhikari, A., Rhoades, H., Winetrobe, H., Fulginiti, A., Astor, R., Montoya, J., et al. (2013). Homelessness experiences, sexual orientation, and sexual risk tasking among high school students in Los Angeles. *Journal of Adolescent Health, 52,* 773–778.

Richie, B. (2012). *Arrested justice: Black women, violence, and America's prison nation*. New York, NY: New York University Press.

Rowan, D., DeSousa, M., Randall, E. M., White, C., & Holley, L. (2014). "We're just targeted as the flock that has HIV": Health care experiences of members of the house/ball culture. *Social Work in Health Care, 53,* 460–477.

Samuelson, A. (2014, August 22). Black transgender women face highest suicide rates. [Weblog post]. *Annenberg Media Center: Health*. Retrieved from http://www.neon-tommy.com

Schmadeke, S., & Gorner, J. (2015, April 20). Anger follows acquittal in rare trial of Chicago cop. *Chicago Tribune*. Retrieved from http://www.chicagotribune.com/news/local/breaking/ct-chicago-police-detective-manslaughter-trial-0421-met-20150420-story.html#page=1

Singh, A. A., & McKleroy, V. S. (2011). 'Just getting out of bed is a revolutionary act': The resilience of transgender people of color who have survived traumatic life events. *Traumatology, 17*, 34–44.

Singh, A. A., Hays, D. G., & Watson, L. S. (2011). Strength in the face of adversity: Resilience strategies of transgender individuals. *Journal of Counseling & Development, 89*, 20–27.

Sontag, D. (2015, April 20). Judge denies transgender inmates' request for transfer. *New York Times*. Retrieved from http://www.nytimes.com/2015/04/21/us/judge-denies-ashley-diamonds-a-transgender-inmate-request-for-transfer.html

Steinmetz, K. (2014, June 9). America's transition. *Time, 183*(22), 38–46.

Strangio, C. (2015, January 28). Hope and resilience for transgender people: Monica Jones victory. *ACLU American Civil Liberties Union of Northern California*. [Web log post]. Retrieved from https://www.aclunc.org/blog/hope-and-resilience-transgender-people-monica-jones-victory

Sue, D. W., & Sue, D. (2013). *Counseling the culturally diverse: Theory and practice (6th ed.)*. Hoboken, NJ: John Wiley and Sons.

Trans Women of Color Collective (TWOCC). (n. d.) [Web log post]. Retrieved from http://www.twocc.us

Vincent, A. R. (2014, September 16). State of emergency for transgender women of color. Stop the unjust arrests of TWOC, #Free Eisha. [Web log post]. *Huffpost Gay Voices*. Retrieved from http://www.huffingtonpost.com/addison-rose-vincent/state-of-emergency-for-tr_b_5792722.html

CHAPTER 9

RACE, SEXUALITY, AIDS, AND ACTIVISM IN BLACK SAME-GENDER PRACTICING MEN'S COMMUNITIES IN POST-APARTHEID SOUTH AFRICA

Leo Wilton

As Africans, we all have infinite potential. We stand for an African revolution which encompasses the demand for a re-imagination of our lives outside neo-colonial categories of identity and power. For centuries, we have faced control through structures, systems and individuals who disappear our existence as people with agency, courage, creativity, and economic and political authority.

As Africans, we stand for the celebration of our complexities and we are committed to ways of being which allow for the self-determination at all levels of our sexual, social, political and economic lives. The possibilities are endless. We need economic justice; we need to claim and redistribute power; we need to eradicate violence, we need to redistribute land; we need gender justice; we need environmental justice; we need erotic justice; we

Talking About Structural Inequalities in Everyday Life: New Politics of Race in Groups, Organizations, and Social Systems, pages 165–182.

need racial and ethnic justice; we need rightful access to affirming and re-sponsive institutions, services and spaces; overall we need total liberation.

We are specifically committed to the transformation of the politics of sexu-ality in our contexts. As long as African LGBTI people are oppressed, the whole of Africa is oppressed.

—*African LGBTI Manifesto/Declaration* (Ekine & Abbas, 2013)

INTRODUCTION

Today, as we approach the fourth decade since the onset of the AIDS epidemic, Black communities globally have represented a substantial disproportionate num-ber of cases of HIV (Human Immunodeficiency Virus) and AIDS (Acquired Im-munodeficiency Syndrome) (World Health Organization [WHO], 2014). South Africa is one of the regions that constitute the highest proportion of HIV infection rates in the world (adult HIV prevalence rate of 19.1% [ages 15–29]), with ap-proximately 6.5 million people living with HIV (Joint United Nations Programme on HIV/AIDS [UNAIDS], 2015). Black South African same-gender practicing men[1] have extremely high HIV infection rates, relative to national general popu-lation estimates in this region of the world (Shisana et al., 2014). The Johan-nesburg/eThekwini Men's Study demonstrated a 49.5% HIV infection rate in Johannesburg and 27.5% HIV infection rate in Durban based on a community based sample of 285 men (aged 18 and older with a median age of 22 and 83.3% identifying as Black); findings also indicated that HIV infection corresponded to gay identification, HIV sexual risk behavior, sex with an HIV-infected person, and an STI (sexually transmitted infection) diagnosis (Rispel et al., 2011). Moreover, another study observed high HIV prevalence rates among same-gender practicing men in Soweto (e.g., 13.2% to 33.9%) (Lane et al., 2011), reflecting one of the largest South African townships where the landmark Soweto uprising occurred among Black South African youth beginning on the morning of June 16, 1976 (Thompson, 2000).[2]

Notably, South Africa represents the first country globally to provide consti-tutional protections pertaining to sexual orientation based on its post-apartheid constitution established with Section 9 of Chapter 2 (Bill of Rights) in 1996, as well as the fifth country in the world to legally recognize same-sex marriage in 2006 (Posel, 2011). Historically, these legal protections were largely in response to the culmination of political activism, grass roots advocacy, and mobilization efforts prior to the implementation of the post-apartheid constitution (Ditsie & Newman, 2001; Gevisser, 1995; Gevisser & Cameron, 1995; Mbali, 2009; Mkh-ize, 2009; Nkoli, 1995; Reddy, Sandfort, & Rispel, 2009). For example, some of the pioneering activist work occurred through the political activism of individuals like Simon Tseko Nkoli,[3] Beverley Palesa Ditsie,[4] as well as organizations such as the Gay and Lesbian Organization of the Witwatersrand (GLOW) and Township AIDS Project (Ditsie & Newman, 2001; Gay and Lesbian Archives of South Africa [GALA], n.d.). For example, the documentary *Simon and I* details key formative organizing efforts of Black same-gender practicing people, with Nkoli commenting, "We are here. We are African and gay" at one rally in Johannesburg (Ditsie & Newman, 2001).

Notwithstanding these historical milestones and progressive legal and political efforts that formulated a global precedence, human rights violations based on gender- and sexuality-based disenfranchisement for Black same-gender practicing people remain a commonplace paradox in South Africa (Ndashe, 2010, 2011; Reddy, 2010; Reid, 2013). Black same-gender practicing women in South Africa experience disproportionate rates of hates crimes through gender-based violence (e.g., "corrective rape") (Mkhize et al., 2010). In 2015, the Brooklyn Museum in New York City in the United States (US) featured the work of human rights activist Zanele Muholi, a Black South African same-gender practicing woman who documents the struggles and experiences of African same-gender practicing women and communities through photography and visual arts (Brooklyn Museum Exhibitions, n.d.). Notably, based on one of Muholi's photography exhibitions at Constitution Hill in South Africa that featured nude African same-gender practicing women couples, *The Guardian* reported that Lulu Xingwana, the Minister of Arts and Culture, brusquely departed the exhibition, indicating that "Our mandate is to promote social cohesion and nation-building. I left the exhibition because it expressed the very opposite of this...It was immoral, offensive and going against nation-building" (Smith, 2010). Furthermore, Black same-gender practicing men and women in South Africa experience stigma, marginalization, discrimination, and violence in connection with socially conservative heteronormative and heterosexist attitudes. In 2012, Thapelo Makhutle, a 24-year-old, Black same-gender practicing man was found dead, with a lacerated throat and his genitals were severed and placed in his mouth, at his home in Kuruman in the Northern Cape in South Africa (Kanani, 2012). Parallel to these human rights violations, the fulfillment of the post-apartheid constitution's legal protections has not been actualized, particularly for Black same-gender practicing communities. According to Reddy (2010), "While we might have an emerging [B]lack middle class, the majority of [B]lack lesbian and gay people are still subjected to major inequalities in our society. This is a factor that goes against the grain of any homogenised view that suggests full equality is achieved, even if LGBT legal protections are in place.... So while the law has opened up a space for citizenship to be claimed, thereby ensuring recognition, inclusion and self-determination, the claim for citizenship is not a special privilege, but a necessary precondition for equal membership in the democratic project and in nation-building" (p. 22).

In the midst of human rights violations, there have been ongoing progressive efforts within Black South African communities that have challenged structural disenfranchisement and subordination among Black same-gender practicing men's communities through a strong sense of agency, resiliency, and solidarity.

Historically, Black same-gender practicing men and women in South Africa have provided strong leadership in addressing the intersection of sexuality- and gender-based subordination (GALA, n.d.). Within recent years, a traditional wedding of two Black same-gender practicing men–Tshepo Cameron Modisane and Thoba Calvin Sithol—was held in the town of KwaDukuza in Kwa-Zulu-Natal (No-femele, 2013) and Zakhele Mbhele, a self-identified Black same-gender practic-ing man, was elected to serve in the parliament in South Africa (Senzee, 2014). Furthermore, in 2013, former Archbishop Desmond Tutu, a Black South African anti-apartheid activist and Nobel peace laureate, while at the age of 81, provided a strident critique about sexuality-based inequalities for same-gender practicing communities at a United Nations Free and Equal campaign, where he indicated, "'I would not worship a God who is homophobic and that is how deeply I feel about this'…'I would refuse to go to a homophobic heaven…I mean I would much rather go to the other place'…'I am as passionate about this campaign as I ever was about apartheid. For me, it is at the same level'…" (BBC News, 2013). These occurrences provide critical engagement pertaining to the complexities of Western international media's negative construction, representation, dehumaniza-tion, and deployment of African/Black communities as "uniformly homophobic" (Ndashe, 2013), while simultaneously recognizing that considerable efforts are needed in addressing the multi-layered complexities of human rights violations, which also exist in Western nations such as the United States (US). These prob-lematic characterizations of African communities, located in Western colonial nar-ratives, marginalize the perspectives of and relegate the substantial human rights grassroots efforts by African same-gender practicing activists, organizations, and movements that have challenged structural subordination (Ndashe, 2013).

Apartheid, involving a racial segregation system (1948–1994) similar to that of Jim Crow segregation in the US, represents a salient socio-historical and –political context for South Africa (Simelela & Venter, 2014; Thompson, 2000). Therefore, based on institutional racism embedded in social, legal, and political disenfranchisement of Blacks and other non-Whites (e.g., Coloured, Indian com-munities) in South Africa (e.g., health care, education, social engagement, etc.) (Thompson, 2000), as well as the regulation of sexuality based, in part, on crimi-nal sodomy laws that were in place historically (Lewis, 2011), apartheid provides a relevant context for understanding global health inequities and socio-structural factors that contribute to the AIDS epidemic in South Africa. Yet, while there is a void in scholarly research on Black South African same-gender practicing men's communities when it comes to examining the linkages between stigma and the AIDS epidemic (Reddy et al., 2009), a key element in addressing HIV-related health inequities in Black South African same-gender practicing men's commu-nities globally relates to the development of innovative models of prevention interventions that are grounded within cross-cutting geographic and culturally congruent contexts. In this context, this chapter will examine socio-historical and -political contexts of the AIDS epidemic in post-apartheid South Africa, theoretical considerations for African sexualities research, structural violence, and human rights in post-apartheid South Africa, and address culturally-relevant prevention strategies regarding HIV-related health inequities for Black South African same-gender practicing men's communities.

SOCIO-HISTORICAL AND –POLITICAL CONTEXTS OF THE AIDS EPIDEMIC IN POST-APARTHEID SOUTH AFRICA

It is beyond the scope of this chapter to provide a full historical trajectory of the AIDS epidemic as situated in post-apartheid South Africa. The overall aim of this section is to discuss fundamental defining socio-historical and –political dimensions that influenced the development of the AIDS epidemic in post-apartheid South Africa. First, HIV was initially constructed as a "homosexual" disease in the 1980s by the South African apartheid government, which did not provide a framework or substantial efforts for intervening and addressing the early phases of the AIDS epidemic (Mbali, 2013). During the early 1990s, with the advent of increasing heterosexual transmission, the premise of the HIV virus as a "homosexual" disease was challenged. Much of the formative discourse about the emergence of the HIV virus involved a focus on conspiracy theories, which—in some instances—were based on colonial legacies of racism (Posel, 2011). During this decade, one of the first major responses to addressing the AIDS epidemic involved the development of the Maputo Statement on HIV and AIDS in Southern Africa (e.g., delineation of prevention efforts, rights of people living with HIV and AIDS), formulation of the National AIDS Coordinating Committee (NACO-SA), and the South African National AIDS Plan, which was endorsed following the first democratic election in post-apartheid South Africa in 1994 (Mbali, 2013). As the substantial increase in HIV infection rates was observed in South Africa during this period, governmental response in addressing the AIDS epidemic was inadequate due to a multitude of factors, including governmental infrastructure, particularly within the context of the complexities of the transition to a new post-apartheid government (Mbali, 2013).

Another major dilemma that contributed to the ineffective response to tackling the AIDS epidemic in South Africa involved government officials from the health sector that ascribed to an initial prevention emphasis that was placed on the cost effectiveness of prevention as compared to conventional science that showed that HIV medicines were able to be utilized in curtailing the epidemic in resource-limited countries (Mbali, 2013). Furthermore, the controversial premise of denialism, or the assertion that the HIV virus did not cause AIDS, and that socio-economic and individual-level factors precipitated the HIV virus, manifested in a dispute between key actors in the government and scientists regarding the origins of the HIV virus (Posel, 2011). At that juncture, Thabo Mbeki, the president of South Africa, was a critical proponent of the idea of denialism, which contributed to undermining HIV research and prevention efforts. For example, according to Thompson (2000), "…[A]lthough Mbkehi was not a scientist, he entered into a controversy about the cause of AIDS, by appointing an AIDS-advisory panel that included several members of the tiny minority of specialists who still disputed the widely accepted theory that HIV causes AIDS" (p. 294). Furthermore, Posel (2011), in broadening this discussion, argues poignantly that the political contexts of sexuality and nation-building under the Mbkehi administration in post-apartheid South Africa provided a complex, nuanced perspective to the articulation of denialism. Posel (2011) noted that:

> Mbeki's so-called denialism produced accusations of bankrupt political leadership, along with international condemnation from a range of places and people....This issue is alleged to have brought the ANC [African National Congress] to internal rupture than any other since 1994....Mbeki revealed his perception that the debate about AIDS was deeply racialised. The call to provide antiretroviral drugs to HIV-positive women, which included a plea to include women who had been raped, he declared had an offensive racist agenda, rooted in stereotypes about the rapacious and violent sexuality of [B]lack men...From this standpoint, allegations about the scale of the epidemic and its sexual vectors—including rape—rested on racist renditions of [B]lack sexuality; to speak about the epidemic in sexual terms carried the accusation of racism. (pp. 135–137)

Following this period, under the current leadership of South African President Jacob Zuma, much of the work on addressing the AIDS epidemic has involved the development of antiretroviral therapies (Mbali, 2013).

THEORETICAL CONSIDERATIONS FOR AFRICAN SEXUALITIES RESEARCH FOR BLACK SOUTH AFRICAN SAME-GENDER PRACTICING MEN'S COMMUNITIES: THE NEED TO UNPACK RACISM, COLONIALISM, AND HETERONORMATIVITY

The building of knowledge on African sexualities has been based, in part, on epistemological and theoretical frameworks in biomedical and social science research that have not incorporated interdisciplinary and intersectional approaches in the study of HIV-related health inequities in a systematic or substantive way for Black South African same-gender practicing men's communities. A significant body of research (Lewis, 2011; Nyanzi, 2011a,b; Posel, 2011; Ratele, 2011; Tamale, 2011a) is relevant here and provides an account of the salience of incorporating intersectional and interdisciplinary approaches as a basis to better understand and develop theoretical formulations that address health inequities within relevant socio-structural domains. In this context, Tamale (2011b) raises several critical points regarding the construct of African sexualities involving the importance of examining the intersection of sexuality and gender—as situated in culture and societal contexts—based on gender systems, reinforcement of power relations (e.g., dominant and subordinate), engaging pluralities of African sexualities that move beyond constricted essentialist binary oppositions in research on sexualities, and unpacking Western colonial hegemony and legacies in the formulation and production of knowledge and theoretical frameworks about African sexualities. According to Tamale (2011b), "The historical trajectory of research on African sexualities began from a place where colonial and imperial interests, biases and agendas defined their parameters in damaging ways. Conceptualised within a tripartite framework of morals, reproduction and dysfunction, the sexualities of Africans were largely constructed as immoral, lascivious and primitive" (pp. 29–30). Moreover, Tamale (2011b) contends that the "colonising project" embedded in research on African sexualities has been situated in the field of public health in HIV and AIDS research. Tamale (2011b) indicates that "...HIV provided the opportunity for a resurgence of the colonial mode of studying sexuality in Africa—racist, moralistic, paternalistic and steeped in liberal thinking...The discourse of 'risk cultural practices' was so intimately bound to the theories and explanations that had emerged on the continent that it became a main resource for public health advocates and policy-makers" (p. 21). However, at the same time, Ndashe (2010) points out that HIV prevention strategies, focused on articulating the salience of documenting the increased HIV vulnerabilities for African same-gender practicing men, have provided a significant formative step in establishing visibility for this often marginalized group. For example, according to Ndashe (2010), "In official policy it has led many states to acknowledge that the community exists and that resources needed to be allocated to cater to their health needs" (p. 8). In particular, Nadashe (2010) contends that the ultimate aim is to develop a solid trajectory for integrating human rights as a core framework for work with African same-gender practicing men's communities.

Furthermore, Lewis (2011), in problematizing the construction of African masculinities and myths based on ideals of sexual deviance, examines the influence of scientific racism on Western medicine (e.g., development of racialized classification systems embedded in hierarchical ordering systems with African people being placed at the lowest realm of the hierarchy). This work can be positioned within scholarly research on the development of the racial worldview as an ideological framework that indicates that race functions based on hierarchies to categorize people into biological and exclusive (unequal) groups that ascribe a binary of superior and inferior (Smedley & Smedley, 2011). More specifically, Lewis (2011) discusses how the sexualities of Khoisan men from southern Africa, for example, were negatively constructed by Western scientists based on a problematic genetics discourse (e.g., constructing the men as being born with one testicle as a basis to denote biological inferiority). The idea of sexual potency of African men based on Eugenic notions was also used to reinforce subordination through power relationships. Lewis (2011) notes that: "Violent methods of policing, punishing or institutionalising [B]lack male bodies was therefore rationalised by beliefs about the rapacity of [B]lack male sexual desire" (p. 203). Furthermore, Lewis argues that a framework based on binary oppositions was utilized to formulate a heteronormative construction of African male sexualities: "African sexuality, therefore, was often defined in relation to reproduction, with the assumption being that Africans could not possibly display homoerotic desires or agencies, which were associated with sophisticated human desires and eroticism" (p. 208). Moreover, building on the work of Foucault (1991) based on the concept of governmentality (e.g., interface of governance [structural] and individuals/systemic processes in the regulation of sexualities), Nyanzi (2011b) contends that the construction of "'otherness'" was used as an ideological framework to reinforce Western superiority and dominance of African peoples in addition to the development of sexual hierarchies. To challenge the faulty logic of essentialist frameworks, Lewis (2011) notes, "Transgressive models in the representation of African sexualities have therefore sought to extricate African sexuality from binaries that define heterosexuality as normatively African and homosexuality as deviant and Western" (p. 209).

STRUCTURAL VIOLENCE AND HUMAN RIGHTS IN POST-APARTHEID SOUTH AFRICA

The analytic probing of colonial frameworks, as described in the previous section, is germane in understanding the nexus of structural violence and human rights considerations that are situated in broader systems of power and domination at the macro-level (e.g., economic, political, legal, health systems) for Black same-gender practicing men's communities in post-apartheid South Africa. In particular, research has demonstrated that structural violence impacts global HIV-related health inequities (Drobac et al., 2013; Farmer, 2005), including human rights violations that facilitate HIV vulnerabilities among Black South African same-gender practicing men's communities (e.g., stigma, discrimination, inequalities, inadequate access to optimal health care, including primary and secondary HIV prevention services) (International Gay and Lesbian Human Rights Commission [IGLHRC], 2007). According to Farmer et al. (2006), "The term 'structural violence' is one way of describing social arrangements that put individuals and populations in harm's way. The arrangements are structural because they are embedded in the political and economic organization of our social world; they are violent because they cause injury to people" (p. 1686). Similarly, Kleinman (2010) articulated that the concept of social suffering as a theoretical framework focused on four components: (1) socio-economic and –political structures influence disease (e.g., interrelationship between structural violence and HIV-related inequities), (2) role of social institutions in contributing to social suffering (e.g., health care institutions such as hospitals and clinics), (3) concepts of pain and suffering involve the individual but also the family and social networks of the individual (e.g., group-level processes that influence suffering), and (4) integration of health and social issues that utilize a multi-faceted approach in addressing these domains (e.g., economic disenfranchisement and high HIV infection rates among Black South African same-gender practicing men). In addition, Kleinman (2000) notes that, "The term structural violence has been used to designate people who experience violence (and violation) owing to extreme poverty. That violence includes the highest rates of disease and death, unemployment, homelessness, lack of education, powerlessness, a shared fate of misery, and the day-to-day violence of hunger, thirst, and bodily pain" (p. 227). Importantly, a substantial proportion of Black South Africans experience considerable economic disenfranchisement with high rates of poverty (e.g., extreme poverty) and unemployment (Alexander, 2013). Building on this idea, the work of Mullings and Schulz (2005) is relevant here and provides an account of the significance of incorporating intersectional approaches as a mechanism to better understand and to develop theoretical formulations that address health inequities within the socio-structural contexts of communities: ." . . . Intersectional theory views race, gender, class [and sexuality] not as fixed and discrete categories or as properties of individuals but as social constructs that both reflect and reinforce unequal relationships between classes, racial groups, genders, [and sexualities]" (p. 373).

Furthermore, Kleinman (2000) indicates that micro-level processes, or the "violences of everyday life," are embedded in structural forces. For example, Kleinman (2000) notes that "The ethnography of social violence also implicates the social dynamics of everyday practices as the appropriate site to understand how larger orders of social force come together with micro-contexts of local power to shape human problems in ways that are resistant to the standard approaches of policies and intervention programs" (p. 227). In this context, global health equity involves examining how macro-level or structural forces work in the everyday lives of people and communities (e.g., with a key emphasis on exploring how disenfranchisement in connection with how resilience, empowerment, and grassroots organizing is manifested at the community level). Global health equity also focuses on investigating power relations that have an impact on communities that experience disenfranchisement based on what Farmer (2005) or Crenshaw (2014) refer to as social axes (e.g., race, gender, social class, sexuality, religion, etc.). For example, Farmer et al. (2013) contend that "Beyond the direct experiences of individuals are social, political, and economic forces that drive up the risk of ill health for some while sparing others" (p. 9) [and] "The health of individuals and populations is influenced by complex social and structural forces; addressing the roots of ill health—including poverty, inequality, and environmental degradation—requires a broad-based agenda of social change" (p. 10).

Building on this construct of structural violence, research has posited that structural violence intersects with human rights violations (Ho, 2007), which contribute to vulnerability to HIV transmission risk (IGLHRC, 2007; World Health Organization, 2015). In this regard, the Universal Declaration of Human Rights, endorsed by the United Nations General Assembly in 1948, provides a relevant framework for human rights considerations (Clapham, 2007). In particular, South Africa had abstained during the voting for the adoption of the Universal Declaration of Human Rights, which was viewed as a mechanism to maintain the racialized system of apartheid. Based on the principles of dignity, liberty, equality, and personhood, the Universal Declaration of Human Rights articulated the salience of individual rights, human rights with respect to defense, civil and political society (e.g., Freedom of movement), spiritual, public, and political freedoms (e.g., religion), and social, economic, and cultural rights (Clapham, 2007). According to Ho (2007), "The theory of structural violence provides a useful framework for the understanding of structural violations of human rights, through an examination of how structures constrain agency to the extent that fundamental human needs are unattainable" (p. 3). The International Human Rights Gay and Lesbian Commission (2007) notes that structural disenfranchisement increases HIV vulnerabilities for Black South African same-gender practicing people involving several human rights principles. Some of the principles that have direct applicability to Black same-gender men's communities include: freedom from unfair discrimination; rights of individuals deprived of their liberty; rights to integrity, dignity, and security of the person; freedom of expression; freedom of association and assembly; right to health; non-discrimination and equality in health services; right to health-related information; right to access means of maintaining sexual health; right to an adequate standard of living; and right to housing.

ADDRESSING HIV-RELATED GLOBAL HEALTH INEQUITIES FOR BLACK SOUTH AFRICAN SAME-GENDER PRACTICING MEN'S COMMUNITIES

Addressing human rights as a framework in understanding HIV-related health care delivery is vital for Black same-gender practicing men's communities in South Africa. Health care delivery cannot be actualized without understanding the intricate underpinnings of addressing structural violence in its broadest form involving macro-level structures that produce structural inequalities (e.g., economic, legal, political, educational systems). Health care delivery must be understood within the context of underlying structural causes of HIV/AIDS as a human rights framework from the standpoint of structural violence. For example, as articulated by Basilico et al. (2013), the emergence of the Alma-Ata International Conference on Primary Health Care (PHC) in 1978 (e.g., access to health care is a right, concept of 'appropriate technology' as a basis to strengthen health care systems, 'critique of medical elitism' to promote community involvement and agency in health care delivery systems, social and economic development through the establishment of primary health care delivery would strengthen intersecting structural systems, comprehensive definition of primary health care) provided a framework for a critique of micro- and –macro level processes and power structures that influence global health equities, particularly in resource-limited communities. In this context, Basilico et al. (2013) contended that the spirit of Alma-Ata was not fully actualized: "The bold vision of Alma-Ata foundered for several reasons. Of great importance, the Alma-Ata Declaration did not specify who would pay for or implement primary health care scale-up worldwide. Signers pledged support for the abstract principles of PHC without a parallel commitment to implementation..." (pp. 80–81). However, the work of Alma-Ata was instrumental through the international alignment of countries as a basis to provide a human rights framework for a critique of macro- and-micro level processes and power structures that have an impact on addressing global health equities to undertake the critical problem of access to health care as a fundamental right.

Moreover, health care delivery may have barriers that prevent understanding the structural contexts of these domains involving macro-level or systemic structures that generate inequalities based on economic and political systems, for example. In addition, the development and engagement of knowledge about the local socio-cultural contexts in which health care delivery occurs is paramount to addressing the needs of Black same-gender practicing men's communities in post-apartheid South Africa. This is important because prevention experts and strategists often attempt to apply a Western model or framework to African peoples in the provision of health services in resource-limited countries (Airhihenbuwa & Webster, 2004), which is often implemented based on the idea of a perceived universal, cost-effective model (Becker et al., 2013). As a result, these models are insufficient and often pathologize the communities that are being served. In particular, the local context is germane in understanding the conceptual frameworks (e.g., cultural values and worldviews) of communities in resource-limited contexts.

It is important to note that culturally-relevant health care delivery work occurs within a context of significant structural barriers (e.g., inadequate access to HIV medications, stigma, marginalization, and complexities of HIV prevention such as HIV testing and engagement in culturally-grounded HIV care). According to Drobac et al. (2013), "When the first AIDS drugs became available in the mid–1990s, skeptics claimed that they were too expensive for poor people. Others argued that stigma would prevent people living with AIDS from seeking care at all and that providers should therefore focus solely on education and prevention" (p. 156). For example, the elements of the Partners in Health's community-based HIV/AIDS care delivery (e.g., enhancing access to primary health care; provision of health care and education for those who experienced poverty; building community partnerships; working on fundamental social and economic community needs; strengthening of public sector health systems; addressing the needs of people in the local community; building technological and communication systems; and distributing global health delivery systems knowledge learned) also involved providing holistic social support (e.g., transportation and food expenses in addition to the provision of "observed therapy" such as observations of adherence to prescribed medications by community health workers). The HIV Equity Initiative illustrated that HIV/AIDS prevention and care was beneficial to the community, which enhanced HIV care delivery systems. As a result, for example, hospital infrastructures were strengthened by building these multi-layered systems while simultaneously addressing the socio-structural needs of communities (Drobac et al. (2013).

Overall, in order to provide optimal services for Black South African same-gender practicing men's communities, a holistic approach is needed that incorporates a focus on structural violence. The aim here is to engage a human rights framework that addresses the effects of social structures that disenfranchise communities. According to Farmer et al. (2013), "The good news is that such biosocial understandings are far more 'actionable' than is widely recognized. There is already a vast and growing array of diagnostic and therapeutic tools born of scientific research; it is possible to use these tools in a manner informed by an understanding of structural violence and its impact on disease distribution and on every step of the process leading from diagnosis to effective care" (p. 2). Kim et al. (2013) also addressed this issue by discussing the problem of the "implementation bottleneck" (e.g., the routing of substantial amounts of resources into global health projects where the delivery and implementation yield is intangible due to inadequate health infrastructure) and "complex strategy problems." For example, "complex strategy problems" involve research and conceptual frameworks pertaining to health care delivery systems necessitating to being applicable and available to global health practitioners. Kim et al. (2013) presented case examples related to Peru, Lesotho, and Swaziland to illustrate his point with respect to accessing funds and building infrastructures to address global health inequities.

A view of global health that critically includes the US provides opportunities for changing our understanding of medicine and public health within its borders. First, there has been a salient socio-historical and –political context related to grassroots advocacy and community mobilization that has influenced this idea. Much of this work has translated into greater health care access, based on activism, for marginalized communities that experience extreme poverty—although there is considerable work that needs to be done in this area in addressing global health inequities. For example, Basilico et al. (2013) states that: "Advancing global health equity demands broad-based and transnational movements….The past few decades have also furnished examples of effective global health activism focused on increasing access to modern medicine and advancing a broader movement for social and economic rights" (pp. 340–341). In addition, the essay, "Realigning Health with Care," Onie, Farmer, & Behforouz (2012) raise critical issues related to the need to expand how we think about product (e.g., redefining how health care is conceptualized such as core necessities related to housing, food, and access to clean water, for example), place (e.g., context and redefining of the concept of place in which health care is provided), and provider (e.g., broadening definitions of health care provider such as local healers and indigenous healing practices). Indeed, according to Onie et al. (2012), "In the last two decades, some health care organizations in the United States have developed delivery models based on more expansive definitions of product, place, and provider…" (e.g., Prevention and Access to Care and Treatment [PACT] program). Moreover, Onie et al. (2012) provide adept illustrations of approaches/strategies that have been utilized related to this area (e.g., Partners in Health focused on people living with HIV and AIDS including integrating accompaniment principles through work with community health workers such as the development of equitable and human rights-oriented partnerships with institutions that communities recognize as reflecting and articulating their objectives and interests.

CONCLUSIONS

Since the onset of the AIDS epidemic, Black communities globally have experienced substantial HIV-related health inequities. There has been a significant void in scholarly research on Black South African same-gender practicing men's communities within the context of the AIDS epidemic. Although South Africa provided a global precedence for the establishment of legal protections based on sexual orientation, ongoing human rights violations occur for Black same-gender practicing men's communities in South Africa as a result of sexuality-related stigma and marginalization. At the same time, there have been progressive efforts within Black South African communities that have challenged structural subordination to provide solidarity with Black same-gender practicing men's communities. In addition, there have been significant limitations in the conceptual frameworks utilized in research on African sexualities for Black South African same-gender practicing men. Traditional models used in research on HIV-related health inequities have not integrated culturally relevant conceptualizations at the core of the analyses. As research has demonstrated that structural violence impacts global HIV-related health inequities, including human rights violations that facilitate HIV vulnerabilities among Black same-gender practicing men's communities, emphasis needs to be placed on these structural determinants. A basic premise of this work involves a paradigm shift that integrates intersectional and interdisciplinary theoretical and methodological approaches in the study of HIV-related health inequities in Black South African same-gender practicing men's communities. One of the core ideas put forth in the development of this work relates to a focus on structural violence based on the intersection of socio-structural factors based on race, culture, gender, social class, sexuality, language, and religion within the context of HIV prevention in Black South African practicing men's communities

NOTES

1.   For the purposes of this chapter, the term same gender practicing men refers to people who practice male-to-male sexual behavior with other men. Although the terms gay and lesbian, for example, have been well documented in the histories of "queer" liberation movements and utilized in contemporary vernacular in South Africa (Gevisser & Cameron, 1995), these identity constructions are based on Western sexuality-based frameworks located in colonial legacies. According to Tamale (2011a), "The dominance of Western theories and perspectives on sexuality stud-

ies and the fact that the main languages of academia are colonial have serious implications for rapidly growing sexualities scholarship on the [African] continent. African feminists and other change agents...constantly struggle to overcome the limitations and encumbrances that come with creating and disseminating cultural-specific knowledge in a foreign colonial language. They understand the capacity of language to confer power through naming and conveying meaning and nuance to sexuality concepts. Concepts such as silence, restraint, choice, gay, lesbian, coming out and drag queen, for example, all carry specific social meanings steeped in Western ideology and traditions" (p. 3). However, the author of this chapter recognizes that the construction of same gender practicing men also constitutes limitations based, in part, on epidemiologic and epistemological frameworks (Nyanzi, 2011a). For example, Boyce Davies (1994), in exploring how Black women's writing engages a (re) negotiation of "ideologies and terminologies" contends that: "The terms that we use to name ourselves...carry their strings of echoes and inscriptions. Each represents an original misnaming and the simultaneous constant striving of the dispossessed for full representation. Each therefore must be used provisionally; each must be subject to new analyses, new questions, and new understandings if we are to unlock some of the narrow terms of the discourses in which we are inscribed. In other words, at each arrival at a definition, we begin a new analysis, a new departure, a new interrogation of meaning, new contradictions" (p. 5). This conceptual framework articulated by Boyce Davies provides applicability to the formative usage of the term Black South African same gender practicing men in this chapter.

2. The Soweto uprisings, also referred to as 16 June, consisted of a multitude of protests of several thousand Black South African youth, which were facilitated by the youth, in Soweto beginning on the morning of June 16, 1976. The youth were protesting the apartheid state-sanctioned usage of the Afrikaans language in the educational system. The Soweto uprisings have been recognized as a critical component of the anti-apartheid movement (Thompson, 2000).

3. The major aspects of the life of Simon Tseko Nkoli cannot be described in one paragraph. However, the objective here is to provide the reader with a brief context of his life. Nkoli was born in Soweto on November 26, 1957. He was a Black South African same-gender practicing man who was a human rights activist (anti-apartheid, gay, and AIDS). In 1984, Nkoli was arrested with 21 colleagues who were involved in the anti-apartheid movement. This group was referred to as the Delmas 22. He was charged with treason (Delmas Treason Trial) by the apartheid government in South Africa. Nkoli is well known for "coming out" as a same-gender practicing man while in prison, which had a substantial im-

pact on the African National Congress (ANC). He engaged in grassroots activism that focused on the adoption of the sexual orientation clause in the Bill of Rights in the post-apartheid South African Constitution. He was a founder of GLOW (Gay and Lesbian Organisation of the Witwatersrand). He was one of the first African gay men who were living with HIV to publicly disclosure his HIV status. He died on November 30, 1998 due to AIDS-related complexities (GALA, n.d.; Ditsie & Newman, 2001).

4. Beverley Palesa Ditsie is a Black South African same-gender practicing women who was born in Orlando, West Soweto. She is a human rights activist. Ditsie is also a musician (e.g., plays the guitar and sings), actress, writer, and filmmaker. She is one of the filmmakers who produced the documentary *Simon and I* that chronicles the life of Simon Tseko Nkoli, her life, as well as the grassroots mobilization efforts of same-gender practicing individuals and communities in South Africa. Based on her activism, Ditsie participated in the Fourth World Conference on Women in Beijing in 1995. She delivered a speech at the conference and indicated "Lesbian rights are women's rights. I urge you to remove the brackets of sexual orientation." She worked closely with Simon Tseko Nkoli on activist projects (Ditsie & Newman, 2001).

REFERENCES

Airhihenbuwa, C. O., & Webster, J. D. (2004). Culture and African contexts of HIV/AIDS prevention, care and support. *Journal of Social Aspects of HIV/AIDS, 1,* 1–13.

Alexander, P. (2013). Affordability and action: Introduction and overview. In P. Alexander, C. Ceruti, K. Mostseke, M. Phasi, & K. Wale (Eds.), *Class in Soweto* (pp. 1–34). Scottsville, South Africa: University of KwaZulu-Natal Press.

Basilico, M., Kerry, V., Messac, L., Suri, A., Weigel, J., Basilico, M. T., Mukherjee, J., & Farmer, P. (2013). A movement for global health equity? A closing reflection. In P. Farmer, J. Y. Kim, A. Kleinman, & M. Basilico (Eds.), *Reimagining global health: An Introduction* (pp. 340–353). Berkeley: University of California Press.

BBC News. (2013, July 26). *Archbishop Tutu 'would not worship a homophobic God.'* Retrieved from http://www.bbc.com/news/world-africa-23464694.

Becker, A., Motgi, A., Weigel, J., Raviola, G., Keshavjee, S., & Kleinman, A. (2013). A movement for global health equity? A closing reflection. In P. Farmer, J. Y. Kim, A. Kleinman, & M. Basilico (Eds.), *Reimagining global health: An introduction* (pp. 212–244). Berkeley: University of California Press.

Boyce Davies, C. (1994). *Black women, writing and identity: Migrations of the subject.* New York, NY: Routledge.

Brooklyn Museum Exhibitions. (n. d.). *Zanele Muholi: Isibonelo/Evidence.* Retrieved from https://www.brooklynmuseum.org/exhibitions/zanele_muholi/

Clapham, A. (2016). *Human rights.* New York, NY: Oxford University Press.

Crenshaw, K. (2014). The structural and political dimensions of intersectional oppression. In P. R. Grzanka (Ed.), *Intersectionality: A foundations and frontiers reader* (pp. 16–21). Boulder, CO: Westview Press.

Ditsie, B. P., & Newman, N. (2001). *Simon and I.* San Francisco, CA: California Newsreel.

Drobac, P., Basilico, M., Messac, L., Walton, D., & Farmer, P. (2013). Building an effective rural health delivery model in Haiti and Rwanda. In P. Farmer, J. Y. Kim, A. Kleinman, & M. Basilico (Eds.), *Reimagining global health: An introduction* (pp. 133–183). Berkeley: University of California Press.

Ekine, S., & Abbas, H. (Eds.). (2013). African LGBTI manifesto/declaration. *Queer African Reader.* (p. 52). Cape Town, South Africa.

Farmer, P. (2005). On suffering and structural violence: Social and economic rights in the global era. In P. Farmer, *Pathologies of power: Health, human rights, and the new war on the poor* (pp. 29–50). Berkeley: University of California Press.

Farmer, P., Kim, Y. J., Kleinman, A., & Basilico, M. (2013). Introduction: A biosocial approach to global health (pp. 1–14). Berkeley, CA: University of California Press.

Farmer, P., Nizeye, B., & Keshavjee, S. (2006). Structural violent and clinical medicine. *PLOS ONE, 3,* 1686–1690.

Foucault, M. (1991). Governmentality. In G. Burchell & C. Gordon (Eds.), *The Foucault effect: Studies in governmentality* (pp. 87–104). Chicago, IL: University of Chicago Press.

Gay and Lesbian Archives (GALA). (n. d.). *Till the time of trial: The prison letters of Simon Nkoli.* Johannesburg, South Africa: GALA.

Gevisser, M. (1995). A different right for freedom: A history of South African lesbian and gay organisation from the 1950s to the 1990s. In M. Gevisser & E. Cameron (Eds.), *Defiant desire: Gay and lesbian lives in South Africa* (pp. 14–29). London: Routledge.

Gevisser, M., & Cameron, E. (Eds.). (1995). *Defiant desire: Gay and lesbian lives in South Africa.* London, UK: Routledge.

Ho, K. (2007). Structural violence as a human rights violation. *Essex Human Rights Review, 4,* 1–17.

International Gay and Lesbian Human Rights Commission (IGLHRC). (2007). *Off the map: How HIV/AIDS programming is failing same-sex practicing people in Africa.* New York, NY: IGLHRC.

Joint United Nations Programme on HIV/AIDS (UNAIDS). (2015). *HIV and AIDS estimates.* Geneva, Switzerland: UNAIDS. Retrieved from http://www.unaids.org/en/regionscountries/countries/southafrica

Kanani, B. (2012, June 14). Transgender pageant winner murdered in South Africa. *ABC News.* Retrieved from http://abcnews.go.com/blogs/headlines/2012/06/transgender-pageant-winner-murdered-in-south-africa/

Kim, J. Y., Farmer, P., & Porter, M. E. (2013). Redefining global health-care delivery. *The Lancet, 382,* 1060–0169.

Kleinman, A. (2000). The violences of everyday life: The multiple forms of dynamics of social violence. In V. Das, A. Kleinman, M. Ramphele, & P. Reynolds (Eds.), *Violence and subjectivity* (pp. 226–241). Berkeley, CA: University of California Press.

Kleinman, A. (2010). The art of medicine: Four social theories for global health. *Lancet, 375,* 1518–1519.

Lane, T., Raymond, H. F., Dladla, S., Rasethe, J., Struthers, H., McFarland, W., & McIntyre, J. (2011). High HIV prevalence among men who have sex with men in Soweto, South Africa: Results from the Soweto' Men's Study. *AIDS & Behavior, 15,* 626–634.

Lewis, D. (2011). Representing African sexualities. In S. Tamale (Ed.), *African sexualities: A reader* (pp. 199–216). Cape Town, South Africa: Pambazuka Press.

Mbali, M. (2009). Gay AIDS activism in South Africa. In V. Reddy, T. Sandfort, & L. Rispel (Eds.), *From social silence to social science: Same-sex sexuality, HIV & AIDS and gender in South Africa* (pp. 80–99). Cape Town, South Africa: Human Sciences Research Council Press.

Mbali, M. (2013). *South African activism and global health politics.* New York, NY: Palgrave MacMillan.

Mkhize, N. (2009). Some personal and political perspectives on HIV/AIDS in Ethekwini. In V. Reddy, T. Sandfort, & L. Rispel (Eds.), *From social silence to social science: Same-sex sexuality, HIV & AIDS and gender in South Africa* (pp. 207–215). Cape Town, South Africa: Human Sciences Research Council Press.

Mkhize, N., Bennett, J., Reddy, V., & Moletsan3, R. (2010). *The county we live in: Hate crimes and homophobia in the lives of Black lesbian South Africans.* Cape Town, South Africa: Human Sciences Research Council.

Mullings, L., & Schulz, A. J. (2005). Intersectionality and health: An introduction. In A. J. Schulz & L. Mullings (Eds.), *Gender, race, class, and health: Intersectional approaches* (pp. 3–20). New York, NY: John Wiley & Sons, Inc.

Ndashe, S. (2010). The battle for the recognition of LGBTI rights as human rights. In A. Katharina & J. Luckscheiter (Eds.), *Perspectives: Political analysis and commentary from Africa* (pp. 4–9). Cape Town, South Africa: Heinrich Boll Foundation Southern Africa.

Ndashe, S. (2011). Seeking the protection of LGBTI rights at the African commission of human and people's rights. *Feminist Africa, 15,* 17–38.

Ndashe, S. (2013). The single story of 'African homophobia' is dangerous for LGBTI activism. In S. Ekrine & H. Abbas (Eds.), *Queer African reader* (pp. 155–164). Cape Town, South Africa: Pambazuka Press.

Nkoli, S. (1995). Wardrobes: Coming out as a Black gay activist in South Africa. In M. Gevisser & E. Cameron (Eds.), *Defiant desire: Gay and lesbian lives in South Africa* (pp. 249–257). London, UK: Routledge.

Nofemele, L. (2013, April 7). *Pair tie bold know.* Retrieved from: http://www.iol.co.za/news/south-africa/kwazulu-natal/pair-tie-bold-knot-1496499#.VZmmAcvbK70

Nyanzi, S. (2011a). From minuscule biomedical models to sexuality's depths. In S. Tamale (Ed.), *African sexualities: A reader* (pp. 47–49). Cape Town, South Africa: Pambazuka Press.

Nyanzi, S. (2011b). Unpacking the [govern]mentality of African sexualities. In S. Tamale (Ed.), *African sexualities: A reader* (pp. 477–501). Cape Town, South Africa: Pambazuka Press.

Onie, R., Farmer, P., & Behforouz, H. (2012). Realigning health with care, *Stanford Social Innovation Review, Summer Edition,* 28–35.

Posel, D. (2011). 'Getting the nation talking about sex': Reflections on the politics of sexuality and nation-building in post-apartheid South Africa. In S. Tamale (Ed.), *African sexualities: A reader* (pp. 130–144). Cape Town, South Africa: Pambazuka Press.

Ratele, K. (2011). Male sexualities and masculinities. In S. Tamale (Ed.), *African sexualities: A reader* (pp. 399–419). Cape Town, South Africa: Pambazuka Press.

Reddy, V. (2010). The battle for the recognition of LGBTI rights as human rights. In A. Katharina & J. Luckscheiter (Eds.), *Perspectives: Political analysis and commen-*

tary from Africa (pp. 18–23). Cape Town, South Africa: Heinrich Boll Foundation Southern Africa.

Reddy, V., Sandfort, T., & Rispel, L. (2009). (Eds.). *From social silence to social science: Same-sex sexuality, HIV & AIDS and gender in South Africa.* Cape Town, South Africa: Human Sciences Research Council.

Reid, G. (2013). *How to be a real gay: Gay identities in small-town South Africa.* Scottsville, South Africa: University of Kwa-Zulu-Natal Press.

Rispel, L. C., Mecalf, C. A., Cloete, A., Reddy V., & Lombard, C. (2011). HIV prevalence and risk practices among men who have sex with men in two South African cities. *Journal of Acquired Immune Deficiency Syndromes, 57,* 69–76.

Senzee, T. (2014, May 30). *South Africa gets its first openly gay parliamentarian.* Retrieved from: http://www.advocate.com/world/2014/05/30/south-africa-gets-its-first-openly-gay-parliamentarian

Shisana, O., Rehle, T., Simbayi, L. C., Zuma, K., Jooste, S., Zungu, N., Labadarios, D., Onoya, D., et al. (2014). *South African National HIV prevalence, incidence and behavior survey, 2012.* Cape Town, South Africa: Human Sciences Research Council Press.

Simelela, N. P., & Venter, W. D. (2014). A brief history of South Africa's response to AIDS. *South African Medical Journal. 104,* 249–251.

Smedley, A., & Smedley, B. D. (2011). *Race in North America: Origin and evolution of a worldview* (4th ed.). New York, NY: Westview Press.

Smith, D. (2010, March 2). South African minister describes lesbian photos as immoral. *The Guardian.* Retrieved from http://www.theguardian.com/world/2010/mar/02/south-african-minister-lesbian-exhibition

Tamale, S. (2011a). Introduction. In S. Tamale (Ed.), *African sexualities: A reader* (pp. 1–7). Cape Town, South Africa: Pambazuka Press.

Tamale, S. (2011b). Researching and theorizing sexualities in Africa. In S. Tamale (Ed.), *African sexualities: A reader* (pp. 11–36). Cape Town, South Africa: Pambazuka Press.

Thompson, L. (2000). *A history of South Africa.* New Haven, CT: Yale University Press.

World Health Organization (WHO). (2014). *The global HIV/AIDS epidemic.* Geneva, Switzerland. Retrieved from https://www.aids.gov/hiv-aids-basics/hiv-aids-101/global-statistics/

World Health Organization (WHO). (2015). *UNAIDS action framework: Universal access for men who have sex with men and transgender people.* Author: UNAIDS.

PART II

STRUCTURAL INEQUALITIES AND INSTITUTIONS

CHAPTER 10

A CRITICAL EXAMINATION OF EDUCATIONAL DISPARITIES IN ASIAN AMERICAN AND PACIFIC ISLANDER COMMUNITIES

Dina C. Maramba and Xavier J. Hernandez

Current research has shown that the United States (US) is becoming increasingly racially diverse (U.S. Census Bureau, 2012). According to the United States Census Bureau (2012), the Asian American population grew at a faster rate than all the major race groups from 2000 to 2010. By the year 2030, the Asian American and Pacific Islander (AAPI) population is projected to reach 26.7 million (National Commission on Asian American & Pacific Islander Research in Education [CARE], 2011). As the US population becomes increasingly diverse, the rapid growth of the AAPI population will continue to make a profound impact on US culture and society. One area of impact involves the response of educational institutions to the growing numbers of AAPI students. Given that education has always been and will continue to be an important part of contributing to the betterment of the country, the demand for a diverse, well-educated population is undoubtedly essential, especially within a competitive global economy. Equally important is the ability for all populations to have equitable access to educational

Talking About Structural Inequalities in Everyday Life: New Politics of Race in Groups, Organizations, and Social Systems, pages 185–203.
Copyright © 2016 by Information Age Publishing

institutions, especially in light of the long history of de facto and de jure exclusion that has served as a major obstacle in educational opportunities across racial/ethnic groups throughout history. Given these concerns, it is critical to pay attention to the diverse needs of students and ways that the educational system can provide successful learning environments for AAPIs.

Despite their projected numbers of population growth, AAPIs continue to be a population that is often misunderstood and misrepresented within the educational arena. We argue that ongoing misperceptions influence how AAPIs progress through and experience the education pipeline. Thus, to have a clearer understanding of AAPIs and their educational experiences, we divide our discussion in three main sections. In the first section of our chapter, we will briefly describe the heterogeneous demography of the Asian American and Pacific Islander (AAPI) population, thereby problematizing the AAPI category. The second section will take a closer look at particular challenges that AAPIs face as an aggregated statistical group and explore how disaggregated ethnic data can reveal a more accurate picture of the needs and capabilities of specific AAPI populations. In particular, we begin this section by covering the pervasive model minority stereotype, a persistent misperception that interweaves itself through many aspects of the educational pipeline. Complementing this discussion, we will include aspects of how the model minority stereotype influences classroom interaction, pedagogy, and curricula as it relates to AAPIs. We also explore some of the unexpected pressures on AAPI students as a result of the model minority myth. In addition, we include the topic of affirmative action, as it is an important national topic that ultimately blankets and influences the discourse on the educational experiences of AAPIs. In the last section of the chapter, we consider the implications for the AAPI education pipeline. In particular, we cover how national initiatives and educational institutions can continue to play a role in working towards creating a more equitable educational pipeline with particular attention to the AAPI population.

It is important to mention that we approach our discussion within a theoretical framework that acknowledges race as a socially constructed categorization rather than an objective classification of people based on a common ancestry or phenotype (Omi & Winant, 2014). Throughout history, public policies that have sought to restrict the civil rights of racial and ethnic minorities have defined racial categories in various ways that perpetuated stratified life chances for certain people of color. For example, Irish and Eastern European immigrants were not considered "White" until their political support was needed to combat demands for civil rights equality from people of color in the early 20th century (Roediger, 2005). Furthermore, Filipino/a Americans, now the second largest Asian American ethnic population (U.S. Census Bureau, 2012), were previously considered as "Malay" or their own racial category separate from Asian until their populations began to flourish and the government sought to exclude Filipinos from civil rights, such as inter-racial marriage, property ownership, and immigration that only applied to Asians (or "Mongolians" as they were often referred at the time)

(Takaki, 1989). Therefore, we approach our research and review of Asian American and Pacific Islander experiences in education with the understanding that such categorizations are incredibly fluid and constantly evolving in both historical and contemporary contexts.

We further construct our critiques of and implications for the educational experiences of AAPI students within a social justice framework. This includes recognizing that all groups should be fully recognized and affirmed in their quest for equal participation in a democratic society; that they are self-determined and interdependent (Adams, Bell, & Griffin, 2007; Darder, 2012). A social justice approach entails acknowledging the inequitable distribution of resources and access to particular forms of knowledge (e.g. education). Within the context of our discussion, it is recognizing that race, racism, and racial structural inequalities exist and ultimately influence the experiences of racialized groups. Social justice works toward finding democratic ways to effectively address these issues. Accordingly, it means that institutions and individuals must work toward creating conditions that equitably serve and benefit all groups.

AAPIS: A CLOSER EXAMINATION OF DISAGGREGATED STATISTICS, DEMOGRAPHICS, AND OUTCOMES

Several researchers contend that while it is important to acknowledge aggregated AAPI data, it is even more critical to examine the disaggregated data that focuses on specific ethnic groups within the AAPI population (Hune, 2002, 2011; Maramba, 2011; Pak, Maramba, & Hernandez, 2014). Our intention here is threefold: to problematize the AAPI category and its relation to the Model Minority Stereotype; engage in a discussion about how we understand AAPI experiences in the educational pipeline; and ultimately address the implications for institutions that have a stake in the success of the AAPI population.

The US Census counts 48 different Asian ethnic groups under the Asian Americans and Pacific Islander category. These diverse populations include but are not limited to the following: Asian Indian, Bangladeshi, Cambodian, Chinese, Filipino, Hmong, Japanese, Korean, Laotian, Pakistani, Taiwanese, Thai, and Vietnamese. The Pacific Islander populations include but are not limited to the following: Chamorro, Fijian, Guamanian, Mariana Islander, Native Hawai'ian, Saipanese, Samoan, Tahitian, Tongan, Micronesian, and Melanesian (CARE, 2008; U.S. Census Bureau, 2012). By virtue of the sheer number of ethnic groups and the vast diversity that comprise the category, the attempt to have a precise definition of the AAPI population is virtually impossible. Chew-Ogi and Ogi (2002) described the AAPI population as biomodal, because the distribution of AAPI characteristics tends to form two opposite extremes. Language, immigration history, generational status, and socioeconomic status are only a few characteristics that further reinforce the extreme differences between AAPI ethnic groups. Such differences are not merely due to naturally occurring statistical variance, but rather they are the product of distinct racialized experiences and institutions that have created stratified life chances throughout history. Due to the varied history of US immigration laws and political relationships with particular countries, Asian and Pacific Islander immigrants have entered the US under categorically different circumstances. For example, the Immigration and Naturalization Act of 1965 gave preference for college-educated professionals, particularly in sciences, technology, engineering, and medical fields, to enter the US (Takaki, 1989). More recently, other Asian groups entered as refugees from Southeast Asia, such as the Vietnamese, Hmong, Burmese, and Bhutanese populations (Chan, 1991; Vang & Trieu, 2014). Many of these refugees lacked formal educations or the ability to choose their place of settlement, thus depriving them of many resources needed to aide their transition to the US. Furthermore, not all AAPI groups "immigrated" to the US. In the case of Native Hawaiians and US territories such as Guam, Samoa, Marshall Islands, and Micronesia, these populations were annexed and colonized by the US (Trask, 1999).

The difference in languages is vast and also directly impacts AAPI educational attainment and opportunities for socioeconomic mobility. For example, 79% of Asian American students and 43% of Pacific Islanders speak another language other than English at home, and 31% of the overall AAPI population speaks English less than "very well" (U.S. Census Bureau, 2012). In addition, over 300 languages exist among Asian and Pacific Islander ethnic groups, which are far more numerous and diverse than nationality-based categorizations. Recognizing language differences and language proficiencies have major implications for educational institutions as they will have to be prepared to address the various needs and capabilities of English language learners. With regard to socioeconomic status, disaggregated data indicate that a number of AAPI populations live below the national poverty line of 12.4%. According to the CARE Report (2008), Southeast Asians (Hmong, Cambodian, Laotian and Vietnamese) compared to their AAPI counterparts have much higher poverty rates (37.8%, 29.3%, 18.5% and 16.6% respectively); for Pacific Islander populations, all fall below the national poverty level (Marshallese, 38.3%, Samoan, 20.2%, Tongan, 19.5%, Native Hawaiian, 15.6% and Guamanian, 13.6%) (CARE, 2011). These statistics, which include language proficiencies and poverty rates, are other important contextual factors to consider especially with regard to understanding how educational access to better-resourced schools and support services increase the potential for educational success.

With regard to AAPI public K–12 enrollment, from 1979–2009, AAPI student enrollment grew from 600,000 to 2.5 million. For AAPI undergraduates, enrollment increased from 235,000 to 1.3 million over the same 30-year period (CARE, 2011). Statistics also indicate that from 2006–2008, the number of AAPI adults (25 years or older) who have not attended college varies widely by ethnic group. For example, compared to Asian Indians (20.4%), Japanese (27.8%) and Koreans (29.3%) who have a lower percentage of adults who have not attended college, Cambodian, Laotian, Hmong and Vietnamese (65.8%, 65.5% , 63.2% and 51.1%, respectively) populations have a much higher percentage of adults who have not attended college. Upon closer examination, if we look at actual educational attainment of AAPIs who attended college and eventually earned a bachelor's degree, the numbers continue to be quite disproportionate. While 40.5% of Asian Indians, 46.8% of Koreans, and 43.9% of Japanese college students eventually earned bachelor's degrees, in contrast, numbers were much lower for Southeast Asian and Pacific Islander groups. Only 25.2% of Hmong, 25.6% of Laotian, 28.8% of Cambodians, 20.3% of Samoans, 15.0% of Tongans, and 17.2% of Native Hawaiian persisted through college to the completion of a bachelor's degree.

Perhaps even more compelling is the type of institutions that AAPI students attend. Contrary to popular belief, a larger proportion of AAPI students attend two-year colleges as opposed to four-year institutions. Over a twenty-year period, AAPI enrollment in public two-year colleges has consistently been higher than AAPI students attending public four-year colleges and universities. As of 2005, 47.3% of AAPIs attend two-year colleges as opposed to 38.4% of AAPIs who attend four-year institutions. Moreover, AAPIs who attend a two-year college have a higher number of risk factors that are related to lower rates of completion compared to AAPIs at four-year institutions. These risk factors include: lack of a high school diploma, part-time enrollment, caring for dependents, and working full time while enrolled (CARE, 2011).

This brief overview of the disparate socioeconomic, cultural, and educational characteristics of the AAPI population illustrates many of the gross overgeneralizations that are made when this extremely heterogeneous group is homogenized under one umbrella category. In the next section, we discuss how the misclassification of AAPIs from these multiple demographic perspectives lays the foundation for interpersonal and institutional challenges throughout the educational pipeline for AAPI students.

AAPIS IN EDUCATION: CHALLENGES AND MISPERCEPTIONS

For almost five decades, Asian Americans have been labeled as a "model minority" within the US racial landscape (Peterson, 1966), suggested as a textbook example of the fulfillment of the American dream and value of democracy and meritocracy. Perhaps the most commonly used reference points are statistics that indicate that Asian American household income is significantly above the national average (almost $70,000, compared to the national average of $51,000), as is their educational attainment (49.2% with a Bachelor's degree or higher, compared to 28.7% of the general population) (U.S. Census Bureau, 2012). When these figures are compared to those of other racial minorities—Native Americans, African Americans, and Latinos—a false causal link is established: Asian Americans are flourishing in this country *because* they are Asian. This argument is supported by far less quantifiable or empirical evidence, which claims that Asian Americans' perceived unique cultural traits of hard work, discipline, and sociopolitical passivity are seen as inherent racial characteristics that are the antithesis to those displayed by other minorities ("Success Story of One Minority Group in the US," 1966). Within this framework, Asian Americans are bolstered as the model for how others should act: hardworking, non-complaining, independent, and self-sufficient (Suzuki, 2002; Wu, 2002). The underlying assumption of this perspective on race relations is that all groups work within an equitable context, therefore establishing genetics and "culture" as the only rational causes for the significant differences among the groups, thus blaming Native Americans, African Americans, and Latinos as the causes of their own shortcomings.

This image of Asian Americans as a model minority is most commonly utilized in the field of education, as schools' direct connections to the governance of behavior and access to upward socioeconomic mobility are in direct conversation with the tenets of the model minority stereotype. When the model minority stereotype is put into practice within educational environments, perceptions of Asian Americans as an over-achieving, monolithic entity are detrimental not only to Asian Americans, but to all under-represented student populations, whether those populations are classified by race, ethnicity, gender, religion, socioeconomic status, or any other variable.

When Asian Americans are evaluated based on such broad racial statistics, what is very easily overlooked is the fact that these misleading statistics, and false perceptions used to reinforce the model minority image, represent datasets that are either very widely distributed or skewed toward a specific subgroup of Asian Americans, thus the bimodal distribution of AAPIs at the opposite extremes of educational achievement (Chew-Ogi & Ogi, 2002). Touting Asian American income levels and educational attainment, specifically, overlooks the immigration policies that on the one hand, selectively skewed the Asian immigrant population toward college-educated professionals who were needed to fill shortages within the US labor market, and on the other hand, displaced other Asian Americans from their native land (both in Asia and in the US) with little to no resources to aid in the transition (Park & Park, 2005; Takaki, 1989). Within this context of immigration history, statistics that espouse Asian American income levels also overlook the fact that Asian Americans are more likely to live in multiple generational households with more wage earners than a traditional nuclear American family. The average American household has 2.6 persons, while the average Asian American household has 3.1 (U.S. Census Bureau, 2012), a result of immigration policies that favor family reunification and employment practices that do not always honor educational and professional credentials of recent immigrants, forcing them to remain dependent on other family members (Buenavista, 2013).

These incredibly different contexts of the "push" and "pull" factors of immigration have facilitated categorically different experiences within the Asian American population that are exemplified through the significant differences in educational access and attainment between Asian American subgroups (Museus, Maramba & Teranishi, 2013; Teranishi, 2010). The stereotype that "all Asians are the same," or that they possess a universal temperament that predestines them toward success, that their educational success is attributed to strict parenting practices, ignores centuries of history, both in America and abroad, which have shaped the ethnic, religious, and other sociopolitical cultures of people of color in extremely different ways (Chan, 1991; Takaki, 1989, Wu, 2002). For example, Chua (2011), among other things stereotypically attributes the success of Chinese students to the strict disciplinary practices of Chinese parents, as if these cultural characteristics are immutable belief systems that are devoid of context and adaptation. Consequently, there have been a number of scholarly critiques challenging Chua's line of thought (e.g. Chang, 2011; Poon, 2011) mainly arguing and complicating the grand narratives that exist about Asian Americans by factoring in the residual legacies of US public policies and their effects on the educational experiences of all people of color. Without this critical understanding of who Asian Americans are as a whole, and how they came to embody these characteristics and conditions, the educational policies that supposedly serve them will continue to come up fundamentally lacking.

The Model Minority and Influences on Classroom Interactions and Pedagogy

Extant literature on AAPI educational experiences demonstrates the persistent role of the model minority myth in perpetuating a culture of stereotype threat that is detrimental to the academic achievement and overall well-being of AAPIs (Cress & Ikeda, 2003; Huang, 2012; Trytten, Lowe, & Walden, 2012), contributing to intra-racial tension among AAPIs (Abelmann, 2009; Espiritu, 1992) and inter-racial tension among all students (Lee, 2009; Yoo & Castro, 2011). Furthermore, the views of AAPIs as a high achieving, monolithic group are further reflected through the perspectives of teachers and administrators, who often use the model minority as rationale for ignoring students' educational and emotional needs, assuming that they are naturally doing well, and if they are in need of assistance, they will explicitly ask for it (Liang & Sedlacek, 2003; Ng, Lee, & Pak, 2007; Suzuki, 2002). The continued perception of AAPIs as a model minority that has overcome explicit institutional discrimination in the US contributes to the exclusion of Asian Americans from K–12 secondary school curricula that seek to address these histories and their contemporary legacies (Chang, 2002; Coloma, 2013; Tintiangco-Cubales et al., 2014). This is also evident at the postsecondary level where courses about the AAPI experience are lacking. Research studies have shown that the limited curricula have a profound impact on students' identity, validation, and sense of belonging at the college level (e.g. Maramba, 2008; Maramba & Museus, 2012; Maramba & Palmer, 2014).

Within the classroom setting at all educational levels, Asian American students must face the effects of their erasure from the curricula. The need for Asian Americans to be reflected in educational courses on American history is not merely a pursuit of superficial or tokenized recognition, but a struggle to have their stories acknowledged and validated by the institutions that are tasked with creating and preserving knowledge in our society (Coloma, 2013). When students of all races are unable to engage in dialogues about the Asian American experience, including the discriminatory immigration laws that affected Asians from 1882–1965, the internment of Japanese Americans during World War II, or the role of Asian Americans in the civil rights movements of the 1960s and 1970s, then the curriculum of US history creates a singular image of Asian Americans. Rather than acknowledging Asian Americans as active participants in the social, economic, political, and cultural development of the US, they are seen as perpetual foreigners who have not made any valid contributions to American society (Wu, 2002). This misinformed perspective of American history contributes to the dehumanization of Asian Americans from yet another aspect of their educational environment, and poses a direct obstacle to inter-cultural understanding between students of different racial and ethnic backgrounds, and in some cases can even devolve into the self-hatred of one's own identity by Asian American students (Tintiangco-Cubales et al., 2014).

The convergence of these factors within an educational environment is illustrative of the symbolic power of the model minority stereotype and the social construction of race. While a multitude of empirical evidence exists that is a testament to the educational disparities among AAPIs (Museus, Maramba, & Teranishi, 2013; Teranishi, 2010), and ethnic studies scholarship has long established that race is a social construction rather than a marker of any sort of biological or genetic difference (Omi & Winant, 2014), the Asian American experience reveals that ideals behind antiquated ideologies still persist in new forms. In other words, even if race is not real, racism still is. The explicit and implicit forms of discrimination that students face as a result of their AAPI identity poses a new set of challenges regarding what it means to be Asian American and/or Pacific Islander within an educational context.

The Model Minority and Unexpected Pressures on AAPI students

The mythical development of the model minority image as a natural attribute of the AAPI identity rather than a stereotype fabricated to preserve racial hierarchies has created widespread ramifications on the ways that AAPI students view themselves and one another. Internally, the pressure to conform to expectations of natural excellence has led to increased levels of stress and anxiety among AAPI students, who are led to believe that they are somehow "less" Asian if they are unable to excel academically (Garrod & Kilkenny, 2007). As a population that predominantly consists of the second generation (American-born children of immigrants), AAPI students are also constantly reminded of the sacrifices their parents made as immigrants and their need to legitimize these sacrifices through academic achievement and upward social mobility, further drawing explicit linkages between elitism and their AAPI identity (Gim Chung, 2001; Maramba, 2008).

The assignment of academic excellence as a cornerstone aspect of the AAPI identity creates both inter- and intra-racial conflicts in educational settings. AAPIs are much more likely to be targets of bullying and other forms of explicit antagonism, seen by other students as curve-breakers and nerds who are actively withdrawn from social and extra-curricular life (Koo, Peguero, & Shekarkhar, 2012; Lee, 2009). Even within the AAPI population, students are also known to project the model minority stereotype onto other AAPI students. Students who seek to combat the model minority position themselves as a more modern, holistic, or well-adjusted AAPI, while still establishing other AAPIs as the "backwards" model minorities whose parents oppress their personal and academic freedom with tyrannical Asian cultural practices (Abelmann, 2009; Trytten, Lowe, & Walden, 2012). While these actions are some form of resistance to the model minority, they still act to preserve the model minority discourse within the educational setting by simply deflecting these stereotypes onto other AAPIs who hold less social and cultural capital within the White mainstream. Moreover, these acts of resistance may have a profound effect on AAPI students' mental well-being. Thus, the availability of student services and counseling become severely needed resources for AAPI students. The following section discusses emerging issues that surround student services, with a particular emphasis on educational institutions to take a more proactive stance toward holistically and equitably serving students in and out of the classroom.

Model Minority Influencing Student Services

The lack of understanding of fundamental AAPI experiences leads to further challenges at the institutional level. For example, when teachers assume that AAPI students are more inclined toward academic excellence, they are less willing to offer counseling and guidance to these students even when they are in need, assuming instead that the student is simply lazy and beyond reproach (Ng, Lee, & Pak, 2007). The assumption that AAPIs are not in need of institutional support is also bolstered by Western cultural values of independence and the ability to openly question and engage with authority figures, particularly in the educational setting. Teachers, counselors, and other administrative professionals who serve AAPI students place the onus on these students to express their concerns freely, while giving little to no consideration to Asian cultural values of deference to authority and apprehension toward social services such as academic or mental health counseling (Liang & Sedlacek, 2003). However, a report by Suzuki (2002) illustrates the dramatic changes in student use that occur within a student services center when they create active outreach toward AAPI students through the hiring of an Asian American counselor. Whereas little to no AAPI students visited counseling when there were no AAPI staff members, the hiring of an Asian American counselor increased AAPI student usage of the center significantly. Suzuki's example illustrates the need for institutions to critically evaluate their assessments of the student body in order to ensure the best possible outcomes of engagement and student success. The case of AAPI students illustrates that there are multiple ways to determine student needs that are not always readily observed.

Within the context of institutional needs to move beyond limited understandings of AAPI students, the next section will further explore the ways that AAPI identity can be more holistically understood within the educational environment as more than a mere category of social and ancestral difference.

UNDERSTANDING ACHIEVEMENT GAPS IN EDUCATIONAL ACCESS AND ATTAINMENT

A significant example of the similarities and differences between AAPI subgroups is found in research on the achievement gap between AAPI elementary school students and their White peers. Research of AAPI students as third and seventh graders by V. Pang, Han, and J. Pang (2013) illustrates that several aspects of the immigrant family experience contribute to disparate math and reading skills among this population. Several ethnic groups showed less developed reading skills than their White counterparts, due to both their parents' lack of proficiency with the English language as well as students' lack of exposure to cultural practices that would expose them to the US vernacular, such as reading the newspaper or playing with educational toys (p. 43). Furthermore, contrary to the expectation that AAPIs are naturally adept in math, AAPI students also showed much lower proficiency in seventh grade math when compared to their third grade evaluation. This downward trajectory was also attributed to students' language proficiency and their inability to comprehend the advanced and abstract vocabulary of higher levels of math (p. 44). The findings of this study illustrate that AAPI educational needs are not just confined to the classroom, but are part of an overall need to bridge the cultural dissonance that occurs between immigrant families and the predominantly White educational institutions that serve them. Furthermore, while V. Pang, et al. illustrate the benefits of examining the AAPI population at a deeper level than the aggregate category, the varying commonalities across ethnicities at their multiple points of comparison (math and reading comprehension, evaluated at third and seventh grade) also highlight the need to identify shared needs among AAPIs at a level that is somewhat more broad than simply ethnic group yet somewhat more narrow than race. These intersections between the immigrant experience and educational outcomes continue through to the highest levels of the educational pipeline, where colleges and universities have been battling with the issue of diversity through the medium of affirmative action for decades. The following section explores affirmative action and the precarious position that AAPIs are often placed on this topic.

AFFIRMATIVE ACTION AND AAPIS

Although affirmative action within an educational setting deals primarily with the process of college admissions, it is undoubtedly one of the most salient issues in education and US society as a whole. The ramifications of affirmative action delve into all levels of education as a growing number of jobs in the economy require college degrees, and therefore a growing number of students seek to gain entry into higher education. Within this context of increased competition and pressure to enter college, the practice of using affirmative action to actively consider race as a variable in college admissions has spurred larger societal debates about the role of race in the US in general and the educational system more specifically. It is upon this relationship between race and academic opportunity that the current affirmative action debate is situated.

The Asian AAPI population adds a significant perspective to affirmative action discourse because of AAPIs' seemingly paradoxical relationship to terms such as "minority" and "diversity" that are tantamount to arguments in favor of affirmative action. While on the one hand, they are seen as a racial minority within the wider US landscape, AAPIs are often viewed as "honorary Whites" who are part of the majority within a higher education context (Kim, 1999). Although they are often touted as part of diversity metrics in college publicity campaigns, AAPIs are often shut off from fellowships, research grants, and student affairs and services that are designed to promote diversity and campus engagement among "minority" students on college campuses (Abelmann, 2009). As a result, the AAPI community has become extremely divided regarding the benefits of affirmative action. While some believe that AAPIs both contribute to and benefit from diverse campus communities, others believe that the considerations of race undermine the meritocracy of higher education, which would theoretically favor a majority of AAPIs who reside in the upper echelon of academic achievement. This disconnect, both within the AAPI community and the educational discourse at large, was made apparent during the most recent Supreme Court case regarding affirmative action in college admissions, *Fisher v. University of Texas* (2013).

The plaintiff, Abigail Fisher, a White woman who was arguing against the use of race-conscious admissions as part of the university's process of holistic review, argued that the position of Asian Americans was evidence that proved that affirmative action was both unnecessary and unfair. Fisher argued that the exclusion of Asian Americans from affirmative action considerations undermined academic merit and was also antithetical to the purpose of affirmative action by excluding a racial minority group (Brief for Petitioner, 2011). The defense, in both oral and written arguments, claimed that Asian Americans were not an under-represented population at the university, with their enrollment numbers hovering between 17–20% of the entering freshman class despite being only 4% of the state's overall population (University of Texas, 2011; U.S. Census Bureau, 2012). Furthermore, AAPIs who supported the university's use of affirmative action through amicus briefs stated that AAPI students will benefit from a diverse campus, and affirmative action will help the recruitment and retention of under-represented AAPI ethnic groups who are marginalized by other factors such as class and language proficiency. With such diverse academic, social, economic, political, and cultural factors influencing the issues of access and equity in higher education, the inclusion of AAPIs within an affirmative action framework could help to foster more productive dialogues regarding the multiple dimensions of diversity as an educational interest, even if such considerations would not affect Asian Americans on as widespread of a level as Black and Latino/a students at the University of Texas (Brief of *Amici Curiae*. Advancing Justice, et al., in Support of Respondents).

TOWARD A CRITICAL DISAGGREGATION OF ASIAN AMERICAN DATA

Analyzing statistics at the macro level are useful for certain broad contexts, but they become particularly problematic in the field of educational policy, which places incredible emphasis on local control at all levels. Jurisdictions of governance within the educational system rarely extend past city, let alone county or state, borders. For most teachers and especially students, the educational experience rarely extends beyond the immediate classroom setting. Therefore, to rely solely on data at the national level runs the risk of placing undue importance on variables that are completely irrelevant to the lived experiences of students. This slippery slope can become particularly problematic for AAPIs, as immigration policies and chain migration patterns have skewed AAPI population density significantly in terms of both *where* AAPIs are and *which* AAPIs reside in these various population clusters. One-half of AAPIs live in only three states (California, New York, and Texas), and overall, 75 percent of AAPIs live in 10 states (the aforementioned three, plus New Jersey, Hawaii, Illinois, Washington, Florida, Virginia, and Pennsylvania) (U.S. Census Bureau, 2012). These demographic analyses present foundational evidence that establishes that AAPIs cannot be considered as a homogeneous entity, because they are a complex population with varying statistical trends that are reflective of multiple historical and legal contexts that have effectively shaped the AAPI experience, particularly as it relates to education.

A more critical form of disaggregation can also be applied to higher education demographics of AAPIs. As discussed previously, almost 60% of AAPIs are immigrants, with a significant number having immigrated since 2000. Furthermore, 64% of AAPIs are adults aged 25 and over (U.S. Census Bureau, 2012). When these numbers are compared with the number of AAPIs students currently in higher education, it becomes clear that the presence of AAPIs in colleges and universities is far less prevalent than national statistics regarding educational attainment may imply. These statistics within the AAPI demographic regarding immigrant and adult populations, when compared with current higher education enrollment statistics, raise critical questions about whether educational attainment statistics as they relate to AAPIs are a testament to the success of the education system or the immigration system. A closer look at the demographics of the AAPI population illustrates that a significant proportion of AAPI college degrees have been obtained in immigrants' home countries, under a significantly different social, economic, and cultural context of higher education that does not always translate to the increased cultural capital for traditionally labeled second-generation college students in the United States (Buenavista, 2013; Teranishi, 2010). Without trivializing the higher education pursuits of Asian and Pacific Islander professionals who used degrees obtained in their home country as a foundation toward upward mobility in the US, the data on AAPIs in higher education only suggests that Asian and Pacific Islanders are attaining education, but not necessarily how AAPIs are accessing education in a US context. The conflation of these two outcomes thus overlooks tremendous shortcomings that continue to plague the educational pipeline, and further illustrates that disaggregation is not merely about ethnicity but also about a multitude of factors that plague educational data collection at a systemic level from the K–12 system through postsecondary education. Given these discussion points, the AAPI identity cannot be considered as a simple marker of racial ancestry or physical phenotype, but rather must also be acknowledged as the product of a multitude of factors that can influence individuals who are homogenized underneath one umbrella category in very divergent ways.

THE AAPI EDUCATION PIPELINE: IMPLICATIONS FOR RESEARCH, PRACTICE, AND POLICY

Addressing the AAPI Education Pipeline effectively requires first acknowledging that there is an imperative need to fully include AAPIs in the education discourse at the local, state, and national levels. It is important to recognize that AAPI ethnic groups come with distinct language proficiencies, socioeconomic statuses, immigration histories, and educational attainment, among many other factors that directly influence educational outcomes. Furthermore, as discussed previously, more critical discussion needs to take place about what it means for AAPIs to be included in the education arena. What does it mean to compare AAPI students to one another, as well as students from other racial/ethnic groups? It is from this context that educators can then fully engage in conversations about the implications for research, practice, and policy. How this takes place may look different depending on varying social, political, and academic contexts. For example, a number of initiatives taking place at the national level have challenged the ways that we frame discussions around AAPIs and their access to education. The Asian Pacific Islander American Scholarship Fund (APIASF) is a non-profit national organization and the largest of its kind in the country that assists AAPI students entering postsecondary educations, both at the community college and university levels. According to Neil Horikoshi, President and Executive Director, the APIASF "create[s] opportunities for Asian American and Pacific Islander students to access, complete and succeed after postsecondary and education….and help(ed) develop future leaders who excel in their careers, serve as role models in their communities, and contribute to a vibrant America"(APIASF, 2014). APIASF was established in 2005 and has supported students from all 50 states and US territories. Since then, 56% of the scholarship recipients were the first generation college students and 58% of 2011–2012 recipients are from families who are living at or below the poverty line. In addition, 83% of the first three cohorts are now college graduates. Through a holistic evaluation of the needs and capabilities of AAPI students and their communities, APIASF has helped recognize and address underserved AAPIs, especially with regard to college access and financial need.

The National Commission on Asian American and Pacific Islander Research in Education (CARE) is another important entity in the national arena. CARE consists of a national commission, research advisory group, and a research team based at the University of California, Los Angeles whose goal is to "engage realistic and actionable discussions about the mobility and educational opportunities for Asian American and Pacific American Islanders...and provide much needed and timely research on key issues and trends related to access and participation of Asian Americans and Pacific Islanders in higher education" (CARE, 2010, p. v). An important aspect of CARE's work is its collaboration with APIASF. Their collaborative relationship has proven effective as they bring together both the practice of direct service to underserved AAPIs and complement this with the importance of documenting and offering solutions that show the relevance of AAPIs in higher education research and policy priorities. As a result of their collective efforts, CARE has disseminated major research reports about the postsecondary concerns and continues to advocate for AAPIs and challenge the national education agenda. Their reports have helped make an impact on creating a clearer picture of the educational disparities among the AAPI ethnic populations.

Second, a large part of our chapter emphasized the importance of more accurate data focused on AAPIs. As discussed in the previous section, critical scholarship that addresses the holistic conditions of AAPIs will help create a better understanding of the diverse array of AAPI needs and capabilities (Hune 2011; Maramba, 2011). The methods by which data is collected, analyzed and disseminated at the local, state and national levels will have a profound impact on the way we tell the multitude of stories that comprise AAPI experiences. Data collection methods that do not directly reflect the diversity of the student body can prove detrimental to students and reduce the practice of data collection to mere social categorization rather than an active method of researching and assessing the students whom institutions serve.

A recent key movement for Asian Americans and Pacific Islanders in higher education is the AAPI data quality campaign. The data quality campaign was initiated by CARE and the White House Initiative on Asian Americans and Pacific Islanders (WHIAAPI) in a 2013 gathering called the iCount symposium. The collaborative efforts of CARE and WHIAPPI resulted in three main goals: (1) "raise awareness about and bring attention to the ways in which data on AAPI students reported in the aggregate conceals significant disparities in educational experiences and outcomes between AAPI sub-groups, (2) aim to provide models for how postsecondary institutions, systems and states have recognized and responded to this problem by collecting and reporting disaggregated data," and "(3) work collaboratively with the education field to encourage broader reform in institutional practices related to the collection and reporting of disaggregated data of AAPI students" (CARE, 2013, p. v). This is a pivotal moment in bringing to the national forefront the fundamental importance of data disaggregation.

Third, and perhaps even more essential is *how* this information is ultimately used by constituents who are responsible for creating better education environments for AAPIs. More specifically, the ways in which programs, activities, and policies are carried out by K–12 teachers, staff, higher education student affairs professionals, faculty, and administrators will be very important. An example of how one might understand the importance of advocates' and constituents' roles in creating better environments for AAPI students is through the 2008 formalization Asian American and Native American Pacific Islander Institutions (AANAPISIs). Included as part of the College Cost Reduction and Access Act of 2007, AANA-PISIs are postsecondary institutions that are the newest of federally designated Minority Serving Institutions (MSI) whose goals are to increase accessibility and positive outcomes for low-income and underserved students. In order for a higher education institution to be eligible for designation as AANAPSI, they must have at least a 10 percent enrollment of AAPI students, a minimum threshold of low-income students, and lower educational and general expenditures per student (CARE, 2010, Park & Teranishi, 2008; Teranishi, Maramba, & Ta, 2011). Currently, there are 153 institutions eligible to become AANAPISIs; however, only 78 are designated and only 21 are funded (CARE, 2013). Most of these institutions are located in California, Hawaii, Illinois, New York, Massachusetts, Maryland, Texas, Washington, and Guam. Furthermore, the majority of eligible AANAPISIs are public two-year colleges (55.3%) as compared to four-year institutions (44.7%) (CARE, 2013; Teranishi et al., 2012).

Moreover, the formalization of AANAPISI designation has provided opportunities and resources for currently funded AANAPISIs to implement programs and activities on their campuses directly catered toward the needs of AAPI students. The outcomes of these implemented programs and activities are important in understanding the impact that the designation has on higher education institutions. In an effort to further support AANAPISIs, APIASF and CARE developed the Partnership for Equity in Education through Research (PEER). With the assistance of Kresge Foundation, Lumina Foundation, USA Funds, and Walmart Foundation, the creation of PEER is yet another example of working collaboratively in furthering the potential for AANAPISIs and the students they serve to succeed. By working together, PEER and campus constituents (student affairs practitioners, staff and administrators) work towards identifying effective practices and intervention programs that help build capacity for the AANAPISI institutions. Currently, PEER is working with three AANAPISIs: DeAnza College (Cupertino, CA), Community College of San Francisco, and South Seattle College. The co-investigative process involving researchers (PEER) and key campus administrators and staff of the three campuses is a positive step towards increasing AAPI college completion and effectively addressing the needs of AAPI students. Another key endeavor is the recent creation of the Center for Minority Serving Institutions at the University of Pennsylvania. Although not specifically focusing on AANAPI-SIs, the center serves as a resource for funders, policy makers, and scholars by providing information on issues related to MSIs. It also serves as a support system for MSIs by offering among many other things grant opportunities, collaborative opportunities, and partnerships to ensure success for their student populations.

All of these efforts to address the AAPI education pipeline are still relatively new, with APIASF being one of the first to be established in 2005. Efforts such as these must continue, as they will work towards not merely dispelling the model minority stereotype but moving toward deeper discussions and understanding about AAPI educational experiences. Incorporating holistic research that is quantitative and qualitative, institutional and interpersonal, and historical and contemporary creates a more accurate picture of varied AAPI populations and highlights the urgent need for disaggregated data collection among Asian American students along multiple axes. A critical analysis of the historical and contemporary conditions of AAPIs reveals a wide array of needs and capabilities that are dependent on a myriad of factors. As it relates to education specifically, educational policy, research, and practice can utilize the case of AAPIs as a strong lens through which to analyze issues of equality versus equity, or whether student concerns are best addressed via a universally applied method or one that takes certain contexts into closer consideration. Therefore, working toward critical methods of disaggregating and analyzing Asian American data can contribute to more effective implementation of promising practices that will not only benefit AAPIs, but will inevitably illustrate ways that educators can continue to serve all students in a more positive manner. It is indeed a social justice imperative that will reap innumerable outcomes for institutions and the students that attend them.

REFERENCES

Abelmann, N. (2009). *The intimate university : Korean American students and the problems of segregation*. Durham, NC: Duke University Press.

Adams, M., Bell, L. A., & Griffin, P. (Eds.). (2007). *Teaching for Diversity and Social Justice* (2nd edition). New York, Routledge Publishing.

Asian & Pacific Islander American Scholarship Fund (APIASF). Today's minds, tomorrow's future. (2014). *APIASF: Asian & Pacific Islander American Scholarship Fund. Today's Minds, Tomorrow's Future*. Retrieved July 23, 2014, from http://www.apiasf.org/welcome.html

Brief of Amici Curiae Members of Asian American Center for Advancing Justice, et al. in Support of Respondents, Fisher v. University of Texas at Austin, 2011 U.S. Briefs 345; 2012 U.S. S. Ct. Briefs LEXIS 3305 (2012).

Brief for Petitioner, Fisher v. University of Texas at Austin, 2011 U.S. Briefs 345; U.S. S. Ct. Briefs LEXIS 2263 (2012).

Buenavista, T. L. (2013). Pilipinos in the middle: Higher education and a sociocultural context of contradictions. In D. C. Maramba & R. Bonus (Eds.), *The "other" students:*

Filipino Americans, education, and power (pp. 259–276). Charlotte, NC: Information Age Publishing.

Chan, S. (1991). *Asian Americans: an interpretive history*. Boston, MA: Twayne Publishers.

Chang, M. J. (2002). The impact of undergraduate diversity course requirement on students' racial views and attitudes. *Journal of General Education, 51*(1), 21–42.

Chang, M. J. (2011). Battle hymn of the model minority myth, *Amerasia Journal, 37*(2), 137–143.

Chew-Ogi, C., & Ogi, A. Y. (2002). Epilogue. In M. K. McEwen, C. M. Kodama, A. N. Lee, S. Lee, & C. T. H. Liang, (Eds.). *Working with Asian American college students: New directions for services,* (97), 91–96.

Chua, A.(2011). *Battle hymn of the tiger mother*. New York, NY: Penguin Books.

Coloma, R. S. (2013). Invisible subjects: Filipina/os in secondary history textbooks. In D. C. Maramba & R. Bonus (Eds.), *The "other" students: Filipino Americans, education, and power* (pp. 165–182). Charlotte, NC: Information Age Publishing.

Cress, C. M., & Ikeda, E. K. (2003). Distress under duress: The relationship between campus climate and depression in Asian American college students. *NASPA Journal, 40*(2), 74–97.

Darder, A. (2012). *Culture and power in the classroom: A critical foundation for the education of bicultural students*. Boulder, CO: Paradigm Press.

Espiritu, Y. (1992). *Asian American panethnicity: Bridging institutions and identities*: Philadelphia, PA: Temple University Press.

Fisher v. University of Texas, 570 U.S. _____ (2013).

Garrod, A., & Kilkenny, R. (2007). *Balancing two worlds: Asian American college students tell their life stories*: Ithaca, NY: Cornell University Press.

Gim Chung, R. H. (2001). Gender, ethnicity, and acculturation in intergenerational conflict of Asian American college students. *Cultural Diversity and Ethnic Minority Psychology, 7*, 376–386.

Huang, K. (2012). Asian American mental health on campus. In A. Agbayani & D. Ching (Eds.), *Asian Americans and Pacific Islanders in higher education* (pp. 231–250). Washington, DC: NASPA.

Hune, S. (2002). Demographics and diversity of Asian American college students. In M. K. McEwen, C. M., Kodama, A. N. Lee, S. Lee, & C. T. H. Liang (Eds.), Working with Asian American College students: *New Directions for Services*, 97, 11–20.

Hune, S. (2011). Educational data, research methods, policies, and practices that matter for AAPIs. *AAPI Nexus: Asian Americans & Pacific Islanders Policy, Practice and Community, 9*(1), 115–118.

Kim, C. J. (1999). The racial triangulation of Asian Americans. *Politics & Society, 27*(1), 105–138.

Koo, D. J., Peguero, A. A., & Shekarkhar, Z. (2012). The "model minority" victim: Immigration, gender, and Asian American vulnerability to violence at school. *Journal of Ethnicity in Criminal Justice, 10*, 129–147.

Lee, S. J. (2009). *Unraveling the "model minority" stereotype: Listening to Asian American youth* (2nd ed.). New York, NY: Teachers College Press.

Liang, C. T., & Sedlacek, W. E. (2003). Attitudes of White student services practitioners toward Asian Americans. *NASPA Journal, 40*(3), 30–42.

Maramba, D. C. (2008). Immigrant families and the college experience: Perspectives of Filipina Americans. *Journal of College Student Development, 49*(4), 336–350.

Maramba, D. C. (2011). The importance of critically disaggregating data: The case of Southeast Asian American college students. *AAPI (Asian American Pacific Islander) Nexus Journal: The Role of new research data, & policies for Asian Americans, Native Hawaiians, & Pacific Islanders, 9*(1 & 2), 127–133.

Maramba, D. C., & Museus, S. D. (2012). Examining the effects of campus climate, ethnic group cohesion and cross cultural interaction on Filipino American Students' sense of belonging in college. *Journal of College Student Retention, 15*(1), 495–522.

Maramba, D. C., & Palmer, R. T. (2014). The role of cultural validation in the college experience of Southeast Asian American college students. *Journal of College Student Development, 55*, 515–530.

Museus, S. D., Maramba, D. C., & Teranishi, R. T. (Eds.). (2013). *The misrepresented minority: New insights on Asian Americans and Pacific Islanders and their implications for higher education.* Sterling, VA: Stylus.

National Commission on Asian American and Pacific Islander Research in Education [CARE]. (2008). *Asian Americans and Pacific Islanders Facts, not fiction: Setting the record straight.* New York, NY: Author.

National Commission on Asian American and Pacific Islander Research in Education [CARE]. (2010). *Federal higher education policy priorities and the Asian American and Pacific Islander community.* New York, NY: Author.

National Commission on Asian American and Pacific Islander Research in Education [CARE]. (2011). *The relevance of Asian Americans & Pacific Islanders in the college completion agenda.* New York, NY: Author.

National Commission on Asian American and Pacific Islander Research in Education [CARE]. (2013). *iCount: A data Quality Movmeent for Asian Americans and Pacific Islanders in Higher Education.* New York, NY: Author.

Ng, J. C., Lee, S. S., & Pak, Y. K. (2007). Contesting the model minority and perpetual foreigner stereotypes: A critical review of literature on Asian Americans in education. *Review of Research in Education, 31*(1), 95–130.

Omi, M., & Winant, H. (2014). *Racial formation in the United States from the 1960s to the 1990s* (3rd ed.). New York, NY: Routledge.

Pak, Y. K., Maramba, D. C., & Hernandez, X. J. (2014). *Asian Americans in higher education: Charting new realities.* San Francisco, CA. Jossey-Bass.

Pang, V. O., Han, P. P., & Pang, J. M. (2013). Asian American and Pacific Islander students: Third graders and the achievement gap. In R. Endo & X. L. Rong (Eds.), *Educating Asian Americans: Achievement, schooling, and identities* (pp. 29–48). Charlotte, NC: Information Age Publishing.

Park, E. J., & Park, J. S. (2005). *Probationary Americans: Contemporary immigration policies and the shaping of Asian American communities.* New York, NY: Routledge.

Park, J. J., & Teranishi, R. (2008). Asian American and Pacific islander serving institutions: Historical perspectives and future prospects. In M. Gasman, B. Baez, & C. Sotello Viernes Turner, *Understanding Minority-Serving Institutions* (pp. 111–126). Albany: State University of New York Press.

Peterson, W. (1966, June). Success story: Japanese-American style. *New York Times Magazine, 21.*

Poon, O. A. (2011). Ching Chongs & Tiger Moms: The "Asian invasion" in U.S. higher education. *Amerasia Journal, 37*(2). Retrieved from: http://hyphenmagazine.com/blog/2011/09/ching-chongs-and-tiger-moms-asian-invasion-us-higher-education

Roediger, D. R. (2005). *Working toward whiteness: How America's immigrants became white.* New York, NY: Basic.

Success story of one minority group in the U.S. (1966, December). *US News and World Report,* 71–74.

Suzuki, B. H. (2002). Revisiting the model minority stereotype: Implications for student affairs practice and higher education. *New Directions for Student Services, 97,* 21–32.

Takaki, R. (1989). *Strangers from a different shore: A history of Asian Americans.* Boston, MA: Little Brown.

Teranishi, R. T. (2010). *Asians in the ivory tower: Dilemmas of racial inequality in American higher education.* New York, NY: Teachers College Press.

Teranishi, R. T., Maramba, D. C., & Ta, M-H. (2012). Asian American Native American Pacific Islander Serving-Institutions (AANAPISIs): Mutable sites of intervention for STEM opportunities and outcomes. In R. T. Palmer, D. C. Maramba, & M. Gasman (Eds.), *Fostering success of ethnic and racial minorities in STEM: The role of minority serving institutions* (pp. 168–80). New York, NY: Routledge.

Tintiangco-Cubales, A., Kohli, R., Sacramento, J., Henning, N., Agarwal-Rangnath, R., & Sleeter, C. (2014). Toward an ethnic studies pedagogy: Implications for K–2 schools from the research. *Urban Review, (March),* 1–22. doi: 10.1007/s11256-014-0280-y

Trask, H. K. (1999). *From a native daughter: Colonialism and sovereignty in Hawaii.* Honolulu, HI. University of Hawaii Press.

Trytten, D. A., Lowe, A. W., & Walden, S. E. (2012). "Asians are good at math. What an awful stereotype": The model minority stereotype's impact on Asian American engineering students. *Journal of Engineering Education, 101*(3), 439–468.

U.S. Census Bureau. (2012). *American FactFinder.* Retrieved from http://factfinder2.census.gov.

University of Texas at Austin. (2011). *Student characteristics Fall 2011.* Retrieved from http://www.utexas.edu/academic/ima/sites/default/files/SHB11–2Students.pdf.

Vang, C. Y., & Trieu, M. M. (2014). *Invisible newcomers: Refugees from Burma/Myanmar and Bhutan in the United States.* Washington, D.C.: The Asian Pacific Islander Scholarship Fund.

Wu, F. H. (2002). *Yellow: Race in America beyond black and white.* New York, NY: Basic.

Yoo, H. C., & Castro, K. S. (2011). Does nativity status matter in the relationship between perceived racism and academic performance of Asian American college students? *Journal of College Student Development, 52*(2), 234–245.

CHAPTER 11

RACIALIZED PERSPECTIVES ON THE PRISON INDUSTRIAL COMPLEX

Alex L. Pieterse

We need to be wary of the limitations of single-issue politics that seek to separate racist repression at home from militarism abroad or gender violence in the family from state violence against whole communities
—Sudbury (2004 p. 10)

Since its inception, the United States has quested for a democracy complicit in, conflicted with, and in almost every sense tormented, if not crippled, by racial inequality and racist demagoguery. The history of US racism is intricately linked to its economic system and acquisition of material wealth.
—James (2000 p. 483)

The American Black man has never known law and order except as an instrument of oppression. The law has been written by white men, for the protection of white men and their property, to be enforced by white men against Blacks in particular and poor folks in general.
—Lester (quoted in Staples, 1975, p. 15)

Talking About Structural Inequalities in Everyday Life: New Politics of Race in Groups, Organizations, and Social Systems, pages 205–223.

"But white people live somewhere," I said. "And nobody arrests them for obstructing pedestrian traffic."

"That's because that's not where the crime is. The crime is out there." He jerked a thumb in the direction of Brooklyn.

"Low-class people," he said, he said, "do low-class things"

—Taibbi (2014, p. 114)

Irrespective of the language of equality, rights, and liberty that framed the Declaration of Independence, the United States (US) continues to be a society defined by social stratification, most clearly observed in the phenomenon of race (Marger, 2011). The manner in which such social stratification impacts various racial groups within the US is perhaps no more clearly evident than when looking at current rates of incarceration and detention. Given this centrality of race, in the current chapter, I review the nexus of race, economics, and state-sanctioned violence within the US and examine this phenomenon by focusing on the over-representation of men and women of African descent within the US prison system, a phenomenon also known as racialized hyper-incarceration (Miller, 2013). Additionally, I invite discussion on two possible responses to racialized hyper-incarceration, namely prison abolition and restorative justice.

The quotations by Sudbury, James, Lester, and Taibbi that introduce the chapter remind us that social injustice is not located in singular, independent issues. Instead, we recognize that oppression is a multi-faceted, interconnected phenomenon, with all aspects serving the core dynamic of domination and subjugation. As such, I argue that the Prison Industrial Complex (PIC) has to be understood as a deliberate and calculated tool for the maintenance of the White power structure within the US. The goal of this chapter, therefore, is to examine the role that racial group membership plays in patterns of incarceration as experienced by Black Americans. To do this, I locate the discussion within the framework of power disparities as created by, and maintained through, the colonial dynamic of White domination and Black subjugation (Williams, Pieterse, DeLoach, Bolden, Ball, & Awadalla, 2010). Furthermore, I advance the argument that an effective response to racialized hyper-incarceration has to include attention to all aspects of power disparities, particularly as it relates to education, employment, income, and the current political structure (Davis, 2009).

RACE, INEQUALITY AND JUSTICE

The past few decades have witnessed a significant increase in the rate of incarceration in the US (see Raphael & Stoll, 2013). Recent data indicates that the US, while comprising five percent of the world's population, holds 25% of the world's prisoners (Lichtenstein, 2011). Furthermore, with People of Color being significantly over-represented within the prison population, and with the manner in which the prison industry contributes to the health of the US economy (Thompson, 2012), some scholars have described this nexus of forced labor and incarceration as a type of neo-slavery (Gilmore, 2000). Within a racialized society such as the US (Smedley & Smedley, 2011), racial oppression is most clearly seen in social structures that intentionally serve to perpetuate dominance and subordination, through an inequitable distribution of resources and opportunities (Neville & Pieterse, 2009). As such, the judicial system and accompanying prison industry provide a clear illustration of the manner in which social institutions are utilized in the maintenance of race-based oppression and discrimination. However, to fully understand the manner in which race accounts for such significant disparities in incarceration rates, we first have to pause and examine the legacy of racial inequality and inequitable wealth distribution in the US. Using humor, Butler (1997) captures the tension that exists between the rhetoric of equality and the reality of inequality:

> Imagine, for example that the issue before a court is whether it is appropriate, in a school district with a history of discrimination, to lay off of a more senior white teacher in order to allow a black teacher to keep her job. The "law" says look at the Constitution but you and I know that the answer is not found there. If you woke up one of the framers of the Constitution in the middle of the night and asked him, he would say something like this "Wait a minute, Niggers teach school??! How did they escape from my plantation?" (p. 16)

This vignette illustrates the contradiction between the vision of freedom and equality outlined in the US constitution, and the actual manner in which equality and freedom is exercised. It is now common knowledge that the framers of the US constitution omitted larger swathes of the population from their definition of all men (women, enslaved individuals, Native Americans, etc.). Some would argue that the manner in which the US constitution was framed was precisely in order to maintain power in the hands of a wealthy elite, at the expense of enslaved individuals, indentured servants, indigenous peoples, and those of lower socio-economic status (See Zinn, 2005). Therefore, the current phenomenon in which global wealth is being increasingly concentrated in the hands of a few represents a long and perverse tradition in Western capitalism (Yates, 2012). Accordingly, Taibbi (2014) provides several illustrations of the manner in which race and low-income continues to have a direct impact on the misapplication of justice within American society. One example Taibbi presents is the discrepancy between the lack of indictments associated with high-level financial crime, and the increased frequency of criminal prosecution for petty crime and minor drug offenses such as the possession and sale of very small amounts of marijuana. The recent death of Eric Garner, a Black American male who died as a result of an illegal restraining procedure while being arrested for unlawfully selling cigarettes on a street in Staten Island, New York provides a grotesque illustration of many elements of injustice within the judicial system (Queally & Semuels, 2014). These elements include the disproportionate use of force, otherwise know as police brutality, the misguided focus on petty offenses, and the racialized aspect of the abuse of power in the US (Cashmore & McLaughlin, 2013; Coker, 2003).

Within a racialized society such as the US, racial group membership becomes much more than a demographic marker, however, and plays a critical role in issues of justice and equity (Bobo, 2011). The following illustration therefore speaks to this racialized inequity and begins to highlight the building blocks of racialized hyper-incarceration in the US.

The fortune 500 club represents the 500 most profitable companies within the US. When looking at the racial composition of Fortune 500 chief executive officers (CEOs) as of 2014, Black CEO accounted for 1.2 percent of all Fortune 500 CEOs. In other words, only 6 out of 500 CEOs of the most profitable companies in the US are Black. Contrast that statistic to another which is equally disheartening. As of 2010, 22% of US children were living in poverty as defined by the US Census Bureau (2010). This means that 16,400,000 children were living in households with an annual income of less that $20,000. Of these children 38 % were Black (6,232,2000) while 12% (1,968,000) were White suggesting a White to Black ratio of 1.3. In other words, for every one White child living in poverty, there are three Black children living in poverty, a ratio that is even more disturbing considering that Whites comprise 77.9% of the US population while Blacks make up 13.1% (US Census Bureau, 2010). Consider then how these disparities in wealth and income might play out in the context of racialized hyper-incarceration in the US. Furthermore, consider that racial disparities in incarceration are entirely consistent with disparities found in other social sectors such as education, wealth, and health where Black Americans tend to have consistently worse outcomes than their white counterparts (Pager & Shepherd, 2008; Smedley, 2012).

CURRENT RACIAL STATUS OF US PRISON POPULATION

We have already noted the rapid increase in the prison population, and the manner in which men and Women of Color are disproportionately represented in US prisons. Importantly, although recent data from the sentencing project suggests a decline in the rates of incarceration of Black men and women, as of 2013 Black men remain 6.4 times more likely to be incarcerated than White men and Black women, and 2.8 times more likely than White women (Goode, 2013). Given the shift from the initial goal of incarceration, namely one of rehabilitation and correction (Barnes, 1921), to a system that now focuses primarily on punishment and labor (Loury, 2008; Rhodes, 2001), a brief review of this transition is required.

Scholars have noted that there are many, often conflicting reasons provided for the dramatic increase in the prison population and the manner in which a prison sentence is now more punitive than corrective. Raphael and Stoll (2009) suggest that an increased focus on public safety, and an increased appetite for punishment among the US population has led politicians to aggressively pursue longer prison sentences as a matter of public policy. Others would postulate that the nexus of global capitalism and neo-liberal policies are to blame given the manner in which the worlds' poor are both exploited and simultaneously punished for their poverty (Reynolds, 2008; Sudbury, 2005). Scholars have also utilized racial dynamics as a possible contributing factor in the shift from rehabilitation to punishment noting that racial projections of violence and partisan political attitudes are also associated with the increased rates of incarceration, particularly among Black American men (Keen & Jacobs, 2009). A perfect illustration can be found in the 1988 presidential election in which then candidate George W. H. Bush's "tough on crime" posture was considered to be a turning point of sorts. During Bush's presidential campaign, a pivotal moment occurred with the decision to use Willie Horton, a Black man from Massachusetts, as the face of violent crime. Some political scientists view this tactic as being rather influential in the ultimate election of President Bush, and providing an illustration of how racial symbolism has been utilized to manipulate public sentiment (Tonry, 2010). In sum, scholars agree that the increase in rates of incarceration are associated with unemployment, income inequality, poverty, racial conflict, and conservative political policies and attitudes. Furthermore, these factors are associated with increases in incarceration independent of increases in criminal activity (Chang & Thompkins, 2002).

In reflecting on racial aspects of hyper-incarceration, many point to the policies of the Reagan and Clinton administrations as critical in understanding the shift to more aggressive policing, harsher mandatory sentencing, and its accompanying effect on Black Americans (Alexander, 2012; Loury, 2008). Ronald Reagan's so-called "War on Drugs" significantly expanded state police's power and introduced mandatory sentencing for relatively minor drug offences. Bill Clinton's 1994 Violent Crime Control and Law Enforcement Act allocated 9.9 million dollars for prison construction. Additionally, Clinton's welfare reform stripped away a significant safety net for individuals and communities experiencing persistent poverty, and to some extent institutionalized a connection between the welfare and criminal justice systems in the US (Brown, 2002; McCorkel, 2004). Finally, the privatization of the prison industry provided further incentive for the expansion of the prison system, and thereby the prison population (Subdury, 2004; Western, 2006). This confluence of a national and political appetite for punishment, injection of capital into prison construction, and a growing private prison industry driven by profit, and stripping away of welfare benefits, arguably laid the foundation for the most significant and unprecedented rise in the prison population in the history of the US—a phenomenon that has been partially driven by the imprisonment of record numbers of People of Color.

Data indicates that in 1973, the US rate of incarceration sat at 100 individual per 100,100 of the population. Currently, the rate of incarceration sits at 725 per 100,000. When including the percentage of individuals either under supervision or parole, we find that 3.1 percent of the US population (approx. 7,000,000) individuals are under some type of correctional supervision (Western & Wildeman, 2009). A paradox associated with these numbers is that while incarceration rates are increasing, levels of historical major crimes (homicide, armed robbery, assault) have decreased significantly (Alexander, 2012; Raphael & Stoll, 2013), a paradox that should provide us with a sense of disquiet. Furthermore, this paradox is consistent with data suggesting that factors such as unemployment, income inequality, and poverty are greater predictors of incarceration than criminal activity necessarily (Chang & Thompkins, 2002). If rates of imprisonment are rising, while rates of major crimes are decreasing, then the utility of hyper-incarceration has to be questioned.

A closer examination of the data therefore provides important insights into what has driven the rise in the prison population. Note the following description from Western and Wildeman (2009):

> From 1980 to 2004, the percentage of young white men in prison or jail increased from 0.6 to 1.9 percent. Among young white men with only a high school education, incarceration rates were about twice as high. At the dawn of the prison boom, in 1980, the incarceration rate for young black men, 5.7 percent, was more than twice as high as that for low-education whites. By 2004, 13.5 percent of black men in their twenties were in prison or jail. Incarceration rates were higher in the lower half of the education distribution. More than one in five young non-college black men were behind bars on a typical day in 2004. (p. 228)

It has to be noted that women in general and Black women specifically are also impacted by a disproportionate representation in the prison population (Isaac, Lockhart, & Williams, 2001). O'Brien (2006) notes that the likelihood of a woman going to prison in her lifetime has increased from a 0.3% chance in 1974 to a 1.8% chance in 2001 with the likelihood of a Black woman going to prison being five times higher than that of her White counterpart. To further illustrate, irrespective of the fact that at the turn of the century Black Americans accounted for 12.3% and White Americans accounted for 75% of the total US population, in 2002 36,000 Black women were imprisoned compared to 35,400 White women, a significant and disturbing disparity (Roberts, 2004).

Much of the discussion associated with the rapid rise in incarceration of Black individuals centers around the impact of drug laws that provide a more severe sentence for a minor drug infraction (Isaac, Lockhart, & Williams, 2010). Subsequently, recent decreases in rates of incarceration of Black men and women also appear to be associated with changes in sentencing of drug offenses (Goode, 2013). The crack-cocaine phenomenon of the 1990s provides a useful discussion point for the relationship between drugs and hyper-incarceration.

The racial imagery associated with the crack-cocaine epidemic of the 1990s has been well documented, largely informed by the focus on crack-cocaine, a type of cocaine that was cheaper and therefore more accessible to Black Americans (Alexander, 2012). While powder cocaine was more likely to be used by White Americans, the focus of attention on crack-cocaine resulted in a distorted imagery of drug use, coupled with fictitious allegations of violence associated with drug use (Leigey & Bachman, 2007). The resulting imbalance in drug sentencing—

lighter sentences for powder cocaine and harsher sentences for crack-cocaine—resulted in an unequal application of the law with Black Americans receiving much harsher and more frequent prison sentences than White Americans. This phenomenon led legal scholars to question both the legality and equity of the sentencing laws as is evidenced in the following quotation from a legal discussion on drug-related sentencing guidelines:

> Whatever its causes, the heavily disproportionate impact of federal crack penalties on Black defendants raises serious questions of equal protection. Why blacks have borne the brunt of the unusually harsh sentences prescribed for trafficking in crack cocaine ultimately matters less than whether Congress knew blacks would bear this burden. And it turns out Congress did know. It turns out, in fact, that the association between blacks and crack cocaine played a significant role in shaping public and congressional perceptions of drug abuse in 1986. (Sklansky, 1995, p. 1290)

The specter of crack-cocaine therefore provides an important and useful illustration of the intersection of race, socio-economic status, and justice in US society.

Turning back to rates of incarceration, the data suggests that in general the most consistent variable associated with incarceration is that of poverty (Loury, 2008) Additionally, sociological research indicates that higher concentrations of low-income populations appears to be associated with higher incidences of crime (Evans, 2004). When considering the role of race, historically segregated neighborhoods were noted to be a contributing factor to higher rates of incarceration, with Black neighborhoods tending to be more impoverished and therefore experiencing higher rates of crime and arrest (Massey & Denton, 1993). More recent research also implicates poverty as a factor associated with criminality. Findings suggest that poverty reduction interventions are positively associated with crime reduction, irrespective of the racial make-up of the neighborhood or community (Hannon & DeFina, 2005).

In sum, an understanding and critique of racial disparities within the US prison population needs to take into account the racialized nature of US, the disparities in wealth and income, the impact of both individual and systemic racism within the judicial system, and the intentionality of race-based oppression in the service of maintaining power among the White elite. Our discussion therefore leads us to adopt the Prison Industrial Complex as a framework in which to further understand the connections between race, economics, and incarceration.

THE PRISON INDUSTRIAL COMPLEX

Drawing on President Dwight Eisenhower's 1960 description of the military industrial complex in which he warned of the potential of misplaced power associated with the nexus of corporate power and the US military, scholars and social activists have labeled the relationship between prison and corporations as the Prison Industrial Complex (Davis, 2009; Thompson, 2012). The Prison Industrial Complex has been described as a "a symbiotic and profitable relationship between

politicians, corporations, the media, and state correctional institutions that gener-
ates the racialized use of incarceration as a response to social problems rooted in
the globalization of capital" (Sudbury, 2004, p. 12). Brewer and Heitzeg (2008)
go further in elucidating the nexus of a racialized social order, global capitalism,
and the function of mass incarceration:

> The extreme racialization of criminal justice and the rise of the prison industrial
> complex are directly tied to the expansion of global economy, the decline of the
> industry, and rise of the minimum wage service sector in the United States, and the
> growth of privatization of public services. (p. 636)

Note, the prison as an industry has multiple aspects to it. First, the prison industry
functions as a corporation. Here, we refer to the privatization of prisons and the
corporatization of the prison industry into for profit businesses that are listed on
the stock exchange. Examples of these corporations include the Corrections Corporations of America, stock listing CXW, and Avalon Correctional Services Inc.,
stock listed as City PK. In 2011, Correction Corporations of America listed its net
income as 162.51 million dollars and total assets at 3.1 billion dollars. Current
stock for CWX is trading at roughly $39 (Google Finance, n.d.).

Second is the type of labor prisoners engage in, and the extent to which this
labor can be utilized by for profit companies. Under the Prison Industry Enhancement Certification Program (PIECP), created by Congress in 1979, corporations
are allowed to enter joint ventures with state prisons. Through this act, prison-
made products can be sold to government agencies, public organizations, and
markets in other countries. The following advertisement captures this aspect of
the prison industry as informed by the PIECP:

> If you are a labor-intensive business and need unskilled or semi-skilled workers,
> you may want to operate in a Connecticut prison. We supply the workers, the space,
> and security. You supply the equipment, supervise the eager and carefully screened
> workers and control hiring and termination. (Chang & Thompkins, 2002, p. 54)

Given the higher rates of incarceration of People of Color in the U.S, it is under-
standable that some have viewed the exploitation of labor in the prison industry
as analogous to a new type of slavery (Gilmore, 2000; James, 2000). It is also
evident therefore that adopting a myopic approach to understanding the role of
prisons in society, i.e. only in the context of law and order (see Raphael & Stoll,
2013), fails to appreciate the complex relationships that account for a systematic
approach to the maintenance of economic power, at the cost of social exploitation
and subjugation of People of Color in the US. Although a more complete analysis
of the Prison Industrial Complex would include the manner in which disenfranchised Whites are also impacted by, and utilized in this system of domination, the
present discussion however is limited to the experience of Black Americans. As
such, we note that very few analysts have utilized the colonial analysis of Frantz
Fanon (1965), as a lens through which to understand racialized hyper-incarcera-

tion (see Staples, 1975). Fanon, a psychiatrist born in Martinique under French colonization, provided an analysis of the psychological impact of colonization as well as a critique of the colonizers' use of violence and economics as tools of societal oppression. In this regard, Fanon viewed the violence perpetrated by the colonizer, both psychic and physical, in combination with economic exploitation as the central weapons of domination. Fanon's critique therefore has direct implications for the current US penal system. Even a cursory review of the US penal system leads one to observe the nexus of state sanctioned violence, economic exploitation, and racialization. Note the following conclusion offered by scholars from the Fanon project:

> The prison industrial complex is a very deliberate and calculated product of the white power structure in the United States. It reifies the colonial relationship and power disparity between Africans and Whites. Particularly oppressive for Africans in the US, the expansion of prison has resulted in the neo-commoditization of Black bodies in a capitalist system with roots in the original commoditization of the African body, labor. Thus, Black incarceration serves a deliberate and specific purpose in sustaining white terror, power, and domination. (Williams et al., 2010, p. 164)

Accordingly, scholars have articulated the devastating impact of the Prison Industrial Complex and on Black individuals in the US (Belk, 2006; Smith & Hattery, 2010). Drawing attention to one area, Chandler (2003) has highlighted the health needs of Black women during incarceration. Given that Black women are disproportionately impoverished, Black women who are incarcerated enter the prison system with higher rates of chronic and serious health concerns. With little to no control of their bodies, the violence associated with incarceration represents a significant threat to the physical health of Black women who often enter prison in an already vulnerable state (Chandler, 2003). The impact of the Prison Industrial Complex on Black women has also been described as occurring at both individual and community levels (Sokoloff, 2003). Community level impacts include: (1) The removal of resources for women who remain in the community; (2) The loss of potential employment; (3) The burden of child-care for the children of women left behind by imprisonment; and (4) The creation of less stable communities. Individual impacts include: (1) Exposure to inadequate health care and substance abuse treatment; (2) Exposure to higher rates of infections (e.g., HIV; Hepatitis); (3) Exposure to sexual victimization; and (4) Difficulty in maintaining contact with and custody of children.

With regard to the impact of incarceration on children, the following has been noted. Children of an incarcerated parent are more likely to be placed in foster care or have disciplinary problems at school. Additionally, emerging evidence suggests that children of an incarcerated parent are more likely to exhibit poorer academic performance, have higher internalizing effects such as anxiety and depression, higher rates of behavioral and conduct disorders, higher rates of homelessness, higher rates of infant mortality and finally experience significant disruptions in attachment and bonding with their parents (Johnson & Easterling, 2012; Wildeman & Western, 2010). In sum, the data suggests that incarceration has adverse behavioral, social, and health-related effects on families (Roberts, 2004). It is also clear that the effects of hyper-incarceration extend well beyond the individual who is imprisoned, and has a direct impact on the larger Black community in the US.

A CYCLE OF OPPRESSION: BEFORE AND AFTER PRISON

At the beginning of our discussion, we were reminded by Sudbury (2004) that when seeking to understand oppression, adopting a single-issue focus is insufficient. With regard to the mass incarceration of Black men and women in the US, it is true that this phenomenon represents one aspect of a larger system of oppression that continues to shape and structure the lives of People of Color in the US (Belk, 2006). As such, we now review two related phenomena associated with racialized hyper-incarceration, namely 'school-to-prison,' and 'post prison rehabilitation' or re-entry.

School to Prison—The idea that structural factors prior to incarceration are associated with higher rates of imprisonment of People of Color is illustrated by disciplinary aspects of the public school system in the US. Reporting data from various sources, Krueger (2010) offers the following, rather bleak picture, of public school discipline from a race-based perspective: Black students account for 32% of all school suspensions while accounting for only 17% of the public school population; practices of suspension and expulsion are highest for Native American students (38%), followed by Black students (32%), Latino students (20%), and White students (15%). In sum, Krueger (2010) states:

> Many scholars, educators and activists are arguing that there exists an institutionalized collaboration between public schools and the juvenile justice system, and that with the help of criminal-justice-oriented educational policies and practices, disruptive students are systematically removed from the classroom and placed in suspension rooms, regional truancy offices, and juvenile detention facilities. (p. 385)

Approaching the school-to-prison pipeline from a different perspective, data suggests that individuals who do not have a high school diploma are up to five times more likely to go to prison than individuals who have graduated from high school. While this statistic holds true across racial groups, a significant disparity within this phenomenon still exists. Black American men with no high school diploma are five times more likely to be incarcerated than their White counterparts. Furthermore, for these men, the lifetime likelihood of going to prison is 60% (Pettit & Western, 2004; Western, 2006). Although a more complete analysis of school based disciplinary procedures is beyond the scope of the current discussion, it does however suggest that the manner in which Black children are treated in the public educational system, coupled with the higher rates of poverty among Black children, is part of a larger cycle of oppression. This cycle is seen to bear its fruit in a system that more frequently targets Black individuals for arrest (Taibbi, 2014), and a system that will send more Black individuals to prison at a higher frequency than their White counterparts, even when getting arrested for the same crime (Demuth & Steffensmeier, 2004; Sommers & Elsworth, 2001).

Reintegration and Reentry—The manner in which individuals re-enter society, following a term of imprisonment is also instructive when seeking to understand the larger cycle of racialized oppression within the US. Uggen, Manza and Thompson's 2006 review of the impact of criminal conviction on civic participation paints a disturbing description of a new class of American, namely the "felon class:

> A 'felon class' of more than 16 million felons and ex-felons represents 7.5 percent of the US population, 22.3 percent of the Black adult population and 33.4 percent of the Black male adult population. (p. 284)

Furthermore, these authors remind us that the number of explicit and implicit barriers facing convicted felons are substantial and represent a significant impediment to reintegration and full participation in civic and family life. These barriers include the inability to vote, higher rates of unemployment, restrictions on access to public housing and other social benefits, and the ability to be easily identified as a convicted felon due to public records now easily available in many states. Additionally, returning to a community which continues to face poverty, unemployment, crime, drugs and demoralization puts the ex-prisoner in a particularly vulnerable position, and increases the chance of offending or re-offending (Seiter & Kadela, 2003) When considering the nexus of social class and race, Wakefield and Uggen (2010) remind us that not only is incarceration directly related to social stratification, incarceration also appears to exacerbate social stratification within the US. Post incarceration data indicates that the earning income of inmates is consistently lower post-incarceration than pre-incarceration (Western 2002). In fact, Black men who have been incarcerated display a lifetime reduction in income earning of 4% (Wakefield & Uggen, 2010).

It is well known that gainful employment is associated with lower rates of recidivism (Visher, Winterfield & Coggeshall, 2005). As such, it is not surprising that public policy has included a focus on job training and job readiness for released prisoners. Research, however, suggests that the results of these programs are mixed. Visher et al. (2005) present findings from a meta-analysis of eight job readiness programs showing no effect on recidivism. Seiter and Kadela (2003), on the other hand, provide evidence to suggest that some prisoner reentry programs are associated with lower levels of recidivism including vocational training programs, drug and alcohol treatment programs, and pre-release programs. The authors do, however, indicate that factors such as lack of social services and greater community instability are positively associated with higher rates of recidivism. Given the fact that many incarcerated individuals have experienced multifactorial structural inequalities, it is clear that programs that do not attend to the underlying socio-economic conditions might have less efficacy in countering recidivism (Seiter & Kadela, 2003).

The current approach to reduction in recidivism is such that responsibility for not reoffending lies with the individual and less so with the structures and environment that often are influential in the initial offense. There appears to be less focus on addressing systemic issues associated with pre-incarceration, incarceration, and post-incarceration (see Latessa, 2012). Thus, the argument I am making here is that programs and policies that attempt to address high rates of incarceration by focusing on a reduction in recidivism, while important, might also be misguided if they do not also attend to conditions associated with racial oppression. Although a patchwork approach to remediating racialized hyper-incarceration might have some utility, and clearly has pragmatic benefits, prison abolition and restorative justice have been offered as more viable alternatives to addressing the mass imprisonment of people of Color within the US.

PRISON ABOLITION AND RESTORATIVE JUSTICE; APPROACHES FOR DECARCERATION

Prison Abolition

As we conclude our review of the current status of racialized incarceration in the US, we stop to consider potential alternatives to moving forward. In Michelle Alexander's *The New Jim Crow: Mass Incarceration in the Age of Colorblindness* (2012), she leaves us to ponder various approaches to reducing mass incarceration including securing true juries of peers, reinvigorating the civil rights movement, reclaiming it from the domain of layers, engaging civil disobedience, and educating the general populace on the nature of racialized incarceration. Although these approaches are valid, have historical legitimacy, and have the potential for change, they also require the activist to work within the current system. Audre Lorde's (2001) reference to the masters' tools not being able to dismantle the masters' house might have particular relevance here. Perhaps, what is needed instead is the creation of a new system that resists, confronts, and expels those foundational constructs associated with this neo-slavery, this neo-Jim Crow, this racialized hyper-incarceration.

Remember that various authors have identified the globalization, income inequality, state violence, political conservatism, racial oppression, and gender oppression as the critical foundations of racialized hyper-incarceration within the Prison Industrial Complex. As Subdury (2004) reminds us, focusing on a single-issue is a limited approach to challenging oppression and hegemony. In this regard, abolition of prisons presents a viable option as it represents a challenge to all the systems associated with the maintenance and promulgation of prison as a legitimate vehicle for punishment and rehabilitation. The prison abolition movement therefore is a broad based approached to social change. As such, it focuses on the following: social factors associated with the higher likelihood of criminal offense; rethinking the definition of crime; eradicating racialized structures associated with higher arrest and incarceration such as police harassment, police violence, and surveillance, eliminating racial bias within the judicial system, and exposing color-blind policies that have the effect of institutionalizing racial bias. Russell and Carlton's (2013) definition of abolition provides a useful summary of the goals of the prison abolition movement and builds on the historical use of the term abolition, when referring to the eradication of slavery

> Abolition stated broadly refers to political visions and activist practices that ulti-mately strive for the eradication of prison, policing and surveillance. Abolitionist campaigns build strategies for decarceration and align with the struggles of crimi-nalized, imprisoned and oppressed communities. The injustices associated with the racialized dimensions of mass incarceration are frequently emphasized by abolition-ists, and understood and historicized as continuations of other racist structures and institutions. (p. 474)

Abolition relies on the notion of intersectionality, especially as it relates to gender, race, and social class: "Intersectional critiques focus on dynamic forces, such as racialization and gendering, rather than static identity categories, and recognize how intersecting forces shift and transform the operation of power across particu-lar institutional fields" (Russell & Carlton, 2013, p. 481).

Prison abolition as a viable approach to decarceration, and as a way in which to redress the racialized hyper-incarceration is a direct challenge to the very foun-dations on which the prison industry exists. Prison abolition therefore could in-clude the following strategies: (1) Reorientation of wealth distribution through narrowing the income gap; (2) Addressing poverty as a core construct of social disintegration; (3) Decreasing the militarization of the police and redistributing funding to social issues; (4) identifying and eliminating state sanctioned violence of which prison represents an integral part (e.g., solitary confinement, psychologi-cal abuse, capital punishment etc.); (5) Attending to school based discipline and disrupting the school-to-prison phenomenon; (6) Providing communities of color with a greater sense of sovereignty by decreasing police presence, and empower-ing of community leaders and educators to apply culturally relevant programs to violence reduction; (7) Fostering political activism and self-esteem enhancement; (8) Educating for non-violent confrontation and educating the public at all levels about the nature of ongoing racial and economic oppression; (9) The provision of tools for activists (e.g., de-investing in for-profit prison corporations); (10) Facili-tating social action such as mass demonstrations outside courthouses and prison complexes; (11) Meticulous documentation of police abuse; and (12) Urgent re-search on the psychosocial effects of poverty. (Davis & Rodriguez, 2000; Meiners & Winn, 2010).

The strategy being advocated here calls for a comprehensive approach to ra-cialized hyper-incarceration. Prison abolition as a remedy applies not only to the end of prison as we know it, but also to the elimination of those oppressive social conditions which are both directly, and indirectly associated with the Prison In-dustrial Complex and the accompanying mass incarceration of People of Color.

Restorative Justice

As previously noted, the current and prevailing paradigm in criminal justice is one of retribution. Given the manner in which prison is such a dominant part of our social landscape, the ability to envision a different process is so challenging that supporters of prison abolition, decarceration, and restorative justice are routinely viewed as naive, utopian, idealists, or other terms meant to convey a sense of paternalistic condemnation (Davis & Rodriguez, 2000). I would argue, however, that in order to imagine change, one first has to believe that change is necessary and, furthermore, that change is possible. In this regard, restorative justice offers another chance to imagine and believe. Restorative justice at its core focuses on reparation as opposed to retribution (Bazemore, 1998). It seeks to restore, rather than restrain, to repair rather than just punish. Note the goals of restorative justice as defined by Morrison and Ahmed (2006):

> Restorative justice aims to empower participants, through fostering accountability and responsibility between those affected by harmful behavior. To this end, it seeks social and emotional resolution that affords healing, reparation, and reintegration, which in turn ameliorates efforts to prevent further harm. (p. 210)

To this end, restorative justice is more interested in bringing together the perpetrator and the victim, with the victim's rights and reparation being more prominent than any interest of the state. Clearly, restorative justice presents a direct challenge to the Prison Industrial Complex, which primarily serves the interest of the state, and increasingly serves the interests of global corporatization. Furthermore, irrespective of the aggressive approach to policing and sentencing, the US continues to have some of the highest crime rates in comparable countries. Note the following comparison of crime rates between New Zealand and the US, taken from the New Zealand Ministry of Justice (2000). I focus on New Zealand here, as New Zealand has been one of the foremost countries to adopt a restorative justice approach. Although it is unclear to what extent the New Zealand restorative justice approach is associated with the crime statistics reported below, it is clear that there is a significant disparity in rates of crime between the US and New Zealand.

Type of Crime	Rate for 100,100 – US	Rate per 100,000 NZ
Murder/Manslaughter	5.5	1.7
Robbery	114.9	46.2
Forcible Rape	32	13.7
Aggravated Assault	323.6	71.2

Given the relevant recency of restorative justice approaches in Western societies, moving forward it would be important to examine the links between restorative justice, recidivism, and reduction in crime. The manner in which a country like New Zealand has embraced restorative justice within its legal system, as well as the significantly lower rates of major crime hints at an important role that restorative justice might play in reduction of crime and accompanying rates of incarceration.

There is, however, emerging evidence suggesting that restorative justice approaches are associated with positive outcomes. Specifically, restorative justice programs have been noted to significantly reduce recidivism when compared to programs that use non-restorative approaches (Latimer, Dowden, & Muise, 2005). It is also encouraging to note that there are numerous examples of restorative justice programs and its applications exists across many settings and disciplines including education, social work, corporate regulators and high profile instances such as South Africa's truth and reconciliation commission (Roche, 2006). Furthermore, when one considers racialized aspects of culture, it could be argued that for Black Americans, restorative justice might be a more culturally appropriate approach to both reductions in incarceration and crime, given the Afro-centric values of community and relationship (Schiele, 1994). Additionally, given the social structure of pre-colonial African societies who focused more on repair than punishment (Van Ness & Strong, 2013), restorative justice could also be a culturally consistent approach for a community that continues to lack in sovereignty and autonomy. Abolition or prisons and restorative justice are therefore two approaches that deserve further interrogation with regard to the adoption of strategies and approaches to the reduction and elimination of racialized hyperincarceration in the US.

In conclusion, racialized hyper-incarceration can be thought of as a logical extension of race and classed based policies that seek to maintain systems of oppression. The Prison Industrial Complex presents a useful illustration of the nexus between race, economics, political ideology and power. In order to challenge this hegemony, prison abolition and restorative justice are offered as two viable options and should be the starting point in our attempts to restore what has been lost.

REFERENCES

Alexander, M. (2012). *The new Jim Crow: Mass incarceration in the age of color blindness*. New York, NY: The New Press.

Barnes, H. E. (1921). The historical origin of the prison system in America. *Journal of the American Institute of Criminal Law and Criminology*, 35–60.

Bazemore, G. (1998). Restorative justice and earned redemption: Communities, victims, and offender reintegration. *American Behavioral Scientist, 41*, 786–815.

Belk Jr, A. G. (2006). *A new generation of native sons: Men of Color and the prison-industrial complex*. Washington, DC: Joint Center for Political and Economic Studies.

Bobo, L. D. (2011). Somewhere between Jim Crow & Post-Racialism: Reflections on the racial divide in America today. *Daedalus 140*, 11–36.

Brewer, R. M., & Heitzeg, N. A. (2008). The racialization of crime and punishment: Criminal justice, colorblind racism, and the political economy of the prison industrial complex. *American Behavioral Scientist, 51*, 625–644.

Brown, E. (2002). *The condemnation of little B*. Boston, MA: Beacon Press.

Butler, P. (1997). Brotherman: Reflections of a reformed black prosecutor. In E. Close (Ed.), *The Darden dilemma: 12 black writers on justice, race, and conflicting loyalties* (pp. 1–9). New York, NY: Harpers Collins Publishers

Cashmore, E., & McLaughlin, E. (2013). *Out of order: Policing Black people.* New York, NY: Routledge.

Chandler, C. (2003). Death and dying in America: The prison industrial complex's impact on women's health. *Berkeley Women's LJ, 18,* 40–60.

Chang, T. F. H., & Thompkins, D. E. (2002). Corporations goes to prisons: The expansion of corporate power in the correctional industry. *Labor Studies Journal, 27,* 45–69.

Coker, D. (2003). Foreword: Addressing the real world of racial injustice in the criminal justice system. *The Journal of Criminal Law and Criminology, 93,* 827–882.

Davis, A. (2009). Masked racism: Reflections on the prison industrial complex. In P. Rothenberg (Ed.), *Race, class, and gender in the United States: An integrated study* (8th ed., pp. 643–647). New York, NY: Worth Publishers.

Davis, A. Y., & Rodriguez, D. (2000). The challenge of prison abolition: A conversation. *Social Justice, 27,* 212–219.

Demuth, S., & Steffensmeier, D. (2004). Ethnicity effects on sentence outcomes in large urban courts: Comparisons among black, white and Hispanic defendants. *Social Science Quarterly, 84,* 994–1011.

Evans, G. (2004). The environment of childhood poverty. *American Psychologist, 59,* 77–92.

Fanon, F. (1965). *The wretched of the earth.* New York, NY: Grove Press.

Gilmore, K. (2000). Slavery and prison: Understanding the connections. *Social Justice, 27,* 195–205.

Goode, E. (2013, February 27). Incarceration rates for Blacks have fallen sharply reports shows. *The New York Times.* Retrieved from http://www.nytimes.com/2013/02/28/us/incarceration-rates-for-blacks-dropped-report-shows.html

Google Finance: Stock market quotes, news, currency conversions & more. (n. d.). Google. Retrieved March 1, 2015, from http://www.google.com/finance

Hannon, L., & DeFina, R. (2005) Violent crime in African American and White neighborhoods: Is poverty's detrimental effect race-specific? *Journal of Poverty, 9,* 49–67.

Isaac, A. R., Lockhart, L. L., & Williams, L. (2001). Violence against African American women in prisons and jails: Who's minding the shop. *Journal of Human Behavior in the Social Environment, 4,* 129–153.

James, J. (2000). The dysfunctional and the disappearing: Democracy, race, and imprisonment. *Social Identities, 6,* 483–493.

Johnson, E. I., & Easterling, B. (2012). Understanding unique effects of parental incarceration on children: Challenges, progress, and recommendations. *Journal of Marriage and Family, 74,* 342–356.

Keen, B., & Jacobs, D. (2009). Racial threat, partisan politics, and racial disparities in prison admissions: A panel analysis. *Criminology, 47,* 209–238.

Krueger, P. (2010) It's not just a method! The epistemic and political work of young people's lifeworlds at the school-prison nexus, *Race Ethnicity and Education, 13,* 383–408.

Latessa, E. (2012). Why work is important and how to improve the effectiveness of correctional reentry programs that target employment. *Criminology and Public Policy, 11,* 87–91.

Latimer, J., Dowden, C., & Muise, D. (2005). The effectiveness of restorative justice practices: A meta-analysis. *The Prison Journal, 85,* 127–144.

Leigey, M. E., & Bachman, R. (2007). The influence of crack cocaine on the likelihood of incarceration for a violent offense: An examination of a prison sample. *Criminal Justice Policy Review, 18,* 335–354.

Lichtenstein, A. (2011). A "labor history" of mass incarceration. *Labor: Studies in Working-Class History of the Americas, 8,* 5–14.

Lorde, A. (2001). The master's tool will never dismantle the master's house. In K. K. Bhavnani (Ed.), *Feminism and race* (pp. 89–92). New York, NY: Oxford University Press.

Loury, G. C (2008). *Race, incarceration, and American values.* Cambridge, MA: Boston Review Books.

Marger, M. N. (2011). *Race and ethnic relations: American and global perspectives* (9th ed.). Belmont, CA: Cengage.

Massey, D. S., & Denton, N. A. (1993). *American apartheid: Segregation and the making of the underclass.* Cambridge, MA: Harvard University Press.

McCorkel, J. (2004). Criminally dependent? Gender, punishment, and the rhetoric of welfare reform. *Social Politics: International Studies in Gender, State & Society, 11,* 386–410.

Meiners, E. R., & Winn, M. T. (2010) Resisting the school to prison pipeline: The practice to build abolition democracies. *Race Ethnicity and Education, 13,* 271–276.

Miller, R. J. (2013). Race, hyper-Incarceration, and US poverty policy in historic perspective. *Sociology Compass, 7,* 573–589.

Morrison, B., & Ahmed, E. (2006). Restorative justice and civil society: Emerging practice, theory, and evidence. *Journal of Social Issues, 62,* 209–215.

Neville, H. A., & Pieterse, A. L. (2009). Racism, white supremacy, and resistance: Contextualizing Black American experiences. In H. A. Neville, B. N. Tynes, & S. O. Utsey (Eds.), *Handbook of African American Psychology* (pp. 159–174) Thousand Oaks, CA: Sage Publications.

New Zealand Ministry of Justice. (2000). *New Zealand compare to the USA: Violent crime.* Retrieved from http://www.justice.govt.nz.

O'Brien, P. (2006). Maximizing success for drug-affected women after release from prison. *Women & Criminal Justice, 17,* 95–113.

Pager, D., & Shepherd, H. (2008). The sociology of discrimination: Racial discrimination in employment, housing, credit, and consumer markets. *Annual review of sociology, 34,* 181.

Pettit B., & Western B. (2004). Mass imprisonment and the life course: Race and class inequality in US incarceration. *American Sociological Review, 69,* 151–169.

Queally, J., & Semuels, A. (August 1, 2014). Eric Garner's death in NYPD chokehold case ruled a homicide. *LA Times.* Retrieved from http://www.latimes.com/nation/nation-now/la-na-nn-garner-homicide-0140801-story.html

Raphael, S., & Stoll, M. A. (2009). Why are so many Americans in prison? In S. Raphael & M. A. Stoll, (Eds.), *Do prisons make us safer? The benefits and costs of the prison boom* (pp 27–72). New York, NY: Russell Sage Foundation.

Raphael, S., & Stoll, M. A. (2013). *Why are so many Americans in prison?* New York, NY: Russell Sage Foundation.

Reynolds, M. (2008). The war on drugs, prison building, and globalization: Catalysts for the global incarceration of women: *NWSA Journal, 20,* 72–95.

Rhodes, L. (2001). Toward and anthropology of prisons. *Annual Review of Anthropology, 30,* 65–83.

Roberts, D. E. (2004). The social and moral cost of mass incarceration in African American communities. *Stanford Law Review, 56,* 1271–1305.

Roche, D. (2006). Dimensions of restorative justice. *Journal of Social Issues, 62,* 217–238.

Russell, E., & Carlton, B. (2013). Pathways, race and gender responsive reform: Through an abolitionist lens. *Theoretical Criminology, 17,* 474–492.

Schiele, J. H. (1994). Afrocentricity as an alternative world view for equality. *Journal of Progressive Human Services, 5,* 5–25.

Seiter, R. P., & Kadela, K. R. (2003). Prisoner reentry: What works, what does not, and what is promising. *Crime Delinquency, 49,* 360–390.

Sklansky, D. A. (1995). Cocaine, race, and equal protection. *Stanford Law Review, 47,* 1283–1322.

Smedley A., & Smedley, B. D. (2011). *Race in North America: Origin and evolution of a worldview* (4th ed.). Boulder, CO: Westview Press.

Smedley, B. (2012). The lived experience of race and his health consequences. *American Journal of Public Health, 102,* 933–935.

Smith, E., & Hattery, A. J. (2010). African American men and the prison industrial complex. *Western Journal of Black Studies, 34,* 387–397.

Sokoloff, N. J. (2003). The impact of the prison industrial complex on African American women. *Souls, 5,* 31–46.

Sommers, S. R., & Elsworth, P. C. (2001). White juror bias: An investigation of prejudice against Black defendants in the American courtroom. *Psychology, Public Policy, and the Law, 7,* 201–229.

Staples, R. (1975). White racism, black crime and American justice: An application of the colonial model to explain to explain crime and race. *Phylon, 36,* 14–22.

Sudbury, J. (2004). A world without prisons, resisting militarism, globalized punishment, and empire. *Social Justice, 31,* 9–30.

Sudbury, J. (2005). Celling black bodies: Black women in the global prison industrial complex. *Feminist Review, 80,* 162–179.

Taibbi, M. (2014). *The divide: American justice in the age of the wealth gap.* New York, NY: Random House.

Thompson, H. A. (2012). The prison industrial complex: A growth industry in a shrinking economy. *New Labor Forum, 21*(3), 38–47. The Murphy Institute/City University of New York.

Tonry, M. (2010). The social, psychological, and political causes of racial disparities in the American criminal justice system. *Crime and justice, 39,* 273–312.

Uggen, C., Manza, J., & Thompson, M. (2006). Citizenship, democracy, and civic reintegration of criminal offenders. *The ANNALS of the American Academic of Political and Social Science, 605,* 281–310.

US Census Bureau. (2010). *Income, poverty, and health insurance coverage in the United States.* Report P60–239. Washington, DC: US Government Printing Office.

Van Ness, D. W., & Strong, K. H. (2013). *Restoring justice: An introduction to restorative justice.* London, UK: Andersen Press.

Visher, C. A., Winterfield, L., & Coggeshall, M. B. (2005). Ex-offender employment programs and recidivism: A meta-analysis. *Journal of Experimental Criminology, 1,* 295–315.

Wakefield, S., & Uggen, C. (2010). Incarceration and stratification. *Annual Review of Sociology, 36,* 387–406.

Western, B. (2002). The impact of incarceration on wage mobility and inequality. *American Sociological Review, 67,* 526–544.

Western, B. (2006.) *Punishment and inequality in America.* New York, NY: Russell Sage Foundation.

Western, B., & Wildeman, C. (2009). The Black family and mass incarceration. *The ANNALS of the American Academy of Political and Social Science, 621,* 221–242.

Wildeman, C., & Western, B. (2010). Incarceration in fragile families. *The future of children, 20,* 157–177.

Williams III, O., Pieterse, A. L., DeLoach, C., Bolden, M. A., Ball, J., & Awadalla, S. (2010). Beyond health disparities: Examining power disparities and industrial complexes from the views of Franz Fanon. *Journal of Pan African Studies, 3,* 151–178.

Yates, M. D. (2012). The great inequality. *Monthly Review, 63,* 1–18.

Zinn, H. (2005). *A people's history of the United States.* New York, NY: Harper Collins.

CHAPTER 12

THE EFFICACY OF PROGRAMMATIC INITIATIVES ON IMPROVING THE GRADUATION RATES OF BLACK MALE COLLEGIANS

Jameel A. Scott, Kourtney P. Gray,
Christopher C. Graham, and Robert T. Palmer

INTRODUCTION

Over the past decade, many scholars have called attention to the challenges and obstacles that Black males face in accessing and succeeding in college (Cuyjet, 1997, 2006; Harper, 2006, 2012; Jackson & Moore, 2006, 2008; Palmer & Wood, 2012; Strayhorn, 2008, 2010, Wood, 2012, 2013, 2014). Studies have covered a multitude of topics on Black male college students, including low socio-economic status (Palmer, Davis, & Hilton, 2009; Scott, 2012) and academic preparation (Davis & Palmer, 2010; Kimbrough & Harper, 2006; Palmer & Davis, 2012). However, the fact remains that within the last 40 years, there has been little to no improvement in the graduation rates of Black male college students on a national

Talking About Structural Inequalities in Everyday Life: New Politics of Race in Groups, Organizations, and Social Systems, pages 225–239.
Copyright © 2016 by Information Age Publishing

level (Harper, 2006, 2012; Palmer et al., 2009; Palmer, Wood, Dancy, & Stray-horn, 2014; Strayhorn, 2008). Black men account for only 4.3% of the total en-rollment at four-year postsecondary institutions in the United States (US), which reflects the same percentage now as in 1976 (Cuyjet, 2006; Harper, 2006, 2012; Palmer et al., 2014; Strayhorn, 2008). Given the relatively flat enrollment and degree completion rates among Black males, the information presented herein may assist in increasing the retention and graduation rates of this sub-population of students.

In this chapter, we will first discuss fundamental impediments related to pre-kindergarten through 12th grade (PK–12) that influence access to higher education for Black males. Second, we will provide a brief overview of the experiences of Black males in higher education pertaining to their involvement in clubs and orga-nizations, with a particular emphasis on the ways these initiatives help to facilitate retention and graduation for this demographic of students. Third, using a strength-based approach, we will analyze two higher education institutions, and discuss the efficacy of programmatic initiatives on increasing the success rate of Black males. This chapter concludes with implications and recommendations for institutional practices. It is assumed that the practices identified, albeit not exhaustive, could assist many universities in increasing their retention and graduation rates among Black males.

Our understanding of Black students' experiences in postsecondary education has been shaped by racialized institutional structures and researchers' biases that may serve to reinforce negative stereotypes of this group. It is well documented that there are racialized structures that have impeded the success of Black stu-dents, which will be addressed in this chapter (Cuyjet, 1997, 2006; Jackson & Moore, 2006, 2008; Palmer et al., 2014). For example, these racialized structures are manifested by the lack of serious targeted support provided for Black students and the overarching assumptions about this group. These assumptions have influ-enced the ways in which professors and administrators teach and provide services to this population. In particular, many college and university administrators would rather analyze why Black students drop out of school, as opposed to analyzing high-achieving Black students, in order to determine best practices to help support their success. The educational structures for Black male college students, such as low numbers of Black faculty and racial profiling in and out of the classroom, have been noted to be impediments to Black male student success.

The impediments that influence academic outcomes and experiences of Black male college students present themselves in many ways, including the egregious racial profiling case of Black male students at SUNY Oneonta in 1992, which was recently chronicled in the film *Brothers of the Black List* (Gallagher, 2014). This incident made national headlines when a school official provided the police with the names of Black male students at the college that resulted in police interroga-tion of these students. Following the report of an older White woman that she was assaulted by a young Black male, several SUNY Oneonta Black male students were subjected to police interrogation vis-à-vis being removed from classrooms, residence halls, and buses, etc. This incident involving the racialized trauma of Black male college students had a far-reaching impact on the emotional and academic outcomes of the students (e.g., transferring to other institutions, leaving school, etc.). This case provides implications for the continued focus on the role of racialized social structures that influence the educational experiences for Black male college students.

Indeed, scholarship on Black students has assumed a deficit model (Fries-Britt 1997; Harper, 2009; Jackson & Moore 2006, 2008; Palmer et al., 2014; Wood & Palmer, 2015), which arguably has contributed to these racialized structures. For example, researchers have viewed and studied Blacks from a deficit-based framework, usually asking questions like, "How many are failing?" "Why are Black students dropping out?" and "Why are Black students in remedial classes?" In order to assist in shifting the tide on the current trends in research for Black students and challenge some of the impeding structures, this chapter approaches these research questions with a strength-based perspective in mind. This critical approach shifts the conversation from a focus on Black student failures to an emphasis on their achievements with resiliencies associated with navigating educational institutions (Harper, 2012). In this context, this chapter will focus on two universities that Harper (2012) identified as effective in increasing the graduation rates of Black male collegians. The recognition of these institutions indicates that some universities have been purposeful about increasing Black male success through targeted support programs and services. Moving beyond a deficit-based approach and incorporating a strength-based approach, this chapter will study two universities to better understand promising practices to help higher education officials improve the completion rates of Black male students.

CHALLENGES TO THE ACCESS AND SUCCESS OF BLACK MALES IN POSTSECONDARY EDUCATION

There is a tremendous amount of literature that highlights the problems that Black males encounter in PK–12, making it difficult for them to access and succeed in postsecondary education (Cuyjet, 1997; Davis, 2003; Howard, 2013; Jackson & Moore, 2006, 2008; Palmer et al., 2014; Wood & Palmer, 2015). Academic problems hindering the educational progress of Black males begin early (Davis, 2003; Epps, 1995; Garibaldi, 2007; Howard-Hamilton, 1997; Wood & Palmer, 2015). For example, Black males are less likely to attend schools that are funded equally to their White counterparts. This funding disparity between school districts is intricately connected to the kind of resources that their schools are able to provide for students. Moreover, schools with more resources are able to offer smaller classes, which positively contribute to student learning and achievement (Garibaldi, 2007; Jackson & Moore, 2006, 2008; Perry, Steele, & Hilliard, 2003; Wood & Palmer, 2015). This places Black students at a disadvantage, given that they disproportionately attend schools with fewer resources and larger class sizes.

Moreover, because Black students attend PK–12 schools that receive less funding, these schools typically are not able to provide the latest books, laboratories, instructional material, and technology compared to those that receive more funding (Garibaldi, 2007; Jackson & Moore, 2006, 2008; Wood & Palmer, 2015).

Another factor that contributes to the disproportionate under-preparedness of Black males in higher education is academic tracking. Academic tracking promotes inequality because students who are placed in high-achieving academic tracks are exposed to more complex and challenging classroom instruction than those who are placed in low-achieving academic tracks (Oakes, Gamoran, & Page, 1992). Moreover, existing empirical research shows that Black males are overrepresented in low-ability or remedial tracks (Cuyjet, 1997, 2006; Harper, 2006, 2012; Jackson & Moore, 2006, 2008; Strayhorn, 2008), even when their scores on standardized assessments are equal to or better than their White peers (Garibaldi, 2007; Jackson & Moore, 2006, 2008; Wood & Palmer, 2015).

Not only are more Black males likely to be placed in lower academic tracks, they are more likely to be found in special education programs (Jackson & Moore, 2006, 2008; Strayhorn, 2008; Wood & Palmer, 2015). While Black males are overrepresented in remedial courses, they are underrepresented in gifted education programs as well as advanced placement (AP) courses (Jackson & Moore, 2006, 2008; Wood & Palmer, 2014). Research indicates that participating in gifted education and AP courses is important because these programs and courses have a positive impact on a variety of achievement outcomes, such as higher scores on standardized college entrance assessments, which is tied to more completed years of education (Jackson & Moore, 2006, 2008; Wood & Palmer, 2015). Thus, the under-representation of Black males in gifted educational programs and AP courses negatively influences their preparation and subsequent success (Jackson & Moore, 2006, 2008; Perry et al., 2003). Contributing greatly to the under-representation of Black students in gifted education or AP courses is the racially-biased perception among teachers, counselors, and school administrators that Black students are intellectually inferior and not capable of coping with the rigorous curriculum of AP programs.

The under-representation of qualified teachers among educators who serve large numbers of Black students is another contributor to their lack of preparedness for success in higher education. Research shows that core academic classes in high-poverty schools are more likely to be taught by a teacher unfamiliar with the field, as compared to low-poverty schools (Jackson & Moore, 2006, 2008; Wood & Palmer, 2015). Since Black students are more likely to attend these schools compared to their White counterparts, they experience disproportionate challenges in comparison to their White peers as they continue their educational trajectory beyond PK–12.

In addition to being minimally qualified, teachers' low expectations can hinder the achievement of Black males (Davis, 2003; Garibaldi, 2007; Palmer et al., 2009; Strayhorn, 2008; Wood & Palmer, 2015). Teachers and counselors are far more likely to impose negative expectations upon Black males as it relates to attending college, than upon their White counterparts (Palmer et al., 2009; Wood & Palmer, 2015). Given that, Black students are likely to have lower scores on standardized examinations than their majority counterparts; teachers are more likely to have higher expectations for White students in comparison to students of color. In turn, teacher expectations lead to differences in teacher behavior, which can influence a student's academic performance, suggesting that those expectations can become a self-fulfilling prophecy (Jackson & Moore, 2006, 2008; Wood & Palmer, 2015). For example, research demonstrates that Black males in PK–12 are disproportionately disciplined, more apt to face expulsions, and suspended longer and more frequently than are White students (Garibaldi, 2007; Jackson & Moore, 2006, 2008; Wood & Palmer, 2014). Indeed, Garibaldi noted that in the majority of the 16,000 school districts across the country, Black males had the highest rates of suspensions, expulsions, non-promotions, and the lowest rates of secondary school graduation.

BRIEF OVERVIEW OF BLACK MEN IN HIGHER EDUCATION

Black undergraduate men in higher education routinely encounter racist stereotypes and racial microaggressions that undermine their achievement and sense of belonging (Bonner, 2010; Harper, 2009). Sense of belonging underscores the importance of students feeling like their presence on campus is noticed and valued by faculty, staff, and peers (Strayhorn, 2012). Since many Black men do not feel as if they belong on campus, some drop out of higher education or transfer to other institutional types, such as historically Black colleges and universities (Fries-Britt & Turner, 2002). Their reasoning for transferring is varied, but most often includes wanting support and feeling isolated. Indeed, recognizing the obstacles that Black males encounter as collegians provides a relevant context for the importance of institutional culture and how it can influence Black men on campus.

Additionally, in comparison to their same-race female counterparts, Black men participate less frequently in campus activities, hold fewer leadership positions, and report lower grades (Cuyjet, 1997; Harper, Carini, Bridges, & Hayek, 2004; Palmer & Wood, 2012; Palmer et al., 2014). This research provides a context for the importance of finding ways to engage, connect, and support students who may feel out of place and tend to be less involved in college life. Understanding the lack of belonging among Black men on most college campuses and their lack of engagement provides some insight into the fact that Black male college completion rates are lowest among both sexes and all racial/ethnic groups in US higher education (Harper, 2006; Strayhorn, 2010). Indeed, the six-year graduation rate for Black male students attending public colleges and universities was 33.3%, compared to 48.1% for all students (Harper, 2012). Additionally, the dropout rate for students, particularly Black students, remains relatively high (Palmer &Wood, 2012; Strayhorn, 2010).

Overall, Black male collegians tend to have less social and cultural capital, which refers to non-financial resources, such as social networks and knowledge that stimulate social mobility beyond economic means (Lareau & Weininger, 2009; Palmer & Gasman, 2008). For example, based on the theory of cultural capital, a first-generation Black male college student may have lower cultural capital, which could result in him having more challenges getting through college, compared to someone else with higher cultural capital. Indeed, a student whose parents attended college, and have been exposed to adults from various career fields, such as doctors and professors, may have a slight advantage when it comes to their ability to graduate from college compared to someone who did not. Black men on college campuses are often low in numbers (e.g., Harper, 2012), and due, in part, to racism, their ability to integrate within the campus community and take advantage of campus offerings is diminished. Thus, this decreases their connection to the campus, poses a threat to their academic achievement, and ultimately may increase the dropout rate for this population of students.

What Can Be Done

Given the factors that challenge the access and success of Black men in both PK–12 and higher education, more must be done to better prepare, assist, and support Black male college students. Research in this area provides some strategies that institutions can take to improve, enhance, and ensure success among this population (Alexander, 2009). Harper and Harris (2012) assert that student organizations can be an affirming, supportive way to help Black men navigate the process of earning a degree by providing them with a ready-made peer group. Moreover, convening internal and external stakeholders to consider the theme of Black male success, with the goal of creating programs to address the student concerns, can assist with the integration of Black students (Scott, 2012). For example, the University System of Georgia created an African-American Male Initiative to increase the recruitment, retention, and graduation of Black males within the university system through strategic interventions. The initiative's current efforts are focused on collaborations and partnerships and sharing best practices for enhanced outcomes for Black male students. Furthermore, Townsen (1994) found that if a school makes a concerted effort to increase graduation rates, by increasing faculty involvement, providing mentorship and tutoring on campus, and being attentive to the students' financial aid needs, there is a greater likelihood that their graduation numbers will increase.

Harper and Kuykendall (2012) and Wood and Palmer (2012) provide standards for Black male campus initiatives, which include, making student inequalities transparent and using data to guide institutional activities. They argue that these processes are imperative for campus buy-in and to create a culture of care and concern for young Black men across campus. They also emphasize that Black men should be meaningfully engaged as collaborators and viewed as experts in designing, implementing, and addressing inequalities. Allowing these men to guide and facilitate the process aligns with a culturally relevant approach, and will make for stronger programming and increased success. Including Black collegians as contributors and leaders in the process can enhance their undergraduate experience.

Harper and Kuykendall (2012) as well as Wood and Palmer (2012) further argue that it is important for actions intended to improve academic achievement and student development to be guided by a written strategy that is created in a collaborative manner, including everyone from Black undergraduates to the college president. Improved degree attainment rates must be prioritized over social programming, initiatives must be grounded in research, and efforts must be enhanced by insights from Black male student achievers. Additionally, institutional agents should engage in authentic conversations about racism and its harmful effects on Black male student outcomes. Finally, at every level, institutional agents must be held accountable for improving Black male student retention, academic success, engagement, and graduation rates. Following these standards will provide for an enhanced institution, but more importantly, it will enhance the sense of belonging for Black men. These findings are similar to that of Lynch and Engle (2010), who suggest that postsecondary institutions will increase their Black graduation rates when all faculty and staff, from the university president to teaching assistants, focus strategically on increasing the number of students of color who graduate. Their findings show that "…when colleges focus on student success, all students benefit greatly—particularly students of color" (Lynch & Engle, 2010, p. 2). Therefore, the responsibility to change the educational trajectory for Black students rests not only on the students, but also with those charged with caring for those students—faculty and staff. Promoting active collaboration within campus organizations is one way to engage students in this manner and increase the retention of Black students.

METHODOLOGY

In the previous sections, we examined pertinent literature regarding Black male college students in PK–12 and higher education and discussed some critical elements germane to Black male initiatives. In this section, we discuss the methodology that we used to identify strategies that support colleges and universities. Harper's (2012) report provided a list of schools as well as various statistics related to Black student success rates. We chose two schools included in Harper's study, one comprehensive state university and one public research university, in part, because most Black males that attend a four-year college attend one of these two types of institutions (Thelin, 2004). Then, we researched and analyzed programs at the schools that aim to retain, engage, and graduate Black male students, identifying at least one program that targeted all three. Based on the higher education literature, programs that consist of a mentoring component, academic support component, and informal and social education opportunities are often the most successful at retaining and graduating their students (Ancis, Sedlacek, & Mohr,

2000); therefore, we focused our questions on these three areas. We interviewed program representatives (faculty and staff), asking the following questions:

1. What factors about your program contribute to Black male graduation rates?
2. What informs your practices, i.e., research?
3. What is unique about your program?
4. How have you been able to maintain success at graduating Black male students?
5. How has the success of your Black male students informed your program practices?

In addition to the interviews, we requested documents and viewed public materials located on program websites in order to evaluate the programs' success rates. Finally, we analyzed the two programs to determine similarities and other findings that present promising practices for higher institutions to implement in order to increase Black male graduation rates.

TWO PROGRAMS

This section is dedicated to providing information on two different higher education institutions that are making improvements in graduating Black male college students. We analyzed the programs at The Ohio State University and Towson University in order to identify Black male initiatives that are effective in graduating Black male students.

The Ohio State University

The Ohio State University in Columbus, Ohio, founded in 1870, is a public research university, which is consistently ranked as one of the most selective flagship universities by US News & World Report. Currently, it is the third largest university campus in the US, a member of the Big Ten athletic Conference, and has an enrollment of over 50,000 students (Carnegie Foundation for the Advancement of Teaching, 2013). Ohio State was ranked 10th in the nation in 2006 for the numbers of Black doctoral degrees awarded, and has been lauded for increasing its diversity both racially and socio-economically.

In 2008, the first-year retention rate of Black male students at The Ohio State University was 91.2 % compared to that of White, non-Hispanic males at 93.5% (Ohio State University, 2013). At first glance, this statistic is impressive numerically for male students of any race entering the university in the autumn quarter. The picture four years later is alarming: the Black male four-year retention rate is 33.6%, and the White, non-Hispanic male four-year retention rate is roughly twenty percentage points higher, at 54% (Ohio State University, 2013).

In 2002, the institution's leadership, including the president of the university, felt a sense of urgency to increase the graduation rates of Black men. It was clear that the dismal graduation rate of Black men was a problem and required deliberate attention. Therefore, Ohio State's leadership created the Bell National Resource Center, which has made significant strides in increasing the retention and graduation rates of Black male students. In 2003, one year after the center's creation, the graduation and retention rate of Black males was 46.2 % compared to that of White, non-Hispanic men at 67.5% within five years. In 2008, the Black male graduation rate had risen to 62%.

This initiative has dedicated resources to Black male students, including individual and group counseling, retreats, mentoring and recognition ceremonies for Black men on campus, and academic support. As an example, the Bell National Resource Center hosts an annual *Gathering of Men* event. This event is designed to foster and maintain campus unity among Black males and provides an opportunity for students to network and fellowship with peers, Black faculty and staff, and influential Black men outside of the university (Ohio State University, 2013). Events similar to this are used to engage, motivate, and stimulate academic persistence of Black males at The Ohio State University.

The data collected from the program indicates that there has been an increase in graduation rates among Black men between 2003–2008, and the students credit this program with helping them feel welcome on campus, which assisted with their sense of connection to the institution.

Towson University

Towson University, founded in 1866, is located in Towson, Maryland. Towson University has an enrollment of over 20,000 students and is one of the largest public universities in Maryland. Towson has been ranked by *US News & World Report* and is recognized for producing the most teachers of any university in the state of Maryland. Currently, Towson's student population equals 22,499 students, 14.75% of which are Black students.

Unlike The Ohio State University, Towson University does not have a program that specifically targets Black men, but the school as a whole has taken the charge of increasing the graduation rates of Black men. Institutional leadership has recognized that there is a need to address the relatively low graduation rates nationally for Black male college students. To do this, they crafted several initiatives, including Students Achieve Goals through Education (SAGE). SAGE is a program birthed out of the university's strategic student retention plan. This program uses its resources to support academic achievement and improved graduation rates by providing students with peer and faculty mentorship, weekly conversations about a wide ranges of topics, and academic support. The program also provides students with networking and career-building opportunities and provides them with personal, career, and academic counseling.

The SAGE program has been supported at Towson University since 1986, and has been designed to increase the graduation rates of students of color at the school. Black male students have been targeted through the SAGE program in order to work on increasing their graduation rates. Since the SAGE program began in 2000, the six-year graduation rates for Black male students have improved from 53% to 60% in 2002, and 74% in 2004. Since 2006, the graduation rate has consistently been over 60% for Black male students.

When asked what makes the SAGE program so successful, the administrators credited their mentorship program. This program teams up freshmen students with upper classmen who have similar interests and majors. They meet once a week and the mentors help familiarize the mentees with the campus and the various resources available to them.

DISCUSSION AND RECOMMENDATIONS

The purpose of this chapter is to determine best practices of higher education institutions that increase the graduation rates of their Black male students. A primary concern of the authors of this chapter is a focus on best practices and methods that will increase the graduation rates of Black male college students. Consistent with this theme, we have reviewed pertinent literature on Black male college students, analyzed literature concerning best practices for increasing graduation rates for this population, and analyzed two programs: The Bell National Resource Center at The Ohio State University and Students Achieve Goals through Education (SAGE) program at Towson University. There are several limitations with this study worth noting. The first is that we chose only two universities and analyzed one program at each of the schools. It is difficult to determine causation in both cases and difficult to determine if the Black male graduation rate improved as a direct result of the students being a part of the respective programs. However, institutions may be able to learn or benefit from the content discussed.

Throughout the literature, in addition to our findings, research suggests that institutional leadership must lay the groundwork for improving the graduation rates of undergraduate Black male students. Our research shows that currently, "institutions do not take student retention seriously" (Tinto, 2004, p. 1). There is a plethora of literature on the underachievement of Black male collegians (Cuyjet, 1997, 2006; Palmer et al., 2014; Strayhorn, 2008, 2010; Wood, 2012, 2014; Wood & Palmer, 2015), and many scholars have provided recommendations for improving those alarming statistics. However, there remains a serious issue regarding Black male graduation. Therefore, our first recommendation is that universities take seriously the graduation of Black male students. To do this, they should incorporate this goal into their university strategic retention plans. They should also provide university resources, including financial support, to programs that target achievement for Black male college students. Lastly, universities should enact policies that encourage Black male achievement.

Another common thread between the programs is the emphasis on mentorship. College initiatives should involve a mentorship program, which should include both peer and faculty/staff mentorship programs. Brown, Davis, and McClendon (1999) noted that, in the case of faculty/staff mentors:

Effective mentoring requires that the mentor spend time with the student outside of the classroom. There must be an opportunity for the student to engage with the faculty person outside of the normal venues of academic interaction. The purpose of the mentoring relationship is to supplement classroom (and orientation) information with pragmatic experiences that give the student insights that would otherwise not have been gained. (p. 107)

The above quote distinguishes between mentorship and teaching. Mentorship requires active participation in the life of the student, which has the potential to propel that student to higher levels of achievement (de Janasz & Sullivan, 2004). We recommend that college programs implement intentional mentorship programs that provide personal, academic, and career counseling.

Additionally, universities should promote speaker series within their campus programs. Speaker series allow for Black leaders from within and outside of the university to come in and speak to students. Students may be able to listen to and meet people who they admire or who they have read about. Also, this allows the speaker to discuss their personal struggles and how they overcame them. These programmatic efforts have the potential to assist the students in their efforts to be academically successful at the university. Furthermore, many schools lack the presence of Black faculty. Having a speaker series where Black faculty from other universities comes to campus can expose Black students to Black professionals with advanced degrees of educational and professional attainment. Universities must provide substantial efforts to the recruitment, tenure, and promotion of Black faculty as a basis to develop a supportive network for Black college students. Given that many Black males lack access to positive Black role models, these individuals could provide a sense of role modeling, support, and guidance for Black males, which could enhance their retention and success (Turner, 2004).

It is well documented that many students come to college with a lack of academic preparation, and disproportionately the literature has presented Black students as the least academically prepared due to a multitude of structural barriers (Palmer & Scott, 2012). Thus, colleges should ensure that the campus initiatives provide adequate academic support for its students. To do this, faculty can increase office hours and reach out to students who need the extra attention. Additionally, programs could work with faculty to help identify students in need of help, so that adequate services could be implemented. Services could also be available for students after regular working hours. For example, 24-hour tutoring services and study halls should be available.

Additionally, university-wide assessment of the effectiveness of curricula, programs and other initiatives can be implemented. These results could assist administrators in data based decision-making. Also, schools could ensure that there are cross-program initiatives. For example, the multicultural affairs department could work with academic departments.

Many schools make it the student's responsibility to engage in on campus activities. Administrators should not only take on the responsibility of ensuring that students have viable options for organizations to join, but also play a significant role in encouraging and supporting students in becoming connected to the campus. This could be done by holding seminars in the residence halls addressing the benefits of getting active on campus.

The two programs analyzed in this study incorporated career development in their programs. This is promising because it exposes students to various career options and assists them in working towards their career choice. Universities should find ways to incorporate career development, by way of counseling, workshops, retreats, and seminars in order to help get and keep Black male students on track for graduation.

Lastly, we recommend that universities streamline these initiatives with many of the services that they already provide. The services at both of the universities in this study were connected with current programs. Initiatives at the university should involve communication with faculty, university services, athletic departments, etc., in order to ensure that efforts to assist the students are efficient, well connected with existing programs, and meaningful.

CONCLUSIONS

In 1993, Carter G. Woodson wrote in his seminal work—*The Mis-Education of the Negro*—"The thought of the inferiority of the Negro is drilled into him in almost every class he enters and in almost every book he studies..." (Woodson, 1993, p. 192). Even though this work has been widely read and is widely cited, the mis-education of Black students, particularly male students, is still prevalent. This mis-education is, in large part, due to the overwhelming pieces of literature that focus on a deficit model. Simply put, the challenges of Black males are more cited than the achievements, and the achievements are not researched as frequently as the challenges when deciding on best practices for Black male students. There is a need for more research on the holistic experience of Black students in order to provide a more balanced and equitable perspective. This chapter aimed to alter the conversation surrounding Black male achievement by challenging Eurocentric, deficit-based conceptual frameworks and employing strength-based perspectives in analyzing two universities and how they seek to improve the graduation rates of Black male students. The findings and recommendations discussed in this chapter provide promising practices to help university administrators increase academic outcomes among Black males.

REFERENCES

Alexander, R. T. (2009). *The effects of college mentoring programs on the academic performance, program satisfaction, and predicting students' future involvement* (Doctoral dissertation). Retrieved from http://fordham.bepress.com/dissertations/AAI3373823

Ancis, J. R., Sedlacek, W. E., & Mohr, J. J. (2000). Student perceptions of campus cultural climate by race. *Journal of Counseling and Development, 78*, 180–185.

Bonner II, F. A. (2010). *Academically gifted African American male college students.* Santa Barbara, CA: Praeger.

Brown II, M. C., Davis, G. L., & McMclendon, S. (1999). Mentoring graduate students of color: Myths, Models, and Modes. *Peabody Journal of Education, 74*(2), 105–118

Carnegie Foundation for the Advancement of Teaching. (2013). *Institution lookup.* Retrieved from http://classifications.carnegiefoundation.org/lookup_listings/institution.php

Cuyjet, M. J. (Ed.). (1997). Helping African American men succeed in college: New directions for student services. In M. J. Cujet, (Ed.), *Helping African American men succeed in college: New directions for student services* (pp. 5–15). San Francisco, CA: Jossey-Bass.

Cuyjet, M. J. (Ed.). (2006). African American college men: Twenty first century issues and concerns. In M. J. Cujet, (Ed.), *African American men in college* (pp. 3–23). San Francisco CA: Jossey-Bass

Davis, J. E. (2003). Early schooling and academic achievement of African American males. *Urban Education, 38*(5), 515–537.

Davis, R. J., & Palmer, R. T. (2010). The role and relevancy of postsecondary remediation for African American students: A review of research. *Journal of Negro Education, 79*(4), 503–520.

De Janasz, S. C., & Sullivan, S. E. (2004). Multiple mentoring in academe: Developing the professorial network. *Journal of vocational behavior, 64,* 263–283.

Epps, E. G. (1995). Race, class, and educational opportunity: Trends in the sociology of education. *Sociological Forum, 10*(4), 593–608.

Fries-Britt, S. L. (1997). Identifying and supporting gifted African American men. *New Directions for Student Services, 80,* 65–78.

Fries-Britt, S., & Turner, B. (2002). Uneven stories: Successful Black collegians at a Black and a White campus. *Review of Higher Education, 25*(3), 315–330.

Gallagher, S. (Producer/Director). (2014). *Brothers of the black list.* United States: Independent Media.

Garibaldi, A. M. (2007). The education status of African-American males in the 21st Century. *Journal of Negro Education, 76*(3), 324–333

Howard, T. C. (2013). *Black male(d). Perils and promise in the education of African American males.* New York, NY: Teacher College Press.

Howard-Hamilton, M. F. (1997). Theory to practice: Applying developmental theories relevant to African American males. *New Directions for Student Services, 80,* 17–30.

Harper, S. R. (2006). *Black male students at public universities in the U.S.: Status, trends, and implications for policy, and practice.* Washington, DC: Joint Center for Political and Economic Studies.

Harper, S. R. (2009). Institutional seriousness concerning Black male student engagement: Necessary conditions and collaborative partnerships. In S. R. Harper & S. J. Quaye (Eds.), *Student engagement in higher education: Theoretical perspectives and practical approaches for diverse populations* (pp. 137–156). New York, NY: Routledge.

Harper, S. R. (2012). *Black male student success in higher education: A report from the national Black male college achievement study.* Philadelphia, PA: University of Pennsylvania, Center for the Study of Race and Equity in Education.

Harper, S. R., Carini, R. M., Bridges, B. K., & Hayek, J. (2004). Gender differences in student engagement among African American undergraduates at historically Black colleges and universities. *Journal of College Student Development, 45*(3), 271–284.

Harper, S. R., & Harris II, F. (2012). *A role for policymakers in improving the status of Black male students in U.S. higher education.* Washington, DC: Institute for Higher Education Policy.

Harper, S. R., & Kuykendall, J. A. (2012). Institutional efforts to improve Black male student achievement: A standards-based approach. *Change, 44,* 23–29.

Jackson, J. F. L., & Moore, J. L., III. (2006). African American males in education: Endangered or ignored. *Teachers College Record, 108*(2), 201–205.

Jackson, J. F. L., & Moore, J. L., III. (2008). The African American male crisis in education: A popular media infatuation or needed public policy response. *American Behavioral Science, 51*(7), 847–853.

Kimbrough, W. M., & Harper, S. R. (2006). African American men at historically Black colleges and universities: Different environments, similar challenges. In M. J. Cuyjet (Ed.), *African American men in college* (pp. 189–209). San Francisco, CA: Jossey-Bass.

Lareau A., & Weininger, E. B. (2009). Cultural capital in education research: A critical assessment. *Theory and Society, 32*(5), 567–606.

Lynch, M., & Engle, J. (2010). *Big gaps, small gaps: Some colleges and universities do better than others in graduating African-American students.* College Results Online. Education Trust. Retrieved from http://www.edtrust.org/sites/edtrust.org/files/publications/files/CRO%20Brief-AfricanAmerican.pdf

Oakes, J., Gamoran, A., & Page, R. N. (1992). Curriculum differentiation: Opportunities, outcome, and meanings. In P. W. Jackson (Ed.), *Handbook of research on curriculum* (pp. 570–608). New York, NY: Macmillan.

Ohio State University. (2013, September 13). *Enrollment services—Graduation and retention.* Retrieved from http://oesar.osu.edu/grad_rates.html

Palmer, R, T., & Davis, R. J. (2012). "Diamond in the Rough:" The impact of a remedial program on college access and opportunity for Black males at an historically Black institution. *Journal of College Student Retention, 13*(4), 407–430.

Palmer, R. T., Davis, R. J., & Hilton, A. A. (2009). Exploring challenges that threaten to impede the academic success of academically underprepared Black males at an HBCU. *Journal of College Student Development, 50*(4), 429–445.

Palmer, R. T., & Gasman, M. (2008). "It takes a village to raise a child": The role of social capital in promoting academic success for African American men at a Black college. *Journal of College Student Development, 49*(1), 52–70.

Palmer, R. T., & Scott, J. A. (2012). "All that I got is you:" Low-income Black men's educational journey to and challenges at America's HBCUs. In T. L. Strayhorn (Ed.), *Living at the intersections: Social identities and Black collegians.* New York/London: Information Age Press.

Palmer, R. T., & Wood, J. L. (Eds.). (2012). *Black men in college: Implications for HBCUs and beyond.* New York, NY: Routledge.

Palmer, R. T., Wood, J. L., Dancy, T. E., & Strayhorn, T. (2014). Black male collegians: Increasing access, retention, and persistence in higher education. *ASHE-Higher Education Report Series, 40*(3), 1–136.

Perry, T., Steele, C., & Hilliard II, A. (2003). *Young gifted and Black: Promoting high achievement among African American students.* Boston, MA: Beacon Press.

Strayhorn, T. L. (2008). The invisible man: Factors affecting the retention of low-income African American males. *NASAP Journal, 11*(1), 66–87.

Strayhorn, T. L. (2010). When race and gender collide: Social and cultural capital's influence on the academic achievement of African American and Latino males. *Review of Higher Education, 33*(3), 307–332.

Strayhorn, T. L. (2012). *College students' sense of belonging: A key to educational success for all students.* New York, NY: Routledge.

Thelin, J. (2004). *A history of American higher education.* Baltimore, MD: The Johns Hopkins University Press.

Tinto, V. (2004). *Student retention and graduation: Facing the truth, living with the consequences* (Occasional Paper, 1). Washington, DC: The Pell Institute for the Study of Opportunity in Higher Education.

Townsen, L. (1994). How universities successfully retain and graduate Black students. *The Journal of Blacks in Higher Education, 4*(summer), 85–89.

Turner, S. (2004). Going to college and finishing college. Explaining different educational outcomes. In C. M. Hoxby (Ed.), *College choices: The economics of where to go, when to go, and how to pay for it* (pp. 13–61). Chicago, IL: University of Chicago Press.

Wood, J. L. (2012). Examining academic variables affecting the persistence and attainment of Black male collegians: A focus on performance and integration in the community college. *Race, Ethnicity, and Education, 17*(5), 601–622.

Wood, J. L. (2013). The same…but different: Examining background characteristics among Black males in public two year colleges. *Journal of Negro Education, 82*(1), 47–61.

Wood, J. L. (2014). Apprehension to engagement in the classroom: Perceptions of Black males in the community college. *International Journal of Qualitative Studies in Education, 27,* 785–803.

Wood, J. L., & Palmer, R. T. (2012). Innovative initiatives and recommendations for practice and future research: Enhancing the status of Black Men at HBCUs and beyond. In R. T. Palmer & J. L. Wood (Eds.), *Black men in college. Implications for HBCUs and beyond* (pp. 176–196). New York, NY: Routledge.

Wood, J. L., & Palmer, R. T. (2015). *Black men in higher education: A guide to ensuring student success.* New York, NY: Routledge.

Woodson, C.G. (1933). *The mis-education of the Negro.* Washington, DC: Associated Publishers.

CHAPTER 13

RACIAL INEQUALITIES AND THE ASSESSMENT OF INTELLIGENCE

A Brief Historical and Interdisciplinary View

Lisa A. Suzuki and Cherubim A. Quizon

The creation of this chapter was a collaborative effort between two academics—i.e., an anthropologist and psychologist. While the two disciplines are currently quite distinct, they share important historical and contextual features with respect to the understanding of how racial dynamics and socio-structural inequalities inform theoretical and methodological assumptions in the social sciences. While sociocultural anthropologists focused upon an understanding of the interactions, behaviors, and cultural meanings of race among so-called "racial groups" studied in their naturalistic settings, psychologists examined behaviors under experimental conditions in laboratories (Guthrie, 1976).

> By declaring itself the study of the mind, psychology claimed ownership of all that dealt with animal and human behavior. The new discipline cut a wide swath through the ivy halls of academia at a time when the western Weltanschauung was infected with racism and social Darwinism, and psychology eventually became an important contributor to the era. (p. 29)

Talking About Structural Inequalities in Everyday Life: New Politics of Race in Groups, Organizations, and Social Systems, pages 241–258.
Copyright © 2016 by Information Age Publishing
All rights of reproduction in any form reserved.

In his review, Guthrie noted the checkered 19th century intellectual legacies influencing the birth of psychology that included Social Darwinism (i.e., an adaptation of a biological concept of natural selection and survival of the fittest applied to human groups believed to be in varying "stages" of social evolution); Galton's eugenics (i.e., a social philosophy seeking to apply Darwin's evolutionary principles to the improvement of genetic traits by controlling heredity using the now-widely questioned assumption of distinct biological categories "race"); German psychophysics (i.e., the proposition that the effect of physical processes on mental processes can be measured through an understanding of the structure of the mind); and Mendelian genetics (i.e., the theoretical foundation of genetic inheritance).

The history of the race concept is even more complex in anthropology and especially so in North America as seen in Stocking's (1982) classic collection of essays that shows many of the aforementioned influences shared with psychology. Anthropology in the North American tradition uniquely follows a four-field approach made up of physical/biological, linguistic, archaeological and cultural perspectives used in the study of humans. For this chapter, we focus on historical and contemporary contributions to our understanding of "race" from two of these subfields, physical/biological anthropology as well as cultural anthropology, due to their observable impact on psychologists' scholarly writings on race in general and assumptions about race in the measures of intelligence in particular (Muckle, 2012; Richards, 1998; Smedley & Smedley, 2011).

Against the historical backdrop of the 18th and 19th centuries, before what we now refer to as psychological or anthropological research was named as such, the study of differences between humans grouped in terms of the rubric "race" or "ethnicity" was a central concern. Although there are many reasons for this, most point to larger structural shifts in the sociopolitical organization in European and North American nation states especially in relation to their former colonies, or, as in the case of the United States (US), the formerly enslaved or displaced native populations. Increased population diversity (not limited to "race") in European and North American cities was a hallmark of the period between the two World Wars and was accompanied by increased dependence on the agencies and instruments of the state such as the census, labor and pecuniary laws in the growing cities. This led to the increasing need to describe and a perception that there was a need to control an increasingly diverse population (Christopher, 2005; Takaki, 1998). The history of ideas about "race" on one hand, as well as intelligence testing on the other, is also connected to the growth of academia and scientific disciplines as used in the public sector. This includes the rise of public education, the increased need of a skilled workforce, the use of census data to allocate resources, and in the case of the US, driving federal and state policies on legal definitions of "race" especially of so-called native peoples or of peoples in American territories overseas (cf. Kauanui 2008, McCoy & Scarano 2009). Similar studies abound linking race categories to local sociopolitical histories and a global flow of the history of ideas/race ideologies during and after colonial rule [e.g., Arens, 1975

(Africa); Nobles, 2000 (Brazil)]. The influence of early 20th century American eugenicist social philosophies worldwide has a complex history in which both psychologists and anthropologists on either side of the divide played a part (Lieberman 2001; Richards 1998).

It has often been observed that the emergence of modern-day academic disciplines that examine race in some form or another flourished during periods of European colonial expansion where the existence of peoples of color were inevitably viewed in terms of an inequality that was deemed "natural," observable and self-evident. Findings of racial group differences were used to justify the oppression and marginalization of particular racial groups. For example, by the 20th century, psychological findings of lower intelligence, poor educational achievement, higher rates of mental illness and pathology, greater severity in signs and symptoms of disease, etc. among non-White populations living in Europe and North America were viewed as indicators of innate disparities in mental abilities and mental illness categories.

This chapter serves as a critique of research and clinical assessment practices considering key socio-historical contexts, scientific assumptions, and cultural foundations upon which they were developed. While many test developers claim that the most popular measures utilized in our profession have attained a semblance of cultural validity, the research methods used to support this conclusion problematically focus on linearity and consistency in the absence of context. For example, in the 1960s disproportionately high numbers of Black children were classified in the mentally retarded range based upon standardized intelligence tests (Office of Education, 1969). These same children, however, were found to demonstrate higher levels of ability based upon their functioning in their communities. These children were identified as the "six hour retardate" as their limitations were evident only during school hours.

Challenges were raised indicating that intelligence tests were culturally biased. In 1979, the California Supreme Court ruled that IQ tests are biased against African Americans (*Larry P. v. Riles*, see Valencia & Suzuki, 2000). Graves and Mitchell (2011) note that professional advocates have continually called for a moratorium on the use of intelligence tests with African American children in the determination of special education placement. Concerns were raised regarding overrepresentation of Black children in categories where classifications are based upon clinical judgment and results of intelligence tests. The 2004 reauthorization of the Individuals with Disabilities Education Act no longer requires intelligence testing and some states prohibit their use in assessing learning disabilities.

The preceding text serves as an introduction to disciplinary based perspectives regarding the concept of race highlighting historical and sociopolitical issues pertaining to the development of intelligence tests. The remainder of this chapter will expand upon these features and focus attention on the measurement issues that have led to and maintain structural inequalities for different racial and ethnic groups in the US. We begin our discussion by examining the concepts of race, ethnicity, and culture that have formed the foundation of our multicultural discourse and the historical context in which intelligence-testing practices emerged (i.e., racial typing and discrimination, race and testing, and the social construction of race). The growing importance of understanding context within the social sciences is then addressed highlighting bioecological systems theory, standpoint theory, and intersecting identities. We conclude with a critique of intelligence testing and its contribution to the maintenance of structural inequalities.

RACIAL TYPING AND DISCRIMINATION:
A HISTORICAL PERSPECTIVE

As noted at the beginning of this chapter, racial typing played a critical role in the development of the social sciences. We define racial typing here as a strategy of categorizing human subjects into groups that share physical characteristics (phenotype) that are believed to determine shared behavioral patterns and temperament. These characteristics are believed to be transmitted genetically and remain stable over time. Though not the focus of this chapter, it is important to acknowledge assumptions of heritability that impact racial typing, that is, the assertion that race types/categories are only based on biologically *inherited* or innate characteristics instead of culturally *learned* behaviors. Rushton and Jensen (2005) illuminate the dynamic between genetic and environmental factors:

> Heritability describes what is the genetic contribution to individual differences in a particular population at a particular time, not what could be. If either the genetic or the environmental influences change (e.g., due to migration, greater educational opportunity, better nutrition), then the relative impact of genes and environment will change. (p. 239)

Heritability, while often viewed as archaic in anthropology, human biology and other academic circles, remains relevant for particular groups given political agendas and access to resources.

It can be argued that structural inequalities exist in every society but "race" as a basis for assigning membership into social groups led to the formation of structural inequalities as represented in hierarchies (e.g., hierarchy of intelligence— some racial and/or ethnic groups score consistently higher or lower in comparison to other groups) enabling differential access to resources, power, and privileges.

The current validity of "race" is widely understood as a cultural concept persisting as a form of "folk biology" but not supported by biological data from allied disciplines such as population genetics, human evolution, and anatomical sciences. In 1996, the American Association of Physical Anthropologists stated that:

> The human features which have universal biological value for the survival of the species are not known to occur more frequently in one population than in any other. Therefore it is meaningless from a biological point of view to attribute a general inferiority or superiority to this or to that race. (1996; cited in Lieberman, 2001, p. 72)

The persistence of racial typing, however, suggests that sociocultural forces are perhaps as powerful as biological ones in shaping how we think about "racial groups." Though the biological basis of racial typing has been debunked in 1996 and further dismantled by larger studies such as the outcomes from the Human Genome Diversity Project (Cavalli-Sforza, 2000), racial typing tends to be favored precisely because structural inequalities that are responsible for the marginal social situation of certain populations in North America and Europe (often but not limited to people of color) are easily set aside in favor of an ostensibly biological reason. In short, the inequality is considered "natural" and therefore cannot (or should not be changed). As noted earlier, this perspective has justified marginalization and oppression of particular racial and ethnic groups (e.g., slavery).

Racial typology persists in the US in peculiar forms not found elsewhere in the world where other forms of classification may be paramount (e.g. social class). There are many reasons for the persistence as well as the specificity of how it is conceived of and made actionable, not the least of which is the history of immigration on one hand and the history of territorial expansion on the other. Both of these influenced the development of federal laws that define "race" in terms of genetic purity that, in turn, define an individual's legal and property rights. In the US, for instance, the use of "blood quantum" rules for indigenous communities have played a central role in the social construction of race in ways that significantly contrasted with the First Nations of Canada who do not rely much on ideals of genetic purity in determining ethnic self-identification (Muckle, 2012). In the US, the "one-drop of blood" rule was also used to perpetuate the slave status, second-class citizenship, and segregation of African Americans (Villazor, 2008). "This history of the insidious relationship between race and blood distinctions informs the current normative equal protection laws, which highly scrutinize categorical differences on the basis of blood" (Villazor, 2008, p. 803). Historically, during slavery, the one-drop of Black blood rule applied and anti-miscegenation laws prevented interracial mixing. The Supreme Court has ruled in favor of laws privileging individuals with one-fourth American Indian blood citing "preference had a political purpose of furthering the right of self-government of federally recognized tribes" (p. 803). Similarly, determinations have been made with respect to Native Hawaiians as federal law allows them to "lease properties for ninety-nine years at a rate of $1.00 per year" (p. 805). Indigenous groups must acquire political status in order to access resources associated with their group through documentation of ancestral heritage (blood ties) to establish their "pedigree."

> ... blood quantum rules had the double effect of not only racializing American Indians but also undercutting their right of sovereignty, including their property rights... American Indians in the reservations who lacked the requisite blood quantum were not given property and such lands that would have been allotted to them were made available to whites. (Villazor, 2008, p. 809)

Similar concerns are noted for Native Hawaiians and American Samoans, i.e., only those with 50% American Samoan blood may own property or lease it for more than fifty-five years (see also Kauanui, 2008). These rulings are in direct opposition to culturally-based beliefs of these designated cultural groups with respect to communal ownership of property and allegiance to indigenous leadership practices. It is important to note the indigenous context of these rulings as Native Hawaiians and American Indians have been fighting to establish political and economic redress for past injustices by the U.S. government.

By contrast, government rules for determining First Nations membership in Canada do not rely on blood quantum rules to determine the rigor of indigenous self-identification (Muckle 2012). A systematic survey of race categories using current census classifications worldwide demonstrates that historical factors such as the US structural engagement with African slavery make the term "race" more likely as its primary census question investigating ethnicity whereas in others, it may be understood as ancestry/national origin (e.g., Australia), or in the more unique case of Brazil, a culturally coded set of terms referring to color (i.e., black, white, yellow, brown, etc.; American Anthropological Association, 2006; Christopher, 2005; Nobles, 2000). It is important to note that there also exists, within racial group categorizations and hierarchies, the phenomenon of colorism, which is based upon skin color in the Black community.

RACE AND TESTING

Psychometric testing has become a cornerstone of psychological practice. Critics of the testing movement cautioned that a focus on group differences in the absence of cultural understanding could lead to damaging outcomes. In 1936, Goodenough, creator of the Draw-a-Person Test, a measure of intelligence in children, cautioned members of the American Association for the Advancement of Science (Section H: Anthropology) indicating that as a psychologist she believed that:

> ... the rising wave of interest in intelligence tests swept away the banks of scientific caution and flooded the psychological journals with a torrent of figures on racial differences in "general intelligence." Examination of literature in this field over the past twenty years shows that approximately two-thirds of all the publications dealing with racial differences in mental traits have been concerned with the measurement of intelligence by means of tests designed for use with American or European whites, while a large proportion of the remainder have to do with the even more hazardous problem of comparing races with respect to traits of temperament and personality as indicated by their scores on tests designed to measure these qualities but of very doubtful validity, even for whites. (p. 5)

Goodenough went on to challenge the field regarding the adequacy of sampling of subjects, issues of content validity, and construct equivalence—"test-items from which the total trait is to be judged are *representative and valid samples of the ability in question, as it is displayed within the particular culture with which we are concerned"* (p. 5). The complexities of determining cultural validity were also identified.

> But if we are to look upon intelligence tests as samples of intellectual requirements of a given culture-group, what basis is there left for applying such a sample of tasks to individuals from another group whose cultural patterns differ widely from those of the original group for whom the test was designed? Very little, I think. About all that can be learned from such a procedure is that the cultures are different…(p. 9)

HISTORICAL CONTEXT OF INTELLIGENCE TESTING IN THE US

Goodenough's cautionary notes came nearly a decade after the initiation of early measures of intelligence and aptitude that were used to determine placement and classifications of individuals in educational and employment settings. The first American group administered intelligence test was the Army Alpha and Beta tests employed during World War I.

> Never before in the history of civilization was brain, as contrasted with brawn, so important; never before the proper placement and utilization of brain power so essential to success. (Yoakum & Yerkes, 1920, p vii)

The purpose of these tests were to "(a) aid in segregating the mentally incompetent, (b) to classify men according to their mental capacity, (c) to assist in selecting competent men for responsible positions" (Yoakum & Yerkes, 1920, p. xi). The tests were group administered and efficiently yielded scores for 1,726,966 recruits of which 41,000 were officers. Based upon the test scores, 7,800 men were recommended for immediate discharge and nearly 30% of the remaining men were found to be unable to "read and understand newspapers and write letters home" (p. 12). These men were given a special examination designed for illiterates. The large data set of scores was later examined with respect to racial group differences (Brigham, 1923) with Blacks and newer immigrant groups obtaining the lowest scores.

On a related front, there was growing attention to racial disparities in intelligence based upon cranial capacity. In Lieberman's (2001) review, he noted that early work in this area supported a "Caucasoid>Mongoloid>Negroid" hierarchy of intelligence. This was later revised with Mongoloids at the top. These findings were influenced by social context as indicated in the following excerpt.

> …the 19th-century hierarchy paralleled the height of European world domination, the nonhierarchy of the 20th century reflected world wars, worldwide depression, and the breakup of empires; the "mongoloid>Caucasoid>Negroid" hierarchy followed the economic success of several Asian nations. (Lieberman, 2001, p. 69)

Many scholars and researchers have rejected the racial hierarchy of intelligence given accusations of fatal methodological flaws in studies leading to these findings (e.g., aggregation of diverse populations into racial categories, operationalization of cultural achievements in relation to brain size). Rushton and Jensen (2005) published a review of 30 years of research of research on racial differences in cognitive abilities. They conclude that underlying the Black-White differences is a genetic component and support a hereditarian perspective. Today, most psychologists, educators, and researchers acknowledge contributions of genetic-hereditarian, cultural, and environmental components to intelligence.

Rushton and Jensen cite numerous studies including those conducted with twins reared apart to support their hereditarian explanation. Nisbett (2009), however, points out that these twins are genetically identical and the separate environments in which each was raised were highly similar as well. Thus, the same data can be accounted for by different explanations based upon the perspective of the researcher. For example, Suzuki and Aronson (2005) note that culture affects all psychological phenomena including biological indicators of intelligence often used to support a hereditarian argument. They note alternative explanations for racial and ethnic group differences in intelligence citing stereotype threat [i.e., performance on intelligence tests can be impacted by stereotypes that exist in reference to one's racial ethnic group (Aronson, 2002; Steele & Aronson, 1995)]; mediated learning experiences [i.e., intelligence test performance can be impacted by exposure to information and dynamic assessment procedures (Skuy et al., 2002)]; and relative functionalism (e. g., performance on intelligence tests can be impacted by opportunities for upward mobility, social discrimination, and language).

THE SOCIAL CONSTRUCTION OF RACE, ETHNICITY, AND CULTURE

The following sections clarify and critique definitions of race, ethnicity, and culture. There is definitely overlap in the operationalization of these constructs. Differences in conceptualization are also highlighted based upon how they are applied in international contexts.

Race. Biologically linked racial distinctions have fallen out of favor for many contemporary scholars given that humans are very similar genetically and race has emerged as "primarily a sociological designation, identifying a class sharing some outward physical characteristics and some commonalities of culture and history" ("Race", n.d.). Gladding (2006) provides a more abbreviated and limited definition:

> An anthropological concept that classifies people according to their physiological characteristics, such as skin color, hair texture, and facial features. Race contributes virtually nothing to cultural understanding. (p. 118)

This definition refers to phenotypic characteristics of individuals and does not acknowledge the sociopolitical implications of racial designations. Smedley and Smedley (2011) define race as follows:

... a shorthand term for, as well as a symbol of, a 'knowledge system,' a way of knowing, perceiving, and interpreting the world and of rationalizing its contents (in this case, other human beings) in terms that are derived from previous cultural-historical experience and reflect contemporary social values, relationships, and conditions. (p. 13)

One of the major applications of racial designations is how they are used by the U.S. Census Bureau that adheres to the following identifiers with respect to race (U.S. Census Bureau, "Race" n.d.):

White–A person having origins in any of the original peoples of Europe, the Middle East, or North Africa.

Black or African American–A person having origins in any of the Black racial groups of Africa.

American Indian or Alaska Native–A person having origins in any of the original peoples of North and South America (including Central America) and who maintains tribal affiliation or community attachment.

Asian–A person having origins in any of the original peoples of the Far East, Southeast Asia, or the Indian subcontinent including, for example, Cambodia, China, India, Japan, Korea, Malaysia, Pakistan, the Philippine Islands, Thailand, and Vietnam.

Native Hawaiian or Other Pacific Islander–A person having origins in any of the original peoples of Hawaii, Guam, Samoa, or other Pacific Islands.

The Census 2000 allowed respondents to self identify more than one race.

The racial categories included in the census questionnaire generally reflect a social definition of race recognized in this country and not an attempt to define race biologically, anthropologically, or genetically. In addition, it is recognized that the categories of the race item include racial and national origin or sociocultural groups" (U.S. Census Bureau, "Census 2000 Gateaway," n.d.)

Race information is designated as "critical in making policy decisions, particularly for civil rights...Race data also are used to promote equal employment opportunities and to assess racial disparities in health and environmental risks" (U.S. Census, "Race," n.d.).

As noted earlier, historically anti-miscegenation laws criminalized intimate sexual relationships between whites and nonwhites. Today, growing numbers of interracial and interethnic relationships have further complicated the discourse of race and ethnicity. It is critical that we understand these categorizations when racial and ethnic distinctions become blurred (i.e., mixed race, interethnic).

As noted earlier, racial categorizations reflect political agendas as evidenced by differences when examined in a global context. Designations are often tied to power and social status. In addition to the examples cited earlier (e.g., Canada, Australia and Brazil), it is interesting to note that historically the Japanese were considered "Honorary Whites" when they invested in South Africa (Kawasaki, 2001). Ignatiev's (2009) text *How the Irish Became White*, documents the journey of Irish immigrants coming to American from a homeland where they were treated as members of the lowest caste. They then became oppressors of African Americans in the U.S. Similar accounts are noted for Jewish, Italian and Polish Americans in their drive to become "White" (Roediger, 2005).

The debate regarding the relevance of race continues though many scholars have indicated that racial designations serve primarily sociopolitical agendas. As noted in the preceding discussion despite the ambiguous nature of race as a self-identifier, the implications for members of visible racial groups is potentially quite powerful.

> The fact is, there simply is no scientific basis for the concept of race (Sternberg, et al., 2005), yet being labeled a member of a specific racial group has pervasive and indelible consequences psychologically, educationally, socially, and politically. (Daley & Onwuegbuzie, 2011, p. 295)

Ethnicity. Over time, greater attention in the social science literature has focused on ethnic designations. Ethnicity is "A group classification in which members believe that they share a common origin and a unique social and cultural heritage such as language, *values*, or religious beliefs" (Gladding, 2006, p. 53). Expanded definitions indicate that ethnic classifications may be related to "racial, national, tribal, religious, linguistic, or cultural origin or background" (U.S. Census Bureau, "Ethnicity," n.d.). These ethnic classifications also denote the importance of within racial group differences as noted in the Census racial category descriptions often citing geographic designations. This type of labeling is noted extensively in the social science literature. For example, Rushton (cited in Lieberman, 2001) refers to three racial aggregates identified in part by geographic origin: Caucasoids—people who originally inhabited Europe, North Africa, Western Asian, and India; Mongoloids—people originating in Asia except the west and south (India), in the northern and eastern Pacific, and the Americas and Negroids—people "originating and predominating in sub-Saharan Africa" (p. 76). Lieberman notes the limitations of these definitions given that many geographic regions are not represented in these three groupings.

Despite acknowledgement regarding the importance of race and ethnicity, scholars in the social sciences have been stymied as to how best to integrate the complexities of these constructs in research and clinical practice. For example, our descriptors commonly used in the published literature refer to Black or African American glossing over the within group variance that may exist. Afro Caribbeans living in the US may not identify with either of these designations given their unique histories in America that may not include slavery. Espiritu (1992) advocated for the formation of an Asian American panethnicity enabling Asian subgroups to form cooperative relationships in response to the racism and discrimination that members of this entire group experience.

Culture. The discussion becomes even more convoluted given cultural dimensions that are often tied to race and ethnicity. Race and ethnicity are cultural constructs. Culture reflects the dynamic and intergenerational transference of values, beliefs, and customs. Gladding (2006) provides the following definition.

> The shared *values,* beliefs, expectations, *worldviews, symbols,* and appropriate learned *behaviors* of a *group* that provide its members with *norms,* plans, traditions, and rules for social living. Culture is transmitted from one generation to the next. (p. 40)

It is critical to keep in mind definitions of these constructs even though they may seem quite elusive at times. Race, ethnicity, and culture, while overlapping are not synonymous. Recognizing the fluidity of racial categorizations around the world point to the difficulties in examining the racial construct in the absence of context. It is commonly acknowledged that there exists greater variation within various racial and ethnic groups in comparison to differences between racial and ethnic groups (e.g., panethnicity vs. identification with unique aspects of ethnic subgroupings). This is true for most psychological constructs in relation to racial categories.

REIFYING INTELLIGENCE

Standardized intelligence testing has been identified as "one of psychology's greatest successes" (Benson, 2003, p. 48) as evidenced by the pervasive usage of these measures. In addition, numerous theories and definitions of intelligence have emerged over the years. Fifty-two scholars and researchers endorsed the following definition of intelligence (*Mainstream science on intelligence,* 1994).

> Intelligence is a very general mental capability that, among other things, involves the ability to reason, plan, solve problems, think abstractly, comprehend complex ideas, learn quickly and learn from experience. It is not merely book learning, a narrow academic skill, or test-taking smarts. Rather, it reflects a broader and deeper capability for comprehending our surroundings "catching on," "making sense" of things, or "figuring out" what to do. Intelligence, so defined, can be measured, and intelligence tests measure it well. (p. A18)

On a related front, Sternberg and Kaufman (1998) empirically examined the role of culture in determining what constitutes intelligent behavior.

> Cultures designate as "intelligent" the cognitive, social and behavioral attributes that they value as adaptive to the requirements of living in those cultures. To the extent that there is overlap in these attributes across cultures, there will be overlap in the cultures' conceptions of intelligence… (p. 497)

Despite these differences in aspects of intelligence there are also shared areas as well given the existence of "a common core cognitive skills that underlies intelligence in all cultures, with the cognitive skills having different manifestations across the cultures" (p. 497).

Studies in other countries have yielded unique aspects of intelligence. For example, Azuma and Kashiwagi (1987) found that the phrase "to be highly intelligent" translated to *atama ga yoi* in Japanese. An intelligent person would be someone who possessed social competence, task efficiency, originality, with skills in reading and writing. Females were found to be identified as having greater intelligence based upon social competence and writing. The Baoule of the Ivory Coast valued social skills defined by "being helpful, obedient, [and] respectful, but also being knowledgeable, taking responsibility, and showing initiative in tasks useful to the family and the community" (Dasen, 1984, p. 430). Benson (2003) highlights the importance of understanding how culture and intelligence interact citing literature regarding differences in Western versus Eastern cultural cognitive styles, cognitive processes, and speed of processing.

Despite these findings of definitional differences in different countries, intelligence testing has gained great traction over the years in American society as well as abroad. Testing corporations export tests to other countries where the measures are renormed, restandardized and applied to new populations. Norms refer to the distribution of scores on a particular test by a group of individuals (sample). Standardization means that the test is administered and scored in a consistent manner. An example of the global export of an intelligence test is, the Wechsler Intelligence Scale for Children, one of the most frequently used measures in the US (now in its 5th Edition). In a volume edited by Georges, Weiss, van de Vijver, and Saklofske (2003) authors highlight the usage of this measure in 15 countries. There has also been an increase in terms of numbers of intelligence measures available despite concerns regarding the operationalization of what constitutes intelligence across cultures.

Attention to racial and ethnic group differences in intelligence has continued given that group differences are consistently found on nearly all measures. Thus, a focus on racial differences on intelligence test performance has continued to be used to explain and justify the lower achievement of particular marginalized and oppressed racial and ethnic groups. For example, *The Bell Curve: Intelligence and Class Structure in American Life* (Herrnstein & Murray, 1994) attributed Black-White racial group difference on intelligence tests to a hereditarian explanation based upon the assumption that intelligence is largely genetically determined. This text spurred a firestorm of controversy around the meaning of intelligence test scores.

CONTEXTUALIZING CULTURE, RACE, AND ETHNICITY

As noted earlier there has historically been a considerable disregard in integrating the culture in intelligence research (e.g., six-hour retardate). A disconnect exists between the systemic rhetoric around issues of race, ethnicity and culture and actual testing practices (e.g., Nisbett, 2009; Nisbett et al., 2012). Important advancements in theoretical perspectives have enhanced understanding of context and experience. To this end, we highlight three illustrative examples: Bronfenbrenner's theory of ecological development, standpoint theory, and the growing emphasis placed upon intersectionality and identity. While these theories do not address intelligence per se, they have implications for understanding the complex nature of context and social location factors which have been studied in relation to intelligence.

Bronfenbrenner's Bioecological Theory

While a number of contextually based theories have emerged over the years highlighting the importance of understanding the multiple nested systems in which an individual resides, one of the most popular and often cited theories is Bronfenbrenner's theory of bioecological development (e.g., Bronfenbrenner & Morris, 2006). Bronfenbrenner's theory emphasizes person, context, process (e.g., interaction between person and environment) and time (e.g., immediate to macrotime across generations) in development. The contexts include microsystems in which a person engages (home, school, peer group); mesosystem (larger family unit, religious affiliation); macrosystem (overarching belief and values); exosystem (e.g., economic, political, government and religious system); and Chronosystem which focuses on dimensions of time.

Standpoint Theory

Standpoint theory recognizes that an individual's perspective is shaped by social location and involvement and position in social groups. Hegel explored standpoints by examining the relationship between masters and slaves in the early 1900s (cited in Bowell, n.d.). He noted that the relationship depended to large extent on position, group influence, and how authority was dispensed. Feminist standpoint theory emerged as scholars such as Harding and Hartsock (cited in Harding, 1987) focused on gender perspectives from a feminist viewpoint noting that how one views the world is dependent upon one's position and outlook. Feminist standpoint theory was designed to give voice to marginalized groups who lack social and economic resources and power in comparison to those of the dominant group who have social and political privilege. Critics of feminist standpoint theory note that it served primarily to privilege the voices of White women to the exclusion of women of color. These voices are captured by authors such as Collins (1991) who focused on oppression and historical suppression of Black women.

> Theories advanced as being universally applicable to women as a group on closer examination appear greatly limited by the white, middle-class origins of their proponents. (Collins, 1991, p. 7)

Intersecting Identities

To gain an understanding of the complex nature of social location and situated voices means attending to gender, social class, race, ethnicity, sexuality, and physical capacities (Bowell, n.d.) and intersecting identities. While a number of authors have written on this topic, including Sue and Sue (2013), one of the most frequently cited models is the ADDRESSING framework developed by Hays (2008). The framework is represented by a useful acronym illustrating the multidimensional conceptualization of intersecting identities that can inform our understanding of an individual's embeddedness—**A**ge, **D**evelopmental and acquired **D**isabilities, **R**eligion, **E**thnicity, **S**ocioeconomic status, **S**exual orientation, **I**ndigenous heritage, **N**ational origin, and **G**ender. In order to understand the context of an individual's life, intersecting facets of identity must to be taken into consideration.

The bioecological model, standpoint theory, and the ADDRESSING framework emerge from different disciplines in psychology and counseling and illuminate the need for a greater attention to context and social location. These theories have significant implications for our understanding of intelligence as researchers have examined contextual factors that impact intelligence. These include: socioeconomic status, home environment, test bias, neighborhood characteristics, and parental expectations (Valencia & Suzuki, 2000). Each of these can be related to racial, ethnic, and cultural factors. For example, socioeconomic status is intimately linked to racial group membership as marginalized and oppressed groups often fall within the lowest rungs in terms of income and access to resources. Similarly, these same groups are often at greater risk for neighborhood violence, lack of community resources (e.g., poorer school districts), and lower scores on intelligence tests.

CONCLUDING REMARKS

Reflecting on the information contained in this chapter, the historical foundations of intelligence testing were fraught with racial overtones. The literature on racial typing and the social construction of race, ethnicity, and culture attest to the importance that continues to be placed on these group differences. Researchers and scholars noted a range of scores on the Army Alpha and Beta tests and chose to examine the findings based upon racial group membership. This action was aligned with a sociopolitical agenda, as the scores could have easily been examined with respect to other variables of distinction and found group differences— i.e., socioeconomic status or social class.

Theories promoting an understanding of context and social location support an expansive understanding of how factors related to race, ethnicity, and culture impact intelligence. Applying standpoint theory tells us about the scholars who chose to focus on racial distinctions on test performance assuming that the difference in test scores reflected real and meaningful differences in the racial hierarchy of intelligence. They focused on aggregating the data by racial category and found statistically significant differences. Historically, these findings were often not challenged nor were potential alternative explanations explored. Despite acknowledgement of the problematic nature of these studies, the focus on racial group differences in intelligence continues as investigators attempt to resolve the Black-White test score gap.

What is troubling is that test scores continue to be used to classify individuals and determine to some degree educational and employment opportunities. The growing reliance on high stakes testing has bolstered the usage of tests of aptitude and ability in the schools in the US and abroad. As researchers and clinicians whose work includes attention to constructs like intelligence, we must be vigilant and steadfast in our commitment to address the needs of the marginalized and oppressed. The US represents a particular racialized society whose values and historical focus on racial hierarchies is not consistent with other parts of the world. We must take into consideration power dynamics and the resulting standpoints unique to each individual.

In this chapter, we have attempted to highlight the racial dynamics that formed the foundation of intelligence testing from its early inception. The operationalization of race is blurred given overlaps in terminology and problems with self-identification. Parallel difficulties are also noted with respect to definitions of intelligence and its cross-cultural applications. The growing number of mixed race individuals also poses potential confusion in terms of classification. Theories tell us that individuals must be understood within context, from their particular standpoint, and with respect to intersecting identities. Intelligence tests do not have the capacity to do this. They are limited in terms of the cultural values and norms upon which each test was developed. We must rely upon knowledgeable, sensitive, sophisticated, and culturally competent social scientists to recognize the complexities of the tasks ahead in order to more fully understand and gain more accurate estimates of intelligence. Then and only then will the structural inequalities of intelligence be changed.

We end this chapter by citing the wisdom of African proverbs. As noted in our chapter due to historical and sociocultural factors, our society has reified the notion of race despite vast evidence that the construct is socially constructed. It is clear that when intelligence data is aggregated by race and ethnic groups differences will appear despite acknowledgement that the within group differences are even greater than those that are found between groups. Thus, we find that "The pond you fish in determines the fish you catch." We find what we are looking for, thereby running the risk of reinforcing the sociopolitical and structured inequalities present in our society. In addition, wise African sages also noted the importance of perspective. "When the lion tells the story, the hunter is no longer a hero." We can turn to standpoint theory to help us understand how different social locations impact our findings such as those related to understanding intelligence in cultural context.

REFERENCES

American Anthropological Association. (2006, February). Understanding race and human variation: A public education program. *Anthropology News, 47*(2), 7.

Arens, W. (1975). *A century of change in Eastern Africa*. Boston, MA: Walter De Gruyter, Inc.

Aronson, J. M. (Ed.). (2002). *Improving academic achievement: Impact of psychological factors in education*. San Diego, CA: Academic Press.

Azuma, H., & Kashiwagi, K. (1987). Descriptors for an intelligent person: A Japanese study. *Japanese Psychological Research, 29*, 17–26.

Benson, E. (2003). Intelligence across cultures: Research in Africa, Asia and Latin American is showing how culture and intelligence interact. *APA Monitor, 34*(2), 56.

Bowell, T. (n.d.). *Feminist standpoint theory*. Internet Encyclopedia of Philosophy: A peer reviewed academic resource. Retrieved June 16, 2014 from www.iep.utm.edu/femstan/

Brigham, C. C. (1923). *A study of American intelligence*. Princeton, NJ: Princeton University Press.

Bronfenbrenner, U., & Morris, P. A. (2006). The bioecological model of human development. In R. M. Lerner & W. Damon (Eds.), *Theoretical models of human development. Handbook of child psychology* (Vol. 1, 5th ed., pp. 793–28). New York, NY: Wiley.

Cavalli-Sforza, L. (2000). *Genes, peoples and languages/luiga luca cavalli-sforza* (Mark Seielstad, Trans). New York, NY: North Point Press.

Christopher, A. J. (2005). Race and the census of the Commonwealth. *Population, Space and Place, 11*, 103–118.

Collins, P. H. (1991). *Black feminist though: Knowledge, consciousness, and the politics of empowerment*. New York, NY: Routledge.

Daley, C. E., & Onwuegbuzie, A. J. (2011). Race and intelligence. In R. J. Sternberg & S. B. Kaufman (Eds.), *The Cambridge handbook of intelligence* (pp. 293–306). New York: Cambridge University Press.

Dasen, P. R. (1984). The cross-cultural study of intelligence and the Baoule. *International Journal of Psychology, 19*, 407–434.

Espiritu, Y. L. (1992). *Asian American panethnicity: Bridging institution and identities*. Philadelphia, PA: Temple University Press.

Ethnicity. (n.d.). *Merriam-Webster online*. Retrieved from: http://www.merriam-webster.com/dictionary/ethnicity

Georges, J., Weiss, L. G., van de Vijver, F. J. R., & Saklofske, D. H. (2003). *Culture and children's intelligence: Cross cultural analysis of the WISC-III*. San Diego, CA: Academic Press.

Gladding, S. T. (2006). *The counseling dictionary: Concise definitions of frequently used terms* (2nd ed.). Upper Saddle River, NJ: Pearson.

Goodenough, F. L. (1936). The measurement of mental functions in primitive groups. *American Anthropologist, 38*(1), 1–11.

Graves, S., & Mitchell, A. (2011). Is the moratorium over? African American psychology professionals' views on intelligence testing in response to changes in federal policy. *Journal of Black Psychology, 37*(4), 407–425.

Guthrie, R. V. (1976). *Even the rat was white: A historical view of psychology.* New York, NY: Harper & Row.

Harding, S. G. (Ed.) (1987). *The feminist standpoint reader: Intellectual and political controversies.* Bloomington, IN: Indiana University Press.

Hays, P. A. (2008). *Addressing cultural complexities in practice, second edition: Assessment, diagnosis, and therapy.* Washington, DC: APA Books.

Herrnstein, R. J., & Murray, C. (1994). *The bell curve: Intelligence and class structure in American life.* New York, NY: The Free Press.

Ignatiev, N. (2009). *How the Irish became white.* New York, NY: Routledge.

Kauanui, J., K. (2008). *Hawaiian blood: Colonialism and the politics of sovereignty and indigeniety.* Durham, NC: Duke University Press.

Kawasaki, S. (2001). The policy of apartheid and the Japanese in the Republic of South Africa (1). *Tokyo Kasei Gakuin Tsukiba Jyoshi Daigaku Kiyo. The Proceedings of Tokyo Home Economy Women's College, 5,* 53–79. Retrieved from http://www.tsukuba-g.ac.jp/library/kiyou/2001/4.KAWASAKI.pdf

Lieberman, L. (2001). How "Caucasoids" got such a big crania and why they shrank: From Morton to Rushton. *Current Anthropology, 42*(1), 69–95.

Mainstream Science on Intelligence. (1994, December 13). *The Wall Street Journal,* p. A18.

McCoy, A., & Scarano, F. (2009). *The colonial crucible: Empire in the making of the modern American state.* Madison, WI: University of Wisconsin.

Muckle, R. (2012). *Indigenous peoples of North America.* Toronto, Canada: University of Toronto Press.

Nisbett, R. E. (2009). *Intelligence and how to get it: Why schools and cultures count.* New York, NY: Norton.

Nisbett, R. E., Aronson, J., Blair, C., Dickens, W., Flynn, J., Halpern, D. F., & Turkheimer, E. (2012). Intelligence: New findings and theoretical developments. *American Psychologist, 67*(2), 130–159. doi:10.1037/a0026699

Nobles, M. (2000). History counts: A comparative analysis of racial/color categorization in U.S. and Brazilian censuses. *American Journal of Public Health, 90*(11), 1738–1745.

Office of Education. (1969). *The six hour retarded child: A report on a conference on problems of education of children in the inner city.* Warrentown, VA. ED 38827.

Race (n.d.). In *Merriam-Webster online.* Retrieved from http://www.merriam-webster.com/dictionary/race

Richards, G. (1998). Reconceptualizing the history of race psychology: Thomas Russell Garth (1872–1939) and how he changed his mind. *History of the Behavioral Sciences, 34*(1), 15–32.

Roediger, D. R. (2005). *Working toward whiteness: How America's immigrants became white: The strange journey from Ellis Island to the suburbs.* New York, NY: Basic Books.

Rushton, J. P., & Jensen, A. R. (2005). Thirty years of research on race difference in cognitive ability. *Psychology, Public Policy, and Law, 11*(2), 235–294.

Skuy, M., Gewer, A., Osrin, Y., Khunou, D., Fridjhon, P., & Rushton, J. P. (2002). Effects of mediated learning experience on Raven's matrices scores of African and non-African university students in South Africa. *Intelligence, 30,* 221–232.

Smedley, A., & Smedley, B. (2011). *Race in North America: Origin and evolution of a worldview* (4th ed.). Boulder, CO: Westview Press.

Steele, C. M., & Aronson, J. (1995). Stereotype threat and the intellectual test performance of African-Americans. *Journal of Personality and Social Psychology, 69,* 797–811.

Sternberg, R. J. (2005). Intelligence. In K. J. Holyoak & R. Morrison (Eds.), *Cambridge handbook of thinking and reasoning* (pp. 751–773). New York, NY: Cambridge University Press:

Sternberg, R. J., & Kaufman, J. C. (1988). Human abilities. *Annual Review of Psychology, 49,* 479–502.

Stocking, G. W., Jr. (1982). *Race, culture, and evolution: Essays in the history of anthropology.* Chicago, IL: University of Chicago Press.

Sue, D. W., & Sue, D. (2013). *Counseling the culturally diverse: Theory and practice* (6th ed.). Hoboken, NJ: John Wiley & Sons.

Suzuki, L. A., & Aronson, J. (2005). The cultural malleability of intelligence and its impact on the racial/ethnic hierarchy. *Psychology, Public Policy, and Law, 11*(2), 320–327.

Takaki, R. (1998). *Strangers from a different shore: A history of Asian Americans, updated and revised edition.* Author.

United States Census Bureau. (n.d.). *Census 2000 Gateway.* Retrieved from: http://www.census.gov/main/www/cen2000.html

United States Census Bureau. (n.d.). *Race.* Retrieved from:http://www.census.gov/topics/population/race.html.

Valencia, R. R., & Suzuki, L. A. (2000). *Intelligence testing and minority students: Foundations, performance factors, and assessment issues.* Thousand Oaks, CA: Sage.

Villazor, R. C. (2008). Blood quantum land laws and the race versus political identity dilemma. *California Law Review, 96*(3), 801–837.

Yoakum, C. S., & Yerkes, R. M. (1920). *Army mental tests.* New York, NY: Henry Holt Company.

PART III

ORGANIZATIONAL AND GROUP DYNAMICS AND STRUCTURAL INEQUALITIES

CHAPTER 14

"THE RACE IDEA TENDS TO MAKE PEOPLE WICKED" [1]

An Exploration of Why It Persists

Charla Hayden

DEDICATION: JOYCE FELDER, WHERE ARE YOU?

This paper is dedicated to a woman I have had no contact with since 1967. Yet she remains an ongoing figure for me in relation to the questions this paper explores. Joyce and I met when we served together on a project group related to our brand-new jobs in federal government agencies. We were in our early 20s, both recent college graduates, smart, ambitious, and accomplished. She was B*lack*, I was *White*, and therein lies the crux of our story. When our project was completed, I asked her if she thought we could build an ongoing friendship. She considered the question thoughtfully, and then said, "No." Writing this paper helped me grasp the wisdom behind her response. This paper is for you, Joyce.

---

[1] Boxill (2004)

Talking About Structural Inequalities in Everyday Life: New Politics of Race in Groups, Organizations, and Social Systems, pages 261–284.

INTRODUCTION

Race is a social construction that has been woven like a basket in the collective psyche of the United States (US) over centuries (Smedley & Smedley, 2011, pp. 1–7). It has held the unconscious projections of disowned elements of the experience of many peoples; the enforcement codes protecting social, economic, and political domination by various groups. And, I propose, it has provided defenses against many unarticulated anxieties, especially a deep sense of inferiority, on the part of such dominant groups. The application of the concept of *race* has been customized over these centuries to fit specific circumstances during which it benefited dominant groups, and because the wider sociocultural context of the times precipitated particular customizations. In this paper, I explore the current use of *race* as a covert, unconscious, social construction in middle class work settings in the US, specifically as it relates to the group of people identified here as *Black*, or *Black* Americans. *Racism* then, which can be seen as conjoined with the idea of *race,* becomes an active accomplice in the pattern of benefits accruing to dominant groups.

I agree with Miles (1993) that the term *race* is "associated with a dangerous, if not ignorant assumption that implies the world is split into very distinct dichotomies, that there is more than one human *race*, [which ignores] the wealth of cultural and ethnic diversity, and, in any case, recent scientific knowledge . . . shows that the 'world's population' could not be legitimately categorized this way." (p. 3) In other words, *race* is a fictitious categorization used to rationalize and defend against the irrational fears and aggression, both conscious and unconscious, of dominant social groups, in this case, mainly *White*, or *White* Americans, of whom I am one. For example, as a child of a US Marine Corps pilot, I lived on the grounds of a US Naval Air Training Center in Florida for two years. To get to elementary school in town all children from integrated housing on the base were loaded into a bus together. When we reached town, we were dropped off at different schools: a brand-new, one-story school for *Black* children and a much older, crumbling but traditional, multiple-story school for *White* children. I wanted to be with all my friends from the base and did not understand our separation, although I noticed some of my classmates at school felt strongly *our* school was "better" because *they* were not there. In 5th and 6th grade, I wasn't conscious enough to ask my parents, who were remarkably fair and open *White* people, why the Navy did not insist that the town's school system keep us together. Now, I understand this represented "going along with" *racist* assumptions that segregation was necessary for reasons that must have been at least acceptable if not desirable to the Navy. (Two years earlier, I had attended a public elementary school on the island of Oahu where students of all *racial* groups were integrated and I had a Chinese teacher whose feet had been bound when she was a girl. I had seen traditional gender oppression up close then, though I did not understand it either—to my 10-year-old mind this too had seemed cruel.) I use these illustrations to demonstrate how we are socialized to participate in ritualized discriminatory patterns everywhere. This begins early in our exposure to culture and represents an unconscious invitation to take the idea of *race* as real, including the belief that *White* skin is a *better* color.

My approach here is to apply selected sociological, psychological, economic, and philosophical frameworks to understand more about how the idea of *race* has contributed to inequalities in everyday work life in the US. Three examples from my own career experiences are provided to demonstrate the nature of the inequalities involved in the construction of *race* in which *Black* Americans are experienced as "the stranger" or "the alien" in their organizations. Through this perceptual field, they become vulnerable to serving multiple unconscious and socioeconomic purposes in current post-modern conditions influencing all types of organizations. The effect of these conditions, which became clearly discernible in the last quarter of the 20th century, will be looked at in the "world of work" involving *white*-collar professional roles held by *Black* Americans. It is important to note that more tangible inequalities in employment, income, wealth, education, health, and other elements affecting individuals representing a multiplicity of racial/ethnic backgrounds have been well documented in the Pew Research Center's Study on the Unequal Distribution of Wealth in the U.S. (Kochhar, Fry, & Taylor, 2009) and The Stanford Center on Poverty and Inequality Report (2014).

THE TRANSITION FROM MODERNITY TO POST-MODERNITY

In the early years of the global transition from *modernity* to *post-modernity,* the US Civil Rights Movement (1954–68) went into an eclipse from which in my view it never fully reemerged. Significant civil rights legislation was passed during the 1960s and 70s in reaction to the tidal wave of killings of prominent *Black,* and *White,* men, and others: women, children, civil rights protestors and workers (Morris, 1986).

The Civil Rights laws, which focused on equal pay, civil rights, and voting rights aligned with related Supreme Court decisions to draw attention to the social and economic inequalities experienced by groups of Americans for whom many of the post-war benefits of an expanding economy were inaccessible because of the color of the skin they lived in the "epidermalization of inferiority" as Frantz Fanon (1952) had earlier described (as cited in Davids, 2011, p. 12). Fanon's work emphasized how B*lack* people who had been colonized lost threads of their original cultural identities while trying to fit into the cultures of their colonizers—a sure-fire invitation to the sense of being "less than." The new laws, however, did not, could not, address the underlying discriminatory mechanisms at work. They did provide avenues for legal redress of the easily documented disadvantaging that people of color experienced, and demonstrated that the attention of a broad swath of Americans had been captured—at least temporarily.

DEFINING POSTMODERNISM AND ITS EFFECTS
ON THE IDEA OF RACE

In *Postmodernism is Not What You Think: Why Globalization Threatens Modernity,* Lemert (2005) introduces a key question: "Does the modern world still realistically offer what for so long it had promised? . . . However much we may retreat into controversy, as if the fire of political battle can truly rekindle moral hope, the somber realities of the modern world are hard to get around" (p. 3). Lemert then offers several key global observations (presaging the Stanford Poverty Center's 2014 findings): overall individual income is in decline while economic systems are driving productivity and cumulative wealth upward; employment systems are offering fewer family wage jobs; inequalities in income and social status are growing worse—most dramatically in the U.S.; and global food and water resources continue to diminish rapidly (pp. 3–4).

The aspirations of *modernism*, which held steady from the late 1700s Enlightenment until the latter part of the 20th century, held promise of economic progress, social equality, freedom from want, and even peace, which was to be realized through the rational exercise of human intellect. In other words, *"modernism* had extended an optimistic, progressive promise that if people worked hard at legitimate endeavors their circumstances would get better, for their children, if not for themselves." (Lemert, 2005, p. 4)

Postmodernism, as seen by Lemert (2005), concerns itself with questions like, "Is anyone better off?" (p. 4). He then provides an interesting hypothesis regarding a widespread fear that the optimistic spirit of "we can make things better" (the *modernist* framework) is failing:

> It is surely not by coincidence that the debates over the meaning of social identity are most viciously engaged at the very time when changes in world politics have provoked a related but no less urgent debate. The two entail each other. As the world changes according to indecipherable laws, identity itself becomes every bit as unstable a social thing as the suddenly decentered world economic system. . . . It is obvious that the destabilizing of the modern world is associated with a curious, but undeniable, energizing of identity as the topic of widespread political interest. (p. 131)

Lemert (2005) describes social identity as a "claim to rights in a social space." Any 'social identity' is a set of social attributes a particular environment makes available to particular individuals. It differs from an individual's 'ego identity,' which is something s/he may apply to altering the social identity already received. Though social space may or may not exist in actual physical terms, it is clear that individuals, across their many differences, live every bit as much in the imaginary but durable space the wider social context offers them and which may include superior or inferior statuses. "Who we are—or, if the moral landscape allows it, who we choose to be—is always unrelentingly a determination made in order to locate oneself in social space. . . 'Identity politics' then relate to those without 'proper official identification' finding access to occupying social territories that were previously closed to them. When people affiliate with a national, ethnic, religious, or sexual identity, they are claiming these as legitimate social locations" (p. 131)—places to stand in. So, why are these questions about identity so crucial in the *post-modern* era? Lemert's response is that for centuries much of the modern world was constructed by dominant, colonizing, Western cultures which are now losing hegemony in the post-modern period.

> It was, in effect, the sometimes innocent, other times fully cognizant, work of those who, believing in themselves most sincerely, defined the world as the ideal, progressive possibility of the universal Man. That *his* racial, sexual, and gender peculiarities were left unglossed in the vocabulary of liberal humanism does not mean that he, so to speak, or at least some of his own, did not realize that the others who served the universal purposes of his glorious culture were not ever about to remain ultimately quiet. (Lemert 2005, p. 132)

HOW THE HOLOCAUST ILLUMINATED POSTMODERN CULTURAL CONDITIONS

One resource for understanding of how the concept of *race* has been constructed in the latter part of the *modern*, and early *post-modern*, periods is the work of sociologist/historian Zygmunt Bauman (2000). His book, *Modernity and the Holocaust* opens wide a lens we can use to view the rise of the Nazis to power and their capacity to carry out, unimpeded for such a long time, an attempt to exterminate the Jews and other "undesirable groups" of Europe. There are several parallels between the socially-enabled projections the Nazis used to "criminalize" European Jews and then try to eradicate them, and the observable *race-based* projections used to "hold" *black* Americans "in the mind" as unwanted "strangers." According to Bauman, "The Holocaust was born and executed in our modern rational society, at the high stage of our civilization and at the peak of human cultural achievement, and for this reason it is a problem of that society, civilization and culture" (p. x). If we're honest with ourselves, we must turn and face this situation as it relates to the idea of *race* in the U.S.

THE IDEA OF RACIALIZED SPACE AND ITS IMPACT

Jane Smiley's (1995) novel, *MOO*, begins with a tongue-in-cheek description of a mythical university in the Midwest called MOO. However funny, several deep themes emerge early, one of which introduces us to the enactment of what we might call "racialized space." We learn about this as we meet Mary Jackson, a *Black* girl who rides an overnight bus from her home in Chicago to get there and tries to manage her appearance to look "fresh" the next morning (p. 9). The *White* girls Mary encounters at the beginning of the novel are "dressed better than their parents" (p. 9). "Mary had nice clothes, too, ones she had worked hard for over the summer, clerking in a drugstore, and chosen carefully, but it was clear in an instant's acquaintance with Sherri, Keri, and Diane that her clothes were nothing like theirs—too urban and eastern, as if she had consulted New York editions of *Mademoiselle* and they had consulted special Midwestern editions" (p. 9). An earlier chapter includes the story of Keri, "one of those pretty but vapid [*white*] girls" who rented a room in a house where "she could . . . look around [this] tiny, empty room and recognize it perfectly as the mold of the person she was going to become" (p. 12). Mary, however, is troubled by her surroundings: "She could not imagine herself here. She could watch herself walk across the campus, enter classrooms, study in the library, eat in the commons . . . When she thought of the campus or her classes, or even her room, she was absent . . . . No amount of approval from professors [*white*] or partisanship on the part of her friends [*black*] . . . got at the root of the problem—the longer she stayed here, and here was the whitest place she had ever been . . . the less she seemed to exist" (p. 381).

In her essay, *The Social Element: A Phenomenology of Racialized Space and the Limits of Liberalism,* Willett (2004) asks, "What is the space we inhabit as social creatures?" (p. 243). How does the space we find ourselves in affect our sense of individuality and freedom? It's not easy to see all, or even most, of the features of the implicit social landscape, as Lemert (2005) noted in the earlier passage from his work on *postmodernity*. Willett describes how challenging the idea of *racialized space* is:

> Not only are features of the social and physical landscape rarely the focus of our attention, much of what we respond to may not be available for conscious or discursive analysis at all . . . There is, however, one highly visible feature of the social landscape and that is the dimension of *color*. Social observers have puzzled over the fact that long after the end of legal apartheid in the United States, *blacks* and *whites* do not live in the same neighborhoods or join the same churches, private clubs, or civic organizations. It is difficult to understand why this segregation continues long after the demise of publicly sanctioned *racist* ideologies and when the concept of *race* has lost all claim to scientific validity. (p. 244)

The *whiteness* Mary feels in *MOO* has less to do with the prior *racist* experiences she's lived through than the *whiteness* of the space she currently inhabits. The point Willett (2004) makes about *MOO* is that it illustrates how many of us do not have the conceptual resources to grasp the full "impact of *racism* on the space in which we encounter each other" (p. 244).

Please consider the story of *Dr. Marjone Franklin* (name and other details have been changed for privacy), whose impact and skills were systematically inhibited by the *whiteness* of the space in which she worked, including the unconscious fear, envy, and other unspoken and unconscious emotional fields generated by the dominant *White* authority structure there.

MARJONE FRANKLIN, PHD

Dr. Franklin was a powerful, charismatic, *Black,* nursing educator hired into an interdisciplinary education service at a Veterans Administration psychiatric hospital where I worked in the role of administrative officer for the service. The staff included a full array of professional mental health clinicians and a large audiovisual studio staff. Our purpose was to provide both classroom and clinical practice learning opportunities for a wide variety of graduate students from university training programs in the surrounding metropolitan area. Dr. Franklin came from a role in another health system where she administered treatment programs. She was an active leader in the larger community, and an accomplished academician.

At the beginning of Dr. Franklin's appointment in the VA hospital, she was heralded as an innovative pioneer who could lead the nursing education programs toward a more current theoretical base and therefore a higher level of preparation. It seemed the only staff who questioned the appointment of Dr. Franklin to take this role were the nurse educators already there, whose educational preparation was at a "lower" level, and who felt her appointment diminished the esteem in which they were held in the organization. These nurses were well-qualified educators who were *White.* On the surface all the other clinical educators, and the hospital's administrators, were very glad Dr. Franklin had been appointed.

After a few months, Dr. Franklin's open and assertive approach to expressing her views began to be the subject of gossip and rumors among the educators and staff on clinical units. She had decided quickly, as described by several observers, what issues and problems needed to be addressed, and had begun implementing changes using the authority of her role. From my perspective, her entry into this system had not been well thought through by those of us in leadership roles. Once she had been selected, we had not prepared to integrate her role or her approach to leadership, nor had we prepared her for the organization's cultural norms. After some initial tensions related to her approach to her role emerged, we began a journey toward shared influence and collaboration.

A particularly sensitive event involving many of the *Black* staff already there occurred not long before Dr. Franklin joined the hospital. This significant moment in the life of the organization involved the taking up of "voice," and a hope for lessening the blanketing effect of *White space* there. The conference seemed to offer a more open space than the established formal organization.

The education service had sponsored a group relations conference, which is an experiential model for learning about leadership and authority in a temporarily constructed organization (Hayden & Molenkamp, 2004). It was conducted in a building on a large VA campus where most of the staff and participants worked. Toward the end of the conference, during an intergroup event, the *Black* staff attending the conference barricaded the doors to the conference staff's work area, preventing anyone from leaving, turned off the lights, and lit candles. Several tense moments ensued for everyone, but eventually the conference director was able to encourage representatives from the group holding the staff hostage to communicate why they had taken this action. It turned out they had acted in protest against the low-grade levels and wages most of the *Black* staff at this hospital were stuck in. After the conference director agreed to bring the group's representatives to a discussion about this with the hospital director, the doorways were opened and conference events proceeded. A few weeks afterward, however, four of us who had been on the conference staff were "investigated" by a central arm of the national organization, which inquired about our motivation for sponsoring the conference. The suspicion was that we had been motivated to create an "uprising" of the *Black* staff. The investigation concluded with one psychiatrist, a treatment unit director, receiving a written admonishment, while the rest of us were "exonerated." Lemert (2005), whose work we considered earlier, provides potential insight into this episode:

> . . . in the cases of those assigned the inferior social locations, it is, under certain conditions of freedom, the struggle to define a location where before none had existed . . . .When the silent begin to speak, they utter the words that begin to create the discursively initiated and organized, but politically and economically powerful, social space from which the imposition of silence was intended to exclude them. (Lemert, 2005, p. 131)

ANALYSIS

Dr. Franklin deserved to inhabit the social space, which should have accrued to her professional status. However, her story illustrates the concept of *"racialized* space" described by Willett in the essay in which she lists some of the frequent structural impediments to the full exercise of their capabilities by *Black* professionals in the US. Willett posits that our sense of self is very much related to our sense of social space, ." . . contemporary liberal and leftist theory, while opening for philosophical reflection the space that can nourish or destroy us as embodied social subjects" also closes off that reflection by not recognizing the enormous power of a *bourgeois* culture to constrain the rights of individuals and repressed groups" (Willett 2004, p. 245). Dr. Franklin did not "fit" easily in *White space*, nor did she fit into the imaginal *Black space* that was being defined as appropriate for her by the mostly *White* professional hierarchy. She was too clear-headed, outspoken, decisive, rational, and self-confident, i.e., she was claiming the kind of authority generally reserved for *White* males in the social landscape of a VA hospital affiliated with a major university medical center. Dr. Franklin did not fit into the mythical role often prescribed for *Black* women as described by Dr. Rhetaugh Dumas (1985) in her classic paper, *Dilemmas of Black Females in Authority*. Franklin was not willing to reshape herself to fit the "Black Mammy" stereotype and become the emotional and physical caretaker of her coworkers. Instead, she was unconsciously "auditioned" for another mythic character often reserved for *Black* women in leadership: "the strong, powerful, castrating black matriarch" (p. 325). So, in spite of well-intentioned, conscious efforts on the parts of several leaders, including Dr. Franklin herself, to open the clearing for what could be recognized as her important contributions to furthering the mission, gossip and "secret" ridicule continued behind her back. This often flowed into rumors implying that the "powers that be" were afraid to discipline her or terminate her employment because of her *race*.

My own "close encounter" with Dr. Franklin's authoritative approach occurred when she pointed out an ethically questionable choice I had made outside the workplace. She had information about my private life via connections with people in another state. As I listened to her critique, I knew her perspective had a great deal of merit, but I also felt "ambushed" by her addressing me about it. I defended myself against her evaluation of my conduct, but for years afterward, I wondered how much Dr. Franklin's *race* figured into my defense. It was easy to tell myself she shouldn't have taken in third-hand information and directed her criticism at me. At the same time, I believe my reaction to her "censorship" related to her being *Black,* as well as old enough to be my mother. I was defending myself against feelings of shame and humiliation partly because our role reversal related to our racial identities. She held a superior ethical stance, and I knew she was right.

COLOR-BLIND RACISM

A growing body of research has focused on the concept of color-blind racism, an idea originated by L. G. Carr (1997) in *Colorblind Racism* and carried forward by other scholars since then. For example, four types of color-blind racism have been characterized by Eduardo Bonilla-Silva (2006). These include:

- **Abstract liberalism**: EEO and individual choice demonstrate that inequality is non-racial.
- **Naturalization:** Naturally occurring choices by individuals of like others as associates.
- **Cultural racism**: Stereotypical traits, such as laziness and promiscuity, in people of color.
- **Minimization**: Hypersensitive reactions to possible discriminatory events are attributed to people of color (p. 29).

While denigrating humor was directed toward Dr. Franklin in private, as far as I knew the fact that she was *Black* was not discussed overtly—though it seemed to figure significantly in the unspoken dynamic field of an organization filled with *White* space. Instead, the overt social construction fixed around Dr. Franklin related to her "personality." She was said to be "over the top," "stubborn," "difficult to deal with," "concrete," "inflexible," "pushy." The situation as I see it today was that she was a fully self-authorized professional educator, who happened to "live in Black skin," and the patriarchal, *White* system surrounding her could not allow the full impact of her talent to be felt and recognized. She was held in the status of "stranger" or "alien" over many years—in a situation we might call a "crime" of social space, not an unfamiliar experience of *Black* women who take up positions of authority (McRae & Short, 2010, pp. 88–91).

In *The New Jim Crow: Mass Incarceration in the Age of Colorblindness,* Alexander (2010) states that in the post-Civil Rights era, the U.S. has subscribed to color-blind *racism*. Color-blind *racism* refers to attributing racial inequality to nonracial dynamics (p. 103). The types of practices that take place under the cover of color-blind *racism* are "subtle, institutional, and apparently nonracial," but they still rest on the social construction of *race.* These practices are not *racially* overt in character like *racism* under slavery, segregation, and Jim Crow laws. Instead, color-blind *racism* is adopted to support the fiction that *race* is no longer an issue in the US.

Alexander's (2010) argument is that in the post-civil rights legislation era, a new form of "*racial* caste system" has emerged (p. 3). This caste system does not recognize one's skin color as a primary element in its construction. Instead, it constructs a framework of presumed criminality via the "war on drugs," which began in 1982 during the Reagan era, and continues just as forcefully today. Her data are startling; for example, "The United States imprisons a larger percentage of its *black* population than South Africa did at the height of apartheid. In Washington, D.C., it is estimated that three out of four young *black* men (and nearly all those in the poorest neighborhoods) can expect to serve time in prison" (pp. 6–7). Her hypothesis—that "mass incarceration in the United States [has] in fact, emerged as a stunningly comprehensive and well-disguised system of *racialized* social control that functions in a manner strikingly similar to Jim Crow (p. 4). This mass incarceration—"not attacks on affirmative action or lax civil rights enforcement—is the most damaging manifestation of the backlash against the Civil Rights Movement" (p. 11). It is also an extremely effective mechanism for removing *Black* men from the labor pool in the US.

Alexander (2010) attacks the idea of achieving the "American dream" through ambition and persistent hard work as an illusion negatively impacting the broader social view of people with *black* skin in the US. Our current judicial system locks a huge number of *black* Americans out of the mainstream of society and the economy (p. 13). President Clinton, who "wrestled" the crime issue away from the Republicans with a 30 billion dollar crime bill in 1994 toughened the consequences of drug-related crimes with a 5-year lifetime limit on eligibility for welfare assistance as well as a permanent, lifetime ban on eligibility for welfare and food stamps after one conviction for a felony drug offense. "Clinton also made it easier for federally assisted public housing projects to exclude anyone with a criminal history" through his "one strike and you're out" initiative. (p. 57).

Alexander (2010) examines how the criminal justice system deprives *Black* Americans and other people of color of their freedom and most of their civil rights in a systematic, bureaucratized fashion reminiscent of some of the Third Reich's strategies toward the Jews before and during WWII. The "war on drugs," over more than three decades now, has avoided disturbing our illusions of having built a *"race* blind" society, while continuing to enact a new form of enslavement, especially of *Black* American men. Let's examine another form of deprivation directed subtly toward a *Black* American male.

NATHAN SMITH

Nathan Smith occupied one of those roles many organizations invest with high expectations for revolutionizing organizational culture, at least consciously, but with considerable *naivete* and perhaps other, unexplored intentions. He was one of two internal Equal Employment Opportunity (EEO) investigators assigned to the human resources department of a large, public university medical center. He could have been anywhere—in any publically funded organization, which aims to display its commitment to justice, equality, and an unbending intention that no *racial* or other discriminatory practice would ever occur there, even in such a complex system—this one employing more than 20,000 people. Nathan Smith was *Black*, his colleague in the same kind of role was *White*, and also male. They were both around 50 years of age. At the time I joined this organization, as a manager of a different division in the human resources department, Nathan had been hired the previous year. His colleague had been there for a short time as well. Both positions had been difficult to keep filled, and there was continuing dialogue in the human resources leadership team at the time about whether to hire licensed attorneys for these positions—an interesting idea, which I thought represented the organization's unexpressed primary task: to avoid costly lawsuits based on discrimination—more than to assure equality of opportunity.

After two years, I began to notice that most frontline supervisors and staff who had discrimination complaints directed toward them expressed a preference for Nathan Smith to handle their investigations, even though in theory cases were assigned to the investigator whose time was less encumbered at the moment. This preference seemed to hold regardless of the racial identification of the person accused. Around that same time, I began to hear Mr. Smith's work described in the management team as "late, not well-documented, and potentially NOT objective." Shortly after that, I decided I needed to fire a new training specialist I had hired because he refused to meet with me for a preliminary performance feedback discussion during his 90-day "probationary" period. He was a *White* man approximately the same age I was, and I was aware of possible gender dynamics underneath what was happening, but was surprised by the direction the events took. Although his employment contract indicated I had the authority to end his employment without an inquiry, he filed a gender discrimination complaint against me, alleging his gender was the reason I was letting him go. Nathan Smith was assigned to investigate this complaint.

Although I had never before been the recipient of a discrimination complaint, I was familiar with how frightening they could be from hearing the experiences of other managers. The potential for shame, humiliation, job discipline or termination, and perhaps the most painful, confrontation with internal questions about one's conscious and unconscious biases, was palpable. Nathan Smith took up his role professionally. Even though we had worked together in training activities for some time, he didn't console me or punish me. He simply did his job. At the end of the investigation, the EEO Officer for the overall university determined no gender discrimination had occurred. I was very relieved, and I also understood more about why most people preferred to work with Mr. Smith. He did not judge; he looked at the evidence.

Two years later, I transferred into a faculty role in one of the university's professional schools and lost track of what was happening with Nathan Smith. One day he appeared in the hall outside my office—looking ill and somehow "broken." He had lost his position in human resources, but the dean of the school where I taught had agreed to place him in an administrative support role. We both worked there for two more years as I became more disenchanted with the overall organization, and Mr. Smith seemed to become less the effective professional he had once been. When I left, he was nearly invisible in his role except to a few individuals who understood the value of who he had been and could be.

ANALYSIS

This case represents an unconscious effort on the part of the surrounding institution to forcefully project into Mr. Smith an identity as an ineffective, unproductive, unprofessional, and undesirable EEO investigator. What coincided with this process was an implicit debate about what constituted competency in such a delicate and important role, how those competencies should be measured, and who could be allowed to be seen as exercising them. The decisions Mr. Smith took while in his EEO role were understood to be intuitively and factually fair by a variety of people with differing elements of identity. However, the aspects of competency that ended up being measured were timeliness of results reporting, the lucidity and well-argued details in the case files, the ability to verbally articulate findings, and above all, the rational presentation of the reasoning behind recommendations made. Mr. Smith's work did not visually resemble his *White* colleague's work, but the other investigator's work did meet the competency assessments being made by university officials with an interest in measuring role performance in the EEO job.

It is important to note that Mr. Smith carried out his role in ways that made an active projective process easy. He was often late, didn't compose "clean" reports, and was not concise in speaking. I was never clear whether he had made a conscious decision to defy the enforcement of less important job requirements, or he was unaware of the risks he was taking. Given that his emotional and physical health deteriorated greatly during the period I knew him, I would guess that he was not able to consciously or unconsciously fend off the projections of incompetence being pushed onto him. He was institutionally "incarcerated" in some form of inadequacy without completely understanding why.

I would like to emphasize three other elements related to Mr. Smith's identity as a "stranger" or "alien" in the university environment. The first involves his childhood in a rural community, where he was the only *Black* child in his school there. He told me once he had felt well treated in this community though he was aware of feeling like he was "some kind of pet" to adults and other children who regarded him as a harmless and interesting anomaly. In retrospect, I wondered whether this aspect of his early socialization had not provided him with the internal resources that might have prepared him to resist the projections he absorbed later in this professional episode.

The second aspect of this example relates to the discussion by Simon Clarke (2003) of Zygmunt Bauman's (2000) concept of the *stranger*. Bauman stated that "Strangers are not *unfamiliar* people, but they cross or break the dividing line of dualism, they are neither 'us' nor 'them'" (p. 55). Clarke paraphrases Bauman: 'they (the stranger) bring the "outside" "inside" and poison the comfort of order with the suspicion of chaos. The stranger is someone we know things about, who sits in 'our' world uninvited. The stranger has characteristics of an enemy, but unlike the enemy is not kept at a safe distance. . . . The stranger is at once estranged while wholly familiar; the stranger is inside us all' (p. 55). It seems to me that putting a *Black* man, or woman, in an EEO investigator role, which is a relatively common occurrence in the US, is to invoke the unconscious fear of a "stranger" who will adjudicate discrimination complaints unfairly so that *White* people will be treated unfairly, creating a high probability that projective "disowning" similar to the process described will occur.

It also seems to me that *racial* assumptions function as a more subtle but still crippling form of "incarceration" *a la* Alexander (2010). Institutional *racism* is endemic in the structures, rules and practices of institutions, and in this context *racism* becomes self-perpetuating, or an important element of the "institution in the mind" carried by those affiliated with it. Menzies-Lyth (1989) is quoted by Clarke (2003) here: " . . .employees of large institutions tend to internalize the characteristics and central tenets of the institution they are part of and use subtle forms of projective identification to alienate and exclude those who do not appear to fit into the commonly held practices or rules of the institution" (p. 164). In Mr. Smith's case, he was deskilled and lost the significant satisfaction of carrying out a role he had performed very well.

THE IMPACT OF SUPERCAPITALISM AND
RELATED *RACIAL* CONSTRUCTIONS

I find it impossible to identify any cultural element in American life capitalism has not affected. There is a children's fable that provides an apt metaphor for the impact of capitalism, now dubbed *Supercapitalism* by Robert Reich (2008), and quoted by Lemert (2005) on all of us:

One fine morning the residents of a small village awoke to find a very big but not unfriendly beast well settled in the center of their small town and mundane lives. Being by nature trusting and kind, the people repressed fear and welcomed the beast. In spite of its enormous height and girth, and the mass of its settled flesh, the beast posed no threats. All he did, in the most matter of fact way, was to say: "Feed me." The villagers complied. Upon devouring what had been fed, he simply repeated his demand, without inflection, "Feed me." Eventually, without vote or complaint, feeding the beast came to be what the village was about. (p. 5)

The U.S. has been living itself into an all-consuming relationship with capitalism since the first Europeans settled in "New England." It would be naïve not to notice the invasion of marketplace assumptions into every facet of life here. The hegemony it holds over all of our important institutions accelerated greatly during the presidency of Ronald Reagan as related in Peter Singer's (1995) book, *How Are We to Live?: Ethics in an Age of Self-Interest*, and has not abated. In addition, in *Caste, Class and Race,* Oliver Cox (1948) argued that '*race* prejudice' is a consequence of the class structures precipitated by capitalism (as cited in Clarke, 2003, p. 17).

"Modernity made *racism* possible. It also created a demand for *racism*" (Bauman, 2000, p. 61). The endurance of a significant underclass of people of color, in particular, *Black* and *Brown* Americans, has been necessary to fuel political support for neoconservative causes from poor *white* Americans. The social divisions precipitated by the need to consider oneself/one's family "above" others are fueled by capitalist notions of success—a very fragile social construction at best, as the (current) Great Recession has demonstrated. In today's capitalist culture, we tend to see individuals in terms of their social positions. This "authorizes" the subtle abuse of those who do not occupy positions that are socioeconomically 'correct.' If *whiteness* functions in the U.S. as a source of capital, or as 'property,' (Harris, 1993; Lipsitz, 2006), when a person's skin is *Black*, or any shade except *White*, s/he is often de-privileged, i.e., not seen as worthy to occupy respected social space or likely to command the financial resources necessary to occupying it. There are notable exceptions: for example, *Black* authors, musicians, actors, and athletes have often earned positions of respect because of their fame and earnings—though envy and animosity often appear to accompany this respect.

An important element in achieving respected social space is opportunity to succeed in employment. Here, we confront "institutional racism" which at "one level is defined as the 'discriminatory impact of administrative procedures. The other level is a complex interaction between a silent *racist* discourse, which has become embodied within an institution [and] which is reinforced and interacts with individuals within that institution. "In this sense, structure and affect fuel each other and cannot be separated" (Clarke, 2003, p. 26).

There are several specific aspects of employment activity which offer demonstrations of the power of the idea of race in action. These include:

- Discrimination is so routine it is almost invisible [even] to those who actually practice it (Modood, 1997, as cited in Clarke 2003, p. 19).
- Common elements applied to constructing employment disadvantages: poor language skills [used to discredit Nathan Smith's very substantive abilities] and a lack of formal education, whether relevant to the position at hand or not (Modood, 1997, as cited in Clarke 2003, p. 20).
- Application of two broad selection criteria: suitability for requirements of the job, and acceptability (appearance, manner and attitude, maturity, manager's 'gut feeling,' and speech style (Jenkins, 2010, as cited in Clarke 2003, p. 20). Some of the "acceptability" factors described here were negatively applied to Dr. Franklin *after* she was hired.
- Bauman (2000) refers to the lethality of unexamined bureaucracy when he asks "when confronted with the matter-of-fact efficiency of the most cherished among the products of civilization; its technology, its rational criteria of choice, its tendency to subordinate thought and action to the pragmatics of economy and effectiveness (p. 13) . . . just how formal and ethically blind is the bureaucratic pursuit of efficiency" (p. 15). His implicit answer is not blind at all. "The rules of instrumental rationality are singularly incapable of preventing phenomena like the Holocaust, [read slavery] because there is nothing in those rules which disqualifies the Holocaust-style methods of social engineering," [read incarceration] and because of "the bureaucratic culture which prompts us to view society as an object of administration, as a collection of problems to be solved, as 'nature' to be controlled, mastered, and improved or remade . . . ." (p. 18). All that was required in the Holocaust [read Jim Crow] was moral neutrality.

"Astounding moral blindness is possible" (Bauman, 2000, p. 24) especially when there is significant social distance, like the kind described in Miller and Gwynne's (1972) classic study of the hiving off of British citizens with physical and mental disabilities, *A Life Apart*. When there are segregated neighborhoods, schools, churches, stores, and business centers in which *White* and *Black people* live apart—far away from each other's view—there is a "much wider number of people who never face consciously either difficult moral choices or the need to stifle inner resistance or conscience" (p. 24). This kind of moral callousness is not reserved for the leaders of corporations—just consider the workers in a GM plant potentially being grateful their company waited years to report a life-threatening design issue in a given car model, an action that might have shut their factory down, temporarily or finally (The Detroit News' published PDF of the Valukas Report on GM's Ignition Recall, June 5, 2014).

REFLECTIONS FROM GROUP RELATIONS AND
PSYCHOANALYTIC PERSPECTIVES

Before Hitler loomed large on the world stage, Sigmund Freud had this to say, "It is always possible to bind together a considerable number of people in love, so long as there are other people left over to receive the manifestations of their aggressiveness" (from Freud, 1930, p. 114, quoted in Clarke, 2003, p. 59). Building on this idea in a recent book called *Our Racist Heart: An Exploration of Unconscious Prejudice in Everyday Life,* Geoffrey Beattie (2013), a British social psychologist, proposes we are all *racist,* no matter what our conscious intentions are:

> In this book I take a novel approach to this problem. What if both sides are right? What if we all are, at a conscious level, no longer prone to the prejudices of the past based around *race* or ethnicity? But what if at some deeper level, there is some system that is quite capable of operating independently of this conscious system: another system this is more susceptible to biases based on differences in *race* or ethnic background? And what if this system is allowed to operate in particular social contexts without challenge and without any top-down editorial control? (p. 4)

Beattie (2013) goes on to wonder why we, collectively, are able to recognize wrong acts or egregious injustices when we see them but we are amazed that they have come about through a series of apparently harmless acts. It is difficult for us to accept that there is often no person or group who planned or purposely caused such injustices, i.e., no one to blame. It is even more difficult to see how our own actions, through their remote effects, contribute to causing misery. So, here we must return to the social construction of "the stranger"—the object of our fears and our hatred of ourselves turned outward (p. 25).

"The 'stranger' . . . is a psychosocial character who threatens us from within and without—or from the inside out. S/he is a psychological manifestation, a projection and consequent internalization of our fear of difference, of being polluted, of being psychologically invaded by otherness. Who are these strangers . . .?" (Clarke, 2003, p. 4). In his essay, "Psychoanalysis and Racism," Frosh (1989) attributes *racism* to fears about the "safety of the psyche." Whether this fear is based in gender or ethnic otherness: "The *racist* defense, along with the fantasy of 'masculine' order, is part of the hatred of all things modernity brings." (Frosh as cited in Clarke, 2003, p. 5)

To generate resentment toward the "alien," who is hostile and undesirable, there always has to be a minority and majority schism, NOT a relationship of two "territorially established" groups. The weaker group within—the minority—maintains, or is forced to maintain, the "foreigners inside" identity (Bauman, 2000, p. 34), *Black* Americans became a "homeless" people once they had been abducted from their homelands in West Africa, and afterwards at least twelve generations have absorbed projections of themselves as "aliens."

I agree with Clarke (2003) that object relations, or Kleinian analytic theory, which rests on hypotheses and research that developed from observing infants' reactions to their dependency on others for survival can be useful to understanding the objectification of "strangers" or "aliens." Klein's (2002) formulations of *projection and projective identification,* "are at the heart of understanding hatred and discrimination" (Clarke, 2003, p. 9). *Projective identification* is, for Klein, the prototype of all aggressive object relations and a crucial mechanism of defense. *Projection per se* is a relatively straightforward process in which we attribute our own affective states to others—we project *onto* rather than *into. Projective identification,* however, involves a deep split, a ridding of unpalatable parts of the self into some other, forcing them to feel the way we do, or feel how we feel about them" (Clarke, 2003, p. 9) Recent, well-publicized examples of the viciousness of projective processes in American culture include George Zimmerman's shooting of Trayvon Martin, (Alvarez, 2015), Donald Sterling's vitriolic media attacks on Magic Johnson (Dwyer, 2014) and even some of the blog messages vilifying Whitney Houston, that accused her of stealing "a white woman's song" (Vanguard News Network, 2012).

I would like to turn our attention again to Miller and Gwynne's (1972) *A Life Apart...* The researchers described their fluctuating reactions to the residents they saw as follows:

> One day we would be overwhelmed with sympathy and pity for the plight of the disabled, doubly persecuted by their physical handicaps and by the destructiveness of the environment in which they lived. Next day we would see the staff as victims of the insistent, selfish demands of cripples who ill-deserved the money and care that were being so generously lavished upon them. . . .we were not alone in this . . . we can recall [no one] who was not either struggling with the ambivalence displayed in our own oscillations of feeling or else captured by a permanent bias. (p. 7–8)

It seems a short distance from what Miller and Gwynne describe (1972) to *White* people's fears of vulnerability and inferiority in general, especially as those cloud the picture of *race* relations in the U.S. We *Whites* fear being weaker, less capable of having what makes for a full and satisfying life on the planet—an unexplored fear of being "less than." So, we fill our lives with materialist pursuits while tacitly denying material well-being to people of color.

In later works, Miller (1985) went on to explore "the "politics of identity." Miller believed that the processes described by Klein are those through which

> . . . the biological condition of individuality gets transformed into consciousness of individuality. . . we use these processes to attain some coherence in the construct of what is "me." We get rid of the bits that don't fit, the inconsistent and conflicting bits, and attach them to our constructs of the various "not me's" with which we populate our environment. To use the language of open systems, the individual exports chaos from inside and imports order from outside. So long as this import-export process is conducted in fantasy it is safe . . . (p. 385)

When fantasy is allowed to creep into our view of "reality," however, the disowned elements of ourselves we believe we see in others can become disabling, as we saw in the example of Nathan Smith. The third workplace example presented here involves Mr. Albert Johnson, whose story has echoes of Mr. Smith's, but with important differences.

ALBERT JOHNSON

Albert Johnson and I worked together for three years in the human resources department of a large and growing natural foods grocery business with several stores in our city. He had been working there for a few years before I was appointed director of the department, which had nine staff, all of whom represented differing ethnic and social backgrounds. Two years into my tenure, I promoted Mr. Johnson to assistant director of the department, thinking that when I left he would be promoted to the director position. This is the story of why he was not offered the job.

Earlier I had served as a consultant to the board of this company and also conducted employee engagement surveys for them. When the previous human resources director was terminated, I was asked to hold the job temporarily—this ended up being a three-year assignment.

Mr. Johnson, who was close to turning 50, and had worked for more than 25 years as an flight attendant for a national US carrier prior to joining the grocery company as a human resources generalist/recruiter. Over his years with the airline, he had been promoted to lead flight attendant of a group of flight crews. He had also earned a master's degree in cultural anthropology, and flown all over the world.

The human resources department space consisted of two offices, a small conference room, and several cubicles located across from neighboring cubicles used by the finance staff of the corporation. Most of the human resources generalist/recruiters had workspaces in cubicles in the center of a large, open wing of the building from which they could observe everyone else in the space. Mr. Johnson had taken a unique approach to his own work space by devising what appeared to be a kind of "fortress" of higher than eye-level dividers arranged hexagonally around him so that no one could see him unless they walked around to the only opening of his work space—which was opposite a blank wall.

Mr. Johnson seemed to have a great deal of leadership potential, and I was curious about whether/how this might emerge. I saw his cubicle arrangement as a metaphor for his "social space" there. During my tenure with this company, no other *Black* person worked in the building. It seemed to me he was walling out *White* space, though at the time I had no such term to describe the sensation. Like Nathan Smith, Albert Johnson was a talented observer of human beings and a very effective, intuitive assessor of who could work effectively in this company's cultural surround. At one point in its early years, he had selected close to 900 of the first 1000 staff who were still working there.

Gradually, as the full camaraderie and spirit of this fascinating group of human resource staff coalesced, Mr. Johnson took down his fortress, and became more completely a member of the team. He was already known as a kind of folk hero among the frontline staff who worked in the stores—he had "seen and understood" them for years. He was professional, compassionate, clear, and knew the relevant federal and state laws and company policies. It seemed obvious to me that he was the natural successor to the department director role, so I promoted him to assistant director. He now managed the rest of the human resources staff when I was away. A short time before this a new benefits specialist had been hired. After Mr. Johnson was promoted, the new benefits specialist remarked to a colleague that she did not belong there, because, after all, "why should I submit to being managed by an old *Black* man who used to be an airline lackey?!" This was the only biased remark I ever heard about Mr. Johnson and it came from a heterosexual, *White* woman in her mid-30s.

When it was time for me to leave, the question about whether Mr. Johnson should succeed me surfaced in the mind of the newly promoted CEO of the company, a woman I had worked with closely as a coach and mentor, but who requested that I leave abruptly because I disagreed with the new approaches to managing staff she was enacting. I had insisted on firing the benefits person mentioned above, who the CEO had taken into her confidence, which was an additional point of tension between us. Of course, the CEO had the authority to make any decision she chose relative to my employment, and to select my successor. As I left, I did not know who would be chosen, but I observed her passing Mr. Johnson as he ascended the central headquarters stairway, and it seemed to me that she ignored him—another metaphor in social space. An extensive search for a new human resources director was conducted, and a *White* man who was known in the local human resources community was selected. A few months later, Mr. Johnson resigned his position there when he was appointed deputy director of the office of diversity for our state, which was one position away from the governor's office.

ANALYSIS

Mr. Johnson himself was not optimistic about being promoted to the human resources director role. His sexual orientation and a chronic health condition could fuel doubts about his capacities to lead. Whether these factors, in combination with his *race*, contributed to his and others' sense of him as potentially "too weak" to hold a role which required coping with a good deal of stress and political pressures from all sides is impossible to determine. I had some personal concerns about his health, but I knew he had earned the opportunity to provide the kind of human resources leadership the company needed as it grew.

Mr. Johnson was well connected to important people in the company; for example, he had a friendly and mutually respectful relationship with the former CEO/Founder and his wife. Another previous relationship that may have figured in Mr. Johnson's not being promoted was that he had had an intimate relationship with one of the more powerful merchandisers for the company, a man who was so valuable to its financial success that he was given significant autonomy. Though there had been many other public friendships and/or intimate relationships among people in this company, it seemed to me that these two connections represented an imagined, powerful threat to the new CEO who was working to establish her credibility and leadership.

With normative equality and the legal requirements for justice in employment, none of the factors mentioned in this Analysis section, in addition to his *race*, should have figured into the question of whether Mr. Johnson should get the promotion. My speculation, however, is that they did. On the basis of leadership experience, earned respect, knowledge of human resources practice, and contributions to the company's culture, and a relevant educational background, Mr. Johnson should have been the leading candidate for the director position.

I am almost certain that *race* was NOT a point of discussion among those who made the decision to hire a *White* man from outside the company for the director role. It would have been easy to "hide" *race* as a question among the other similarly inappropriate factors (sexual orientation, health status, personal connections) that may have figured in the selection. This example illustrates the ways in which organizational dynamics, which include both the conscious and unconscious social constructions in work settings, deny opportunities to *Black* people as well as others with attributes which have been socially denigrated by dominant groups over time.

I highlight the example of Mr. Johnson because it represents a little explored element of *White* racism in particular. I have observed, and can own experiences of envy and inferiority related to *Black* and other people of color. I believe *Black* Americans in particular are held in the broad unconscious range of *White* experience as stronger, darker survivors, who have come from older, deeper places in our shared racial history than where *we* come from. They are more capable, less oriented toward Western "ways of knowing" in making decisions, and less "artificial," more "substantial," and therefore more powerful in the realm of our collective unconscious. One example from my own experience occurred when I was beginning to learn about the unconscious aspects of groups and organizations. At the second group relations conference I attended, my small study group was consulted to by an incisive and attractive young *Black* man. By the third session of this group, I became aware of wanting to kiss him, to put my mouth over his. As I spoke this wish to the group, I realized that my motive was to shut him up, seduce him, and take his power for myself. The urge to erase him intertwined with and then overwhelmed the erotic elements of the moment, and I had a flickering awareness that other group members had a stake in this as well. Afterwards I had a familiar *White* experience, I believe, when a sense of inherited guilt, a sense of having participated in something ancestral—the sexualization and diminishment of a *Black* man, through wanting to deny his competence and his authority as the group's consultant.

CONCLUSION: CAN WE FIND OURSELVES IN *MORAL SPACE?*

We have examined some of the everyday structural inequalities experienced by people of color, especially *Black* Americans. The tragedy of these inequalities is that they are based in a social fiction: the fantasy there are innate differences between "us" (the *White*-skinned) and "them," (those living in darker skins—a social construction that has coerced them into different "social spaces" in the overall patterns of life in the U.S. I would like to conclude with some ideas that originate in two sources: Charles Taylor's (1989) book, *Sources of the Self: The Making of Modern Identity*, and Cynthia Willett's (2004) essay, *The Social Element: A Phenomenology of Racialized Space and the Limits of Liberalism* already cited here.

In the second chapter of *Sources of the Self*, (1989) Taylor describes "knowing one's identity in a moral space" as a useful framework for looking at identity and why we need to define it, especially now.

> Who am I?. . . To know who I am is a species of knowing where I stand. My identity is defined by the commitments and identifications which provide the frame or horizon within which I can try to determine from case to case what is good, or valuable, or what ought to be done, or what I endorse or oppose. To know who you are is to be oriented in moral space, a space in which questions arise about what is good or bad, what is worth doing and what is not, what has meaning and importance for you and what is trivial and secondary. (pp. 27–28)

Cynthia Willett (2004) also speaks of finding ourselves in moral space: "The Greeks named the crimes that damage social space as acts of *hubris*, and they used the theater as well as the assembly to warn the elites of the consequences of their *hubris* for the social milieu. Western democracy theory today needs to reacquaint itself with ancient legal and moral tools against social domination" (p. 245).

Currently, dominant Eurocentric culture in the US offers a "passive container model of space" (Willett, 2004, p. 254) where individuals seek fulfillment. However, it can be argued that most humans experience the basic unifying factor among us not through individual fulfillment but through a network of social ties and relations extending across time and space. In spite of the *postmodern* emphasis on individuality/identity, our states and communities can be best constructed in ways that protect relationships and make choices meaningful to more than one individual at a time (p. 248).

Willett (2004) points out that choruses in early Athenian drama often portrayed a marginalized segment of society—women, old men, foreigners, underlings, slaves—who were there to deliver messages to the elite, e.g., "Hubris breeds the tyrant." The *hubris* of the elite is shown not only to harm individuals and the relationships among them, but to weaken the fabric holding the community together. In Athenian drama the *demos* (people) had the legal right to charge the elite with arrogance and bring individuals before a court. The liberalism held by many *White* Americans has framed no ethical equivalent to *hubris* (p. 259), nor do we tend to hold ourselves individually accountable. A short time ago I worked with an executive team of nine people, including three professionally accomplished *Black* men. From my perspective as an external consultant, these men, two of whom were typically silent in meetings, offered unspoken commentary on the norms of the group and the culture of the wider organization. My interpretation was that they reflected an underlying pattern of the organization's culture: inviting people of color "to the table," but not to participate fully—to be "seen but not heard." In this drama, I saw reenactments of the stories of the three *Black* Americans I have described in this paper—stories of *White* space, color-blind *racism*, and a *postmodern* world we haven't yet begun to understand.

Not one of us lives and works in a void, but in a space that establishes our power and status, in part, through the color of the skins in which we live—in spite of the entirely imaginary basis for this. Are we capable of seeking a deeper awareness of what's in "our collective unconscious"? Can we adopt practices supporting a *moral* social space to replace our largely *racialized* space? I think the answer rests on whether we have the courage to face inward and bring what we find there into the light for exploration with each other.

REFERENCES

Alexander, M. (2010). *The new Jim Crow: Mass incarceration in the age of colorblindness.* New York, NY: New Press.

Alvarez, L. (2015, February 24). U.S. won't file charges in Trayvon Martin killing. *New York Times.* Retrieved from http://www.nytimes.com/2015/02/25/us/justice-dept-wont-charge-george-zimmerman-in-trayvon-martin-killing.html?_r=0

Bauman, Z. (2000). *Modernity and the Holocaust.* Ithaca, NY: Cornell University Press.

Beattie, G. (2013). *Our racist heart?: An exploration of unconscious prejudice in everyday life.* New York, NY: Routledge.

Bonilla-Silva, E. (2006). *Color-blind racism and the persistence of racial inequality in the U.S.,* Lanham, MD: Roman and Littlefield.

Boxill, B. (2004) Why we should not think of ourselves as divided by race. In M. P. Levine & T. Pataki (Eds.), *Racism in mind,* (pp. 209–224). Ithaca, NY: Cornell University Press.

Carr, L. G. (1997). *Colorblind racism.* Thousand Oaks, CA: Sage Publications.

Clarke, S. (2003). *Social theory, psychoanalysis and racism.* London, UK: Palgrave Macmillan.

Cox, O. (1948). *Caste, class and race.* New York, NY: Monthly Review Press.

Davids, M. F. (2011). *Internal racism: A psychoanalytic approach to race and difference.* London, UK: Palgrave Macmillan.

Dumas, R. G. (1985). Dilemmas of Black females in leadership. In A. D. Colman & M. H. Geller (Eds.), *Group relations reader 2,* (pp. 323–334). Jupiter, FL: A. K. Rice Institute.

Dwyer, K. (2014, May 12). Donald Sterling attacks Magic Johnson in a bizarre interview with Anderson Cooper. *Yahoo! Sports.* Retrieved from: http://sports.yahoo.com/blogs/nba-ball-dont-lie/donald-sterling-goes-on-the-attack-after-magic-johnson-in-a-bizarre-interview-with-anderson-cooper-013351560.html

Fanon, F. (1952) *Black sin, white masks,* Paris, France: Points Publishing.

Frosh, S. (1989). Psychoanalysis and racism. In B. Richards (Ed.), *Crisis of the self.* London, UK: Free Association Books.

Harris, C. (1993). Whiteness as property. UCLA School of Law Research Paper No. 06–5. *Harvard Law Review, 106*(8) 1707–1794.

Hayden, C., & Molenkamp, R. (2004). Tavistock Primer II. In S. Cytrynbaum & D. A. Noumair (Eds.), *Group Relations Reader 3* (pp. 135–157). Waldorf, MD: McArdle Printing, A.K. Rice Institute.

Jenkins, R. (1986), *Racism and recruitment: Managers, organisations and equal opportunity in the labour market.* New York, NY: Cambridge University Press.

Klein, M. (2002). *Love, guilt, and reparation: And other works 1921–1945.* New York, NY: Free Press.

Kochhar, R., Fry, R., & Taylor, P. (2009). *Twenty-to-one: Wealth gaps rise to record highs between Whites, Blacks, Hispanics.* Pew Research Center: Social and Demographic Trends Report. Retrieved from: http://www.pewsocialtrends.org/2011/07/26/wealth-gaps-rise-to-record-highs-between-whites-blacks-hispanics/

Lemert, C. (2005). *Postmodernism is not what you think: Why globalization threatens modernity.* Boulder, CO: Paradigm Publishers.

Lipsitz, g., (2006) *The Possessive Investment in Whiteness: How White people profit from identity politics.* Philadelphia, PA: Temple University Press.

McRae, M. B., & Short, E. L., (2010). *Racial and cultural dynamics in group and organizational life: Crossing boundaries,* Thousand Oaks, CA: Sage Publications.

Menzies-Lyth, I. (1989). *The dynamics of the social.* London, UK: Free Association Books.

Miles, R. (1993). *Race after 'race relations.'* New York, NY & London, UK: Routledge.

Miller, E. J. (1985). The politics of involvement. In A. Colman & M. Geller (Eds.), *Group relations reader 2,* (pp. 383–397). Springfield, VA: Goetz Printing, A. K. Rice Institute.

Miller, E. J., & Gwynne, G. V. (1972). *A life apart: A pilot study of residential institutions for the physically handicapped and the young chronic sick.* London, UK: Tavistock Publications.

Modood, T. (1997). *Ethnic minorities on Britain: Diversity and disadvantage.* London, UK: Policy Studies Institute.

Morris, A. (1986). *Origins of the civil rights movement.* New York, NY: Free Press.

Reich, R. B. (2008). *Supercapitalism: The transformation of business, democracy, and everyday life.* New York, NY: Vintage Books.

Singer, P. (1995). *How are we to live?: Ethics in an age of self-interest.* Amherst, NY: Prometheus Books.

Smedley, A., & Smedley, B. D. (2011). *Race in North America: Origin and evolution of a worldview* (4th ed.). New York, NY: Westview Press.

Smiley, J. (1995). *MOO: A novel*. New York, NY: Anchor Books.

Stanford Center on Poverty and Inequality. (2014). *The 2014 poverty and inequality national report card*. Stanford, CA: Stanford University. Retrieved from web.stanford.edu/sotu/SOTU_2014_CPI.pdf

Taylor, c. (1989). *Sources of the self: The making of modern identity*, Cambridge, MA:. Harvard University Press.

The Detroit News. (June 5, 2014) PDF: Read the Valukas Report on GM's ignition recall. Retrieved from http://www.detroitnews.com/article/20140605/SPECIAL01/140605001

Vanguard News Network. (2012). *Whitney Houston dead*. Retrieved from http://vnnforum.com/shoutthread. Retrieved 5/7/14.

Willett, C. (2004). A phenomenology of racialized space and the limits of liberalism. In M. P. Levine & T. Pataki (Eds.), *Racism in mind*. Ithaca, NY, & London, UK: Cornell University Press.

CHAPTER 15

ANITA HILL AND CLARENCE THOMAS, NAFISSATOU DIALLO AND DOMINIQUE STRAUSS-KAHN

A Group Relations Perspective: Black Women, Feminism, and the Act of Giving Voice

Ellen L. Short

Just my breath, carrying my words out, might poison people and they'd curl up and die like the black fat slugs that only pretended. I had to stop talking.

—*Maya Angelou,* I Know Why the Caged Bird Sings (1969/2015)

For we have been socialized to respect fear more than our own needs for language and definition, and while we wait in silence for that final luxury of fearlessness, the weight of that silence will choke us.

—*Audre Lorde,* Sister Outsider (1984)

Talking About Structural Inequalities in Everyday Life: New Politics of Race in Groups, Organizations, and Social Systems, pages 285–308.

How silences are broken is as important as breaking them.
—*Tricia Rose*, Longing To Tell. Black Women Talk about Sexuality and
Intimacy (2003)

When I say raise your voice, I mean raise your voice wherever you find it.
—*Anita Hill*, Anita. Speaking Truth to Power (2013)

Almost 25 years have passed since the Thomas-Hill hearings. The 20th anniversary of the hearings was observed by a documentary, *Anita. Speaking Truth to Power* (2013) which premiered at Sundance and a book entitled, *I Still Believe Anita Hill. Three Generations Discuss the Legacies of Speaking Truth to Power*, based on a conference held on October 15, 2011, to commemorate the 20th anniversary of the hearings (Richards & Greenberg, 2013; Rothman, 2014).

The Thomas-Hill hearings took place on October 11, 1991 before a Senate Judiciary Committee chaired by then Senator Joseph Biden, who is now the Vice President of the United States. The two individuals called to testify at the hearings were Anita Hill and Clarence Thomas, as well as their witnesses and supporters. Thomas had earlier been nominated by President George H. W. Bush to be appointed to the Supreme Court seat that had been recently vacated by Thurgood Marshall, who was the first African American to be appointed to the United States Supreme Court. President Bush's nomination of Clarence Thomas, who held conservative political views, was opposed by several Civil Rights organizations, including the NAACP, as well as women's groups. The process of confirming Thomas before the Senate Judiciary Committee, however, was stalled not by opposition from these groups, but by Anita Hill, a law Professor at the University of Oklahoma, and a former attorney advisor to Clarence Thomas during his tenure as Assistant Secretary of the U.S. Department of Education's Office for Civil Rights and when he was the head of the Equal Employment Opportunities Commission (EEOC). Hill, in a confidential statement to the Senate Judiciary Committee accused Thomas of having sexually harassed her when she worked for him 10 years earlier, citing repeated instances in which he invited her on dates and engaged in inappropriate discussions of a sexual nature, despite her refusals to date him and to engage in such discussions with him. Hill's statement was investigated by the FBI, deemed inconclusive and then leaked to the public and the press; it was after these events that a decision was made to hold the hearings (Hill, 1997; *History 122*, n.d.). It should be noted that Clarence Thomas vehemently denied Hill's accusations. The hearings to address the accusations and denials were televised and watched by viewers across the country.

As we approach the 25th anniversary of the Thomas-Hill hearings, it is clear that the events that took place before, during, and after those hearings continue to be resonant in American society to this day. This chapter will revisit the Anita Hill and Clarence Thomas hearings with a focus on the Noumair, Fenichel, & Fleming (1992) article, "Clarence Thomas, Anita Hill and Us: A Group Relations

Perspective," which was one of the first articles to analyze this event within a group relations framework. In concert with Noumair et al., this chapter will present analyses and interpretations of the Thomas-Hill hearings and the more recent case of Nafissatou Diallo and Dominique Strauss-Kahn. The Diallo/Strauss-Kahn case was based on an accusation of sexual assault made by Nafissatou Diallo against Dominique Strauss-Kahn in May of 2011 in New York City (Baker & Erlanger, 2011). As with the Thomas-Hill hearings, this case resulted in an ongoing public discourse about sexual harassment in the workplace that occurred in the US and in France. Both cases are intricately connected via the individuals involved, the span of time that separates each case, as well as the structural inequalities that both women experienced as a consequence of their acts of giving voice to their victimization. The cases will be analyzed using a group relations theoretical lens, which will be elaborated upon in another section of this chapter. Additionally, the complexities and structural inequalities inherent in the act of giving voice for Black women and the ways that feminism informs these dynamics will be explored through the interrelatedness of Black feminist, transnational and postcolonial feminisms, and group relations theory that embodies a focus on racial-cultural dynamics.

The terms that will be used to describe racial and cultural identity will be Black and African American in a US context; when appropriate the racial identifier of Black will also include nationality and ethnicity in international/African Diasporic contexts. The terms that will be used to identify and describe forms of violence perpetrated upon Black women will be sexual harassment, sexual assault, rape, and the broader systemic term, gender-based violence, which is violence that is directed against a person on the basis of gender. Gender-based violence constitutes a breach of the fundamental right to life, liberty, security, dignity, and equality between men and women, thereby reflecting and reinforcing inequalities between men and women in heterosexual contexts. The impact of gender-based violence negates the existence of non-discrimination and mental and physical integrity (European Institute for Gender Equality, EIGE, 2015). Ethnoviolence, defined by Helms, Nicolas, and Green (2011) as "violence and intimidation directed at members of ethnic groups that have been marginalized and stigmatized by the dominant or host culture because of their inability or unwillingness to assimilate threatens the dominant group's entitlement to society or community resources," is another term used in this chapter (p. 67). An aspect of ethnoviolence that will be focused on is the relationship it has to race-related trauma and immediate or delayed post-traumatic stress disorder (PTSD) symptomatology for direct cataclysmic racial or ethnic cultural events, vicarious or witnessed cataclysmic events, and racial and cultural microaggressions (Helms et al., 2011).

Finally, the act of Black women giving voice, specifically to incidents of gender-based violence in public domains will be defined as a political act of radical resistance to what hooks (1992) in her book *Black Looks: Race and Representation*, identifies as the *silences*, unaddressed places, for example, within her own or others' personal, political and artistic revolution. In the context of this chapter, silences will be identified as unaddressed places of pain and oppression that have historically been located within the realm of trauma for Black women who have been victimized by gender-based violence and forms of ethnoviolence. Silent places of pain and oppression can also engender experiences of being and feeling silenced, particularly by groups, organizations, and institutions that perpetuate dominance in racist and sexist contexts. Giving voice, therefore, can be defined as the act of individuals from an oppressed group, in this case Black women, coming to voice, articulating a "speech of suffering," a sound that very often no one wants to hear (p. 146). In *Yearning: Race Gender, and Cultural Politics* hooks (1990) states:

> Often when the radical voice speaks about domination we are speaking to those who dominate. Their presence changes the nature and direction our words. Language is also a place of struggle...Dare I speak to oppressed and oppressor in the same voice? Dare I speak to you in a language that will move you beyond the boundaries of domination—a language that will not bind you in, fence you in, or hold you? Language is also a place of struggle. The oppressed struggle in language to recover ourselves, to reconcile, to reunite, to renew. Our words are not without meaning, they are an action, a resistance. Language is also a place of struggle. (p. 146)

In hooks' assessment that language is also a place of struggle, lies one aspect of structural inequality regarding the act of giving voice—the political act of articulating stories, narratives, and testimonies that are often resisted, denied, interrogated, and silenced by groups, systems, and societies.

SELF-ANALYSIS

An integral part of the genesis of my desire to write this chapter comes from a need to place myself in it as an author and as a witness to the aftermath of both incidents as they became the property of the public domain and to position myself in ways that reflect the meaning that both events have had for me at individual and group levels. Upon much reflection, I realized that my positionality involves my identity as a descendent of Black women who did domestic work, like Nafissatou Diallo, in public and private spaces where White people lived and worked. My ancestors who did this labor had a strong work ethic and took pride in their skills and competencies. The work they did made the lives of those they worked for easier while simultaneously making their lives more stressful as they struggled to maintain their own homes and care for their families in the margins. In the homes of their employers they also endured oppression and discrimination doing labor that required them to make intimate contact with those they served while coping with the paradoxical indignities of being rendered hypervisible and/or invisible as well as being patronizingly labeled a "member of the family," but also expendable. Although I am not an immigrant, I am descended from ancestors who endured forced immigration through the Middle Passage and the horrors of enslavement, and I am also descended from those that perpetrated and benefitted from slavery. And, I am also a product of the Great Migration from the south to the north made by my parents. Like Anita Hill, I am a tenured professor at a university, with all of the privileges of that role, tempered by the usual constraints and stressors that are often placed upon Black women academics working in predominantly White academic institutions. I am a counseling psychologist who teaches and conducts scholarly work and consulting focusing on racial-cultural dynamics in groups, organizations, and institutions. I have vacationed, lived and worked in France and could be described as a Francophile. And, like both Nafissatou Diallo and Anita Hill, I have a valence for and a history of giving voice, of telling stories that others didn't or don't want me to tell, and for doing that I have been ignored, punished and even silenced but I have also been praised and rewarded. And, all of the above intersecting identities have shaped my identity as a Black feminist.

I vividly remember watching the Clarence Thomas-Anita Hill hearings in the autumn of 1991, sitting completely riveted before the television in my apartment in a major Midwestern city. And, I had begun to think about and explore feminism in relation to my identity as an African American woman. Therefore, the Thomas-Hill hearings and specifically, the specter of Anita Hill and her forthright and courageous testimony brought forth a multitude of complex feelings and reactions in me.

Although it would be five years before I was introduced to group relations theory, I now realize that watching the Thomas-Hill hearings was an engaging, albeit very disturbing primer for prompting me to reflect on what I was viewing in systemic and complex ways. And, after enrolling in a Counseling Psychology masters program and getting my introduction to group relations from a course and a course-related conference, I read the article written by Debra A. Noumair, Ann Fenichel, and Jennifer L. Fleming (1992), entitled, "Clarence Thomas, Anita Hill, and Us: A Group Relations Perspective." The article was meaningful to me then because of its focus on the Thomas-Hill hearings and for the way that the authors skillfully applied group relations theory, which I was then learning in class, to explain, analyze, and critique the complexities of the events that took place. The authors also provided a group relations lens regarding the impact the hearings had on our views of race, gender, power, and sexual harassment.

In 2011, the year of the 20th anniversary of the Thomas-Hill hearings, another event occurred in New York that captured my attention much in the same ways that the Thomas-Hill hearings had, which was the encounter between Nafissatou Diallo, who was employed as a housekeeper at the Sofitel Hotel in midtown Manhattan and the then head of the International Monetary Fund (IMF), Dominique Strauss-Kahn. The encounter that occurred in that hotel room lead to an alleged sexual assault when Diallo entered the room to clean it and Strauss-Kahn reportedly attacked and sexually assaulted and her (Dickey, 2011; Hawley, 2011). Her subsequent act of reporting the sexual assault, which has also been described as an attempted rape (Baker & Erlanger, 2011), and her act of immediately giving voice to what happened, resulted in the Port Authority police boarding an Air France plane at John F. Kennedy Airport upon which Strauss-Kahn was seated for an overnight flight to Paris, arresting him on charges of a criminal sexual act, attempted rape, and unlawful imprisonment in connection with a sexual assault on Nafissatou Diallo, and "perp walking" and incarcerating him in the Special Victims Unit of the New York Police Department on Rikers Island (Baker & Erlanger, 2011).

As with the Thomas-Hill hearings, this incident resonated with me in multiple ways—the sadness and anger I felt about Nafissatou Diallo's ordeal, my admiration for her regarding the immediacy of her act of giving voice to the experience of her attack, the swiftness with which her alleged attacker, Strauss-Kahn was apprehended, the sensational news and social media coverage of the incident and the events that played out after, were all fascinating to me. Moreover, the transnational impact of this incident and the ensuing conversations and debates across the globe, but specifically on two continents, the US and France about race, gender, power, authority, and gender-based violence in the form of sexual harassment/ assault perpetrated upon women in the workplace by men was riveting (Frosch, 2011; Rouyer, 2013).

Noumair et al. (1992), in their explanation of their need and responsibility to collectively make sense of their "intense feelings" about the Thomas-Hill hearings, cited the political and external as being linked to the psychological and internal and their belief that psychologists have "a responsibility to look at how psychic conflict gets projected and manifested externally as well as internally" (p. 378). I concur with their assessment and as a witness, albeit a public one to events surrounding the Diallo/Strauss Kahn incident, as with the Thomas-Hill hearings, I felt the need to make meaning of what I was feeling, through the lens of group relations theory which provides societal, institutional, systemic and group contexts to events and human behaviors, and feminist theories, which can illuminate and critique existing structural inequalities of these domains.

SIMILARITIES AND DIFFERENCES OF BOTH CASES

In addition to the Diallo-Strauss Kahn incident occurring in the year of the 20th anniversary of the Thomas-Hill hearings, certain details of both events are strikingly similar, while others are quite dissimilar. Both women were Black; Anita Hill, was a tenured law professor at the University of Oklahoma College of Law who, as has previously been mentioned, worked with Clarence Thomas twice (Hill, 1997). Anita Hill was a single African American woman, descended from slaves, the youngest of 13 children, whose family had lived and prospered in the US for generations (Hill, 1997; Mock 2013). Nafissatou Diallo was Guinean, a widow and a mother who immigrated to the US in 2003, applied for asylum and eventually found employment in the Housekeeping Department of the Sofitel Hotel. At the time of both events, each woman was in her 30s and both women accused two prominent men, one an African American man and nominee for a Supreme Court

Justice appointment, the other a White, French, Jewish man, head of the International Monetary Fund (IMF) and, at the time of his arrest, the likeliest candidate to become the next president of France, of sexual harassment and sexual assault, respectively (Dickey, 2011; Hill, 1997).

For Anita Hill and Clarence Thomas, who were both African American and part of what bell hooks (2000) described as "mainstream white conservative culture and politics" (p. 80), what connected them, in addition to race and political affiliations was their representation of the long held, relatively unexplored within race conflicts concerning sexism, gender and power between African American men and women. For Nafissatou Diallo, a working class Guinean woman coping with the stresses of immigration and acculturation in a new country and Dominique Strauss-Kahn, a prominent, privileged, wealthy White French Jewish man, who was an economist, politician, and member of the upper strata of French society, the class differences were stark. However, there was also the unspoken, relatively unexplored connection of their nationalities—the Republic of Guinea (formerly known as French Guinea) a West African country colonized and ruled by France from the late 1800s until 1958 (Embassy of Guinea, Washington, DC, n.d.), and unconsciously held dynamics of the alleged sexual assault being related to historical issues of oppression and dominance of a European country over an African nation/republic.

Additional similarities can be found in the media coverage of the aftermath of both events; in 1991 before the advent of what we identify today as social media, the televised Thomas-Hill hearings were deemed to be a rare and almost surreal event watched by many viewers, or as Kimberlé Crenshaw (1992) described, a beautifully played episode "right out of The Twilight Zone," (p. 402), with the specter of an all White middle aged, male Senate who, although clearly ill at ease with the process of eliciting testimony from Anita Hill, nevertheless were unwavering in their intentions to de-authorize, shame and diminish her, exhibiting, what bell hooks (1992) described as "fierce, sexist interrogation" (p. 82), (Hill, 1997; Mock, 2013). The senators seemed equally uncomfortable with Clarence Thomas, whose testimony evoked anger, rage and declarations of being a victim of a "high-tech lynching" during the hearings (hooks, 1992, p. 81). In contrast, two decades later, the Diallo/Strauss-Kahn incident was covered extensively on television and social and news media outlets around the world (Baker & Erlanger, 2011; Dickey, 2011; Facebook, 2011; Frosch, 2011; Hawley, 2011; Peltz & Hays, 2011; YouTube, 2011). Another of the important differences between the two cases was the global impact; the Thomas-Hill hearings were viewed internationally as an example of US culture as democratic in its exposure of political corruption and pioneering and progressive in the area of civil rights (Ross, 1992), but the uproar was relegated primarily to US and American history and culture. In contrast, the Diallo/Strauss-Kahn case, despite its eventual dismissal in a New York court (Peltz & Hays, 2011), spanned two continents and shed a spotlight on the US's challenged history with societal views of sexual harassment and systemic inequalities of women giving voice to these incidents, seen most vividly via the Thomas-Hill hearings but also in subsequent publically aired incidents of gender-based violence throughout two decades. France, however, a country that often viewed the US's focus on civil rights as extreme and puritanical, seemed to barely have begun acknowledging a long held, culturally sanctioned pattern of tolerating and even openly accepting sexual harassment, particularly in heterosexual contexts (Rouyer, 2013).

Finally, an interesting connection between the two cases was cited by Gloria Steinem (2013), who, in a chapter entitled, "Supremacy Crimes," published in *I Still Believe Anita Hill*, identified Paulette Barnes, Mechelle Vinson and Anita Hill, all Women of Color as the "three great pioneers of protesting sexual harassment." She observed that their strong voices provided a foundation for Nafissatou Diallo to have the courage to come forward to give her voice to her experience of being sexually assaulted by Dominique Strauss-Kahn, which in turn allowed another woman in France to do the same. Steinem contended that although both women lost in the courts, they won in the "court of public opinion." Moreover, Diallo's victory was won much more quickly than Hill's—the evidence of this being the election of Clarence Thomas to the Supreme Court, despite Hill's testimony. In her comparison of the results of the two cases, however, she observed that Strauss-Kahn would never be president of France (Richards & Greenberg, 2013, Loc 2609–2625 of 3397). Steinem's (2013) observations makes clear the historical connection to acts of giving voice to women's traumatic experiences of sexual harassment and gender-based violence and the impact of that history. The next section will provide an application of multiple theoretical lenses through which both cases can be analyzed.

GROUP RELATIONS THEORY, RACE, AND CULTURE

Race and culture have always been integral but not explicitly identified components of group relations theory due to its genesis as a Eurocentric theoretical perspective that embodies a focus on psychoanalysis, object relations (Bion, 1961; Klein, 1946) and systems theories (Lewin, 1951). Thus, although the group relations theoretical lens clearly embodies a cultural perspective that is monocultural, this fact has, for the most part, been unacknowledged.

Developed at the Tavistock Institute for Human Relations, the Group Relations Model was expanded by A. Kenneth Rice, and introduced in the US by Margaret Rioch (Rioch, 1985) a clinical psychologist and the founder of the A. K. Rice Institute for the Study of Social Systems (Khaleelee & White, 2014). The Group Relations Model is derived from theories developed by Wilfred Bion (1961, 1975), Melanie Klein (1946) and Kurt Lewin (1951) (Hayden & Molenkamp, 2004). It is grounded in psychoanalytic and systems theory, and views groups as entities that have developmental life stages, which are often connected to completion of a group task. Embedded levels of group affiliations are often representative of multiple identities, such as race, ethnicity, gender, social class, sexual orientation, religion, as well as professional and social group affiliations (Alderfer, 1994, 1997).

The British psychiatrist and analyst Wilfred Bion (1961, 1975) contributed to the model with his belief that groups were objects that triggered anxieties related to paradoxes of the desire to join versus fears of group rejection, abandonment, and engulfment. He identified what he termed, *basic assumption group functioning* as an often unconscious mode of work group behavior focused on management of anxiety related to the group's primary work tasks. He developed three modes of basic assumption functioning: *dependency*, in which the group exhibits excessive dependence on the formal group leader, *fight/flight*, in which group members fight or flee from the primary task(s), and *pairing*, evidenced by paired members whose positive or adversarial interpersonal dynamics distracts the group from its' primary task(s) and may also represent unconscious expressions of group intimacy and competition. Two more modes of basic assumption functioning were developed later; *oneness* (Turquet, 1985), embodies passive group level participation and fusion with an "omnipotent" leader, and *the fifth basic assumption* or *basic assumption me-ness* (Lawrence, Bain, & Gould, 1996), characterized by withdrawal from and denial of the group, with an emphasis on the self, in narcissistic (e.g., pathological) contexts. Short (2007) expanded on the fifth basic assumption, hypothesizing that detachment from the group is not always pathological, but may be adaptive, indicative of an act of dependency upon oneself, and related to survival of the psyche, for instance, in racial-cultural contexts.

The premise of the group relations model is that group membership creates paradoxical tensions (e.g., between engulfment and/or estrangement by the group) that promote the use of defense mechanisms to alleviate anxieties. Thus, defense mechanisms of *splitting*, in which individuals and groups are divided into polarized entities of good or bad with perceptions that specific qualities are contained in one individual or group and their opposites often occurs (McRae & Short, 2010; Wells, 1990). *Projection* is often the result of individual or group level splitting and involves projecting onto others one's own unacceptable desires and impulses (Kernberg, 1976). The quality of projections related to race and culture is often intricately connected to societal attitudes, expectations, prejudices, and stereotypes, in historical and contemporary contexts (Dalal, 2002). *Projective identification*, an interactive process in which undesirable projections are ambivalently held, can be internalized by individuals and groups who receive the projections; these entities may unconsciously begin to engage in behaviors that are consistent with the projections on behalf of those who have initiated them. It's important to note that the exchange is not random or coincidental; the individuals or groups who are recipients (e.g., containers) of the projections may have an unconscious disposition or valence for expressions of the projected material (McRae & Short, 2010; Noumair et al., 1992; Reed & Nomair, 2000). For example, Noumair et al. (1992) cite Wells (1990) and state that an individual's valence for containment of others' projections is influenced by his/her psychological identity and group identity, which includes any "stereotypic attributions that accompany it," such as a woman [finding] herself elected to cry for the group, or a Black member [finding herself/himself] chosen to carry the group's sexuality or rage" (p. 380). Connolly and Noumair (2000) cite the processes by which race, gender, and sexual orientation are often used as receptacles for the unwanted aspects of the self (e.g., using the other as a container for undesirable aspects of the self). McRae, Kwong, and Short (2007) cite the challenges inherent in Women of Color and White women colluding with racial and gendered stereotypes that serve to disconnect them from engaging in authentic racial dialogue in groups, and McRae and Short (2010) identify these all of these dynamics as embodying racial-cultural aspects of power differentials, authority and class hierarchies that exist in society.

Aspects of group relations theory apply to the Thomas-Hill hearings and the Diallo/Strauss-Kahn case. Basic assumption functioning at group and societal levels is evident in the pairing of Anita Hill and Clarence Thomas and Nafissatou Diallo and Dominique Strauss-Kahn, which in both cases were adversarial pairings connected by gender-based violence allegedly perpetrated by both men. Both pairings, as previously stated, represented what could be described as unspeakable dynamics of within race sexism (Hill and Thomas), as well as oppression related to social class, race, and colonization (Diallo and Strauss-Kahn). Moreover, elements of defense mechanisms of splitting, projection, and projective identification were evident, particularly within the realms of systemic inequalities of Hill and Diallo's acts of giving voice; this phenomenon will be explored in the remaining sections of the chapter. The next section of will focus on feminism, with an emphasis on Black feminist theories and their relevance to both cases.

Black Feminist Standpoint Theory and Feminisms

hooks (2000) in *Feminism is for Everybody*, defines feminism as "a movement to end sexism, sexist exploitation, and oppression." This definition of feminism doesn't imply that men are the enemy and cites all sexist thinking and action as problematic. hooks characterizes the definition as being "broad enough to include an understanding of systemic institutionalized sexism" (p. 1). There are, of course other definitions of feminism/feminisms and feminist frameworks, including socialist, poststructuralist, and transnational (Holvino, 2010), as well as lesbian and queer feminist theory and postcolonial and third wave feminisms (Enns 2010).

For the purpose of this chapter, however, feminism will be defined based on hooks' (2000) definition, Collins (2000/2014) standpoint theory, which represents group knowledge, and US Black feminist thought, which places Black women's experiences and ideas at the center of analyses and focuses on feminism as an activist response to Black women's subordination within intersecting oppressions of race, class, gender, sexuality, and nation. Black feminist thought also incorporates a focus on tension connecting experiences and ideas regarding instances of derogation experienced by women of African descent and the diversity of responses to these experiences, for example, within transnational, global contexts and connections between US Black women's collective historical experiences of oppression that may stimulate the development of a defined standpoint, which in turn may foster Black women's activism. Another aspect of the theory concerns the contributions of what Collins identifies as African American women intellectuals of diverse ages, social classes, educational backgrounds and occupations whose "special relationship" to the larger community of African American women framed Black feminist thought's contours as critical social theory (p. 32). The significance of change is another aspect of US Black feminist thought, as it relates to the ability of the theory to be effective within Black feminism and social justice contexts. The final aspect of the theory is the relationship it has to social justice in humanist contexts. Harris-Perry's (2011) discourse on Black women's recognition and misrecognition in public and private spaces and the crooked room will also be explored. Intersectionalities of group relations, feminist and Black feminist theories will also be identified.

It should be noted that the importance of applying Black feminist theories that embody a focus on intersectionality to highlight structural inequalities of Black women giving voice to gender-based violence and ethnoviolence lies in assessments of the inadequacies inherent in utilizing the dominant feminist lens/analysis exclusively to contextualize and deconstruct these types of traumatic incidents for these populations (Crenshaw, 1992; Enns, 2010; Holvino, 2010). Intersectionality is also deeply embedded in transnational and postcolonial feminisms, which privilege Women of Color and non-Western women (Mendoza, 2002, as cited in Holvino, 2010).

Intersections of Group Relations Theory, Feminist, and Black Feminist Theories

The intersection of group relations theory to feminism and Black feminist theory seems to lie in Noumair et al. (1992) and McRae and Short's (2010) focus on group relations theory and overt and covert institutional processes that impede and/or enhance organizational functioning and illuminate power differentials, authority, racial and class hierarchies that exist in society. Intersections also reside in defense mechanisms often employed by groups to cope with anxieties of group life: splitting, projection, and projective identification in racial-cultural contexts. The enactment of each defense mechanism at group, institutional and societal levels is intricately tied to conscious and unconscious desires to cope with anxieties related to racial-cultural dynamics in which subgroups of individuals become "spokespersons, leaders, scapegoats, heroes/heroines, or enemies based on stereotypic assumptions (Noumair et al., 1992). Connected to all of the above is hooks' (2000) definition of feminism as well as Collins' (2000/2014) Black feminist thought, specifically, her assertion that the ties between what one does and what one thinks is illustrated by individual Black women and can also characterize Black women's experiences and ideas as a group. Collins' assertion can also be connected to ethnoviolent experiences for Black women. For example, the experience of witnessing instances of race and gender-based violence and trauma impacting a Black woman in the public domain and the immediate or delayed post-traumatic stress disorder (PTSD) and other symptomatology that may result in Black women as a group due to their vicarious experiences of these racial/ethnic cultural events (Helms, et al., 2011). Thus, public acts of giving voice by individual Black women in oppressive institutional and societal contexts can evoke psychologically debilitating symptomatology for Black women as a group. However, per Collins (2000/2014), these traumatic experiences can also result in calls to activism, for example, the Black feminists who formed the African American Women in Defense of Ourselves (AAWIDOO) group in 1991, in defense of Anita Hill and the history of Black women enduring negative stereotyped labeling (Crenshaw, 2013), and the global and virtual protests on behalf of Nafissatou Diallo (Facebook, 2011; YouTube, 2011).

Feminist ideology in group relations literature has been explored via the impact of gender, race, sexual orientation, authority, power, and privilege on systemic dynamics as these variables are connected most often to women at group, organizational and institutional levels (Bayes & Newton, 1985; Brazaitis, 2004; Connolly & Noumair, 1997; Dumas, 1985; Gabelnick, 1993; 2004; Gould, 1985; Khaleelee & White, 2014; Malone 2000; McRae, 2004; McRae, Kwong, & Short, 2007; McRae & Short, 2010; Noumair et al., 1992; Reed & Noumair, 2000; Rioch, 1985; Rosenbaum, 2004; Short, 2007; Short & Williams, 2014; Short & Woon, 2009). Strengths of the existing literature are the collectivistic perspectives of the authors' writings that focus on women and places gendered identity and behavior related to authority, power, and leadership, within a contextual framework that reflects embeddedness at multiple levels. Thus, the implications of these authors' work is that it has served to provide important gendered and racialized perspectives to group relations theory and models of conducting group relations consultative and therapeutic work.

The next section will provide analyses of structural inequalities of acts of giving voice regarding the Thomas-Hill hearings and the Diallo/Strauss-Kahn cases.

THE THOMAS-HILL HEARINGS (NEARLY) TWENTY-FIVE YEARS LATER: STRUCTURAL INEQUALITIES OF GIVING VOICE

In their article, Noumair et al. (1992), as three self-identified White women, described themselves as a microcosm of the larger group (e.g., the nation), which at the time of the Thomas-Hill hearings, was led by president George H. W. Bush. They further cited that the group that most strongly identified with Anita Hill were White, highly educated, middle class women like themselves. They located their understanding of this in the differences between levels of privilege for White and Black women; despite being impacted by sexism, White women have unearned privileges stemming from skin color and their proximity to White men while Women of Color have less privilege due to racial oppression. Thus, the authors hypothesized that Black women's positionality necessitated allegiance to race rather than gender and it appeared to the authors that "for black women, supporting Anita Hill meant public disloyalty to a Black man" (p. 381). The authors further state that as White women, from their position of privilege, their identification with and support of Anita Hill affirmed their identities as women. However, Anita Hill as "feminist heroine" served to perpetuate racist myths of Black men (e.g., Clarence Thomas) as a dangerous threat. Noumair et al. (1992) believed that by viewing the Thomas-Hill hearings solely as an outgrowth of patriarchy, "white women were able to remain virtuous by identifying only with the parts of themselves that have been oppressed by sexism and splitting off the parts that have oppressed others through racism" (p. 381).

The hypotheses of Noumair et al., (1992), particularly that of the challenges Black women face concerning their allegiances to race and gender are historically accurate (hooks, 1992, 1990, 2000). In describing Clarence Thomas' enactment of this challenge, Painter (1992) cites that in a struggle between himself and a woman of the same race, Thomas "executed a deft strategy," whereby he occupied the position of "the race," making himself into "the black person," which resulted in Anita Hill becoming a villain, the "black-woman-as-traitor-to the race" (p. 204). According to Painter, black-woman-as-traitor-to-the race has a long history in American culture and was familiar to Black Americans but less familiar to White Americans. Thus, by recasting Anita Hill as villain and linking it to lynching via what Crenshaw (1992) describes as: "Anita Hill as Villain: The Lynching Trope" (p. 417), Thomas succeed in erasing her identity as a "highly educated, ambitious, Black female Republican," and intellectual—an identity that was less acceptable to the public than the stereotype of black female villain/traitor (Collins, 2000/2014; Painter, 1992). This was also an example of within race splitting and projection at the group level (e.g., between an African American man and woman). This defense mechanism of splitting, however, and the projective processes involved, served to transform Clarence Thomas into a victim of racial discrimination, while rendering Anita Hill's race irrelevant regarding her position as an African American woman because sexual harassment and abuse between Black men and women was not related to the history of lynching which was "a tradition based on upon white hysteria regarding black male access to white women" (Crenshaw, 1992, p. 416). Moreover, historically, Black women's relationship to lynching was not that of perpetrator, but of victim either through their own lynching or that of a loved one (Crenshaw, 1992). More recently, Crenshaw (2013) in a chapter entitled, "Stunned But Not Bowed," in *I Still Believe Anita Hill*, cited the trope of lynching to have served as "both shield and sword, to deflect the charges against Thomas, and to forcibly separate Hill and her supporters from Black communal politics" (Loc 2139 of 3397).

What is missing, however, from these analyses is a larger, socio-political perspective on the location of Black women, according to Crenshaw (1992), who wryly stated that the televised hearings allowed America access, not into the "Twilight Zone," but:

... into the place where African-American women live, a political vacuum of era-sure and contradiction maintained by the almost routine polarization of "blacks and women" into separate and competing political camps. (p. 403)

Crenshaw's description of this political vacuum continues:

Existing within the overlapping margins of race and gender discourse and in the empty spaces between, it is a location whose very nature resists telling. This location contributes to black women's ideological disempowerment in a way that tipped the scales against Anita Hill from the very start. (p. 403)

The above descriptions capture Crenshaw's assertion of Black women's experi-ence in American dominant cultural ideology as intersectional. Intersectionality, as described by Crenshaw, conceptualizes and captures the locations of Black women in dominant American social relations as unique and in some ways "unas-similable into the discursive paradigms of gender and race domination" (p. 404). Anita Hill's identity as a Black woman "at the crossroads of gender and race hierarchies," faced with a lack of available and widely comprehended narratives to communicate the reality of her worldview, resulted in her being (mis)perceived (p. 403). This margined location whose nature "resists telling" is reflective of hooks' (1990) assertion of the existence of silences and unaddressed spaces where language is a place of struggle and resistance. The unassimilability of location is also resonant with Black women's vulnerability to ethnoviolence whereby their inability or unwillingness to assimilate threatens the dominant group's entitle-ment to society or community resources. In the Thomas-Hill case ethnoviolence was perpetrated upon Anita Hill first in the form of sexual harassment by her employer, Clarence Thomas, and then, at the hearings via sexist interrogation. Society was embodied by the patriarchy in the form of the all White male senate, and resources were located at the community level within the divisive political environment of Washington, DC, and more importantly, at a national level was the ultimate prize, the vacant seat on the Supreme Court.

Another salient aspect of the Thomas-Hill hearings is a perspective that locates the act of giving voice to gender-based violence in institutionalized, systemic, politicized contexts. As hooks (1992) stated, the Thomas-Hill hearings made it "abundantly clear that coming to voice around sexual harassment is only one stage of a process for any individual female seeking justice." She emphasized that the hearings were not solely an issue of a female coming to voice in a case of sexual harassment but also a complex issue regarding Thomas' Supreme Court appointment and "Hill's relationship to the political system that chose to support and affirm that appointment" (p. 80).

Embedded in hooks' (1992) assessment for the need of an awareness of the systemic challenges related to acts of giving voice to gender-based violence is a clear identification of the existence of systemic institutionalized sexism. She identifies the need for understanding that, even at the start of the hearings, "white supremacist patriarchy had already chosen Thomas" (p. 80). Thus, she cites, there was a need for Anita Hill to have a feminist perspective that would have challenged and subverted the existing system; simply stating her case was not sufficient. As hooks stated, "Subversion requires strategy" (p. 80). Her assessment complements group relations theory's focus on the existence of both overt and covert institutional processes that impede and/or enhance organizational functioning and illuminate power differentials, authority and racial and class hierarchies that exist in society (Noumair et al., 1992; McRae & Short, 2005). Thus, Anita Hill's testimony (e.g., her act of giving voice), in a systemic context that embodies all of the above criteria representative of structural inequalities, is an example of Black feminist standpoint and thought, specifically, Collins' (2000/2014) assertion that the ties between what one does and what one thinks is illustrated by individual Black women (Hill) and can also characterize Black women's experiences and ideas as a group (the experiences of institutionalized sexism and racism that often impede and/or silence the process of coming to voice), for example in ethnoviolent contexts (Helms et al., 2011). The next section will present an analysis of the Diallo/Strauss-Kahn case involving gender-based violence with applications of group relations, Black feminist, transnational, and global feminist theories.

THE DIALLO/STRAUSS-KAHN CASE: TWENTY YEARS AFTER THE THOMAS-HILL HEARINGS: STRUCTURAL INEQUALITIES OF GIVING VOICE

The Diallo/Strauss-Kahn incident occurred in May of 2011. In applying the group relations lens as per Noumair et al. (1992), it would be important to note the involvement of two nations, the US and France and that presidents Barack Obama and Nicolas Sarkozy were the formal, authorized leaders of both countries, respectively. It would also be important to note that this incident occurred in a country that was and is currently led by the first African American president who is married to an African American woman, First Lady, Michelle Obama. It could be said that the Obamas in their pairing, parallel, in overt and covert ways, the pairing of Clarence Thomas and Anita Hill—he parallels of course, have not to do with the adversarial, highly dysfunctional relationship of Thomas and Hill, but with a more idealized, longed for (especially in Black American conscious and unconscious realms) pairing of an African American male (who is also biracial) and female, who represent the US. Thus, Bion's (1961, 1975) basic assumption theory regarding pairing that occurs at group levels is evidenced by paired members whose positive (the Obamas) or adversarial (Thomas and Hill) interpersonal dynamics may also represent unconscious expressions of group intimacy and competition in contemporary and historical contexts.

Black feminist thought is applicable to Nafissatou Diallo's experience of being sexually assaulted by Dominique Strauss-Kahn in connecting experiences and ideas regarding instances of derogation experienced by women of African descent and the diversity of responses to these experiences, for example, within transnational, global contexts and connections between US Black women's collective historical experiences of oppression that Collins (2000/2014) hypothesizes may stimulate the development of a defined standpoint which in turn may foster Black women's activism. Nafissatou Diallo's act of giving voice to her sexual assault by Strauss-Kahn and her documented experiences of culturally sanctioned female genital mutilation (FGM) (also called female genital circumcision/cutting) in the Republic of Guinea, her experience of the death of her husband, other reported instances of sexual assault, as well as the stresses of emigrating to the US, applying for asylum, and acculturation to the dominant American culture, can all be viewed under the rubric of Black feminist transnational and global contexts.

Transnational and postcolonial feminisms expand upon and critique White feminism, and as with Black feminist thought, these feminisms have a focus on intersectionality. However, in addition to a focus on intersections of race, gender, class, and sexuality, there is also a strong emphasis on privileging Women of Color and non-Western women. Transnational and postcolonial feminist frameworks highlight contexts of globalization and global sisterhood that espouses recognition of women's similarities and differences (Mendoza, 2002, as cited in Holvino, 2010). Another important aspect of these feminisms is their perspective about the "long term negative consequences of colonialism," and their goal to deconstruct and "disrupt the power of Western feminists to name problems" (Enns, 2010, p. 5). Thus, the challenge posed by these feminisms to Western feminists is that they become aware of their privilege and tendency to define global issues in terms of Western worldviews; inherent in this challenge is a critique concerning the dichotomous 'us' and 'them' thinking that positions the lives of so called "'3rd world' women in direct contrast with women in 'developed' countries" (p. 5).

hooks (2000), in describing global feminism, cites the challenges inherent in Western feminists' projections of imperialist fantasies onto women from non-Western countries; she emphasizes the importance of understanding the terms colonialism and neocolonialism and of having decolonized feminist perspectives. An example of this would be this would be my labeling of female genital mutilation (FGM) (e.g., by using the word *mutilation,* which is indicative of a distinctly Western feminist-oriented worldview regarding this custom). hooks, in calling for less decolonized feminist perspectives, advocates examining how "sexist practices in relation to women's bodies globally are linked," for example connecting female circumcision with life-threatening eating disorders, which she identifies as being directly related to "culture imposing thinness as a beauty ideal" (p. 46). Collins (2000/2014) also describes a *tension* linking experiences and ideas among women of African descent within a Black diasporic context who share historical and current experiences of derogation, for example, in the forms of gender-based violence and ethnoviolence, but who may differ on the meaning and significance of these experiences.

Nafissatou Diallo's act of giving voice to her experience of sexual assault can be viewed, therefore, within contexts of Black feminist thought, transnational and postcolonial feminisms. The tension that Collins describes resonates with me, however, for in writing about Nafissatou Diallo it seems clear that my location as an African American woman for whom having a US Black feminist/Western lens is a given, creates a space wherein my perspectives have the potential to embody structural inequalities regarding any analyses I may present in this chapter of her act of giving voice to her experiences of sexual assault. Thus, I find myself in a similar space as Noumair et al. (1992), who, as three White women questioned their understanding of their identification with Anita Hill and provided an indictment of White women's need to fragment and/or split off parts of themselves (e.g., oppressed versus oppressor) in order to retain a sense of psychological and group level righteousness and connection. Therefore, as the author of this chapter, it is clear that identification and acknowledgment of existing gendered, within race differences for analyses of Nafissatou Diallo's and Anita Hill's acts of giving voice illuminate the complexities of intersectionality in multiple contexts.

As stated previously, the Diallo-/Strauss-Kahn incident ignited a global conversation about the impact of gender-based violence in the form of sexual harassment in heterosexual contexts within workplace environments. In the United States, because of the Thomas-Hill hearings and subsequent heightened awareness of sexual harassment, through more women giving voice to their experiences, ongoing discussions, legislation, workplace changes, etc., (Mock, 2013), the nation, while not comfortable with this issue, was, by the time of the Diallo/Strauss-Kahn incident, fairly clear about the need for victims to publicly give voice to it and for the courts to address it. In France, however, the French media expressed shock at Strauss-Kahn's arrest, minimized the alleged crime of sexual assault and victimization of Diallo, while simultaneously deflecting discourse of the incident to declarations that sexual relations between men and women were held within domains of right to privacy (e.g., as opposed to public scrutiny), thus ignoring the more salient issues of power inequalities and gender based violence (Rouyer, 2013). In comparing the coverage of the French press to that of the US, Rouyer cited an historical tendency for the French media toward complacency and collusion with Strauss-Kahn's questionable "previous behavior" (e.g., alleged sexual harassment). She further cited the re-emergence of Tristane Banon, a young White French writer who had previously accused Strauss-Kahn of sexual assault in 2003, along with the demonstration of French feminist groups in solidarity with Banon as the impetus for the French press and social media outlets to take the Diallo/Strauss-Kahn incident more seriously. She stated: "The Banon and Diallo affairs worked hand in hand to advance women's rights and constituted a kind of transnational trial by proxy;" she maintained that the "double affair" exposed "gender inequalities in the social construction of legal disputes in France" (p. 190). Thus, the basic assumptive pairing of Banon and Diallo (Bion, 1961, 1975) served to expose structural inequalities regarding gender-based violence in the form of sexual harassment on two continents, as well as embedded cultural dynamics related to patriarchal power and privilege. The pairing of the two women also served to illuminate defense mechanisms of splitting and projection between the US and France regarding institutionalized, systemic attitudes about sexual harassment/assault and the criminal prosecution of perpetrators of this form of gender-based violence.

Per hooks' (2000) call for a decolonized feminist perspective when working with global feminist perspectives, connections between sexist practices in relation to women's bodies globally are linked via collective histories of gender-based violence and ethnoviolence. Thus, connections between feminisms that are global, transnational, and postcolonial, as well as, for example, US Black feminist standpoint/thought are all applicable to institutionalized sexism. Moreover, the emergence of social media has made it possible for historical and contemporary narratives to be merged and shared, resulting in enforced silences that have served to disconnect to be abandoned.

A missing piece of the analyses of Nafissatou Diallo's act of giving voice to her experience of sexual assault, however, was in the location of the incident— the United States. In the ensuing days, weeks and months after the assault, media coverage of Diallo was indicative of structural inequalities related to American society's desire for women who give voice to gender- based violence to be "perfect victims," which was compounded by the devaluation of Diallo based upon her status as a Black immigrant woman. Thus, her immigrant status, highlighted by her reported lack of English fluency, her alleged illiteracy and flawed personal history, as well as reported inconsistencies regarding her story of sexual assault by Strauss-Kahn, all served to make her less than the ideal victim in the public domain (Frosch, 2011).

Anita Hill's unassimability of location resulted in her being (mis)perceived (Crenshaw, 1992). Likewise, Diallo was, as a result of her act of giving voice, according to Harris-Perry (2011), *misrecognized* in the public sphere. Misrecognition can be defined by its opposite—*recognition*, which Harris-Perry defines as "a useful framework because it emphasizes the interconnection between individuals and groups" (Loc 608 of 6298). She further states that, "Individuals from disempowered social groups desire recognition for their group but also want recognition of their distinctiveness from the group" (Loc 608 of 6298). Thus, African Americans dislike the idea of color blindness due to it's suggestion that race is irrelevant to identity; there are paradoxical desires to be recognized and understood as being Black and having a history and culture associated with blackness, while not wanting to be reduced to one's racial identities alone. Harris-Perry cites hooks'(1992) in her book *Black Looks* as equating recognition as a precondition for citizenship and asserting that the act of looking at individuals from marginal groups is a powerful, political act, especially for those who have privilege and power over them.

In locating Nafissatou Diallo within this framework, it seems clear that the misrecognition she may have experienced was a result of her race, gender, and immigrant status—quite literally, it may been easier for the public to condemn her because she was *not* a US citizen. Thus, the collective gaze upon her was indicative of misrecognition by the powerful and privileged American society which she was attempting to acculturate into, and in France, that gaze also embodied misrecognition infused with imperialist, colonial overtones.

Harris-Perry (2011) cites "the misrecognition experienced by Black women who attempt to engage in the public sphere" (Loc 624 of 6298) to be indicative of the crooked room. Thus, the crooked room is directly related to structural inequalities via Black women's citizenship and their "attempts to navigate a room made crooked by stereotypes that have psychic consequences" (Loc 655 of 6298). The image of the crooked room, with what Harris-Perry describes as it's slanted, stereotyped images of Black women is quite powerful when considering the structural inequalities related to Anita Hill's and Nafissatou Diallo's acts of giving voice to their experiences of gender-based violence. The crooked room can be analogized as the symbol of structural inequalities; the women's courageous acts of giving voice could be representative of their resistance to the oppressive experience of being forced to adjust themselves in societal spaces that do not comfortably fit or allow for recognition; spaces that are damaging to them, physically, psychologically, emotionally and intellectually (e.g., that ignore, distort and misrepresent their intersecting identities). In a group relations theoretical context the crooked room, therefore, could be the institutionalized, systemic dynamics that overtly and covertly perpetuate defense mechanisms of splitting, projection and projective identification of Black women in stereotypical ways. Finally, it also embodies the aforementioned unassimilability of location and its relationship to Black women's vulnerability to ethnoviolence whereby their inability or unwillingness to assimilate (e.g., a metaphor in itself for forced adjustment to distorted and potentially damaging spaces), threatens the dominant group's entitlement to multiple societal resources.

CONCLUSION

Crenshaw (2013) states that, "We know now that awareness of sexual harassment has grown exponentially since the hearings" (Loc 2171 of 3397). As we near the 25th anniversary of the Thomas-Hill hearings and the courageous act of Anita Hill in giving voice to her experience of sexual harassment, it is clear that this event will not be forgotten. In an interview for a Time Magazine article about the documentary, *Anita. Speaking Truth to Power*, Hill stated, "We understand not only the past and how it affects us but that it is still a very real and present problem for young women—but that they're tackling it. That's very, very affirming" (Rothman, 2014, p. 54). It seems clear that Nafisssatou Diallo's equally courageous act of giving voice to her experience of sexual assault and the subsequent handling of the Diallo/Strauss-Kahn case reflected a distinct change in the way that gender-based violence is viewed and addressed publicly and in the legal system. Moreover, discussions and protests about gender-based violence are ongoing in the public sphere in global contexts. What seems to be most difficult to change, however, are the broader, deeply embedded dynamics of systemic, institutionalized sexism that give way to structural inequalities that adversely impact women's acts of giving voice to their gender-based violent and ethnoviolent experiences. This continues to be the case in a variety of domains in which Black and African descent women, Women of Color, and White women courageously give voice to their experiences of victimization, resistance, and survival.

This chapter's focus on the importance of examining structural inequalities of giving voice to women's experiences of gender-based violence at all levels (e.g., group, organizational, institutional, and societal), has advocated application of the group relations theoretical lens, using the seminal work of Noumair et al., (1992), US Black feminist (Collins, 2000/2014), and transnational/global and postcolonial feminist (Enns, 2010; Holvino, 2010) lenses to revisit, explore and deconstruct a disturbing and transformative event in our nation's history and to connect it to yet another disturbing event that took place two decades later.. As hooks (1992) stated, "Subversion requires strategy" (p. 80). If we truly view women's acts of giving voice to gender-based violent and ethnoviolent as acts of courageous subversion of institutionalized sexist ideologies and practices, then it will continue to be necessary to employ strategies (e.g., theoretical, activist, systemic, and other types of foundational lenses) to support and honor their voices.

REFERENCES

Alderfer, C. P. (1994). A white man's perspective of the unconscious processes within black-white relations in the United States. In E. J. Trickett, R. J. Watts, & Birman (Eds.), *Human diversity: Perspectives on people in context* (pp. 201–263). San Francisco, CA: Jossey-Bass.

Alderfer, C. P. (1997). Embedded intergroup relations and racial identity development theory. In C. E. Thompson & R. T. Carter (Eds.), *Racial identity theory: Applications to individual, group, and organizational interventions* (pp. 237–263). Mahwah: NJ: Lawrence Erlbaum.

Angelou, M. (1969/1997/2009). [iBooks]. *I know why the caged bird sings*. New York, NY: Random House.

Baker, A., & Erlanger, S. (2011, May 14). I. M. F. chief, apprehended at airport, is accused of sexual attack. *The New York Times*. Retrieved from: http://www.nytimes.com/2011/05/15/nyregion/imf-head-is-arrested-and-accused-of-sexual-attack.html?_r=0

Bayes, M., & Newton, P. M. (1985). Women in authority: A sociopsychological analysis. In A. D. Colman & M. H. Geller (Eds.), *Group relations reader 2* (pp. 309–322). Jupiter, FL: A. K. Rice Institute.

Bion, W. R. (1961). *Experiences in groups*. New York, NY: Brunner-Routledge.

Bion, W. R. (1975). Selections from experiences in groups. In A. D. Colman & W. H. Bexton (Eds.), *Group relations reader 1* (pp. 11–20). Washington, DC: A. K. Rice Institute.

Brazaitis, S. (2004). White women—Protectors of the status quo: Positioned to disrupt it. In S. Cytrynbaum & D. Noumair (Eds.), *Group dynamics, organizational irrationality, and social complexity. Group relations reader 3* (pp. 99–116). Jupiter, FL: The A. K. Rice Institute for the Study of Social Systems.

CBS. (2010, October 20). *Anita Hill vs. Clarence Thomas: The backstory.* Retrieved on 4/7/15 from http://www.cbsnews.com.

Collins, P. H. (2000/2014). *Black feminist thought: Knowledge, consciousness, and the politics of empowerment.* New York, NY: Routledge.

Connolly, M. L., & Noumair, D. A. (1997). The white girl in me, the colored girl in you, and the lesbian in us: Crossing boundaries. In M. Fine, L. Weis, L. C. Powell, & L. Mun Wong (Eds.), *Off-white: Readings on race, power, and society* (pp. 322–332). New York, NY: Routledge.

Crenshaw, K. (1992). Whose story is it, anyway? Feminist and antiracist appropriations of Anita Hill. In T. Morrison (Ed.), *Race-ing, justice, en-gendering power. Essays on Anita Hill, Clarence Thomas, and the construction of social reality* (pp. 402–440). New York: Pantheon Books.

Crenshaw, K. W. (2013). Stunned but not bowed. In A. Richards & C. Greenberg (Eds.), *I still believe Anita Hill. Three generations discuss the legacies of speaking truth to power* [Kindle]. (Loc 1988–2428). New York, NY: Feminist Press at the City University of New York.

Dalal, F. (2002). *Race, colour, and the process of racialization: New perspectives from group analysis, psychoanalysis and sociology.* New York, NY: Brunner-Routledge.

Dickey, C. (2011, July). "DSK maid" tells of her alleged rape by Strauss-Kahn: Exclusive. *Newsweek.* Retrieved on 3/10/2015 from newsweek.com

Dominique Strauss-Kahn Fast Facts.(2015, June 15). Retrieved 1/5/16 from CNN Library, http://www.cnn.com

Dumas, R. G. (1985). Dilemmas of black females in leadership. In A. D. Colman & M. H. Geller (Eds.), *Group relations reader 2* (pp. 323–334). Jupiter, FL: A. K. Rice Institute.

Embassy of Guinea. Washington, DC. (n.d.) Retrieved from http://www.guineaembassyusa.com

Enns, C. Z. (2010). Locational feminisms and feminist social identity analysis. *Professional Psychology: Research and Practice, 41*(4), 1–16. Retrieved on 2/24/2015 from PsychArticles http://0-web.a.ebscohost.com.liucat.lib.liu.edu/ehost/detail/detail.

European Institute for Gender Equality (n.d.) Retrieved http://www.eige.europa.eu.

Facebook community page about feminism. (2011). *We are all chambermaids.* Retrieved on 4/10/15 from http://www.facebook.com/event.php

Frosch, J. (2011, July 4). Strauss-Kahn case aggravates French-US cultural divide. *France 24.com.* Retrieved on 4/11/15 from http://www.france24.com

Gabelnick, F. (2004). Leading institutional transformation: The architecture of change. In S. Cytrynbaum & D. Noumair (Eds.), *Group dynamics, organizational irrationality, and social complexity: Group relations reader 3* (pp. 267–288). Jupiter, FL: The A. K. Rice Institute for the Study of Social Systems.

Gabelnick, F. (1993). Roles of women in the large group: Enduring paradigms in a chaotic environment. [Abstract]. *Group 17*(4), 245–253.

Gould, L. J. (1985). Men and women at work: A group relations conference on person and role. In A. D. Colman & M. H. Geller (Eds.), *Group relations reader 2* (pp. 163–172). Jupiter, FL: A. K. Rice Institute.

Harris-Perry, M. V. (2011). *Sister citizen. Shame, stereotypes, and black women in America.* [Kindle]. New Haven, CT: Yale University Press.

Hawley, C. (2011, July 18). Dominique Strauss Kahn: IMF chief on suicide watch in New York jail. *Huffington Post, The World Post.* Retrieved on 5/23/15 from huffington-post.com

Hayden, C., & Molenkamp, R. J. (2004). The Tavistock primer II. In S. Cytrynbaum & D. Noumair (Eds.), *Group dynamics, organizational irrationality, and social complexity: Group relations reader 3* (pp. 135–156). Jupiter, FL: The A. K. Rice Institute for the Study of Social Systems.

Helms, J., Nicolas, G., & Green, C. E. (2011). Racism and ethnoviolence as trauma: Enhancing professional and research training. *Traumatology 18*(1), 65–74. doi: 10.1177/1534765610396728. Retrieved on 1/15/14 from http://tmt.sagepub.com/content/18/1/65

Hill, A. F. (1997). *Speaking truth to power.* New York, NY: Random House.

History 122: An outline of the Anita Hill/Clarence Thomas debate (n.d.). Retrieved on 4/7/15 from chnm.gmu.edu

Holvino, E. (2010). Intersections: The simultaneity of race, gender and class in organization studies. *Gender, Work and Organization, 17*(3), 248–277. doi: 10.1111/j.1468-0432.2008.00400.x. Retrieved 2/24/15.

hooks, b. (1990). *Yearning race, gender, and cultural politics.* Boston, MA: South End Press.

hooks, b. (1992). *Black looks: Race and representation.* Boston, MA: South End Press.

hooks, b. (2000). *Feminism is for everybody. Passionate politics.* Cambridge, MA: South End Press.

Kernberg, O. F. (1976). *Object relations theory and clinical psychoanalysis.* New York, NY: Aronson.

Khaleelee, O., & White, K. (2014). Speaking out. Global development and innovation in group relations. *Organisational & Social Dynamics 14*(2), 399–425.

Klein, M. (1946). Notes on some schizoid mechanisms. *International Journal of Psychoanalysis, 27,* 99–110.

Lawrence, G. W., Bain, A., & Gould, L. (1996). The fifth basic assumption. *Free Associations, 6*(37), 28–55.

Lewin, K. (1951). *Field theory in social science.* New York, NY: Harper & Row.

Lorde, A. (1984). *Sister outsider. Essays & speeches by Audre Lorde.* Berkeley, CA: Crossing Press.

Malone, R. (2000). A salt-and-pepper consultation: Racial considerations. In E. B. Klein, F. Gabelnick, & P. Herr (Eds.), *Dynamic consultation in a changing workplace* (pp. 81–96). Madison, CT: Psychosocial Press.

McRae, M. (2004). Class, race and gender: Person-in-role implications in taking up the directorship. In S. Cytrynbaum & D. Noumair (Eds.), *Group dynamics, organizational irrationality, and social complexity: Group relations reader 3* (pp. 225–237). Jupiter, FL: The A. K. Rice Institute for the Study of Social Systems.

McRae, M. B., Kwong, A. K., & Short, E. L. (2007). Racial dialogue among women: A group relations theory analysis. *Organizational & Social Dynamics 7*(2), 211–234.

McRae, M. B., & Short, E. L. (2005). Racial-cultural training for group counseling and psychotherapy. In R. T. Carter (Ed.), *The handbook on racial-cultural psychology. training and practice* (vol. 2). New York, NY: John Wiley & Sons.

McRae, M. B., & Short, E. L. (2010). *Racial and cultural dynamics in group and organizational life. Crossing boundaries.* Thousand Oaks, CA: Sage.

Mock, F. (2013). *Anita. Speaking truth to power.* United States: Samuel Goldwyn Films.

Noumair, D. A., Fenichel, A., & Fleming, J. L. (1992). Clarence Thomas, Anita Hill, and us: A group relations perspective. *The Journal of Applied Behavioral Science, 28*(3), 377–387.

Painter, N. I. (1992). Hill, Thomas, and the use of racial stereotype. In T. Morrison (Ed.), *Race-ing, justice, en-gendering power. Essays on Anita Hill, Clarence Thomas, and the construction of social reality* (pp. 402–440). New York, NY: Pantheon Books.

Peltz, J., & Hays, T. (2011, October 24). Dominique Strauss-Kahn rape charges dismissed. *The Huffington Post, The World Post.* Retrieved on 4/10/15 from huffingtonpost. com

Reed, G., & Noumair, D. (2000). The tiller of authority in a sea of diversity. In E. B. Klein, F. Gabelnick, & P. Herr (Eds.), *Dynamic consultation in a changing workplace*, (pp. 51–79). Madison, CT: Psychosocial Press.

Richards, A., & Greenberg, C. (Eds.) (2013). *I still believe Anita Hill. Three generations discuss the legacies of speaking truth to power* New York, NY: Feminist Press. City University of New York.

Rioch, M. J. (1985). Why I work as a consultant in conferences of the A. K. Rice Institute. In A. D. Colman & M. H. Geller (Eds.), *Group relations reader 2* (pp. 365–381). Jupiter, FL: A. K. Rice Institute.

Rose, T. (2003). *Longing to tell. Black women talk about sexuality and intimacy.* New York, NY: Farrar, Strauss & Giroux.

Rosenbaum, S. C. (2004). Group-as-mother: A dark continent in group relations theory and practice. In S. Cytrynbaum & D. Noumair (Eds.), *Group dynamics, organizational irrationality, and social complexity: Group relations reader 3* (pp. 225–237). Jupiter, FL: The A. K. Rice Institute for the Study of Social Systems.

Ross, A. (1992). The private parts of justice. In T. Morrison (Ed.)., *Race-ing, justice, en-gendering power. Essays on Anita Hill, Clarence Thomas, and the construction of social reality* (pp. 11–0). New York: Pantheon Books.

Rothman, L. (2014, March 24). Testify. A documentary takes a fresh look at Anita Hill. *Time. The Culture* (p. 54).

Rouyer, M. (2013). The Strauss-Kahn affair and the culture of privacy: mistreating and misrepresenting women in the French public sphere. *Women's Studies International Forum, 41,* 187–196.

Short, E. L. (2007). Race, culture and containment in the formal and informal systems of group relations conferences. *Organizational & Social Dynamics 7*(2), 156–171.

Short E. L., & Williams, W. S. (2014) From the inside out: Group work with women of color. *Journal for Specialists in Group Work, 39,* 71–91.

Short, E. L., & Woon, J. M. S. T. (2009). Crossing multiple boundaries: Reflections on the Belgirate II experience. In E. Aram, R. Baxter, & A. Nutkevitch (Eds.), *Adaption and innovation. Theory, design and role-taking in group relations Conferences and their applications* (vol. II, pp. 233–242). London, UK: Karnac.

Steinem, G. (2013). Supremacy crimes. In A. Richards & C. Greenberg (Eds.), *I still believe Anita Hill. Three generations discuss the legacies of speaking truth to power* [Kindle] (Loc 2609–2685). New York, NY: Feminist Press at the City University of New York.

Turquet, P. M. (1985). Leadership: The individual and the group. In A. D. Colman & M. H. Geller (Eds.), *Group relations reader 2* (pp. 365–381). Jupiter, FL: A. K. Rice Institute.

Wells, L. (1990). The group as a whole: A systematic socioanalytic perspective on interpersonal and group relations. In J. Gillette & M. McCollom (Eds.), *Groups in context: A new perspective on group dynamics* (pp. 49–85). Reading, MA: Addison-Wesley.

YouTube. (2011, August 22). *Protest in support of Nafissatou Diallo.* Retrieved 4/10/15 from www.YouTube.com

CHAPTER 16

RECLAIMING THE HUMAN

Exploring Caste Through The Lens of Group Relations Conference Experiences

Rosemary Viswanath

INTRODUCTION

I have been associated with human rights and social justice issues for over two decades. These include people's movements, networks, and campaigns, which focus on environmental justice; rights of communities to resources, livelihoods, and equity; human rights; and *Dalit*[1] rights. My work has largely been in the capacity of strengthening these networks and organizations in terms of their institutional processes and strategies with a particular focus on processes of leadership.

While my personal caste background is not known to me, as my paternal and maternal families converted to Christianity several generations ago, it is unlikely given their relatively comfortable social status today, that they were Dalit. My first encounter with caste was when I married an upper caste (Brahmin) Hindu. I have described this aspect of my personal history in an earlier paper (Viswanath, 2009) and about how this was the particular impetus to my working with groups and networks fighting caste-based discrimination. Having been involved in Group Relations Conferences (GRC) for over two decades, its approach and frame-

Talking About Structural Inequalities in Everyday Life: New Politics of Race in Groups, Organizations, and Social Systems, pages 309–334.

works[2], particularly that of systems psychodynamics, have deeply influenced my understanding of systems and organizations.

Group Relations Conferences were first offered by the Tavistock Institute of Human Relations, London, in 1957, based on the pioneering work of W. R. Bion. In India, GRCs were introduced in 1973. The set of conferences and workshops that this chapter primarily refers to are those offered between 2002 and 2013 in which the author was Director, Associate/Co-director, or Consultant. There was a significant effort in these conferences to reach out to potential members from a very diverse set of backgrounds—class, caste, geographical region, gender, working with social sector and corporate organizations—resulting in a very diverse membership in these conferences.

Group Relations Conferences are temporary organizations for learning through direct experience. They are designed to provide a variety of opportunities for members to exercise leadership and authority, unravel and deal with the problems and resistances encountered in doing this, and manage oneself in role. These explorations, experiences, and insights have the potential to lead to transformed ways of being and relating in a range of interpersonal, institutional, and societal spaces. Over time, the design and structure of GRCs have undergone many changes, as they began to be offered in many parts of the world. However, the primary focus on unconscious processes[3] in groups and systems, and learning through direct "here and now" experiences, have remained key features of GRCs.

In my earlier paper (Viswanath, 2009), I indicated how exposure to group relations frameworks helped Dalits involved in the struggle against pervasive caste-based discrimination. For example, I argued that the group relations framework offered an opportunity for individuals to surface deep-seated assumptions, which obstructed the process of freeing oneself from the rules of structural inequality and oppression. I observed this process as a valuable and essential element in the process of social transformation. Until then, most strategies employed by these groups and networks had focused on structural responses targeted at institutional spaces[4]. Exposure to group relations had helped work on a missing quadrant in these set of interventions through uncovering unconscious processes, both individual and systemic, that reinforced internalized oppression.

In this paper, I aim to take these explorations further, using in-depth interviews with Dalit activists and leaders. I also interviewed non-Dalits (most of them happened to have upper caste roots). All those interviewed[5] participated in GRCs and, in my view, have a demonstrated interest in working on caste-based discrimination.

In response to what the experience of participating in the GRC gave them and what they valued, many respondents spoke about how much their participation in a GRC and working on unconscious processes helped in deepening their understanding of how caste dynamics shaped them and their contexts—and in turn shaped their responses to these contexts. They spoke of how a deeper engagement with oneself, integrating disowned parts of self, and facing one's desires and one's fears, supported a new way of engaging with the world. This was a freeing experience. This aspect of personal insights was in tune with the findings in my earlier paper (Viswanath, 2009).

What I am suggesting further is that as GRCs are designed to work on unconscious system dynamics, they are a particularly useful container to work on individual and systemic dynamics around a range of structural inequalities and discrimination that are experienced around caste, gender, race, religion, and sexual orientation. These aspects are more difficult to work on than other hierarchies because we have a way of pushing these hierarchies into the most unspeakable and unreachable realms in the unconscious[6]. In his popular book *Blink*, Gladwell (2006) shows how our unconscious attitudes may even be utterly incompatible with our stated conscious values. With its focus on unconscious processes in groups and systems, GRCs offer opportunities for individuals (without mobilizing too much defensiveness, hopefully) to look at themselves, and what they carry into and from systems. There are certain supportive factors that the GRCs did and can continue to offer to enable work on unconscious systems dynamics. These became evident in the course of the interview conversations. One of the contributing factors to learn experientially about systemic inequalities and dis-privilege was to have diversity in the membership. When the conference membership represents a microcosm of society, it recreates conscious and unconscious societal dynamics. This opened up the opportunity for the implications of difference and diversity to be experienced directly and potentially worked with in the GRCs by Dalits and non-Dalits alike. Many of those interviewed spoke about how the insights that their GRC experience offered on caste and structural discrimination have stayed with them and infiltrated the approaches and stances they take in everyday life—the institutions they belong to and work settings they are part of.

The other insight that emerged from this work is that GRCs are powerful sites to learn about transformation of a system because they are designed to keep the whole system in view. Participants could experience what it meant at an individual level and collectively to be part of a system and take up roles in it. This in turn offered the challenge and opportunity to work with the idea of self and other and how we create the other as a defense against working on certain aspects of the self. The idea that the Brahmin is also in one's mind and not only 'out there,' and that one holds within oneself the same process that is then enacted in society, is both powerful and shattering. It then points to a key requirement of societal transformation—of non-separation from the other. GRCs offer the space for such insights to be generated, which in turn offers the hope for exploring further how society may be transformed.

In the forthcoming sections of this paper, I expand on the insights summarized in the paragraphs above. First, in Section A, I locate caste realities in contemporary India in terms of their impact and implications, offering a backdrop for the further sections. In Sections B and C, I present the reflections from the interview-conversations about how group relations experiences contributed to personal insights and ways to engage more systemically on issues of caste based discrimination. Finally, I conclude in Section D, with examining ways in which GRCs could contribute in more significant ways to work on transforming communities and societies.

SECTION A

Locating Caste Realities in Contemporary India[7]

India often congratulates itself on being the world's largest democracy. Its reality also is that India is perhaps the world's most stratified society. A system of graded inequality on the basis of caste has been part of the Indian subcontinent's history for centuries.

At a basic level, the term caste[8] in English translates into two concepts in the Indian sub-continent, the *varna* and the *jaati*. The earliest mention of the varnas can be traced to the *Purusha Sukta* hymn in the *Rig Veda* (1200–900 BCE) in Vedic India. The varna system divided society into four categories or varnas that are mutually exclusive, hereditary, endogamous and occupation specific- *Brahmins* (priests and teachers), *Kshatriyas* (warriors and royalty) *Vaishya* (traders, merchants, moneylenders), and *Shudras* (those engaged in menial jobs). The lowliest of the low, the untouchables, were *avarna*—not considered worthy of even being a varna. Thus, they were part of the varna system by being excluded from it! The operative category that determines the contemporary social code is the jaati—over 3000 jaatis exist and follow a more complex system of hierarchy and rules of conduct towards each other. The varnas in a way provide a scale of status to which jaatis try to align themselves. However, this scale turns out to be fluid and ambiguous as the rank a jaati claims of itself and that conceded by others may vary (Deshpande, 2011).

Historically speaking, significant challenges to the caste system first came about 1000 years after its introduction from the Buddha (Siddhartha Gautama, around 500 BC) who was a severe critic of the caste system. Basava, a radical and progressive social thinker challenged caste in South India in the 12th century. In the 13th–16th centuries, poet-saints like Ravidas, Kabir, Tukaram, Janabai and Mirabai breached the barriers of caste in their poems and songs. Later, it was in the 19th and 20th centuries when Jotirao Phule, Pandita Ramabai, Swami Achutanand Harihar, Ayyankali, Sree Narayana Guru, Iyothee Thass, B. R. Ambedkar and E. V. Ramasamy Naicker led strong intellectual and movement based traditions that challenged caste and worked for its annihilation.

In his landmark work 'Castes in India,' Ambedkar (1917) argued that 'apart from the distinctive feature of caste being endogamy superimposed on exogamy in a shared cultural ambience, other key features of the caste system were the principle of birth, division of labour, prohibition of inter-dining and untouchability, with graded inequality being its normative anchor (Rodrigues, 2002). It is not the aim of this paper to trace historically the origins, nature, and trajectory of caste over the long period of its existence. These are complex processes and there is no one authoritative view on the subject. Over the centuries, sub-caste (approximated to jaati) categories have been fluid and forms of caste-based discrimination have mutated. However, the caste system and caste based discrimination have persisted and is very much part of the lived experience and a social, political, and economic reality in India today. While the practice of 'untouchability' was legally abolished under India's constitution in 1950,[9] the caste system was not. Thus, the idea of castes remains firmly entrenched in contemporary Indian society, and its accompanying structural inequalities, including the practice of untouchability—the imposition of social, cultural, and economic proscriptions on persons by reason of their birth in certain castes or as outcastes— remains alive, and in fact takes on new forms.

Over one-sixth of India's population, some 167 million people,[10] live a precarious existence because of their rank as untouchables at the bottom of India's pervasive caste system. Dalits, as the untouchables and outcastes have chosen to call themselves, are discriminated against, denied access to land and basic resources, forced to work in degrading conditions, routinely humiliated, forced into servitude, denied basic political rights, and abused by powerful dominant-caste groups (Human Rights Watch, 1999, 2007).

These atrocities through discrimination, violence, and exclusion mostly go unpunished as the dominant castes enjoy both impunity and the state's protection. A series of caste based massacres and acquittals in the state of Bihar in India are one among the many examples of violence and impunity. In July of 1996, members of the Ranveer Sena, the private militia of powerful upper caste Bumihar landlords, allegedly killed 21 Dalit men women and children in Bathani Tola in response to the Dalit labourers demand for a wage increase. All accused were acquitted by the High Court in Patna in 2012. In Laxmanpur Bathe on 1 December 1997, 58 landless poor Dalits were allegedly killed by members of the Ranveer Sena. It was only in 2008 that even charges were pressed. In October 2013, the Patna High court again overturned the verdict of the session's court and acquitted all 26 accused (Krishnan, 2013).

Laws and government policies on land reform and budget allocations for the economic empowerment of the Dalit community remain largely un-implemented. Reservations in government jobs and in higher education as a form of affirmative action or positive discrimination[11] have created some space for progress (Deshpande, 2011). However, with the march of neoliberal ideologies[12] into every conceivable sphere involving the market, health, basic services, and governance, the spaces to debate and claim human rights and entitlements, particularly from the state, are shrinking. For the Dalits, this means that with a shrinking government, the number of government jobs and the hope of implementation of anti-discriminatory laws, both of which were poorly implemented in any case, is reduced even further. The expanded role of the private sector in creating jobs and driving the economy implies that Dalits would be increasingly dependent on a private sector that does not have a track record on social justice or equity issues[13].

In the political sphere, reservations for Dalits at the grassroots level of local governance[14] have brought in some measure of hope in cases where Dalits have been able to surmount massive obstacles or tokenism to claim their political rights. These obstacles are multi-faceted and often in the form of a backlash by dominant castes at the audacity of Dalits who dare to challenge the social order. Dalit villages are collectively penalized for individual "transgressions" through social boycotts, including loss of employment and access to water, grazing lands, and subsidized public distribution shops. For most Dalits in rural India—who are often landless and earn less than subsistence living as agricultural laborers—social and economic boycott means destitution and starvation. Burning and destruction of homes and settlements, killing, lynching, maiming, and raping Dalit women are commonplace ways of putting Dalits in their place and teaching them a lesson. The denial of justice is also starkly evident. Heinous crimes against Dalit men and women do not receive the media attention that other crimes get, police do not register offences, acquittal rates of offenders is high in the cases that do reach courts, trials are deliberately delayed or go on for so long that the justice process is rendered ineffective.

Caste and analogous systems of social and structural stratification and hierarchy prevail as an operating feature of modern societies. They may be more visible in parts of Asia and Africa, but are present in many parts of the world, (e.g. the Roma in Europe and the Buraku in Japan), subjecting millions to inhuman treatment on the basis of being born into a certain caste or similar social group. Though the communities themselves may be indistinguishable in appearance from others in the region, socio-economic disparities are glaring, as are the particular forms of discrimination practiced against them. It is approximated that around 250 million people across the world suffer from caste or work and descent based discrimination, impacting their civil, political, religious, socio-economic and cultural rights[15] and their right to live a life of dignity.

Colonial history attempted to link caste with race, but subsequently many scholars have shown that this was more a matter of orientalism and colonial prejudice than scholarship (Deshpande, 2011). However, what is important to note is that the articulation of caste as a social grouping and the resultant forms of that discrimination (i.e., discrimination based on descent—exclusion, untouchability, denial of constitutional rights and guarantees, violent subjugation and histories of slavery are resonant of internationally recognized forms of racism). This commonality between experiences of caste and race inspired the move by Dalit rights groups across the sub-continent to bring caste within the ambit of the Convention on the Elimination of Racial Discrimination (CERD) of the United Nations, seeing this as an ongoing effort to realize the visions of anti-caste movements initiated in the 19th and 20th centuries.

Studies on caste by sociologists, social anthropologists, and historians coincided with the 18th century colonization of the sub-continent (Thapar, 2000a). As mentioned earlier, these were largely influenced (and limited) by colonial imperialistic worldviews and primarily viewed pre-colonial Indian society as unchanging, with religion (read Hinduism) as its central piece, without looking at the complex interconnections of caste with economics and culture (Thapar, 2000b). Post India's independence in 1947, it seemed like the influence of these imperialistic world views remained strong, and economists who worked on the 'hard' questions of development did not see caste as a relevant area of inquiry, holding the view that this anachronism would weaken and eventually disappear with the process of development or modernization (Jodkha, 2010). The fact that many of them were upper caste themselves could be the unconscious reason why they held the belief that development and markets were essentially secular, rational, and anonymous processes. This resulted in very little focus, in the period from the 1950s to the 1980s, in academic study, public discourse, and policy impact of the realities of caste and caste based dynamics.

Two trends (albeit gradual) at the global level have indirectly influenced a shift in this position post the 1980s. One, with the feminist debate (Batliwala, 2012) gaining ground, there has been an increased willingness to acknowledge the gendered nature of policies and their development outcomes. This trend has also drawn attention to other factors such as caste having policy implications. The second, in the debate on globalization[16] (Viswanath & Chattopadhyay, 2006), there is a growing recognition that non- economic aspects of globalization are as legitimate as the economic, in understanding the phenomena. Thus, subsequent research has recognized the crucial importance of factors such as caste, race, ethnicity, or gender in structuring markets and determining economic outcomes. Mainstream development studies have also undergone a paradigm shift over the last few decades with human, rather than only economic development becoming the focus and index of growth and progress (Jodkha, 2010). These trends have supported the possibility of caste based discrimination being raised as a complex form of discrimination obstructing human development and as a violation of human rights—not just civil and political rights but also economic social and cultural rights[17].

On the political front in India, the collapse of the single-party-dominated political system was the result of the rise of regional parties, which also led to fragmentation and coalition politics. The political motivation to prioritize developmental issues affecting Dalits was low until the advent of the Bahujan Samaj Party (BSP),[18] a national political party with socialist leanings formed mainly to represent people from the Scheduled Castes, Scheduled Tribes and Other Backward Castes as well as minorities. Claiming inspiration from the philosophy of B. R. Ambedkar,[19] and founded in the mid 80s, the BSP was the fourth largest party in terms of seats in the Indian Parliament in 2009 but was routed in the 2014 general election. Notwithstanding its bleak fortunes at the polls, the rise of this party has intensified the debate on identity politics and has been a significant factor in the mainstream discourse on the political significance of the Dalits or at least the Dalit vote.

The period of the late 1980s and 1990s also saw the emergence of autonomous Dalit movements and platforms in the broader civil society arena in India[20]. Their initial interventions aimed to expose and make visible the fact that untouchability and casteism not only exist but is also growing in new forms in contemporary India. In the 2000s, these movements also began to feel the backlash of the state and civil society and had to adopt a more confrontative stance. Numerous studies undertaken by the members of these movements and organizations in solidarity highlighted new forms of discrimination[21]. The failure as well as culpability of the state in the colossal non-implementation of its own policies and laws was challenged head on.

I present a vignette from a massive rally in the national capital of India, New Delhi, in November 2012, which indicates a probable third phase of interventions of these movements in the struggle against caste and caste-based discrimination. In November 2012, over 20,000 Dalit and Adivasi men and women from 14 states of India marched to the national capital as a mark of protest against casteism and called for its annihilation. This was not the first time such a protest march was held. However, on this occasion, the scale and spread of people gathered was larger. Also, this time the nature of the protest and call for action indicated a paradigm shift—from a position of victimhood to one of agency[22]. The Dalits and Adivasis asserted their central role in nation building and maintained that continued oppression and discrimination against them would also imply a loss in the collective potential of the nation and its ideals.

It is difficult both for the oppressed and the oppressor to see how the oppressor also loses in the act of oppression. Such a stance flies in the face of the usual modes of activism which identify the causes of injustice as being 'out there' and therefore seek to implement the righting of historical wrongs and systems of retributive justice as the way to do this[23]. The paradigm shift glimpsed here was the recognition that transformation was not possibly in only a part of the system and necessarily implied working with the whole (which included both the oppressor and the oppressed). In aspiring for a just society that annihilated caste altogether, the Dalits, by relinquishing their victim stance, offered that possibility of the need for working with the whole and not only fixing the other. I will attempt in the next sections to draw some links between the space that GRCs offer and how it could contribute to this transformative stance.

SECTION B

Finding Voice, Claiming Space, Valorizing One's Experience:
Personal Insights on Caste through Group Relations Work

This section and the following are primarily based on qualitative data from in-depth interviews with Dalit and non-Dalits who have engaged with group relations work, as staff or as members in GRCs or workshops that were designed using conceptual frameworks of group relations. The methodology used was to first send email requests for a discussion on the links they experienced between experiences in GRCs and their understanding of caste dynamics. Out of 17 invitations sent out for in-depth interviews (11 Dalits and 6 non-Dalits), 13 responded—9 Dalits (6 Dalit men and 3 Dalit women) and 4 non-Dalits (3 non-Dalit men and 1 non-Dalit woman). Nine of these were face-to-face conversations, and 4 were conducted on the telephone or through Skype. All of those invited to respond had attended at least one GRC, and many had attended more than one conference or a conference and a couple of workshops based on the same conceptual framework. Six of the respondents had also participated in the GRCs in the role of staff or consultants. These GRCs were offered in the period 2002 to 2013 and so the respondents refer to their experiences mostly in this time frame.

I introduced the idea of interviews with a set of indicative questions, which were sent on email requesting for time for a discussion. The questions were framed very broadly and sought to explore from the particular lens of caste and caste based discrimination how group relations experiences and frameworks contributed to social change and social justice. I also sought to explore if GRCs needed to offer something different in order to be more relevant to those engaged in transforming structural and social injustices. Most of the discussions were face-to-face and over a few hours each. This process of co-creating was both energizing and insightful. While the indicative questions were sent and referred to at the start of the discussion, the actual nature of the discussions were conversations that often set the questions aside, and meandered of its own will into what seemed most appropriate and compelling in the moment, leading to new ways of thinking and understanding these dynamics for both the author and those interviewed.

Thus, the way I have structured these insights and offerings are not based on the set of original questions, but my view of common themes from the pool of insights that emerged from these conversations. This formative methodological approach allowed for the richness of inviting what wanted to emerge, from a rather broad context. Methodologically speaking, mapping these responses to specific questions or even a specific context in these conversations becomes difficult. What is interesting is that most people spoke about how the GRC experiences enabled them at a personal level to understand themselves better, helped them intervene more effectively, and recognize with more acuity, caste based dynamics and discrimination in systems they were part of. The aspect of how GRCs could contribute in more systemic ways to social change and social justice were largely left unaddressed. Similarly, the question of what would need to be done to make GRCs more relevant to these needs and agendas was also not engaged with as much.

Group relations conferences are very intense experiences owing both to the fact that they are experiential and that they work on unconscious processes. While a closing session of a conference would usually focus on participants sharing their experiences, particularly their own insights, it is acknowledged that the closing of the conference does not by any means signify closure to learning. Much of the initial insights get affirmed and indeed some insights emerge for people much later—when a 'real life' situation or experience resonates very strongly with one in the conference. This enables people to make sense of their conference experience on a continuing basis. It also happens that in the intense emotional experience of the conference, not everything can be processed and this processing continues, much in the vein of chewing the cud. It may also be the case that the kind of openness and depth with which people shared and co-developed insights in the conversations were also influenced by the fact that I was seen as a person committed both to group relations work and to working to eliminate caste based discrimination. This process created both trust and an exciting atmosphere of building insights co-creatively.

At this point, it may be useful to describe the elements of design of the GRCs that I am referring to in order to contextualize some of the insights that the respondents offer. Typically, these components were designed as a temporary learning organization that provides several opportunities through various events to differentiate how much the experience of the "here and now" (i.e., experiences that are available to a group as data during an ongoing session) is influenced by fantasy (i.e., unchecked assumptions based on both conscious past experience and experience stored in the unconscious). The various events were: Plenaries to introduce events or reflect on overall learnings; Small and Large Study Groups to study here and now group processes; the Social Sensing Matrix to work with dreams and associations as a way to understand the unconscious; an Institutional Event to understand systemic processes, particularly how pictures in the mind of systems impact sub-system relationships and the exercise of authority; Review and Application Groups to reflect on ones experience and develop new perspectives for back home application; and a Yoga Event to help integrate mind, body, and spirit. I shall be referring again to some of these events in Section C.

The conversations with respondents indicated that what was valued about the experience of the GRC was the new language it offered to make sense of one's experiences. When terms like feelings, emotions, dreams, institution, projections, boundaries, relationships, transformation, roles, and personal authority became part of one's vocabulary, it offered a way to be more alert and aware of these issues. Thus, language provided a handle and insight into how one handles oneself in roles, the positions one takes, the conscious and unconscious aspects of these positions, and opened up new possibilities for action in day-to-day life. One respondent stated:

> The GRC gave me the space to reflect on myself and relate to the other. It seemed to me it was the first time I was focusing on the 'I.' It was not easy- it was frightening at times, and joyous too—what seemed to be a process of peeling myself off layer by layer, making me nude, as unconscious elements were brought to the fore—fear, guilt, shame. Relating to my own self more realistically has helped me relate to others. (D, W)

Another respondent stated:

> As a result of the experience in GRCs I realized how the unconscious pops up—how much of stuff we accumulate in the unconscious and how it impacts my behaviour. Until then, I believed that the root cause of my anger was the other person. I have now learnt to reflect and not dismiss what I don't understand or wish to reject. This reflection may take some time, but I continue to develop insights about myself in the process. (D, M)

A very common theme among the Dalits who responded was the suppression of their own needs and feelings, believing they were inferior and unimportant. Finding voice and finding one's personal authority was an act of according oneself one's personhood. This is something Dalits have been denied and have denied to themselves for centuries (Viswanath, 2009).

A respondent said:

> As a Dalit I have learnt to deal only with the present—the past creates fear, I feel there is nothing for me to reclaim from my past. Hence my past becomes untouchable. And as for my future—what can it possibly offer me? Why should I think about it? (D, M)

Some respondents spoke of the design of the GRC and how different events and elements help the connection between mind, body, and soul:

> Dalits have for centuries experienced oppression in the body—and it is important for them to get in touch with what they have stored in the body for generations on end. (nD, M)

> We think as we are Dalits, we are not allowed to say, 'No.' We then eat our emotions, our anger which then affects our body and our mind. I used to suppress what I feel, and what I want to say, always trying to give space to the other, making them important, their needs important. Now I relate to others more authentically. The GRC has resulted in my being more confident, more assertive, and even confrontative—in both family and work spaces. (D, W)

> It is very difficult to be unaffected by a GRC—even rejecting it implies I have to reject my experience with every pore—and that is an act of assertion! (D, M)

Participating in the 2013 GRC gave me self confidence—made me bold. One of the ideas that were really critical to my learning was the 'hierarchy in the mind.' I realized that inferiority was to a large measure created by me in my mind, I felt others could always do better than me. Now I understand that each one has a different role to play including 'the management in the conference.' That has made me much more reality oriented. (D, W)

I knew there would be upper caste and upper class people in the GRC and I wondered if I could survive for 6 days and not run away. It was a challenge I gave myself. (D M)

An experience in the GRC shocked me into reality. In the small group a non-Dalit asked me—is it because you are Dalit that you are not at all assertive? This hurt me a lot—yes, but I began to work on it, and saw some truth in it—which I was not willing to face earlier. (D, W)

Historically, some Dalit activists have been influenced and some involved in far left politics[24] and believed that it was the only hope to throw off an oppressive system. However, many of them became disillusioned and involved in the less radical 'left of centre' form of activism that was prevalent in the not for profit development sector. However, the influence of far-left ideologies led them to believe that the personal was not a matter for focus—and any investment in exploration of one's self, was unnecessary, even irrelevant.

This resulted in a situation of a strong split between the self and the system (with all projections of the oppressor being put onto the system). The prevailing revolutionary belief "I exist for others," unconsciously gave them permission: "I need not examine myself, I need not change." Thus, there was no impetus to address the issue of lack of congruence between one's personal experience, values, and behaviour and the values of the larger organization or the values of the cause that one espoused (in this case, the cause of Dalit liberation).

Some respondents spoke about this:

15 years in the ML movement had taught me to read, interpret, and give speeches and I believed that to be empowerment. I learnt in the GRC to base my insights on my own experience—and I think this is a powerful form of empowerment. (D, M)

I came from an ultra left background and in my worldview everyone who was in a position of power was an exploiter. I took a very counter-dependent stand with authority figures in groups. My first brush with exercising my own personal power and authority consciously was as member of a GRC in 2009. This proved to be a watershed experience for me. A simple example—the GRC had a yoga event and I felt unwilling to participate—as I felt the background and philosophy of yoga was upper caste. That was not the important part! What was important was my implementing the decision not to participate. This was very freeing for me. I was doing what I wanted to do instead of saying to myself—this is part of the structure and a given and I have to follow. (D, M)

SECTION C

Going Beyond the Self and Engaging the System: Group Relations Conferences as a Powerful Container to Work on Systemic and Structural Inequalities

One of the essentials to learn about systemic inequalities and dis-privilege is to have diversity in the membership so that this can be directly experienced and potentially worked with in the conference. In the 2002–2013 period, the author was on the staff of several GRCs in India offered on varying themes of Identity and Authority, Exploring Resistance and Transformation in Organisational and Social Systems, Transformation of Self and Organisation in a Globalised world, Gender and Authority, Managing Differences, and Leadership for Transformation, and a series of workshops on the theme of Listening to the Unconscious. Some had very diverse membership in terms of caste, gender, sexual orientation, religion, race, class, the not-for-profit, corporate and academic sectors, geographical diversity and diversity also in terms of national and international participants. In others, the membership was not as diverse.

On reflection as to what conditions supported non-tokenistic work on caste and hierarchy in a GRC, it seems that this process involved more than the actual theme; it was the presence of a least a few Dalit members owning their Dalit identity, other members who identified with minority and dis-privilege issues, and staff members who did not shy away from these dynamics. This allowed an open acknowledgement of and enabled work on caste based dynamics in the GRC. This aspect of the GRC as a container is reflected in the following statements of some of the respondents:

> The 2013 GRC had people from different backgrounds—most from high families and status and backgrounds. I was Dalit and the 2nd generation in my family to be educated. I wonder if they will also think about untouchability because of the interventions of the Dalits in the conference. (D, W)

> The idea of associating with dreams was a powerful one. Until the experience of the GRC, I thought my dream was mine. When others associated and others associated with the associations- it was mind blowing! The idea that something is exclusively mine has changed forever. (D, M)

Another respondent who has been in both member and staff roles in conferences reflected on a range of experiences:

> Acutely aware of my own upper-casteness, I had to come to terms with my own (upper) caste identity before I could engage with issues of caste with a certain degree of confidence—one aspect was to accept that a part of my name was a clear upper caste signifier. In a workshop on Dalit leadership with a group of Dalit activists, I was extremely anxious and under-confident of my own ability to engage and to question them—I felt underprepared and felt as if I was being watched by Dalit eyes. My own

experience as member in GRCs helped me enormously at that point. I recognized how in my first experience as a member, the staff were a monolithic oppressive unit all fused into one! Gradually I learnt to differentiate and recognize my own projections on them. This experience helped me to work with the feelings and implications of my own upper-casteness in other situations, and to be able to handle the perceived or actual projections on my being upper caste. (nD, M)

Another respondent stated:

I attended my second GRC in 2009 at a time of significant personal transition, moving from a role of state level responsibilities to national level responsibilities. While personal reflection was not something new to me, the GRC space gave me a particular opportunity to address what kind of blocks I have within myself to face the new challenges ahead of me. The idea of influencing a system is powerful in a GRC. I got to understand more about what baggage I needed to leave behind—the baggage of some of my habits, in order that I may take up my role in the new system with an understanding its requirements. I was aware of the danger of simply importing [unconscious] baggage from the old into the new. The idea that there are multiple approaches to influencing a system also came through very powerfully. I feel that were it not for the opportunity to understand and work on these issues, this transition may not have been successful. (D, M)

The idea that one projects internally held hierarchies to protect oneself from facing one's own tendencies to discriminate, comes as a shock to non-Dalits and Dalits alike. The GRCs offered a space to face up to and explore this complex dynamic of 'discovering the Brahmin in the mind'[25]. Many Indian upper caste men and women, who view themselves as progressive, carry the belief that the caste system in India is a thing of the past, and if at all, it rears its ugly head in remote rural villages. This unconscious defense of shielding themselves from the disturbing realities of how caste based discrimination is growing and taking new forms, results in it being very difficult to even have a discussion about this issue in most middle or upper middle class spaces. This combined with a growing neoliberal ethos may result in a view of having done enough for the Dalits and backward castes and the position of "It is time they stopped whining and took responsibility for their own progress."

Experiences in the conferences helped to face the reality that caste was alive and kicking in oneself and in the system. This happened in many subtle but unmistakable ways as articulated by a non-Dalit respondent as follows:

For the privileged class and castes in India caste realities are suppressed in the unconscious. I realized to my shock that casteism was rearing up inside of me in all kinds of ways and I have hardly got rid of it. I saw the Brahmin in me! (nD, M)

This respondent continued by sharing a particular incident in the GRC he participated in as a member in 2003. During the conference, he castigated the organizers for declaring the conference language to be English—and informed the conference administrator that many of the Dalit members were struggling because of this. When the conference administrator, who was a Dalit man, pointed out that this did not seem to be the experience of the Dalit members, this respondent got in touch with how unconsciously he had placed the Dalits as intellectually lesser beings and that he as an intellectually superior upper caste person must take cause for them!

For the Dalits, the process of getting in touch with the shadow—the possible collusion to maintain the status quo in a society ordered by hierarchy—has been a particularly painful reality. One of the respondents stated this quite starkly:

> My first GRC 2003 was like an introduction—I was confused and didn't get the underlying approach. But I persisted. The role consultation was so powerful—my consultant was so tough and so critical—when I described a situation in my family context, the consultant noted that I was playing the role of an oppressor myself! I was first offended and then shocked—but I realized slowly that it was true—I had a Brahmin inside of me too! (D, M)

The following statements from the perspective of both non-Dalit and Dalit respondents highlight the aspect of how GRCs are particularly suited to work on caste dynamics:

> The 2003 GRC with its focus on caste dynamics was the most transformational and most difficult GRC I was a member in. It seemed those learnings have and will stay with me for all time. One you have faced a learning publicly, then you have the ability to face it again and again and work with it in other situations. The personal is public and the personal is political. Seeing your own role in a dynamic, and how one creates that as it unravels in the here and now, can be a transformational experience. (nD, M)

> Many other behavioral interventions such as T groups or team building programmes for instance focus on individual and interpersonal dynamics. The GRC is a space where one works with the unconscious at the level of the group, the system and the institution. Therefore, what in other spaces may be 'written off' as interpersonal and attributed to individual traits or competencies (as a person being outgoing vs. shy, or participative vs. non participative), can be interpreted in a GRC and understood as dynamics of privilege or disprivilege linked to caste. (nD, M)

> I use these insights subsequently in the institutions that I am part of. I have been able to identify and highlight issues of caste and class, even though the attempt by others in the institutions is to damp them down as individual traits. My raising these as issues of caste and class tend to create huge turmoil in the system as the majority there, who are upper class and upper caste, are not ready to see this. I have even raised these as issues of professional ethics and challenged the system, but the resistance in the system to see it as such is very high and they would prefer this be sorted out 'amicably' and at an interpersonal level and not explore these as systemic aspects. (D, M)

Is the boundary of self rigid or permeable? Is my sense of self, as self in context? Does the way I define my identity have a strong component of my relationship to one or many collectives? One hypothesis about why Dalit members learned so much about themselves and caste dynamics in the GRC is because a primary part of their identity is constructed more as 'me in context' rather than 'me as me.' Their sense of belonging to a community of Dalits has been almost essential to their survival. For other castes, particularly upper castes, this is likely to have shifted to a more individualistic sense of self, with increased income levels, modern trends of urban living, capitalistic values and nuclear families all contributing to this sense of individualism.

Interestingly, the capacity to see themselves in context was also the reason the upper caste members who found the GRC very powerful spaces to learn about caste dynamics, learned so much. Most Indians would tend to stay within their caste/class/gender/cultural/religious and social spaces, even in the mind, as the construction of Indian society has very strongly defined prescriptions and proscriptions for staying within similar categories. Thus, people of the same of similar caste backgrounds would form social relationships or networks, stay in the same localities, do business together, inter-marry, etc. Therefore, while they may have a sense of 'me as me,' the social and professional spaces they inhabit would still tend to be 'like me.' As expressed by a non-Dalit upper caste respondent:

> What the GRC throws up is precisely these new contexts in which I find myself. These are not my carefully constructed and maintained usual contexts. This gives me the opportunity to find new 'me's. (nD, M)

What seems to contribute to such learning is the extent to which a member is not caught up within oneself, and is able to focus on 'me in context'—what am I doing to the group?, what is the group doing to me and therefore what am I learning about myself as part of the context? The structure and task of a GRC also offers a unique opportunity to work on not just individuals projecting on an 'other' and the linked projective identification[26] but also the systemic projections by a group on a group of others. Thus, design and spaces in a GRC have a clear contribution to the possibilities of such learning.

In our conversations, I was also seeking to explore why, when respondents mentioned learning about themselves as persons (exercise of personal authority, finding voice), they usually spoke about experiences in the small group formations (the Small Study Groups and the Review and Application Groups). They attributed learning about the dynamics of caste in society to the larger system formations in the conference—such as the Large Study Group, the Institutional Event, and Plenary sessions. What seemed to emerge was that in the large system events the sense of a more visible 'system as a whole' also mobilized in an unconscious way their primary identity in community as a Dalit, and other roles or aspects of their identity were on the back burner.

This was particularly striking in the GRC in 2013, where almost always when a Dalit member spoke in the Large Study Group, it was about being Dalit or a reference to caste or gender hierarchies being experienced. In the Institutional Event (IE) in that same conference a group was formed around caste and race issues. All the Dalit members of the conference were in that group, along with other members who had lent public solidarity to the issue. It was as if by their joining one of the other groups in the IE they would be betraying their Dalitness. However, what transpired was that this group working on caste and race was not 'able' to engage with the rest of the system very much and work on the primary task of the IE (which was to study the picture of the whole conference as an institution as it emerged). Their primary identity was about being members of the sub-group but not as members of the larger system and thus their relationship with the larger system was not explored. It seemed as if by having a group working on caste on behalf of the whole system—the issue was visibilized, and that was seen as 'good enough.' But going further and transforming that into learning about how caste impacted the whole system, and how the whole system needed to transform, was far more difficult and perhaps even threatening. This may also give a clue also to why the respondents did not focus much on the potential of GRCs to help systemic transformation and focused more on its potential for individual transformation.

SECTION D

Group Relations Conferences and Transforming Societies

In this concluding section, I attempt to bring together some of the threads that link work on transformation and group relations, particularly work on transforming painful and difficult social realities. It seems from the voices of the Dalit and non Dalit respondents struggling courageously with understanding, taking ownership and accountability for the dynamics of caste and structural inequalities that they created and recreated within the GRC, that the split between 'me and the other' needed to be worked with and restored if society has to be transformed. As long as the split remains, the recognition that we all are both victims and oppressors becomes difficult to experience and acknowledge.

One aspect of the stance of victimhood is that since 'the other' does not carry the experience of being victimized, the other cannot become part of 'me.' If this is the underlying thesis, then no one else is 'qualified' to work on oppression except the oppressed themselves. The oppressor is often not aware that their act of oppression also results in their being a victim of a different kind—as in the case of an economic blockade of a lower caste group ultimately hurting overall productivity. When we see collective greed, hatred or delusion, and if we are able to see these in ourselves as well, we realize that the victim and oppressor are both inside and outside. We realize we are all victims and we are all oppressors. To explore this split of victim and oppressor requires permission, indeed invitation, to touch and be touched by the 'other.'

This may be one reason why despite many decades of work on Dalit rights, the non-profit sector in India continues to be largely split into organizations that work on caste (these being almost exclusively Dalit organizations) and organizations that work on other development issues. From a psychodynamic perspective, the Dalits unconsciously are left to do the work on caste. This is similar to the dynamic of women's groups in India, and possible many other parts of the world, getting isolated to primarily do work on gender. The challenge seems to be to transform this process so that there is the possibility of partnerships and a sense of permeability to work on this issue, in a way that the ownership of the implications of a caste ridden society can be shared and co-owned by people from all castes and does not get both relegated and delegated only to the Dalits. A belief in and commitment to whole system change is the other necessary condition for such transformation. In this case, it is exemplified by the shift from 'seeking one's rights and entitlements' to annihilating caste and thus transforming society. Once the belief is firm, the strategies will emerge and need to be co-created. Co-creation is not possible unless one is willing to trust and open up space for connection with others. It requires the ability to venture into the unknown and take considerable risks and embrace the other. It requires facing one's fears and expanding one's capacities. This implies at the very minimum deep work on oneself, in fact, an ongoing commitment to work on oneself, is needed in the context of relating with others.

This transformation in approach also requires the recognition that ultimately the Brahmin is in the mind—one's own mind and that of others. The transformation process would involve the willingness to see oneself in the mirror of the other and the willingness to work with one's shadow and one's projections. This may also imply that the thinking in binaries or defined categories needs to shift to thinking about the grays. One is not either Dalit or upper caste, but the possibility that one is a bit of both. We define rigid boxes in order not to have to face the complexities and contradictions within ourselves, and this in turn leads to our projecting inner grays and contradictions onto external boxes of society.

Such a transformation also implies designing inclusive processes—which will include the erstwhile enemy—the upper castes in this case—in the transformation process. This requires the conviction that without such inclusion and without the reclaiming of projections and projective identification processes by all concerned, no transformation of the system is possible. As long as we design processes that are within the scope of our existing capacities and current frameworks, we will self-sabotage the emergence of a larger, more transformatory processes, which necessarily imply an expansion of our capacities.

One may challenge this by saying that this is rather simplistic, and even if the target of oppression is willing to make this shift, will the oppressor? How does the Brahmin in society 'recognize' that oppressing the Dalit hurts himself and hurts society, apart of course, from the basic recognition that it hurts the Dalit? How do those in power 'recognize' their role in system failures (as in the case of the intractability of developed countries in the face of climate change or distorting trade rules)? How does one become willing to give up power? How do we become agents for a new conversation?

The opportunity and in fact the direct experience of seeing oneself as part of a system, and one's relationship to the larger system is one of the ways of doing this. The possibility of experiencing interconnectedness and how much we need the other for our well-being is another aspect of this realization. (In fact, the opposite of this position is one of needing to preserve one's enemy in order to retain a sense of one's identity as separate). This sense of altruism, of love and of compassion, can come only when our measures of society expand from the current measures of economics and power to other aspects such as well-being, sustainability, and wholeness.

While this chapter is focused on the dynamics and destructiveness of caste—these dynamics can be recognized in work with many other kinds of inequalities and forms of discrimination, which make us less humane. The caste system, like other systems of oppression, is pervasive because it has been able to mutate and serve the 'needs' of society. In the serving of these needs, there is a bizarre and deeply unconscious collusion of victim and oppressor, which does not allow a transformative breakthrough. Individual insights are powerful, but these alone do not lead to transformation of systems. We need to transcend the notion of the individual—what is me and mine. For that to happen, we need to transcend individual learning and learn what will heal the system.

This leads me to some more reflections and questions. Are these necessarily linear processes—do we need to work on ourselves first—and only then can we access the connection with the other? Is healing and growth possible only through retribution or reparation or can we call on other processes that are more restorative in nature? I am not sure I have the answers. In my view, the conversations in this chapter do point to the potential of group relations conferences to offer the space for work on both personal and social insights at a deeper level. Whether they can go one step further and establish the connection between personal transformation and social transformation, and that one cannot happen without the other, points to the next challenge for group relations work.

This link between inner transformation and outer—the deep connection between what is inside us and what is outside, is what spiritual work is all about. I believe GRCs can and should become a site for this kind of spiritual work. This is because they can potentially represent the microcosm of the world outside to enable the connections between the inside and outside to be experienced. It would imply that those offering, designing and staffing conferences work towards these being spaces that are inclusive and embrace diversity, and to have the intention to work with issues that arise from this representation. With conferences the world over becoming increasingly difficult to run as financially viable entities this becomes an additional challenge to ensure that membership represents all sections of society. But, it is a challenge we must take on in order to ensure that GRCs contribute to societal transformation in more powerful, direct ways.

Currently in conferences we work on achievement, competition, ambition, desire, creativity, complexity, passion, pace, dealing with change and turbulence. We need to create the space as well for work on love, simplicity, wanting less, cherishing others, slowing down, mindfulness, paying heed to our intentions, and caring for the whole system. This would create the much-needed space to work on broader societal agendas such as justice, peace, and a more humane and sustainable world. This implies that those directing and staffing conferences see their work as social, political, and spiritual. Without such an approach, the space for courage, generosity, compassion, and wisdom is limited. We may have rich personal insights but more than ever before we need to generate the hope for transformation.

NOTES

1. The caste system involves the division of society into a hierarchy of unequal social groups where basic rights and duties are assigned based on birth and are not subject to change. The Dalits are outcastes falling outside the traditional four broad caste groups of Brahmin, Kshatriya, Vaishya, and Shudra. While originating in Vedic Hinduism over 3000 years ago, the notions of caste have infiltrated in practice all other religions in the Indian sub-continent to a greater or lesser extent—be it Christianity, Islam, Buddhism, Jainism, or Sikhism, and remains alive and strong in contemporary Indian society.

   The word Dalit literally means broken, ground-down, downtrodden, or oppressed. Those previously known as untouchables, depressed classes, and harijans are increasingly adopting the term Dalit to highlight the persecution and discrimination that they face routinely. Dalit refers to one's caste rather than class; it applies to members of those castes who bear the stigma of untouchability because of the extreme impurity and pollution ascribed to their traditional occupations, and constitutes roughly 17% of India's population. First used in the context of caste oppression in the 19th century, the term Dalit was popularized in the 1970s by untouchable writers and members of the revolutionary Dalit Panthers (a name inspired by the Black Panthers of the United States) as a political act.

   The official term is Scheduled Castes (abbreviated as SC) as they are enumerated in the Constitution of India along with Scheduled Tribes (ST) as historically disadvantaged. Similar to the use of the term Dalit, the Scheduled Tribes prefer to use the term *Adivasi*, which means 'original people of the land.' Adivasi is an umbrella term for a heterogeneous set of ethnic and tribal groups claimed to be the aboriginal population of India. They comprise about 8.6 % of the population of India.

2. Group Relations is a method of study and training in the way people perform their roles in the groups and systems to which they belong. The frameworks developed are associated closely with the work of the Tavistock Institute in the United Kingdom and A. K. Rice Institute for the Study of Social Systems in the United States, and subsequently developed in many other parts of the world including India. To know more about group relations theory, its application in particular to group relations conferences, its history and theoretical underpinnings refer the 'Theory' page of the website www.grouprelations.com

3. The conscious part of the mind processes information, stores memory and also interacts with the environment and this is the part we are in touch with and call our mind. Our own experiences, various experiments, and clinical data indicate that much of human experience is relegated to a 'part of the mind,' which is very difficult to access, the unconscious, which indicates not a physical place but a process. Sigmund Freud is credited with developing the term unconscious and subsequently Carl Jung also developed the ideas. Experiences stored in the unconscious are often anxiety provoking or frightening and hence repressed. At the same time, the unconscious is a rich storehouse of resources of creativity and risk taking if one can work through one's defenses against accessing the data. We spend a good deal of psychic energy keeping unconscious data from surfacing to the conscious part of the mind. The more one can access unconscious data, the more one frees energy to be used consciously. Whenever these unconscious experiences resonate with here and now experiences, one 'acts out' beyond one's awareness whatever is held in the unconscious that had resonated, through processes such as projection, transferences and a range of unconscious defenses. This more often than not leads to unexpected and unplanned for consequences, the oddities of human behavior. Research in neurosciences has kindled interest in unconscious processes, which was earlier mostly the preserve of psychoanalysts.

4. These were interventions to ensure access to resources, influencing law and policy, and ideologies to influence institutions such as education, judiciary, police, policy makers, governance, media, and politics (Viswanath, 2009).

5. When I quote from the in-depth interviews, I have used D, M to indicate that the respondent was a Dalit man and D, W for a Dalit woman; similarly nD, M for a non-Dalit man and nD, W for a non-Dalit woman respondent.

    While I am not in a position to name and acknowledge each individual whose insights and experiences have informed this paper at various points, I would like to particularly salute my colleagues with and linked to the National Campaign for Dalit Human Rights for their keenness to risk the engagement in learning opportunities over the last two decades of our association in different spaces and their generosity in sharing their insights.

I am grateful also to Marijke Torfs whose insightful comments on the first draft of this paper helped me immensely.

6. In a workshop in October 2013 titled "Listening to the Unconscious," a member offered a dream in which a woman in a swimsuit was trying to retrieve a packet from the rear end of a large freezer. An apt way of describing the inaccessible and unspeakable!

7. This section relies significantly on information from the National Campaign on Dalit Human Rights (n.d.). I have relied on many sections of their website (http://www.ncdhr.org.in/Dalit-rights-situation) as well as information from personal engagements with activists and leaders of the campaign.

8. The English word caste comes from the Portuguese *casta* indicating race- breed- ancestry. The Indian (Sanskrit) terms varna and jaati have different meanings as indicated in the text. By using the term caste the notions of race have perhaps tended to get superimposed on the notions of varna and jaati.

9. Following the nation's independence in 1947 from British rule, Article 17 of the Indian Constitution (1950) abolished untouchability and has forbidden its practice in any form. The Untouchability (Offences) Act 1955 was amended in 1976 and is now known as "Protection of Civil Rights Act, 1955. It was a long 42 years after Independence that the Indian Parliament enacted the Scheduled Castes/Scheduled Tribes (Prevention of Atrocities) Act, 1989 and subsequently the Scheduled Castes/Scheduled Tribes (Prevention of Atrocities) Rules, 1995, in recognition of the fact that SCs and STs have been suffering exclusion and exploitation, discrimination and atrocities at the hands of dominant caste forces and needed protection and moral and legal redress. (See, http://annihilatecaste.org/wp-content/uploads/2012/10/Peoples-Report-on-PoA-Act-2012.pdf)

10. Census of India, http://censusindia.gov.in. The SCST presentation dated October 28, 2013 informs that as per the Census of India 2011, the number of scheduled castes is 201.378 million out of the total population of 1.21 billion, which accounts for 16.6% of the population.

However, the actual figures of those discriminated on the basis of caste would be much higher because as per the Constitution only those who are Hindus, Sikhs, or Buddhists would be enumerated as scheduled castes. In reality, a large number of Christians and Muslims are also scheduled castes, but at some point their ancestors converted, most likely to escape the tyranny of caste. The irony is that conversion did not guarantee their not being discriminated on the basis of caste.

11. Affirmative action or positive discrimination (known as employment equity in Canada, reservation in India, and positive action in the US) is the policy of providing special opportunities for and favoring members of a disadvantaged group who suffer from discrimination. The nature of positive discrimination policies varies from region to region. Some countries, such as India, use a quota system, whereby a certain percentage of jobs or school vacancies must be set aside for members of a certain group. In some other regions, specific quotas do not exist; instead, members of minorities are given preference in selection processes. Source http://en.wikipedia.org/wiki/Positive_discrimination

12. Neoliberalism—the doctrine that market exchange is an ethic in itself, capable of acting as a guide for all human action, has become dominant in both thought and practice throughout much of the world since 1970 or so, shrinking the spaces for socially just alternatives. The belief in the supremacy of 'free' markets to drive and govern human affairs, obliterates the public's voice in public affairs and substitutes the bottom line in place of people's basic obligation to care for one another. See Harvey (2005) for more on neoliberalism.

13. The Economic and Political Weekly (EPW) (Saxena, Donker, & Ajit, August 11, 2012) reported a first-of-its-kind study at the University of Northern British Columbia, Canada, "Corporate Boards in India: Blocked By Caste?" It found that nearly 93% of board members of the thousand top Indian companies (accounting for four-fifths of market capitalization of all companies listed in the major stock indices in India) were upper caste members—46% Vaishya and 44% Brahmin. The backward castes put together vis-a-vis OBCs (other backward castes) and SCs/STs, who would together constitute over 60% of India's population, were a meagre 3.8% and 3.5% respectively. Caste linked affiliations among upper castes thus remain the primary factor for entry into corporate boards, over considerations such as experience or merit.

14. There is a percentage of reserved seats in both rural (*panchayats*) and urban local self-governance bodies (municipalities), depending on the population of scheduled castes in the constituency.

15. The International Dalit Solidarity Network (IDSN) is an international network working for the elimination of caste discrimination globally. (See, http://idsn.org/caste-discrimination/ & http://idsn.org/country-information.)

16. See http://ifg.org/about/position-statement/ for a definition of economic globalization.

17. Economic, social and cultural rights (ESCR) include the right to self determination, equality for men and women, the right to work and favorable conditions of work; the right to form and join trade unions, the right to an adequate standard of living, including adequate food, clothing, and

housing; the right to physical and mental health and healthcare; the right to social security; the right to a healthy environment; and the right to education, the protection of the family and right to social security.

Economic, Social, and Cultural Rights are an important part of the international human rights law. It is recognized that civil and political rights and economic, social, and cultural rights are indivisible and interdependent. The first comprehensive international instrument encompassing both sets of rights, i.e., civil and political rights and the economic, social, and cultural rights is the Universal Declaration of Human Rights (UDHR). The International Covenant on Economic, Social, and Cultural Rights (ICESCR) remains the principal instrument on economic, social, and cultural rights. As of November 2005, 149 countries have ratified the Covenant. Other key international instruments that have a bearing on caste based discrimination include the Convention on the Elimination of All Forms of Racial Discrimination (1965) (CERD), the Convention on the Elimination of All Forms of Discrimination against Women, 1979 (CEDAW), the Convention on the Rights of the Child, (1989) (CRC) and Conventions of the International Labour Organization.

18. Bahujan literally means people in majority. (See http://en.wikipedia.org/wiki/Bahujan_Samaj_Party)

19. Dr B. R. Ambedkar (14 April 1891–6 December 1956), was an Indian jurist, politician, philosopher, anthropologist, historian and economist. As independent India's first law minister, he was principal architect of the Constitution of India. Born into an untouchable Mahar family, he was the beloved icon for Dalit emancipation. Ambedkar was emphatic about the fact that India's deeply entrenched social inequities and caste loyalties were its most serious obstacle to democratic participation and a shared sense of citizenship and nationhood.

The following words of Ambedkar: "My final words of advice to you are educate, agitate, and organize; have faith in yourself. With justice on our side, I do not see how we can lose our battle. The battle to me is a matter of joy. The battle is in the fullest sense spiritual. There is nothing material or social in it. For ours is a battle not for wealth or for power. It is battle for freedom. It is the battle of reclamation of human personality" is the inspiration for this paper's title.

20. I am particularly grateful to Dr. SDJM Prasad for this analysis of the autonomous Dalit movements, the nature of leadership it called for, and reflections on its future.

21. Several organizations have brought out studies and papers on caste based discrimination in the last decade or so. National Campaign on Dalit Human rights (www.ncdhr.org), Indian Institute of Dalit Studies (www.dalitstudies.org.in), International Dalit Solidarity Network (http://idsn.org), IDEAS (Madurai), Human Rights Watch (http://www.hrw.org),

and National Safai Karamchari Andolan are some of the organizations. Only some of these organizations have websites as indicated, and even so, details of all their publications and papers are not available on the internet.

22. See Campaign to End Untouchability and Atrocities" at http://annihilatecaste.org

23. Archbishop Desmond Tutu describes beautifully the power of restorative justice in his introduction to the 'Truth and Reconciliation Commission of South Africa Report' in VOLUME ONE (http://www.justice.gov.za/trc/report/finalreport/Volume%201.pdf). "Certainly, amnesty cannot be viewed as justice if we think of justice only as retributive and punitive in nature. We believe, however, that there is another kind of justice—a restorative justice which is concerned not so much with punishment as with correcting imbalances, restoring broken relationships—with healing, harmony, and reconciliation."

24. Referred to as ML (Marxist-Leninist) groups they are seen subscribing to ultra left communist ideologies. Many of these groups today are banned by the state and operate underground. They began with armed struggles against feudalism and now increasingly these struggles are directed against the state.

25. The term 'Brahmin in the mind' first came up in the Group Relations Conference in 2003 when a Dalit member who headed a political movement, acknowledged this insight in the closing plenary. That GRC which focused specifically on the issue of caste had a Dalit collective 'Dappu' as one of the sponsoring organizations. Subsequently Gouranga Chattopadhyay developed this idea and a short workshop was directed by him sponsored by HID Forum. Discussions have been ongoing with organizations working on Dalit rights to offer a conference on this theme

26. Projective identification is a psychological term was first introduced by Melanie Klein of the Object Relations School of psychoanalytic thought in 1946. It refers to a psychological process in which a person projects (this is an unconscious process) a thought or belief that they have onto a second person. In most common definitions of projective identification, there is another action in which the second person is changed by the projection and begins to behave as though he or she is in fact actually characterized by those thoughts or beliefs that have been projected. (See, http://psychology.wikia.com/wiki/Projective_identification)

REFERENCES

Ambedkar, B. R. (1917). *Castes in India*. New York, NY: Grove Press.

Baltiwala, S. (2012) *Changing their world: Concepts and practices of women's movements* (2nd ed.). Association for Women's Rights in Development (AWID) retrieved from www.awid.com

Deshpande, A. (2011) *The grammar of caste: Economic discrimination in contemporary India.* New York, NY: Oxford University Press.

Gladwell, M. (2006) *Blink, the power of thinking without thinking.* New York, NY: Penguin Books.

Harvey, D. (2005) *A brief history of Neoliberalism,* New York, NY: Oxford University Press.

Human Rights Watch. (1999). *Broken people: Caste violence against India's Untouchables.* India. South Asia Edition 2000, Books for Change.

Human Rights Watch. (2007). *Hidden apartheid: Caste discrimination against India's "Untouchables"* (Report). Retrieved from www.hrw.org

Jodhka, S. S. (2010). Engaging with Caste: Academic discourses, identity politics and state policy. In *Working Paper Series.* Indian Institute of Dalit Studies and UNICEF.

Krishnan, K. (2013). Battle for justice and democracy Laxmanpur-Bathe. *Economic & Political Weekly. XLVIII* (45 & 46, Nov 16, 2013), 10–12.

National Campaign on Dalit Human Rights. (n.d.). Retrieved from http://ncdhr.org.in/Dalit-rights-situation

Saxena, R., Donker, H., & Ajit, D. (2012). Corporate Boards In India: Blocked by Caste? *Economic and Political Weekly, XLVII,* (32, August 11, 2012), 39–43.

Thapar, R. (2000a). Ideology and interpretation of Early Indian history. In R. Thapar , *History & beyond* (pp. 1–22). Oxford, UK: Oxford India Paperbacks, Oxford University Press.

Thapar, R. (2000b). Durkheim and Weber on Theories of Society and Race relating to pre-colonial India. In R. Thapar, *History & Beyond.* (pp. 23–59). Oxford, UK: Oxford India Paperbacks, Oxford University Press.

Viswanath, R. (2009). Identity leadership and authority: Experiences in application of group relations concepts for Dalit empowerment in India. In E. Aram, R. Baxter, & A. Nutkevitch (Eds.), *Adaptation and innovation Vol II. Theory design and role-taking in group relations conferences and their applications* (pp 179–196). London, UK: Karnac Books.

Viswanath, R., & Chattopadhyay, G. P. (2006). Whose globe is it anyway? In E. B. Klein & I. L. Pritchard (Eds.), *Relatedness in a global economy* (pp. 31–56). London, UK: Karnac Books.

ABOUT THE AUTHORS

Dr. Rebecca Rangel Campón is an assistant professor of psychology at Seton Hall University. She holds degrees in counseling and art therapy from Teachers College, Columbia University and Lesley University. She is a current fellow of the New York State Psychological Association and director of mentorship for the Latina Researchers Network. Her clinical and research interests focus on trauma, discrimination, cultural competency, Latino mental health and social justice. Rebecca is also a Licensed Creative Arts Therapist with a specialty in Art Therapy serving Spanish-speaking populations in Boston, Denver and most recently, in New York City.

Christopher C. Graham is a higher education administrator and passionate inclusive leader. His innovative, passionate, and diverse background is truly a remarkable story. He currently serves as the Assistant Director of Fraternity and Sorority Life for one of the largest fraternal communities in the country. He earned his bachelors degree from Winston-Salem State University. He went on to earn a master's degree in College Counseling Student Development in Higher Education from the 2nd ranked counseling program in the country at The University of North Carolina at Greensboro. Chris aspires to become a chief student affairs officer and ultimately become a college president. He is passionate about underrepresented populations, especially the access, persistence, and success of Black

Talking About Structural Inequalities in Everyday Life: New Politics of Race in Groups, Organizations, and Social Systems, pages 335–343.

male collegians. He is an active member in the Southern Association of College Student Affairs, NASPA, Association of Fraternity and Sorority Advisors, and Alpha Phi Alpha Fraternity, Inc.

Kourtney Gray is a doctoral student at Louisiana State University. He previously worked for Indiana University as a program coordinator with the Indiana Memorial Union. He is interested in the experiences of Black males in higher education, with a particular emphasis on black male leadership development. His other research interest includes experiences of new professionals of color, and social activism on the college campus.

Dr. Nyasha Grayman-Simpson is Assistant Professor of Psychology at Goucher College located in Baltimore, MD. Her scholarship focuses on African American cultural practices and positive psychological, social, emotional, and spiritual functioning. She is author/co-author of several articles and book chapters on the topic, including, "'We who are Dark...:' The Black Community According to Black Adults in America," "Black Community Involvement and Subjective Well-being," and "Positive Psychology in African Americans" in Handbook of Positive Psychology in Racial and Ethnic Minority Groups: Theory, Research, Assessment, and Practice. Dr Grayman-Simpson received her Ph.D. in Counseling Psychology from New York University.

Dianne Ghiraj is a graduate of the Mental Health Counseling program at Long Island University—Brooklyn. She obtained her License in Mental Health Counseling in 2015 and is currently working on achieving her CASAC. Dianne Ghiraj is employed at Montefiore Medical Center under the Division of Substance Abuse.

Schekeva "Keva" P. Hall, Ph.D., has devoted her early career interests to exploring identity development for diverse Blacks living in the U.S. She has worked independently and collaboratively with other scholars on exploring racial identity development in Black West Indian American populations. Her more recent projects have focused on the outcomes of both Caribbean and U.S. socialization systems on the various social and intrapersonal identities of Black West Indian Americans. Keva interests also include exploring body image. She has explored intersections of racial/cultural identity development and body image for women including diverse Blacks in the U.S. Her 2008 "My Good Hair" interactive art exhibition illustrated how Black hair has been used to highlight cultural relatedness among Black women. Keva continues to explore how this form of cultural identity can be used clinically to explore race and relatedness in the therapeutic relationship. Keva holds a doctorate in Counseling Psychology from Columbia University. She is currently a Postdoctoral fellow at Albany Medical Center where she works with a clinical eating disorder population, designs psychoeducation support groups for bariatric population and does clinical work in the community.

Charla Hayden, M.A., is a freelance organizational consultant and a Board Member of the A.K. Rice Institute for the Study of Social Systems.

Krista Herbert is an adjunct instructor of psychology at William Paterson University. She received her master's degree in Clinical and Counseling Psychology from William Paterson University and is pursing her license to be a professional counselor. She also holds a degree in Psychology and Gerontology from the Richard Stockton College of New Jersey. Ms. Herbert's research focuses on psychological implications of chronic illness in college students. She is also interested in research focusing on the manifestation and impact of microaggressions on physical and mental health of marginalized people. Currently, Ms. Herbert volunteers in a research lab in the Cancer Prevention and Control Program at Mount Sinai School of Medicine.

Xavier J. Hernandez is a PhD student in the Department of Education Policy, Organization, and Leadership at the University of Illinois at Urbana-Champaign. He received his MA degree in Asian American studies from San Francisco State University and his BA degree in criminology, law, & society from the University of California, Irvine. He has also studied abroad at the University of the Philippines, Diliman. His research interests include Asian American college preparation, access, and retention with a particular focus on the influence of extracurricular involvement on Asian American educational experiences.

Aisha Holder is a Doctoral Candidate pursuing a Ph.D. in Counseling Psychology at Fordham University. She has co-authored articles on racial microaggressions published in the American Psychologist and Professional Psychology Research and Practice journals. She has also co-authored a chapter on culturally competent vocational assessments published in the Handbook of Multicultural Assessment (3rd Ed.). Until April 2012, Aisha was a Vice President at JPMorgan Chase (JPMC) in the Corporate Training group as a facilitator and project manager. Prior to joining Corporate Training, Aisha worked in the Career Advancement Program (CAP) in the Career Development Group as a career advisor and project manager. Aisha began her career as an Associate in the Human Resources Associate Program, a management program at JPMC. After completing the Associate's program, Aisha assumed the role of Human Resources Business Partner in the Retail Financial Services and Investment Banking divisions of JPMC.

Dina C. Maramba is Associate Professor of Student Affairs, Administration and Asian and Asian American Studies at the State, University of New York (SUNY) at Binghamton. With over 10 years of experience as a student affairs practitioner, among her many roles included working with first generation students and facilitating their success in college. Her research focuses on equity, diversity and social justice issues within the context of higher education. Her interests include how educational institutions (MSIs and PWIs) and campus climates influence access and success among students of color, underserved and first generation college students. Her books include The Other Students: Filipino Americans, Education and Power (with Rick Bonus); Fostering Success of Ethnic and Racial Minorities in STEM: The Role of Minority Serving Institutions (with Robert T. Palmer and Marybeth Gasman); The Misrepresented Minority: New Insights on Asian Americans and Pacific Islanders and their Implications for Higher Education (with Samuel Museus and Robert T. Teranishi). Having presented her research at the national and international level, her work includes publications in the Journal of College Student Development, Journal of College Student Retention, Research in Higher Education and Educational Policy. Dr. Maramba is a recipient of the 2011 Award for Outstanding Contribution to Asian/Pacific Islander American Research in Higher Education by ACPA.

Jacqueline S. Mattis, Ph.D. is Professor in the University of Michigan's Department of Psychology and Director of the Center for the Study of Black Youth in Context (CSBYC). Mattis's research focuses on the role of religion and spirituality in the positive psychological development of African Americans. She explores the factors that contribute to altruism, compassion, empathy and optimism. Her research has been published in numerous academic journals and texts including The Journal of Community Psychology, the Journal of Adult Development, Personality and Individual Differences, Violence Against Women, and The Journal of Clinical Child Psychology and in textbooks published by Oxford University Press and the American Psychological Association. She teaches graduate as well as undergraduate courses on the topics of culture, religiosity and spirituality, and positive psychological development. She is a recipient of a Positive Psychology Young Scholars Award. She is also the recipient of the 2011 Martin Luther King, Jr. Award for outstanding teaching, mentorship, service and commitment to social justice. She is co-author and co-editor with Fulya Kurter of a case-centered handbook entitled Culturally sensitive counseling from the perspective of Turkish practitioners (Bahcesehir University Press).

Dr. Kevin Nadal is the Executive Director of the Center for Lesbian and Gay Studies at the City University of New York (CUNY) Graduate Center, as well as an Associate Professor of Psychology at John Jay College of Criminal Justice—CUNY. He is the President-Elect of the Asian American Psychological Association, the co-president of the metro New York Chapter of the Filipino American National Historical Society (FANHS), and a FANHS National Trustee. He is author of over 60 publications, including the book Filipino American Psychology: A Handbook of Theory, Research, and Clinical Practice (Wiley, 2011) and That's So Gay! Microaggressions and the Lesbian, Gay, Bisexual, and Transgender Community (American Psychological Association, 2011).

Janee V. Nesbitt is a alumna of Long Island University where she received her Masters of Education in Mental Health Counseling. She also received her Bachelor's degree in Black Studies and English Literature at the State University of New York at New Paltz, where she researched gender identity in her thesis, African Womanism and/or Black Feminism. Her research work focuses on the importance of Nommo (individuals ability to self name and self define), often focusing on identity development from multiple lenses (societal, internal and etc.) and developing interventions to counteract negative identity development. Janee currently works as a family therapist in the child welfare system.

Robert T. Palmer is an associate professor in the Department of Educational Leadership and Policy Studies at Howard University. His research examines issues of access, equity, retention, persistence, and the college experience of racial and ethnic minorities, particularly within the context of historically Black colleges and universities. Dr. Palmer's work has been published in leading journals in higher education, such as The Journal of College Student Development, Teachers College Record, Journal of Diversity in Higher Education, Journal of Negro Education, College Student Affairs Journal, Journal of College Student Retention, The Negro Educational Review, and Journal of Black Studies, among others. Since earning his PhD in 2007, Dr. Palmer has authored/ co-authored well over 100 academic publications. His books include Racial and ethnic minority students' success in STEM education (2011, Jossey-Bass), Black men in college: Implications for HBCUs and beyond (2012, Routledge), Black graduate education at HBCUs: Trends, experiences, and outcomes (2012, Information Age Publishing), Fostering success of ethnic and racial minorities in STEM: The role of minority serving institution (2012, Routledge), Community colleges and STEM: Examining underrepresented racial and ethnic minorities (2013, Routledge), STEM models of success: Programs, policies, and Practices (2014, Information Age Press), Black male collegians: Increasing access, retention, and persistence in higher education (2014, Jossey-Bass), Understanding HIV and STI Prevention for College Students (2014, Routledge), Black men in higher education: A Guide to Ensuring Success (2014, Routledge), Exploring diversity at historically Black colleges and universities: Implications for policy and practice (2015, Jossey-Bass), Hispanic serving institutions: Their origins, and present, and future challenges (2015, Stylus), the African American students' guide to STEM Career (forthcoming, Greenwood Publishing), Black men in the academy: Stories of resiliency, inspiration, and success (2015, Palgrave Macmillan), and Graduate Education at HBCUs: The Student Perspective (Routledge, forthcoming). In 2009, the American College Personnel Association's (ACPA) Standing Committee for Men recognized his excellent research on Black men with its Outstanding Research Award. In 2011, Dr. Palmer was named an ACPA Emerging Scholar and in 2012, he received the Carlos J. Vallejo Award of Emerging Scholarship from the American Education Research Association (AERA). Furthermore in 2012, he was awarded the

Association for the Study of Higher Education (ASHE)-Mildred García Junior Exemplary Scholarship Award. In 2015, Diverse Issues in Higher Education recognized Dr. Palmer as an emerging scholar. Later that year, he also received the SUNY Chancellor's award for Excellence in Scholarship and Creative Activities. This prestigious award is normally given to a full professor.

Alex L. Pieterse is an Associate Professor who is affiliated with the Counseling Psychology Program at the University at Albany—SUNY. He received his Ph.D. in Counseling Psychology from Teachers College, Columbia University, New York. Dr. Pieterse's scholarship focuses on psychosocial aspects of racism including health related outcomes and anti-racism advocacy. His research has been published in several professional journals and he is currently an Associate Editor for the Journal of Psychology in Africa. In addition to his academic appointment, Dr. Pieterse also serves as a diversity consultant and maintains a private psychotherapy practice.

Dr. David P. Rivera is an associate professor of counselor education at Queens College, City University of New York. A counseling psychologist by training, his practical work includes consultations and trainings on a variety of cultural competency issues. Dr. Rivera holds degrees from Teachers College, Columbia University, Johns Hopkins University, and the University of Wyoming. His research focuses on cultural competency development and issues impacting the marginalization and wellbeing of people of color and oppressed sexual orientation and gender identity groups, with a focus on microaggressions. Dr. Rivera is currently board co-chair of CLAGS: Center for LGBTQ Studies, on the executive committee of the APA's Society for the Psychological study of Lesbian, Gay, Bisexual, and Transgender Issues, a consulting editor of the journal Psychology of Sexual Orientation and Gender Diversity, and an adviser to The Steve Fund. He has received multiple recognitions for his work, including national honors from the American Psychological Association, the American College Counseling Association, and the American College Personnel Association.

Cherubim Quizon is Associate Professor in the Department of Sociology, Anthropology and Social Work, at Seton Hall University. Born and raised in the Philippines, she came to the United States to train in Art History before pursuing a PhD in Cultural Anthropology at Stony Brook University. She co-edited (with Patricia Afable) an influential centenary volume on the living display of Filipinos at the St. Louis World's Fair, using field and museum research to underscore the agency of those displayed, their interlocutors, and their descendants. Her principal research examining US colonial-era collections of Bagobo indigenous textiles and through the lens of contemporary fieldwork in the origin community has been published in the US, Europe and Asia. Her current research looks into the transnational identities and citizenship claims of indigenous peoples explored through the framework of visual anthropology.

Jameel Alexander Scott earned his BA from Morehouse College, M.Th. from Drew University and M.S. from the University of Pennsylvania. Jameel also holds an Advanced Graduate Certificate from the University of Maryland, College Park in higher education economics and finance. Mr. Scott has authored over 10 book chapters, and more than 20 newspaper, journal, and magazine articles. Mr. Scott's writing is centered on student retention in high school and college and financial management for college students. Currently, Mr. Scott is a Ph.D. student at Old Dominion University.

Ellen L. Short, Ph.D., is an Associate Professor of Counseling in the Department of Counseling and School Psychology in the School of Education at Long Island University/Brooklyn. Dr. Short received an M.A. in Counseling Psychology from Northwestern University and a Ph.D. in Counseling Psychology from New York University. Her areas of specialization in teaching, scholarly research and publishing are: Group dynamics focusing on race, ethnicity, gender and culture, multicultural assessment of intelligence tests and social justice/multicultural counseling. She teaches courses on counseling theory and skills, group work, multicultural counseling, substance abuse and high-risk behavior, career counseling, consultation counseling, and grief counseling. Dr. Short has spent nearly two decades working in the field of group relations and has served as a consultant at group relations conferences in the United States and internationally. She has also directed Group Relations Conferences at Teachers College, Columbia University and New York University. She is the co-author of "Racial and Cultural Dynamics in Group and Organizational Life: Crossing Boundaries" (Sage, 2010). She is affiliated with the A.K. Rice Institute for the Study of Social Systems and the New York Center for the Study of Groups, Organizations and Social Systems.

Lisa A. Suzuki, Ph.D., is an Associate Professor in the Applied Psychology Department, Steinhardt School of Culture, Education and Human Development, at New York University. She is the senior editor of the Handbook of Multicultural Assessment now in its 3rd edition (Suzuki & Ponterotto, 2008), and co-editor of the Handbook of Multicultural Counseling currently in preparation for the 4th edition (Casas, Suzuki, Alexander, & Jackson, in progress). She is a graduate of the Counseling Psychology Program at the University of Nebraska-Lincoln and has been a faculty member at Fordham University and the University of Oregon. Her current research interests are in the areas of multicultural assessment and qualitative research methods.

Nenelwa Tomi is a multidisciplinary artist, creator, and educator. She currently serves as Assistant Director of Admissions and Coordinator of International Recruitment at Goucher College. Ms. Tomi is co-founder of All Things Africa, a start-up aimed at unifying Africans across the diaspora through culture, cause and community-building. As a Tanzanian American, she hopes to become a pioneer in the field of International Education to create connections in spite, and because of our differences, while working towards the betterment of the African Diaspora.

Rosemary Viswanath is a post graduate in Management from Indian Institute of Management Bangalore (1984), and a graduate in Mathematics from St Stephens College Delhi (1982), India. She works on Organization Consulting, Strategic Visioning & Planning, Change Management and Leadership Coaching with a wide range of organisations and networks—not for profit, government systems, and corporate orgnaisations, both in India and internationally. She has privileged working with organisations and institutions that impact society and macro social processes through their work on human rights, development and its impacts, social justice, dalit human rights, equity, environmental justice, women's rights & empowerment, and alternative structures and visions of society and governance. She was until recently Director of EQUATIONS, a national research campaign and advocacy organisation focusing on the impact of tourism on local communities. She also serves in governance and advisory roles in several nonprofit trusts and foundations. Rosemary has been intensively involved in Group Relations Conferences, based on the work initiated at the Tavistock Institute of Human Relations in the UK. In this arena since 1989, she has been in Director as well as consulting staff roles in over 30 Group Relations Conferences and workshops based on these methodologies in India, the UK, France and the Netherlands.

Dr. Carolyn M. West is Associate Professor of Psychology and winner of the 2013 Distinguished Teaching Award at the University of Washington. As an award-winning scholar, Dr. West has authored or co-authored more than 40 journal articles and book chapters. She is editor/contributor of Violence in the Lives of Black Women: Battered, Black, and Blue, which was published by Routledge in 2002 (winner of the 2004 Carolyn Payton Early Career Award). In recognition of her scholarship, she received the first Bartley Dobb Professorship for the Study and Prevention of Violence (2005-2008).

Dr. Wendi Williams is a counseling psychologist and is on faculty at Long Island University—Brooklyn in the department of Counseling and School Psychology. Her work centers on the development, implementation and evaluation of school and community-based health and educational interventions that promote optimal health and well-being among urban youth and their families and the practitioners that will work with them. She engages research for action and social change and implements interventions that will build critical consciousness among participants. Her intent is to facilitate awareness to the connection between physical, mental and spiritual health and wellness among populations disconnected from these relationships. Dr. Williams is affiliated with the American Psychological Association (APA), Society for the Psychology of Women (Section One- Black Women).

Leo Wilton, Ph.D., is an Associate Professor in the Department of Human Development in the College of Community and Public Affairs at the State University of New York at Binghamton. His primary research interests include health disparities (primary and secondary HIV prevention); community based research and evaluation; and Black psychological development and mental health. Dr. Wilton's scholarly research on the AIDS epidemic focuses on the intersectionality of race, gender, and sexuality, as situated in macro- and –micro-level inequalities in Black communities, both nationally and internationally. He teaches courses on Black Families, Black Child and Adolescent Development, Psychology of Racism, Psychology of HIV and AIDS, and research methods. Dr. Wilton is a recipient of the Chancellor's Award for Excellence in Teaching in the State University of New York (SUNY). He completed a PhD degree in counseling psychology at New York University, predoctoral clinical psychology fellowship in the Department of Psychiatry at the Yale University School of Medicine, a three-year postdoctoral research fellowship in HIV behavioral research and evaluation at New York University, and a postdoctoral summer fellowship in the Empirical Summer Program in Multi-Ethnic Research at the University of Michigan. He is a lifetime member of the Association of Black Psychologists and affiliated with the A.K. Rice Institute and New York Center for the Study of Groups, Organizations and Social Systems.

Made in the USA
Middletown, DE
02 February 2021